# Sexual politics in revolutionary England

Manchester University Press

POLITICS, CULTURE AND SOCIETY IN EARLY MODERN BRITAIN

General Editors
Alastair Bellany, Alexandra Gajda, Peter Lake,
Anthony Milton, Jason Peacey, Abigail Swingen

This important series publishes volumes that take a fresh and challenging look at the interactions between politics, culture and society in early modern Britain and beyond. It seeks to counteract the fragmentation of current historiography by encouraging a variety of methodological and critical approaches to this period of dramatic conflict and change that fundamentally shaped the modern world. The series welcomes volumes covering all aspects of sixteenth, seventeenth and eighteenth-century history, including the history of Britain's growing imperial ambitions and global reach.

To buy or to find out more about the books currently available in this series, please go to: https://manchesteruniversitypress.co.uk/series/politics-culture-and-society-in-early-modern-britain

# Sexual politics in revolutionary England

Samuel Fullerton

MANCHESTER UNIVERSITY PRESS

Copyright © Samuel Fullerton 2024

The right of Samuel Fullerton to be identified as the author of this work has been asserted in accordance with the Copyright, Designs and Patents Act 1988.

Published by Manchester University Press
Oxford Road, Manchester M13 9PL

www.manchesteruniversitypress.co.uk

British Library Cataloguing-in-Publication Data
A catalogue record for this book is available from the British Library

ISBN 978 1 5261 7590 8 hardback
ISBN 978 1 5261 9586 9 paperback

First published 2024
Paperback published 2026

The publisher has no responsibility for the persistence or accuracy of URLs for any external or third-party internet websites referred to in this book, and does not guarantee that any content on such websites is, or will remain, accurate or appropriate.

EU authorised representative for GPSR:
Easy Access System Europe – Mustamäe tee 50,
10621 Tallinn, Estonia
gpsr.requests@easproject.com

Typeset by Newgen Publishing UK

# Contents

| | |
|---|---|
| *List of figures* | *page* vi |
| *Acknowledgements* | vii |
| *List of abbreviations* | ix |
| Introduction | 1 |
| 1 Sexual satire and partisan identity, 1637–42 | 29 |
| 2 Mobilisation, escalation and sexual polemic, 1642–46 | 69 |
| 3 Toleration and its discontents, 1646–48 | 106 |
| 4 The porno-politics of regicide, 1648–51 | 147 |
| 5 Contesting reformation, 1649–53 | 187 |
| 6 Discipline and debauchery, 1654–59 | 226 |
| 7 The Restoration and beyond | 265 |
| Conclusion | 279 |
| *Bibliography of archival sources* | 289 |
| *Index* | 296 |

# Figures

0.1 Frontispiece to *A wonder woorth the reading*, STC 14935 (1617). © The British Library Board. Reproduced by permission of the British Library. Shelfmark C.127.g.17 — page 15

1.1 Frontispiece to *Articles ministred by His Majesties commissioners . . . against John Gwin*, E.177[20] (1641). Image courtesy of the William Andrews Clark Memorial Library, University of California, Los Angeles. Shelfmark BX5199.G9 G9* — 46

1.2 Frontispiece to *A new sect of religion descryed*, Wing B4295A (1641). Image courtesy of the Houghton Library, Harvard University. Shelfmark *EC65 B7395 641n — 50

3.1 Frontispiece to Daniel Featley, *The dippers dipt*, E.268[11] (1645). Image courtesy of the William Andrews Clark Memorial Library, University of California, Los Angeles. Shelfmark BZ F288d 1645* — 114

3.2 Frontispiece to *An exact diurnall of the parliament of ladyes*, E.386[4] (1647). Image courtesy of the Beinecke Rare Book and Manuscript Library, Yale University. Shelfmark Ij N416 647E — 128

4.1 Frontispiece to Thomas Hobbes, *Leviathan*, Wing H2246 (1651). Image courtesy of the William Andrews Clark Memorial Library, University of California, Los Angeles. Shelfmark f B1222 1651* — 177

5.1 Frontispiece to *The Ranters declaration*, E.620[2] (1650). © The British Library Board. Reproduced by permission of the British Library — 196

6.1 Frontispiece to *The Quakers dream*, E.833[14] (1655). © The British Library Board. Reproduced by permission of the British Library — 251

7.1 Frontispiece to [Roger L'Estrange], *The committee*, Wing L1226 (1680). Image courtesy of the William Andrews Clark Memorial Library, University of California, Los Angeles. Shelfmark Pam coll. Folio Drawer — 275

# Acknowledgements

The acknowledgements section has always been my favourite part of any scholarly monograph, and so it is a true pleasure now to thank the many people and institutions who made this book possible.

First, I must acknowledge the generous financial and institutional support of several key benefactors. This project began as a PhD dissertation at the University of California, Riverside, and I owe a great debt to various campus organisations there for getting me to the archives early and often. Major portions of the research were conducted during short-term fellowships held at Brown University's John Carter Brown Library, the Huntington Library, the Newberry Library, UCLA's William Andrews Clark Memorial Library, and Yale's Beinecke Rare Book and Manuscript Library. I am most grateful to Peter Lake and the Department of History at Vanderbilt University, where I served as a postdoctoral fellow in 2020–21. It is difficult to imagine how this book could have been completed at all without those pivotal years in Nashville.

Many thanks are due to Meredith Carroll, Laura Swift, and the rest of the team at Manchester University Press for their help and patience in steering me through the publication process. I am equally grateful to the series editors for their enthusiasm and to the anonymous readers for their helpful comments on the manuscript. I should also take this opportunity to thank Cambridge University Press for permitting me to reproduce sections of a 2021 article (Samuel Fullerton, 'Fatal Adulteries: Sexual Politics in the English Revolution', *JBS* 60:4 (2021), 793–821) in Chapter 4.

Next, I wish to recognise the many librarians and archivists who aided in locating and identifying materials in repositories across the USA and Great Britain. The Beinecke, the British Library, Harvard's Houghton Library and the Clark graciously provided the images that appear throughout the following chapters. In California, the staff of UCR's Tomás Rivera Library have supported this project since my time as a graduate student, and they proved equally important during its final stages. I owe a special debt to the staff of Vanderbilt's Jean and Alexander Heard Library, who kept me topped up on research materials despite the enormous logistical challenges imposed by the Covid-19 pandemic.

One of the great joys of this profession is its people, and I am deeply thankful for the friends and colleagues who shared references, listened to conference papers, and generally kept me in good spirits during this project's long gestation. Richard Bell, Michael Bennett, David Como, David Cressy, Jordan Downs, Jeremy Fradkin, the late Matt Growhoski, Joel Harrington, Joel Halcomb, Catherine Hinchliff, Steve Hindle, Chris Kyle, David Magliocco, Noah Millstone, Michael Questier, Tim Reinke-Williams, Talya Sarna, Sandy Solomon, Hillary Taylor, Sonia Tycko and Vanessa Wilkie provided much advice and good cheer from San Marino to the Skinners Arms. Ed Legon, Jason Peacey, Isaac Stephens and Laura Stewart provided helpful early readings of individual chapters, while Alastair Bellany and Jonathan Koch gamely took on the whole thing in draft. I am especially grateful to Ann Hughes and Sue Wiseman, both of whom have read and discussed this material with me over many years while offering much encouragement and guidance in the process; Ann in particular has fielded more queries, and suffered through more half-baked prose, than any one person should have to endure over the course of a single project. This book is much the better for all of their insights. Any faults that remain are, of course, my own.

There are two people without whom this book could not have been written. The first is Tom Cogswell, who suggested the topic to me during my inaugural year as a graduate student, and who has read (and re-read) nearly everything I have written since. Beyond providing a bottomless well of mentorship and an unparalleled editorial pen, Tom taught me how to be a historian. If there is anything useful to be found in these pages, it is entirely to his credit.

The second person I must single out is Peter Lake. Peter was responsible for my two-year stint at Vanderbilt, where much of this book was initially revised and restructured, and my immense intellectual debt to him and his work will be abundantly clear in what follows. Far more crucial to the book's successful completion, however, has been Peter's generosity, patience and good humour in even the most trying of circumstances – among which must be numbered the pandemic years, when we spent many bibulous afternoons discussing early modern sex-talk from a safe distance in his back garden.

Finally, I thank the many friends who have struggled, not always successfully, to pull me out of the seventeenth century and into the twenty-first; Malcolm Baker and Jesse Carrillo, and especially Nina Martyn, for providing safe harbour in London over many years; and my family, for their continual love and support. My last and greatest debt is to Molly Kessler, through whom all things are possible.

# List of abbreviations

| | |
|---|---|
| *A&O* | C. H. Firth and R. S. Rait (eds), *Acts and Ordinances of the Interregnum, 1642–1660* (3 vols, London, 1911) |
| Add. MS | Additional Manuscripts |
| BL | British Library, London |
| Bod. | Bodleian Library, Oxford University |
| Braddick, *Fury* | Michael Braddick, *God's Fury, England's Fire: A New History of the English Civil Wars* (London, 2008) |
| BRBML | Beinecke Rare Book and Manuscript Library, Yale University |
| Capp, *Culture Wars* | Bernard Capp, *England's Culture Wars: Puritan Reformation and Its Enemies in the Interregnum, 1649–1660* (Oxford, 2012) |
| *CJ* | *Journals of the House of Commons* (London, 1802) |
| Como, *RP* | David R. Como, *Radical Parliamentarians and the English Civil War* (Oxford, 2018) |
| *CSPD* | *The Calendar of State Papers, Domestic* |
| CUL | Cambridge University Library |
| DWL | Dr Williams's Library, London |
| *EHR* | *The English Historical Review* |
| ERO | Essex Record Office, Chelmsford |
| *Gangraena I, II, III* | Thomas Edwards, *Gangraena*, E.323[2] ([16 February] 1646) (*I*); Thomas Edwards, *The second part of Gangraena*, E.338[12] ([28 May] 1646) (*II*); Thomas Edwards, *The third part of Gangraena*, E.368[5] ([28 December] 1646) (*III*) |
| Gianoutsos, *Manhood* | Jamie A. Gianoutsos, *The Rule of Manhood: Tyranny, Gender, and Classical Republicanism in England, 1603–1660* (Cambridge, 2021) |

| | |
|---|---|
| HEHL | The Huntington Library, San Marino, California |
| HJ | *The Historical Journal* |
| HLQ | *Huntington Library Quarterly* |
| HR | *Historical Research* |
| HRC | The Harry Ransom Center, University of Texas at Austin |
| Hughes, *Gender* | Ann Hughes, *Gender and the English Revolution* (London, 2012) |
| JBS | *Journal of British Studies* |
| LJ | *Journals of the House of Lords* (London, 1767–1830) |
| LRO | Lancashire Record Office, Preston |
| Marshall, *Toleration* | John Marshall, *John Locke, Toleration and Early Enlightenment Culture: Religious Intolerance and Arguments for Religious Toleration in Early Modern and 'Early Enlightenment' Europe* (Cambridge, 2006) |
| MITM | [John Crouch], *The man in the moon* |
| NLS | National Library of Scotland, Edinburgh |
| NRO | Norfolk Record Office, Norwich |
| ODNB | Colin Matthew (ed.), *Oxford Dictionary of National Biography* (Oxford, 2004) |
| P&P | *Past & Present* |
| Purkiss, *Literature* | Diane Purkiss, *Literature, Gender and Politics During the English Civil War* (Cambridge, 2005) |
| 'Rump Songs' | The Huntington Library, San Marino, California, HM 16522 ('A Collection of Poems + Ballads') |
| Sharpe, *IW* | Kevin Sharpe, *Image Wars: Promoting Kings and Commonwealths in England, 1603–1660* (New Haven, CT, 2010) |
| SHC | Somerset Heritage Centre, Taunton |
| Smith, *CRW* | Nigel Smith (ed.), *A Collection of Ranter Writings: Spiritual Liberty and Sexual Freedom in the English Revolution* (London, 2014) |
| SRO | Staffordshire Record Office, Stafford |
| TNA | The National Archives of the UK, Kew |
| TRHS | *Transactions of the Royal Historical Society* |
| Turner, *Libertines* | James Grantham Turner, *Libertines and Radicals in Early Modern London: Sexuality, Politics and Literary Culture, 1630–1685* (Cambridge, 2002) |
| WACML | William Andrews Clark Memorial Library, University of California, Los Angeles |

Dates remain in the Old Style, although the year is taken to begin on 1 January. I have retained original spellings in contemporary sources while silently expanding contractions. Seventeenth-century pamphlet titles have been shortened wherever possible to save space; for pre-1800 texts, the place of publication is London unless stated otherwise. Generally, references to printed texts come from the British Library's Thomason Collection (catalogued in G. K. Fortescue (ed.), *Catalogue of the Pamphlets, Books, Newspapers, and Manuscripts . . . Collected by George Thomason, 1640–1661* (2 vols, London, 1908)); in these citations, bracketed dates represent the date of Thomason's acquisition. Citations for non-Thomason pamphlets are to the Wing and/or STC references listed in the English Short Title Catalogue (http://estc.bl.uk). Biblical quotations are taken from the King James Version.

# Introduction

On 4 October 1652, more than three years after the English Revolution reached its climax with the execution of King Charles I, the London bibliophile George Thomason acquired a short pamphlet authored by the puritan bookseller Michael Sparke. Sparke's tract, entitled *A second beacon fired by Scintilla*, was fixated on a particular problem: the 'poysoning and most Blasphemous Books' that had overrun English print culture since the early 1640s. His list of offending titles, all tending to 'the dishonour of God, scandall of Religion, the decay of Piety, and the disgrace of your Government', was long and varied, but Sparke found one aspect of these new 'Ranting, Scandalous and Libellous' texts especially abhorrent: their 'Bawdery and Scurrility', exemplified by 'that Fiery flying Roll of [the Ranter Abiezer] Copps', which had 'term[ed] the Holy Bible the Scripturian Whore' and advocated for sexual promiscuity. For Sparke, as for many early modern moralists, such talk posed a profound danger to the kingdom's political and spiritual well-being. His reaction was instinctual – and surprising. 'Was not one hanged in Qu[een] Elizabeths dayes for a Book' like Coppe's, the bookseller wondered? Moreover, had he not 'of late seen many Books, that had they been published in the Bishops dayes, how had a man suffered'? To find Sparke, an enthusiastic publisher of vicious attacks against those very same bishops, thinking fondly on the days of episcopal press licensing speaks to the depths of his concern.[1] In revolutionary England, at least according to the *Second beacon*, lascivious language had grown entirely out of control.

Another pamphlet, published anonymously in March 1650 in response to the outrageous sexual satires of the republican Henry Neville – whose 'Ribauldry and Bawdery', it argued, qualified him 'to be made grand Secretary to all the Pimps in Europe' – summarised the contemporary case against public sex-talk in equally strong terms. For this author, the very act of reading Neville's bawdy language was traumatic. 'When first I perused it', he wrote,

> it made my eyes to water, my hands to shake, my heart to tremble, my senses astonished with a just amazement, and finally, it almost stroke an universall Palsey through my hole microcosme; in a word, me thoughts Hell it selfe could not be fuller fraught with more diabollicall expressions.[2]

Engaging with such lurid material was therefore not just immoral, but potentially life-threatening. What a shame, he reflected regretfully, that the days 'when the Author, of any scurrulous, or scandalous Pamphlet was soundly lasht' had 'become meere strangers unto us'.[3]

Both pamphlets were correct: things had not always been this way. Many Tudor and early Stuart authorities shared Sparke's fears about the corruptive power of lewd language. As a result, explicit sex-talk had only rarely appeared in print prior to 1640, thanks to the oversight of ecclesiastical press licensers and the London Stationers' Company as well as an independent collection of cultural, moral and religious injunctions against its public dissemination. This, in turn, relegated most obscene, libellous and politically subversive sexual material to underground scribal and oral forms that lay safely beyond the reach of anxious regulators. English print culture therefore remained almost entirely devoid of graphic sex-talk before the outbreak of civil war, even as it swirled violently through less conventional channels of discourse.

By the 1660 Restoration of King Charles II, much had changed. Sex was omnipresent in late Stuart England: printed satires gleefully described 'carnal passages betwixt a Quaker and a Colt' while foreign pornographies circulated among the London elite; female actors regularly appeared onstage for the first time in English history, and in 1675, so did a dildo; and the new king publicly trumpeted his extramarital affairs while contemporaries gossiped about the size of his penis.[4] This was a far cry indeed from Jacobean England, where, in Laura Gowing's words, 'it was positively virtuous not to be able to describe sex'. Instead, as Valerie Traub writes, by the early 1660s English polemicists, publicists and readers had 'reconfigured the terms of what could be said and written about sex in public'.[5] Sparke, who died in 1653, was surely rolling in his grave.

This book explores that dramatic transformation as it unfolded during the English Revolution of 1640–60. Following the Anglo-Scottish Bishops' Wars and the subsequent collapse of press licensing in England, partisan writers intrigued by the potential polemical value of explicit sex-talk took advantage of the chaos to propel it into print for the first time in English history alongside the outbreak of civil war. From there, sexual politics grew increasingly graphic and correspondingly more subversive, driven in part by the necessities of military mobilisation and partly by enterprising publishers striving to corner mid-century England's lucrative print marketplace. When the Stuart dynasty regained the throne in 1660, those novel lexicons – now widely available in print and primed for further appropriation – provided the ideological basis for both Charles II's pleasure-centred self-representation as well as that of his moralising godly opposition while also laying crucial discursive groundwork for the eighteenth-century phenomenon that Faramerz Dabhoiwala has recently dubbed the West's 'first sexual revolution'.[6]

To tell that story, this book presents a new narrative history of the English Revolution. The following chapters explore how partisan muckrakers, catalysed by the frantic pace of civil war politics, transformed once-taboo sexual tropes and stereotypes into a set of coherent – and ultimately quite potent – public political discourses. This study offers a novel take on the revolutionary period in several senses: first, as an empirical political history that places sex and gender at the centre of its analysis; second, as a challenge to longstanding assumptions about the origins of Restoration sexual culture; and, third, as an argument for the broader significance of England's mid-seventeenth-century civil wars and interregnum to the history of Western sexuality writ large. In the process, by charting the development of a single strain of polemic across the entire period, it offers an opportunity to 'think the English Revolution whole' in a way that has rarely been attempted in specialist scholarship.[7]

Its most important objective is exploratory. Although literary scholars and historians have often commented on the lurid content that flooded into English print culture after 1640, none have yet undertaken a full analysis of mid-seventeenth-century sex-talk, much less an account of its polemical development over two decades of political upheaval. That story – the unprecedented sexualisation of English public discourse between 1640 and 1660 – is my primary focus, and while a comprehensive account lays beyond the scope of any one book, I hope here to provide a useful starting point for future scholarship.

Next, this book charts the ways in which mid-century polemicists applied explicit sex-talk to politics. In particular, it argues that patriarchal and post-Reformation ideas about the political and moral significance of sexual (im)morality came to provide a unique collection of satirical stereotypes, libelous critiques and inventive metaphors through which partisan commentators could debate the conflict's most pressing issues. That development was due in part to the special epistemological appeal of human sexuality, which stemmed from a host of early modern moral, spiritual and cultural contexts; but equally important was its broad accessibility, for almost everyone in early modern England possessed a basic understanding of sexual pleasure, pregnancy and birth. Those concepts therefore translated readily to partisan propaganda in ways that more abstract frameworks did not: as Robert Darnton has written for a later period, sex could do 'for ordinary people what logic does for philosophers'.[8] They eventually fired the imagination of Charles II himself, who, after his 1660 accession, set about adopting a radical strand of interregnum royalist sexual politics for his own personal brand. In making explicit the connections between politics and sex-talk during the English Revolution, therefore, this analysis also sheds light on that relationship after the Restoration, at a time when the two were more explicitly linked.

Lastly, this book proposes that the sexualisation of English public culture during the 1640s and 1650s can provide a new way of thinking about the history of Western sexuality writ large. Although most (but, importantly, not all) of the polemicists responsible for propelling graphic sex-talk into print after the outbreak of civil war showed very little interest in promoting sexual liberty, the sheer volume of sexually explicit material circulating in revolutionary England was virtually impossible for contemporary readers to ignore. Equally important was the budding connection – sometimes latent, sometimes explicit – between sexual discourse and sexual practice, as contemporaries discussed, denounced and defended their (and others') personal sexual histories with surprising candour. By publicising sex-talk like never before, in short, partisan pamphleteers unwittingly rendered sexuality itself less susceptible to moral control. That collective – albeit largely unconscious – decision would resonate in England, and beyond, for at least a century to follow.

## Some preliminary definitions

First, a word on terminology. I have employed the analytical category of 'sexual politics' as shorthand for the disparate array of sexual polemics that surged into print after 1640. The feminist scholar Kate Millett famously defined sexual politics as intrinsically coercive, patriarchal and violent, rooted in the domination of women by men and virtually pervasive in modern public culture.[9] In one sense, this book follows Millett's argument by asserting that in civil war England, women's bodies served as a primary conceptual battlefield over which mid-century polemicists staked their respective claims to moral, religious and political legitimacy. However, it also expands on her definition to encompass myriad different and often competing ways in which contemporary discourses of sex and the body collided with early modern ideas about church, state and society. In doing so, I echo scholars like Frances Ferguson and Kathleen Lubey, among others, who have linked sex-writing (both early modern and modern) with a more complex and potentially revolutionary set of epistemological positions than were allowed for in Millett's pioneering work.[10]

In what follows, I pay particular attention to a form of creative sex-writing that I, following earlier commentators, have dubbed 'porno-politics'.[11] By this, I mean a contemporary mode of political theorising in which graphic sexual metaphors were employed to describe, and eventually even explain, political change. From the mid-to-late 1640s, contemporaries marshalled a potent figurative language of infidelity, sexual violence and monstrous birth in which protagonists as diverse as the national church and King Charles himself were reimagined as lovers engaged in heterosexual, procreative intercourse with dramatic consequences for the kingdom. As we will see, mid-century porno-politics appeared in a variety of ideological and thematic guises, although generative language proved particularly useful for partisan theorists struggling to explain the upside-down world in which they found themselves after 1640.[12] These pornified truth-claims thrived especially in the years surrounding the regicide, and as Susan Wiseman and Rachel Weil have shown, they continued to shape English political theory after the Restoration.[13]

Print – especially the short-form pamphlets, single-sheet broadsides and serial newsbooks collectivised under the broad label of 'cheap print' – provides the bulk of my evidence. Mid-seventeenth-century print culture has received considerable scholarly attention, and this book strives to contribute to that rich historiography by highlighting the ways in which the so-called 'print explosion' of 1640/41 amplified modes of political discourse previously considered too transgressive for the medium.[14] In doing so, it does not ignore the complex interlinkages between oral culture, manuscript and print that persisted throughout the revolutionary period; nor does it neglect the commercial motivations of publishers who embraced graphic sex-talk primarily for profit's sake.[15] Both perspectives are essential for appreciating the long-term impact of the mid-seventeenth-century printing revolution for English political and sexual culture alike after 1660.

This book is about print, but it is also about the more complicated category of 'public culture'. I do not want to suggest that the two are synonymous, for historians have shown that manuscripts could be 'public' documents, too, insofar as they were also intended to be absorbed and acted upon by a broad readership.[16] Even so, contemporaries certainly distinguished between private and public arenas of discourse when it came to evaluating the appropriateness of explicit sex-talk: proof can be found in, on the one hand, the extremely frank sexual language that accompanied courtroom discussions of sexual crime throughout the early modern period and, on the other, the near-total absence of such language from English print prior to 1640.[17] By 'public culture', then, I mean a collection of political and social processes – including a burgeoning kingdom-wide news culture and growing contemporary interest in (and access to) parliament – that, alongside the 1640/41 printing revolution, have been identified by some scholars with the emergence of England's first proto-modern 'public sphere'. Although I am not especially invested in the particulars of that debate, it is clear that the revolutionary period transformed contemporary thinking about the necessity and ease of participating in national politics.[18] It is thus the intrusion of politicised sex-talk into that process (which, given that such language was often explicitly intended to reveal 'private' practices to the wider world, was necessarily a complicated one), and its impact on English political and sexual culture in turn, with which this book is chiefly concerned.

### Early modern sexuality in context/s

Sex, as it is understood here, encompasses the full spectrum of human erotic activity – penetrative and non-penetrative, hetero- and same-sex, consensual and non-consensual – as well as the correspondingly broad collection of contemporary teachings related to human sexuality that circulated throughout seventeenth-century English society: beliefs that, with very few exceptions, stemmed from a basic assumption that the only legitimate forms of sexual contact occurred within the bounds of heterosexual marriage. Christian morality, supplemented by a cultural obsession with bodily comportment and personal reputation, provided much of the inspiration for such teachings, which stretched beyond the pulpit into nearly every facet of early modern English society.[19] As we will see, contemporary ideas about sexual morality took on especial significance during the civil wars, when the rending of the body politic – and the physical violence it entailed – placed the human body at the very centre of the kingdom's collective political consciousness. As such, they deserve some extended attention here.

In early modern Britain, as in eighteenth-century France, bodies served as emblems and barometers of social, spiritual and cosmic (dis)order.[20] This in turn lent personal sexuality an enormous political and moral significance. According to the puritan moralist John Dod, for example, adultery was 'worse then eyther theft or murder', because the adulterer 'doth not onely destroy his owne soule, but . . . the soule of another also'.[21] Equally telling is the letter that the clergyman Richard Baxter received in July 1655 from a minister whose addiction to 'the practise of selfe pollution' (i.e. masturbation) had encouraged him to make 'many an attempt against my owne life'. While he apparently survived those ordeals, another contemporary was not so lucky: after the Staffordshire man Thomas Cooke was accused of having 'Buggered a Mare' that same year, the shame of the 'scandale' caused his son to hang himself.[22] Sex – and especially sexual malfeasance – was no trivial matter for early moderns.

Nor could it be, considering the extraordinary emphasis placed on the regulation of sexual crime by Tudor and early Stuart authorities. Early-seventeenth-century English sexual culture has been summarised as a 'system of public discipline' in which 'the right to have sex, and to form a family', was a communal affair. Thus, church courts regularly mandated behavioural or financial penance for extramarital unchastity, while local communities employed rowdier festive rituals to shame sexual criminals. Many social historians have suggested, in Martin Ingram's words, that 'the authorities' view that the legal regulation of personal behaviour was fundamental to the maintenance of social order was at least to some extent shared by the mass of the governed'; others, however – primarily historians of gender – have argued instead that those who suffered most from these patriarchal regulatory systems (i.e. women) were unlikely to embrace public discipline as readily as the male householders generally responsible for enforcing it. Nevertheless, and although new scholarship on the late medieval period has challenged the uniquely repressive character of early Stuart moral control, most scholars agree that the Jacobean and Caroline regimes policed sexual activity to a remarkable degree.[23]

As those oppressive regulatory structures attested, early moderns endowed sex with an enormously complicated range of political and religious meanings. Consider the story of King David's adultery, narrated in 2 Samuel 11. In the biblical account, David is so overcome by lust for Bathsheba, wife of the Israelite soldier Uriah, that the king orders Uriah to his death on the front lines of an ongoing war so that he can lie with her unencumbered. Later, David is thoroughly chastised by God for his sins. But although the king's adultery (and, of course, Uriah's murder) was obviously criminal, early modern exegetes drew many different meanings from this episode. Was the lesson that all kings were inherently rapacious? Or that all people, royal or otherwise, were susceptible to lust? Or, indeed, that David's long and exceptional reign demonstrated how the natural glory of monarchy might overcome even gross moral error?[24] Even within the restrictive boundaries of contemporary morality, the political implications of human sexuality were unendingly complex.

Two further contexts proved especially influential in shaping early modern English sexual culture. First were widespread patriarchal assumptions about the intrinsic intellectual, spiritual and moral inferiority of women to men, among which numbered a truism about the endless depths of female libidinousness in comparison with the natural chastity associated with proper masculinity.[25] Second, but no less pervasive, was the contentious influence of Europe's long Reformation, which suffused English political culture throughout the period.[26] Not only, therefore, was sex inseparable from early modern politics; it was also inextricably connected with contemporary debates about gender, religion and popular culture. This, in turn, made sexual politics a uniquely potent tool for commenting on the sociopolitical upheavals of revolutionary England.

## Methodologies

This book takes the form of an empirical narrative history. Beginning with the Anglo-Scottish troubles of July 1637 and concluding several decades after the 1660 Restoration, it charts the development of explicit sex-talk into a distinctive mode of public politicking during the English civil wars and interregnum. I recognise that this chronological structure entails several unavoidable pitfalls. In addition to all the usual concerns – the possibility of undue repetitiveness, for instance, or of rehashing large chunks of the period's too-familiar political history – it also fails to honour calls from literary scholars to queer the historiography by offering alternative, non-chronological accounts of human sexuality past and present. (On this reading, historicism itself is seen to be complicit in the construction of heteronormativity, as nearly every chronological history of sexuality engages, explicitly or implicitly, with the modern binary of hetero/homo.)[27] However, a narrative approach is essential for capturing the nuance and breadth of English sex-talk as it developed in print after the outbreak of civil war; indeed, without it, we miss the opportunity to appreciate the echoes, appropriations and inversions that linked the sexual politics of 1641 with those of 1659 (and beyond), and therefore to explore key continuities that tied together the entire revolutionary period. I hope I will also be forgiven for pitching this account at a slightly more accessible level than is commonplace for specialist scholarship, in hopes that readers unfamiliar with the context might still find it useful.

Throughout, we will focus on the innovative ways in which partisan polemicists applied graphic sex-talk – often, but not exclusively, in print – to politics. Mid-century sexual polemic took a dazzling range of medial and thematic forms, from bulky heresiographies to single-sheet broadsides and proto-pornographic verse. In what follows, we will encounter moralising censures of sexual corruption, often blamed by contemporaries on the ongoing revolutionary upheavals; acrid satires, including unprecedented *ad hominem* commentary on the sexual histories of England's most revered political leaders; and creative adaptions of familiar cultural tropes, like the Protestant vision of Catholicism as the biblical Whore of Babylon, for novel porno-political ends. Early modern England was also home to a thriving (scribal) culture of erotic writing prior to the outbreak of civil war, and these texts, too, surged into print with increasing frequency during the revolutionary decades. Indeed, after the regicide of Charles I, some partisan theorists even began to advocate for new models of human sexual practice itself, as libertine Ranters preached a novel doctrine of divine promiscuity while cavalier poets embraced a worldly ethos of drink and casual sex in response to Cromwellian moral discipline: both prime examples of the astounding creativity engendered by the period's political strife.²⁸

I have chosen to embrace, rather than to anatomise, this disparate array of polemical modes. As we will see, none escaped the general escalation in graphic description prompted by the English Revolution; nor were their authors spared the criticisms of contemporary moralists like Michael Sparke, who argued that such language threatened to drag its consumers – and, consequently, the entire kingdom – into sexual anarchy by virtue of the fantasies it engendered. In what follows, therefore, lurid accounts of puritan 'holy sisters' copulating with their brethren in secret conventicles are situated side-by-side with horrified descriptions of monstrous births. Each attests, in its own way, to the unprecedented sexualisation of English public discourse after 1640.

This approach, too, presents methodological challenges. First, the sheer variety of sex-talk available to contemporary pamphleteers makes it impossible to offer a quantitative analysis by any conventional metric.²⁹ Moreover, although this study routinely addresses textual disparities in format, timbre and polemical purpose, it does not pay sustained attention to certain genres – such as medical textbooks or familial advice literature – that were not directly mired in the ongoing conflict.³⁰ This includes the vexed debate over the origins of seventeenth-century English pornography, about which I have very little to say here.³¹ Nor do I follow other scholarly commentators in delineating strict etymological boundaries between degrees of sexual explicitness: categories which, Melissa Mohr has argued, were only just coming into existence during the early modern period.³² Instead, this book focuses on the comprehensive evolution of English sexual language between 1640 and 1660, and its corresponding influence on the political history of the period.

Finally, a word on reception. Throughout this book, we will encounter evidence of contemporaries who bought, read and discussed the vicious sexual polemics that whirled across revolutionary England. My analysis relies especially heavily on the collecting habits of the London bookseller George Thomason, who purchased nearly every text discussed in the following chapters and often helpfully annotated his copies with the date of acquisition.³³ Yet reader responses to those texts are relatively rare, limiting the degree to which we can assess their broader impact. The astonishing array of different purposes to which they could be put – from sophisticated political commentary to mundane sexual arousal – complicates the question even further. All that can be said for certain is that explicit sex-talk continued to appeal to readers throughout the period, and that English printers and publishers proved increasingly willing to respond in kind.

## Historiographies

Broadly speaking, historians are no strangers to sexual politics. Since the early 1980s, a vast historiography has traced these themes across early modern Europe and beyond.[34] Yet while they have periodically featured in other subfields of British history, 'sexual politics' as such rarely surface in political histories of Tudor and Stuart England.[35] The omission is conspicuous, especially given the inherently gendered qualities of the era's dominant political metaphors. As Alastair Bellany notes, this failure to take 'contemporary discourses of sexuality . . . seriously as political languages' has hampered modern scholars from appreciating critical aspects of seventeenth-century English history.[36] One central objective of this book, therefore, is the rehabilitation of human sexuality as an important, even essential, lens for assessing the political culture of the period.

In doing so, it also attempts to bring the political history of the English Revolution up to speed with other areas of the historiography. By documenting early modern England's complex and competing patriarchal belief systems, for instance, scholars of seventeenth-century gender politics have revolutionised our understanding of early Stuart kingship on the eve of the civil war.[37] Historians of England's 'post-Reformation public sphere', meanwhile, have investigated the prejudices and polemics that divided English Catholics, conformist Protestants, puritans and radicals for many decades following the religious upheavals of the early sixteenth century: disputes that, given the age-old equation between theological heterodoxy and sexual corruption, often invoked sexual politics in their most grotesque and vicious forms.[38] Elsewhere, scholars have continued to explore the histories of libel, publicity and 'popularity' to great effect.[39] The best of this work has convincingly reconstructed many of the period's deep-seated anxieties about disorder, inversion and the world-turned-upside-down, with transformative consequences for our broader picture of seventeenth-century political history.[40]

Nevertheless, with only a few exceptions, none of this scholarship has yet inspired historians of the English Revolution to analyse in any great detail the sexual polemics that entered print after 1640. Indeed, barring some recent comments on the theoretical connection between Hobbesian materialism and Restoration libertinism, not even the otherwise excellent historiography of English pornography has much to say about the mid-century's role in that genre's rapid early modern evolution.[41] Among political historians in particular, this neglect has stemmed largely from the influence of the revisionist movement of the 1970s and 1980s, which rejected huge swathes of contemporary partisan print as fundamentally unfit for analysis.[42] As a result, mid-century sex-talk remained largely unexplored for many years, even as scholars in adjacent fields charted important links between sex, print and political revolution across early modern Europe.[43]

For many earlier historians, the earthiness of the sources also proved a powerful disincentive. In 1961, H. N. Brailsford wrote, 'it is amazing how many rhymes a royalist scribbler can find for "whore"; the modern reader can supply yet another; it begins with b'. Other twentieth-century assessments were equally scornful, from Hyden Rollins's 1923 description of several mid-century ballads as 'pure doggerel' to Charles Carlton's dismissal of other cheap royalist publications as 'downright tasteless . . . piece[s] of nonsense'.[44] Anonymous modern commentary on seventeenth-century manuscripts leaves a similar impression. On one anti-puritan verse satire, a later writer has scrawled, 'is not this Archbishop Frewens handwriting? It is no great credit to him.' A poetic miscellany in Cambridge University Library bears an equivalent note: 'There is not much that is new in this MS', it reads; 'most of it has been printed, excepting the indecencies, which are very gross, even to me who profess[es?] not to be squeamish'. As attested by J. B. Williams's 1910 adjudication that the scandalous output of royalist polemicists was altogether 'quite unquotable', the sensibilities of disapproving readers have until recently precluded many of these sources from scholarly consideration outright.[45]

The same biases are evident in modern editions of seventeenth-century manuscripts, many of which purposefully omit the sexual from their transcriptions. The 1848 edition of *The Diary of Walter Yonge* silently excised all evidence that Sir Henry Marten kept a mistress, while even Rollins, who made 'no apology' for the 'frankness of language' catalogued in his collection of civil war ballads, excluded two exceptionally scurrilous stanzas from one entry in the interest of 'purify[ing] coarseness of diction'.[46] Similarly, the widely used Halliwell edition of Sir Simonds D'Ewes's correspondence does not include most of the sexual material present in the original manuscript, including a graphic description of Sir Francis Bacon as an effeminate sodomite.[47] Nor was this practice limited to previous generations: in the 1991 edited calendar of Richard Baxter's correspondence, for instance, the letter quoted above in which a self-loathing young minister begs Baxter for guidance on how to cure his masturbation addiction (a plea that runs to more than two pages in manuscript) is reduced to a single sentence.[48] Sexual politics therefore have not only been neglected, but sometimes actively repressed, by modern scholars.

Only recently have they begun to receive serious attention. The groundbreaking study was Susan Wiseman's pioneering 1991 analysis of republican porno-politics, which proposed to treat 'political theory and scurrilous polemic' as two parts of 'a continuum of political discourses' that mingled promiscuously during the revolutionary decades.[49] Other literary scholars, among them Sharon Achinstein, Joad Raymond, Diane Purkiss and Nigel Smith, have followed suit in an array of studies documenting the rhetorical and theoretical connections between mid-century literary culture and contemporary sex and gender ideologies.[50] Even more productively, Melissa Mowry and James Grantham Turner have traced the development of specific veins of civil-war sex-talk during the 1640s and 1650s into full-blown political pornography after the Restoration.[51] Yet none of these scholars has yet attempted, as this book does, to move beyond genre in order to assess the broader transformations that assailed English sexual polemic during the revolutionary upheavals. By taking the widest possible view, this analysis in turn provides a new framework for analysing individual strands of mid-century sex-writing.

Historians have been slower to join the chorus. Even so, since the publication of Ann Hughes's 1995 analysis of the Levellers' 'vivid language of sexual contrast', gender and print historians in particular have produced several important studies of revolutionary-era sex-talk.[52] Especially notable has been the work of David Underdown and Jason McElligott, which catalogued the appeal of explicit sexual rhetoric for royalist polemicists anxious to attract the support of conservative anti-puritan readers during the later 1640s. In a different vein, Jamie Gianoutsos has traced the role of 'classical discourses of tyranny and gender' in undermining Stuart rule during the early-to-mid-seventeenth century, while Bernard Capp has addressed another aspect of mid-century sexual politics in his study of the interregnum culture wars.[53] Yet despite these valuable contributions, relatively little has been done to integrate sex-talk into the standard political history of the period.[54] Meanwhile, even less attention has been paid to its significance for the general historiography of Western sexuality.

This book sets out to address those lacunae by marrying the historiographies of early modern gender and sexuality with the narrative political history of the English Revolution for the first time. It is an approach that offers considerable dividends for both fields. Moreover, by watching as partisan writers melded a disparate array of sexual stereotypes, libellous satires and political theories into coherent political languages after the outbreak of civil war, we can appreciate not only the centrality of sex-writing to mid-century political culture, but also the possibilities afforded by that culture towards the transformation of other contemporary discursive modes. As such, this study offers a structural model for future work as well as a series of specific claims about the historical and historiographical significance of mid-seventeenth-century sex-talk.

Finally, this book argues that the English Revolution deserves attention from historians of Western sexuality more broadly. From the pioneering work of Lawrence Stone to Faramerz Dabhoiwala's recent exploration of the West's 'first sexual revolution', most scholars have privileged the promiscuous Restoration court of Charles II, rather than the bloody upheavals that preceded it, as the most important seventeenth-century influence on the development of English sexual modernity. As I will show, however, late Stuart sexual culture owed a considerable debt to the English Revolution, which ushered frank discussions of human sexuality into print for the first time in the kingdom's history. On this account, that process was the unintended consequence of short-term decisions made by political actors with (mostly) little-to-no interest in fostering sexual liberty – here, I follow James Grantham Turner in recognising that 'world-changing ideas' can make 'their first appearance as farce' – but that made it no less significant.[55] The ultimate result, to borrow Valerie Traub's phrase, was the birth of England's first 'sexual public', as contemporary readers collected, consumed and contested graphic descriptions of human sexual activity like never before.[56] The historiographical implications of this argument will be explored further in the conclusion. The remainder of this introduction briefly sketches the most important themes of English sexual politics as they developed during the century-and-a-half preceding the outbreak of civil war – and, just as importantly, the methods employed, largely successfully, by Tudor and early Stuart authorities to silence them.

## Sexual politics in Tudor and early Stuart England

Early modern sexual politics began with monarchy. Sex and kingship were intimately intertwined, due to the ancient patriarchal tenet that kings served as both fathers and husbands to their loving subjects: 'soveraigns marry', read one illustrative proverb, 'for the good of the state, whereof they must be more amarous & jealous, than of wives, and children'.[57] Important, too, was the political myth of the 'king's two bodies', which bifurcated royal power into two distinct forms – one personal, physical and mortal ('the body natural'), the other constitutional, metaphysical and eternal ('the body politic') – said to meld promiscuously within every sitting ruler.[58] In both senses, the royal body served a powerful legitimising purpose; but kingly sexuality could be dangerous, too, and wayward monarchs risked unseemly comparisons with the numerous oversexed tyrants – like Sextus Tarquinus, the rapacious tormentor of chaste Lucretia – who populated the classical tradition revered by sixteenth- and seventeenth-century commentators.[59]

As Kevin Sharpe has shown, Henry VIII walked this line more carefully than any of his predecessors by 'present[ing] his private, sexual body as a public representation of his rule'.[60] Many of his successors proved similarly adept at navigating the sexual politics of early modern monarchy: Elizabeth I, facing down a host of misogynistic stereotypes, repudiated criticisms of her femininity, her singlehood and her parentage with an amalgam of positive tropes (unmarried virgin, loving wife, nurturing mother) that undermined contemporary assumptions about the dangers of female rule; James I, already a self-proclaimed father-king to his Scottish subjects when he inherited Elizabeth's crown in 1603, declared himself England's new loving 'Husband'; and even the abstemious Charles I held up his bounteous marriage to Henrietta Maria of France as both a literal and metaphorical symbol of English political harmony.[61] In the process, these rulers – including, at times, Elizabeth – refined a conjugal metaphor for patriarchal kingship that situated their subjects in the role of obedient, loving wives.

As good patriarchs, English monarchs were responsible for the moral well-being of their people. In the sixteenth century, both Edward VI and Elizabeth excelled in this role, the latter by exercising strict control over the romantic escapades of her courtiers.[62] Similarly, in 1631, Charles won praise for his handling of the notorious Castlehaven case, when he promptly sentenced to death an Irish peer accused of rape and sodomy. (The king even forbade female spectators from attending the trial for fear that overhearing a recitation of the crimes might damage their modesty.)[63] In contrast, the lurid scandals that haunted James's court tarnished his public image. None were more damning than the so-called Overbury affair, which began when Lady Frances Howard divorced her aristocratic husband, the third earl of Essex, in 1613 on grounds of impotence before quickly remarrying one of the king's favourites. Worse still, when she was later found to be guilty of murder, the king could not bring himself to execute either her or her new husband and sent them into quiet exile instead.[64] During the years that followed, in pamphlets like *A wonder woorth the reading* (1617), contemporary moralists reported tales of malformed offspring delivered by English women – complete with alarmingly monstrous images – as providential signs of God's mounting displeasure with the kingdom.[65] Such stories reflected a burgeoning cultural binary between the corrupt, licentious 'court' and a virtuous, purifying 'country' that would haunt James and his successor for many years to come.[66]

Sexual politics therefore provided a potent framework for critiquing kingly failures. Nearly every monarch who ruled between 1509 and 1640 learned this lesson in one form or another. Henry VIII's scandalous marital saga, and especially the executions of Anne Boleyn and Catherine Howard for adultery, cemented his court's reputation for sexual disorder.[67] Elizabeth's perpetual bachelorhood led both hostile Catholic commentators and her own Protestant subjects to excoriate her presumptive partners, and eventually (in the Catholics' case) even the queen herself,

# A WONDER WOORTH THE READING,

OR

A True and faithfull Relation of a Woman, now dwelling in Kentstreet, who, vpon Thursday, being the 21. of August last, was deliuered of a prodigious and Monstrous Child, in the presence of diuers honest, and religious women to their wonderfull feare and astonishment.

LONDON
Imprinted by *William Jones* dwelling in Redcrosse-streete 1617.

Figure 0.1 *A wonder woorth the reading* (1617)

as promiscuous and debauched.[68] James's alarmingly close relationships with his male favourites inspired dark whispers about his sexuality, while Charles's devotion to his French Catholic wife prompted his godly subjects to wonder if their king had been seduced and emasculated by his foreign, popish queen.[69] In making these claims, some critics of royal policy even turned their sovereigns' beloved conjugal metaphor on its head: in one instance, during the 1620s, an unknown satirist condemned the 'wanton Duke' of Buckingham for disrupting the marriage between 'the Kinge and his Wyfe the Parliament' by having 'rape committed' on the body politic.[70] The explosive nature of such critiques necessarily relegated them to manuscript and oral forms, for reasons to be discussed shortly; but they remained potent nonetheless.[71]

Indeed, for some subjects, royal favourites like Buckingham represented one of the kingdom's most serious threats. Drawing on an ancient trope frequently employed by the Roman historian Tacitus, hostile commentators identified such figures as 'evil counsellors': conniving, self-serving advisors who misled their patron monarchs for personal gain.[72] Especially frightening was their access to the sacred royal body, which opened the door for sexual corruption. Most alarming of all was the spectre of same-sex intimacy, characterised under a catch-all term for gross sexual deviance, 'sodomy' (or, alternatively, 'the sin that cannot be named'). James's relationship with Buckingham was so suspicious in this regard that scribal poets labelled the duke an alluring 'Ganymed[e]', Jove's boy-lover from classical myth, who James's 'marrow so had wasted'.[73] It is difficult to imagine a more damning indictment of royal misgovernment – albeit one that circulated, again, entirely in manuscript.

Underlying most of these concerns was another fundamental obsession with the vitality of English Protestantism. From its faltering beginnings, England's long Reformation brought a virulent strain of sexual politics to the archipelago derived from the brutal polemics that had volleyed between Luther and his Catholic critics since the 1520s. After Henry VIII's break with Rome, his Protestant subjects happily joined in, lampooning Catholic monks as sodomites and the Roman episcopacy as pimps and whoremongers.[74] Simultaneously, English evangelicals led by the polemicist John Bale crafted an apocalyptic interpretation of the Catholic church as the biblical Whore of Babylon and its spiritual hierarchy of pope, bishops and priests as her monstrous children.[75] For reformers who viewed the pope as Antichrist, the staggering variety of these allegations made sense (what else would one expect of a satanic creed except a total inversion of proper morality?), and popish diabolism justified in turn the Protestants' deployment of vulgar slanders that contrasted sharply in tone with their moralising agenda.[76] They were challenged in turn by Catholic apologists who drew on contemporary accounts of sectarian depravity – such as the horrors of Anabaptist Munster, where Protestant radicals established a short-lived utopian kingdom in which the polygamous doctrine of a shared 'community of women' was made legal – in order to decry the Protestant heresy (and, often, errant fellow Catholics) as equally immoral and depraved.[77]

No English ruler engaged with those discourses more readily than Elizabeth, whose reign featured skirmishes with Catholic polemicists at home and abroad as well as a prolonged standoff with evangelical puritans who criticised the queen's lukewarm commitment to reformation by adapting Bale's apocalyptic anti-popery to dismiss any remnants of Catholic ecclesiology in the national church (most of all, Elizabeth's bishops) as the Babylonian Whore's bastard offspring.[78] In both cases, the regime fought fire with fire. The queen's ministers licensed covert libels against its Catholic enemies in manuscript and anonymous print, and they were even more aggressive in utilising anti-puritan satire against her Protestant critics.[79] When, in the 1580s, Presbyterian activists writing under the moniker of 'Martin Marprelate' published a string of printed attacks on Elizabeth's bishops laced with accusations of bigamy, adultery and cuckoldry, Elizabethan authorities responded by hiring penmen of their own to produce a mélange of cheap pamphlets and burlesque stage-plays ridiculing the godly leadership as lecherous, sex-obsessed hypocrites who preached moral reformation while secretly wallowing in lust.[80] A decade prior, genuine Protestant sectarians like the Family of Love had received equally short shrift from regime-sponsored pamphleteers who followed earlier critics of the Munster Anabaptists in focusing on the promiscuous implications of the familists' 'antinomian' theology, which dictated that God's grace granted true believers total freedom from the moral law.[81]

Elizabethan leaders' enthusiastic sponsorship of sexual politics in these quasi-official forms is particularly striking because the reign also witnessed sustained regime efforts to suppress overtly obscene, subversive and libellous sex-talk from public discourse. As Debora Shuger has observed, unlike in Catholic Europe, there were no laws on the books in Tudor and early Stuart England that specifically forbade the publication of obscenity; but this was not from lack of trying. Edward VI, following the model of Calvin's Geneva, attempted to ban the printing of immoral and unseemly language in 1551, and Elizabethan puritan legislators made several similar attempts to outlaw 'lewd & wanton discourses of love' decades later.[82] Yet even in the absence of such laws, most graphic sex-talk remained limited to manuscript and oral circulation before 1640.

That was due largely to the kingdom's increasingly confident press licensing system. First established under Elizabeth and periodically revitalised by the Stuarts, the various mechanisms employed by Elizabeth's bishops and the London Stationers' Company to regulate England's burgeoning print marketplace were highly effective at protecting it from the period's most potentially destabilising sexual politics: most notably, criticisms of the state, the monarchy, or the national church.[83] In theory, this meant that graphic sex-talk – including straightforward eroticism – which did not directly impinge on politics could circulate freely; and, indeed, from the 1580s, English writers inspired by the work of Renaissance eroticists like Pietro Aretino had produced a flurry of lascivious scribal verses in which graphic allusions to female genitalia ('cunnye', 'cunt') collided with frank descriptions of intercourse.[84] But although this tradition, which reached its peak with Thomas Nashe's comically sensual 'Choice of Valentines', did not unduly alarm Elizabeth's ministers while it remained in manuscript, the authorities occasionally did act against overtly erotic material when it appeared in print. Consider, for instance, the 1599 'Bishops' Ban', which outlawed the printing of satires and epigrams in general and singled out a few specific pamphlets to be publicly incinerated. Although the texts in question were undoubtedly political, they were also sexually explicit, and some scholars have argued that it was ultimately their eroticism which convinced regime leaders to act.[85] Whatever its architects' motives, the 1599 ban succeeded in limiting genuinely obscene sex-talk to manuscript for nearly four decades to follow.[86]

Again, this still technically left a mass of minorly bawdy poetry and prose free to enter print. But even this less obviously graphic canon unsettled other commentators who worried about the impact of such lurid material on English social harmony. Arbiters of genteel culture, for one, mobilised the humanist principles embodied in Erasmus of Rotterdam's enormously successful *De civilitate morum puerilium* (1530) to oppose the printed dissemination of explicit sex-talk in the vernacular, although they generally remained happy to allow classical Roman erotica to circulate in its original Latin.[87] Even more vociferous were English puritans, who extrapolated from a broader Calvinist physiology of sin that drew no material distinction between reading bawdy books and engaging in illicit sex-acts to insist that that erotic writing of any sort – from the patently obscene to the mildly bawdy – served only to 'corrupt mens mindes, pervert good wits, allure to baudrie, induce to whordome, suppresse vertue & erect vice'.[88] Interestingly, these objections did not prevent many sober Protestant ministers from embracing the undeniably eroticised spiritualist language of the biblical Song of Songs (a quasi-ecstatic tradition also beloved of many early modern Catholics and genuine Protestant sectarians alike).[89] Nevertheless, the godly repeatedly took to print during the half-century before 1640 to

Introduction 19

bemoan 'the wanton and dissolute education' of England's 'youth' by 'ribaldous words', 'filthy rimes' and 'unchristian Songs'.[90]

The profusion of mild bawdry in printed jest-books and verse collections throughout the period suggest that very few readers took the puritans' warnings seriously.[91] Indeed, many contemporaries displayed an evident fondness for ribald humour, such as two Caroline officials who joked about 'having gott yours [wife] with childe' in private correspondence.[92] Still, others remained anxious about lascivious language. The decidedly non-puritan Nicholas Ferrar reportedly burned his books on his deathbed in 1637 in recognition of the 'filthy lusts' they engendered in readers. Even collectors of erotic poetry in manuscript documented their unease at its moral implications. One early Stuart transcriber of a lurid satire on London prostitutes thus scribbled, 'pray my love tell nobody from whom this song comes, for I am ashamed to owne it', on the back of their copy. Another lewd miscellany from the period bears a handwritten note begging, 'let nobody see this booke'.[93]

Altogether, then, prewar England's patchwork of regulatory mechanisms ensured that most graphically sexual language remained confined to manuscript and oral forms, although the active suppression of objectionable material occurred only sporadically. It seems that while English printers and publishers recognised the potential selling power of lewd books (as evidenced by the steady production of bawdy jestbooks, murder pamphlets and mildly erotic verse throughout the Tudor and early Stuart periods), they were generally too fearful of censure to risk violating the period's various injunctions against truly obscene, libellous or politically subversive sex-talk. Yet while those safeguards were broadly effective in keeping graphic sex-writing from print, they were not always compatible with one another. Consider the case of the puritan pamphleteer William Prynne, who indicted the 'Unchast, Obscene, and Amorous wordes' of Caroline court theatre in his 1633 *Histriomastix* only to run afoul of regime leaders (and, ultimately, lose the tips of his ears) for obliquely describing Queen Henrietta Maria as a whore in a four-word index entry.[94] At the same time, Charles I's ongoing patronage of a small group of court poets and dramatists – whose bawdy (scribal) verses seemed to celebrate, in the poet Thomas Carew's words, the triumph of 'unrestrayned Appetite' over the 'fetter[s]' of 'chastitye' – proved similarly perplexing for his godly subjects, who struggled to square the king's apparent support for such blatant eroticism with his swift prosecution of Castlehaven in 1631.[95]

Such conflicts were a natural result of the strange state of English sexual politics by the end of the early Stuart period: widely constrained from print by a variety of regulatory mechanisms, yet mutating into ever more violent and complex forms in circumspect manuscripts and oral exchanges. One final example illustrates this paradoxical arrangement. When Buckingham was impeached by the House of Commons for crimes against the kingdom in 1626, parliamentary prosecutors compiled a lengthy account of the duke's 'Adulteryes and the like' that they presumably intended to deploy during the trial. But once the proceedings began, Buckingham's accusers balked: rather than revealing what they knew about the duke's sexual exploits to the listening parliament-men, they alluded to his lechery only obliquely. Similarly, during the duke's concurrent trial in the Lords, it was announced that the 'scandall' of Buckingham's 'personall behavior' was neither 'fitt . . . to speake, nor for the howse to heare'.[96] In both cases, a prevailing cultural allergy to public sex-talk – not to mention the potential royal outrage that might have greeted the revelation of Buckingham's sexual crimes – succeeded in silencing his opposition on this count despite all of their preparatory work. But it could not prevent Charles's subjects from continuing to slander Buckingham's chastity in manuscript; and, two years later, the duke was assassinated by John Felton, a voracious consumer of such literature.[97]

All told, while sex-talk circulated in English print prior to 1640, it did so only in relatively mild forms. As the gruesome fate of William Prynne attested, great danger awaited any contemporaries bold enough to employ it directly – publicly, at least – against the state, its ministers and its royal head. Instead, such criticisms were limited (alongside most explicitly erotic writing and similarly scabrous personal libels) almost entirely to manuscript and oral culture throughout the Tudor and early Stuart periods. It would take the outbreak of civil war across all three Stuart kingdoms to finally propel them into print.

Before turning to that story, let me conclude with one final caveat. The sexual politics of mid-seventeenth-century England are not for the faint of heart. Obscenities dot many of the following pages, in some cases with alarming frequency, and the blatant misogyny that underlay all aspects of early modern gender ideology is difficult to escape even in the absence of outright vulgarity.[98] Because the mounting pitch of mid-century sex-talk is itself crucial evidence towards my argument, and in the interest of faithfully documenting the brutal polemical milieu in which these discourses emerged, I have refrained from censoring or skirting the language of contemporary sources even when it is patently offensive. At all points, my intention is to treat this material as seriously, and as thoroughly, as possible; to do any less would only perpetuate its damaging scholarly effacement. In the process, however, I also want to acknowledge its impact on contemporary men and (especially) women, for whom the period's vicious sexual polemics were inevitably demeaning, frequently harmful and occasionally fatal. For that reason, as much as any other, they deserve our attention.

# Notes

1 Michael Sparke, *A second beacon*, E.675[29] ([4 October] 1652), pp. 5, 7, 11.
2 *New news from the Old Exchange*, E.595[6] ([16 March] 1650), pp. 4–5.
3 Ibid., p. 1.
4 [Alexander Brome], *The Rump*, E.1833[4] ([21 June] 1660), p. 6; William Wycherley, *The country-wife*, Wing W3738 (1675), pp. 70–1; Robert Latham and William Matthews (eds), *The Diary of Samuel Pepys* (11 vols, Berkeley and Los Angeles, CA, 1970–83), iv, pp. 136–8. See also David Foxon, *Libertine Literature in England, 1660–1745* (New York, NY, 1965).
5 Laura Gowing, *Common Bodies: Women, Touch and Power in Seventeenth-Century England* (New Haven, CT, 2003), p. 83; Valerie Traub, *Thinking Sex with the Early Moderns* (Philadelphia, PA, 2016), p. 116.
6 Faramerz Dabhoiwala, *The Origins of Sex: A History of the First Sexual Revolution* (London, 2012).
7 I borrow this phrase from Steven Pincus, Tiraana Bains and A. Zuercher Reichardt, 'Thinking the Empire Whole', *History Australia* 16:4 (2019), 610–37.
8 Robert Darnton, 'Sex for Thought', *New York Review of Books* (22 December 1994).
9 Kate Millett, *Sexual Politics* (New York, NY, 1970), ch. 2.
10 Frances Ferguson, *Pornography, the Theory: What Utilitarianism Did to Action* (Chicago, IL, 2004); Kathleen Lubey, *What Pornography Knows: Sex and Social Protest Since the Eighteenth Century* (Stanford, CA, 2022).
11 For other uses of this term, see Susan Wiseman, '"Adam, the Father of all Flesh": Porno-Political Rhetoric and Political Theory in and after the English Civil War', in James Holstun (ed.), *Pamphlet Wars: Prose in the English Revolution* (London, 1992), pp. 134–57; Turner, *Libertines*; Purkiss, *Literature*.
12 For similar language in a later context, see Lisa Forman Cody, *Birthing the Nation: Sex, Science, and the Conception of Eighteenth-Century Britons* (Oxford, 2005); Carol Blum, *Strength in Numbers: Population, Reproduction, and Power in Eighteenth-Century France* (Baltimore, MD, 2002).
13 Wiseman, '"Adam, the Father of all Flesh"'; Rachel Weil, 'Sometimes a Scepter is Only a Scepter: Pornography and Politics in Restoration England', in Lynn Hunt (ed.), *The Invention of Pornography: Obscenity and the Origins of Modernity, 1500–1800* (New York, NY, 1993), pp. 125–53. See also Darnton, 'Sex for Thought'.
14 Joad Raymond, *The Invention of the Newspaper: English Newsbooks, 1641–1649* (Oxford, 1996); Joad Raymond, *Pamphlets and Pamphleteering in Early Modern Britain* (Cambridge, 2003); David Zaret, *Origins of Democratic Culture: Printing, Petitions, and the Public Sphere in Early-Modern England* (Princeton, NJ, 2000); Jason Peacey, *Print and Public Politics in the English Revolution* (Cambridge, 2013); Como, *RP*.
15 Adam Fox, *Oral and Literature Culture in England, 1500–1700* (Oxford, 2000); Andrew Pettegree, *The Book in the Renaissance* (New Haven, CT, 2011).

16 Noah Millstone, *Manuscript Circulation and the Invention of Politics in Early Stuart England* (Cambridge, 2016).
17 For a useful discussion of 'public' and 'private' sources, see Peter Lake and Isaac Stephens, *Scandal and Religious Identity in Early Stuart England: A Northamptonshire Maid's Tragedy* (Woodbridge, 2015).
18 Peacey, *Print and Public Politics*.
19 Faramerz Dabhoiwala, 'Lust and Liberty', *P&P* 207 (2010), 89–179.
20 Dorinda Outram describes bodies as 'the most basic political resource' in pre-revolutionary France: *The Body and the French Revolution: Sex, Class and Political Culture* (New Haven, CT, 1989), p. 1.
21 John Dod, *A plaine and familiar exposition*, STC 6974 (1618), p. 290.
22 DWL, DWL/RB/2/5.62; SRO, Q/SR/291, no. 3.
23 Dabhoiwala, *Origins of Sex*, pp. 31, 40; Martin Ingram, *Church Courts, Sex and Marriage in England, 1570–1640* (Cambridge, 1994), pp. 31 (quoted), 278–80. See also G. R. Quaife, *Wanton Wenches and Wayward Wives: Peasants and Illicit Sex in Early Seventeenth Century England* (London, 1979); Martin Ingram, 'Ridings, Rough Music and Mocking Rhymes in Early Modern England', in Barry Reay (ed.), *Popular Culture in Seventeenth Century England* (London, 1985), pp. 166–97; D. E. Underdown, 'The Taming of the Scold: The Enforcement of Patriarchal Authority in Early Modern England', in Anthony Fletcher and John Stevenson (eds), *Order and Disorder in Early Modern England* (Cambridge, 1985), pp. 116–36. Cf. Laura Gowing, *Domestic Dangers: Women, Words, and Sex in Early Modern London* (Oxford, 1996), on attitudes towards public discipline; and Martin Ingram, *Carnal Knowledge: Regulating Sex in England, 1470–1600* (Cambridge, 2017), on early Tudor sexual culture.
24 See for example Phillip Stubbes, *The anatomie of abuses*, STC 23376 (1583), sig. H3r; William Prynne, *Histriomastix*, STC 20464 (1633), p. 962; BRBML, Osborn MS b200, p. 240; Alexandra Walsham, ' "The Fatall Vesper": Providentialism and Anti-Popery in Late Jacobean London', *P&P* 144 (1994), 36–87, at 69–70.
25 Alexandra Shepard, 'Gender, the Body, and Sexuality', in Keith Wrightson (ed.), *A Social History of England, 1500–1750* (Cambridge, 2017), pp. 330–51; Margaret R. Sommerville, *Sex and Subjection: Attitudes to Women in Early-Modern Society* (London, 1995).
26 Braddick, *Fury*, p. xxiii.
27 Jonathan Goldberg and Madhavi Menon, 'Queering History', *PMLA* 120:5 (2005), 1608–17.
28 Michael Braddick, 'Mobilisation, Anxiety and Creativity in England during the 1640s', in John Morrow and Jonathan Scott (eds), *Liberty, Authority, Formality: Political Ideas and Culture, 1600–1900* (Exeter, 2008), pp. 175–94.
29 As does the frequency with which commonplace sexual insults – most notably, 'whore' – were deployed as generic attacks on perceived corruption rather than specific allegations of unchastity: Alexandra C. Lumbers, 'The Discourses of Whoredom in Seventeenth-Century England' (DPhil thesis, Oxford University, 2005).

30 For which see Christopher Durston, *The Family in the English Revolution* (Oxford, 1999); Mary E. Fissell, *Vernacular Bodies: The Politics of Reproduction in Early Modern England* (Oxford, 2004); Roy Porter and Leslie Hall, *The Facts of Life: The Creation of Sexual Knowledge in Britain, 1650–1950* (New Haven, CT, 1995).

31 But see Samuel Fullerton, 'The "Holy Sister" Anatomized: Religious Polemic and Erotic Writing in England, 1640–1660', *Journal of Modern History* (forthcoming).

32 Melissa Mohr, 'Defining Dirt: Three Early Modern Views of Obscenity', *Textual Practice* 17:2 (2003), 253–75; Melissa Mohr, *Holy Shit: A Brief History of Swearing* (Oxford, 2013). See also Joan DeJean, *The Reinvention of Obscenity: Sex, Lies, and Tabloids in Early Modern France* (Chicago, IL, 2002); Karen Harvey, *Reading Sex in the Eighteenth Century: Bodies and Gender in English Erotic Culture* (Cambridge, 2004).

33 Lois Spencer, 'The Politics of George Thomason', *The Library* 5:14 (1959), 11–27; Lois Spencer, 'The Professional and Literary Connections of George Thomason', *The Library* 5:13 (1958), 102–18.

34 See, for example, Katherine Crawford, *The Sexual Culture of the French Renaissance* (Cambridge, 2010); Lyndal Roper, *Oedipus and the Devil: Witchcraft, Sexuality and Religion in Early Modern Europe* (London, 1994); Robert Darnton, *The Great Cat Massacre and Other Episodes in French Cultural History* (New York, NY, 1984); and below.

35 E.g., Henric Bagerius and Christine Ekholst, 'Kings and Favourites: Politics and Sexuality in Late Medieval Europe', *Journal of Medieval History* 43:3 (2017), 298–319; Seth Koven, *Slumming: Sexual and Social Politics in Victorian London* (Princeton, NJ, 2006); Anna Clark, *Scandal: The Sexual Politics of the British Constitution* (Princeton, NJ, 2004).

36 Alastair Bellany, 'The Murder of John Lambe: Crowd Violence, Court Scandal and Popular Politics in Early Seventeenth-Century England', *P&P* 200 (2008), 37–76, at 46.

37 Alexandra Shepard, *Meanings of Manhood in Early Modern England* (Oxford, 2003); Cynthia B. Herrup, *A House in Gross Disorder: Sex, Law, and the 2nd Earl of Castlehaven* (Oxford, 1999); Herrup, 'The King's Two Genders'; Frances E. Dolan, *Dangerous Familiars: Representations of Domestic Crime in England, 1550–1700* (Ithaca, NY, 1994).

38 Lake and Stephens, *Scandal and Religious Identity*; Marshall, *Toleration*; Peter Lake with Michael Questier, *The Antichrist's Lewd Hat: Protestants, Papists and Players in Post-Reformation England* (New Haven, CT, 2002); Kristen Poole, *Radical Religion from Shakespeare to Milton: Figures of Nonconformity in Early Modern England* (Cambridge, 2000); Frances E. Dolan, *Whores of Babylon: Catholicism, Gender, and Seventeenth-Century Print Culture* (Ithaca, NY, 1999).

39 Peter Lake, *Bad Queen Bess?: Libels, Secret Histories, and the Politics of Publicity in the Reign of Queen Elizabeth I* (Oxford, 2016); Alastair Bellany and Thomas Cogswell, *The Murder of King James I* (New Haven, CT, 2015); Debora Shuger, *Censorship and Cultural Sensibility: The Regulation of*

*Language in Tudor-Stuart England* (Philadelphia, PA, 2006); Peter Lake and Steven Pincus (eds), *The Politics of the Public Sphere in Early Modern England* (Manchester, 2007); John Walter, '"The Pooremans Joy and the Gentlemans Plague": A Lincolnshire Libel and the Politics of Sedition in Early Modern England', *P&P* 203 (2009), pp. 29–67; Andrew McRae, 'The Literary Culture of Early Stuart Libeling', *Modern Philology* 97:3 (2000), 364–92.

40 Susan Amussen and David Underdown, *Gender, Culture and Politics in England, 1560–1640: Turning the World Upside Down* (London, 2017); Alastair Bellany, *The Politics of Court Scandal in Early Modern England: News Culture and the Overbury Affair, 1603–1660* (Cambridge, 2002); Peter Stallybrass and Allon White, *The Politics and Poetics of Transgression* (Ithaca, NY, 1986); Christopher Hill, *The World Turned Upside Down: Radical Ideas During the English Revolution* (London, 1975).

41 For English erotic writing prior to 1640, see Ian Frederick Moulton, *Before Pornography: Erotic Writing in Early Modern England* (Oxford, 2000). On early modern 'pornography' more broadly, see Peter Wagner, *Eros Revived: Erotica of the Enlightenment in England and America* (London, 1988); Walter Kendrick, *The Secret Museum: Pornography in Modern Culture*, 2nd ed. (Berkeley, CA, 1996); James Grantham Turner, *Schooling Sex: Libertine Literature and Erotic Education in Italy, France, and England, 1534–1685* (Oxford, 2003); Harvey, *Reading Sex*; Kathleen Lubey, *Excitable Imaginations: Eroticism and Reading in Britain, 1660–1760* (Lewisburg, PA, 2012); Julie Peakman, *Mighty Lewd Books: The Development of Pornography in Eighteenth-Century England* (Basingstoke, 2003); Roger Thompson, *Unfit for Modest Ears* (Totowa, NJ, 1979); Hunt (ed.), *Invention of Pornography*; David O. Frantz, *Festum Voluptatis: A Study of Renaissance Erotica* (Columbus, OH, 1989); Foxon, *Libertine Literature*. An important exception is Sarah Toulalan, *Imagining Sex: Pornography and Bodies in Seventeenth-Century England* (Oxford, 2007). For the libertine earl of Rochester's debt to Hobbesian thinking, see James William Johnson, *A Profane Wit: The Life of John Wilmot, Earl of Rochester* (Rochester, NY, 2004).

42 Richard Cust and Ann Hughes, 'Introduction: After Revisionism', in Richard Cust and Ann Hughes (eds), *Conflict in Early Stuart England: Studies in Religion and Politics, 1603–1642* (London, 1989), pp. 1–46; Susan D. Amussen, 'The Irrelevance of Revisionism: Gender, Politics, and Society in Early Modern England', *HLQ* 78:4 (2015), 683–701.

43 See, for example, Robert Darnton, *The Forbidden Best-Sellers of Pre-Revolutionary France* (New York, NY, 1996); Sarah Maza, *Private Lives and Public Affairs: The Causes Célèbres of Prerevolutionary France* (Berkeley, CA, 1993); Lynn Hunt, *The Family Romance of the French Revolution* (Berkeley, CA, 1992).

44 H. N. Brailsford, *The Levellers and the English Revolution* (Stanford, 1961), p. 404; Hyden E. Rollins (ed.), *Cavalier and Puritan: Ballads and Broadsides Illustrating the Period of the Great Rebellion, 1640–1660* (New York, NY, 1923), p. vii; Charles Carlton, *Going to the Wars: The Experience of the English Civil Wars, 1638–1651* (London, 1992), pp. 77, 365n55.

45 East Sussex Record Office, FRE 600, p. 4; CUL, MS Add.4138; J. B. Williams, 'Alderman Atkins and the Thomason Tracts', *Notes and Queries* 11:1 (1910), 205.
46 George Roberts (ed.), *Diary of Walter Yonge* (London, 1848), p. 113 (cf. BL Add. MS 35331, fol. 16r); Rollins (ed.), *Cavalier and Puritan*, p. viii (relevant stanzas on p. 424).
47 James Orchard Halliwell (ed.), *The Autobiography and Correspondence of Sir Simonds D'Ewes* (2 vols, London, 1845), i, pp. 190–2 (cf. BL, Harley MS 646, fol. 59r); J. Sears McGee, *An Industrious Mind: The Worlds of Sir Simonds D'Ewes* (Stanford, CA, 2015), pp. 18, 27–8.
48 N. H. Keeble and Geoffrey F. Nuttall (eds), *Calendar of the Correspondence of Richard Baxter* (2 vols, Oxford, 1991), i, p. 187 (cf. DWL, DWL/RB/2/5.62).
49 Wiseman, '"Adam, the Father of all Flesh"', p. 135.
50 Sharon Achinstein, 'Women on Top in the Pamphlet Literature of the English Revolution', *Women's Studies* 24 (1994), 131–63; Raymond, *Invention*, pp. 180–2; Purkiss, *Literature*; Nigel Smith, *Literature and Revolution in England, 1640–1660* (New Haven, CT, 1994).
51 Melissa M. Mowry, *The Bawdy Politic in Stuart England, 1660–1714: Political Pornography and Prostitution* (Aldershot, 2004); Turner, *Libertines*.
52 Ann Hughes, 'Gender and Politics in Leveller Literature', in Susan D. Amussen and Mark A. Kishlansky (eds), *Political Culture and Cultural Politics in Early Modern Europe: Essays Presented to David Underdown* (Manchester, 1995), pp. 162–88, at 177. Christopher Hill's early work on the Ranters also deserves mention: *World Turned Upside Down*, pp. 197–230.
53 David Underdown, *A Freeborn People: Politics and the Nation in Seventeenth-Century England* (Oxford, 1996), ch. 5; Jason McElligott, 'The Politics of Sexual Libel: Royalist Propaganda in the 1640s', *HLQ* 67:1 (2004), 75–99; Gianoutsos, *Manhood*, p. 4; Capp, *Culture Wars*. See also David Cressy, *England on Edge: Crisis and Revolution, 1640–1642* (Oxford, 2006), pt 3; Jason Peacey, '"Hot and Eager in Courtship": Representations of Court Life in the Parliamentarian Press, 1642–9', *Early Modern Literary Studies* 15 (2007); Lloyd Bowen, 'The Bedlam Academy: Royalist Oxford in Civil War News Culture', *Media History* 23:2 (2017), 199–217; Mark Stoyle, 'The Road to Farndon Field: Explaining the Massacre of the Royalist Women at Naseby', *EHR* 123:503 (2008), 895–923; Hughes, *Gender*.
54 But see Alastair Bellany, 'Railing Rhymes Revisited: Libels, Scandals, and Early Stuart Politics', *History Compass* 5:4 (2007), 1136–79, at 1165–6; Sharpe, *IW*, pp. 332–3; Weil, 'Sometimes a Scepter', pp. 136–7; Toulalan, *Imagining Sex*, pp. 37–42; Purkiss, *Literature*, pp. 141–2; Thompson, *Unfit for Modest Ears*, p. 13.
55 Turner, *Libertines*, p. xvii.
56 Traub, *Thinking Sex*, p. 116.
57 BRBML, Osborn MS fb77, fol. 24r.
58 Ernst H. Kantorowicz, *The King's Two Bodies: A Study in Medieval Political Theology* (Princeton, NJ, 2016), pp. 9–10.
59 Gianoutsos, *Manhood*.

60 Kevin Sharpe, *Selling the Tudor Monarchy: Authority and Image in Sixteenth-Century England* (New Haven, CT, 2009), p. 71.
61 *CJ*, i, p. 143, for James. For Elizabeth, see David Cressy, *Dangerous Talk: Scandalous, Seditious, and Treasonable Speech in Pre-Modern England* (Oxford, 2010), p. 61; Carole Levin, *The Heart and Stomach of a King: Elizabeth I and the Politics of Sex and Power*, 2nd ed. (Philadelphia, PA, 2013), p. 87. For Charles, see Ann Baynes Coiro, ' "A Ball of Strife": Caroline Poetry and Royal Marriage', in Thomas N. Corns (ed.), *The Royal Image: Representations of Charles I* (Cambridge, 1999), pp. 26–46.
62 At least until the 1590s, that is: Paul Hammer, 'Sex and the Virgin Queen: Aristocratic Concupiscence and the Court of Elizabeth I', *Sixteenth Century Journal* 31:1 (2000), 77–97.
63 Herrup, *A House in Gross Disorder*, pp. 50, 91.
64 Bellany, *Court Scandal*; David Lindley, *The Trials of Frances Howard: Fact and Fiction at the Court of King James* (London, 1993).
65 *A wonder woorth the reading*, STC 14935 (1617). See also David Cressy, *Travesties and Transgressions in Tudor and Stuart England: Tales of Discord and Dissension* (Oxford, 2000), ch. 2.
66 Richard Cust, 'The "Public Man" in Late Tudor and Early Stuart England', in Lake and Pincus (eds), *Politics of the Public Sphere*, pp. 116–43.
67 G. W. Bernard, 'The Fall of Anne Boleyn', *EHR* 106:420 (1991), 584–610; David Starkey, *Six Wives: The Queens of Henry VIII* (London, 2003), pp. 681–4.
68 Lake, *Bad Queen Bess?*; Freddy Cristóbal Dominguez, *Radicals in Exile: English Catholic Books during the Reign of Philip II* (University Park, PA, 2020).
69 James Knowles, 'To "Scourge the Arse / Jove's Marrow So Had Wasted": Scurrility and the Subversion of Sodomy', in Dermot Cavanagh and Tim Kirk (eds), *Subversion and Scurrility: Popular Discourse in Europe from 1500 to the Present* (Aldershot, 2000), pp. 74–92; Dolan, *Whores of Babylon*, pp. 97–101.
70 Bod., MS Eng. Poet. C. 50, fol. 14r.
71 Jamie Gianoutsos, 'Criticizing Kings: Gender, Classical History, and Subversive Writing in Seventeenth-Century England', *Renaissance Quarterly* 70:4 (2017), 1366–96.
72 Millstone, *Manuscript Circulation*.
73 BL, Add. MS 22603, fols 33v–4r.
74 Stephen Haliczer, *Sexuality in the Confessional: A Sacrament Profaned* (Oxford, 1996); Frances E. Dolan, 'Why Are Nuns Funny?', *HLQ* 70:4 (2007), 509–35; Helmut Puff, *Sodomy in Reformation Germany and Switzerland, 1400–1600* (Chicago, IL, 2003).
75 Paul Christianson, *Reformers and Babylon: English Apocalyptic Visions from the Reformation to the Eve of the Civil War* (Toronto, 1978).
76 Peter Lake, 'Anti-Popery: The Structure of a Prejudice', in Cust and Hughes (eds), *Conflict in Early Stuart England*, pp. 72–106, at 73. See also Karl Gunther, *Reformation Unbound: Protestant Visions of Reform in England, 1525–1590*

(Cambridge, 2014), ch. 2; John N. King, *English Reformation Literature: The Tudor Origins of the Protestant Tradition* (Princeton, NJ, 1982), p. 94.

77 Roper, *Oedipus and the Devil*, pp. 81–94; Ariel Hessayon, 'Early Modern Communism: The Diggers and Community of Goods', *Journal for the Study of Radicalism* 3:2 (2009), 1–49; Thomas A. Fudge, 'Incest and Lust in Luther's Marriage: Theology and Morality in Reformation Polemics', *Sixteenth Century Journal* 34:2 (2003), 319–45. For similarly vicious intra-Catholic polemics, see Peter Lake and Michael Questier, *All Hail to the Archpriest: Confessional Conflict, Toleration, and the Politics of Publicity in Post-Reformation England* (Oxford, 2019).

78 Christianson, *Reformers and Babylon*, p. 48.

79 Steven W. May and Alan Bryson, *Verse Libel in Renaissance England and Scotland* (Oxford, 2016), p. 11; Lake, *Bad Queen Bess?*

80 Joseph Black, 'The Rhetoric of Reaction: The Martin Marprelate Tracts (1588–89), Anti-Martinism, and the Uses of Print in Early Modern England', *Sixteenth Century Journal* 28:3 (1997), 707–25. See also Lake with Questier, *Antichrist's Lewd Hat*, ch. 13.

81 Christopher Carter, 'The Family of Love and Its Enemies', *Sixteenth Century Journal* 37:3 (2006), 651–72. See also Christopher W. Marsh, *The Family of Love in English Society, 1550–1630* (Cambridge, 1994).

82 Shuger, *Censorship and Cultural Sensibility*, pp. 59–65, quoting p. 64.

83 Cyndia Susan Clegg, *Press Censorship in Elizabethan England* (Cambridge, 1997), pp. 30–40; Anthony Milton, 'Licensing, Censorship, and Religious Orthodoxy in Early Stuart England', *HJ* 41:3 (1998), 625–51; Joseph Lowenstein, *The Author's Due: Printing and the Prehistory of Copyright* (Chicago, IL, 2002).

84 E.g., Folger Shakespeare Library, MS V.a.399, fol. 25r; BRBML, Osborn MS b62, p. 110. See also Moulton, *Before Pornography*; Frantz, *Festum Voluptatis*.

85 Lynda E. Boose, 'The 1599 Bishops' Ban, Elizabethan Pornography, and the Sexualization of the Jacobean Stage', in Richard Burt and John Michael Archer (eds), *Enclosure Acts: Sexuality, Property, and Culture in Early Modern England* (Ithaca, NY, 1994), pp. 185–200; Alan Bray, *Homosexuality in Renaissance England* (New York, NY, 1995), p. 33; Moulton, *Before Pornography*, p. 28.

86 Thomas Cogswell, 'Underground Verse and the Transformation of Early Stuart Political Culture', in Amussen and Kishlansky (eds), *Political Culture and Cultural Politics*, pp. 277–300.

87 Shuger, *Censorship and Cultural Sensibility*, pp. 108–9; Anna Bryson, *From Courtesy to Civility: Changing Codes of Conduct in Early Modern England* (Oxford, 1998); Jacques Revel, 'The Uses of Civility', in Roger Chartier (ed.), *A History of Private Life*, Volume III: *Passions of the Renaissance*, trans. Arthur Goldhammer (Cambridge, MA, 1989), pp. 167–205, at 168; Richard Cust and Peter Lake, *Gentry Culture and the Politics of Religion: Cheshire on the Eve of Civil War* (Manchester, 2020), pp. 85, 120–1, 263.

88 Stubbes, *Anatomie of abuses*, sig. P8v.

89 See, for instance, John Coffey, *Politics, Religion and the British Revolutions: The Mind of Samuel Rutherford* (Cambridge, 1997), pp. 85–7, 104–7.
90 John Dod and Robert Cleaver, *A godlie forme of householde government*, STC 5386 (1612), pp. 260, 288, 321.
91 For this material, see Moulton, *Before Pornography*, pp. 22–3; Pauline Croft, 'Libels, Popular Literacy and Public Opinion in Early Modern England', *HR* 68:167 (1995), 266–85, at 273; Peter Lake, 'Deeds Against Nature: Cheap Print, Protestantism and Murder in Early Seventeenth-Century England', in Kevin Sharpe and Peter Lake (eds), *Culture and Politics in Early Stuart England* (Stanford, CA, 1993), pp. 257–83, at 259–60.
92 TNA, SP 16/447, fol. 163v.
93 CUL, MS Baker Mm.1.46, pp. 399–400; BL, Add. MS 23229, fol. 43v; Folger Shakespeare Library, MS V.b.110, p. 1. For another example, see TNA, SP 16/441, fols 31r–v.
94 Prynne, *Histriomastix*, p. 65 (quoted), sig. Rrrrrr4r.
95 BL, Add. MS 21433, fols 135r–6r.
96 BL, Add. MS 4155, fols 143r–4v; CUL, MS Gg.4.13, p. 114. See also Bellany and Cogswell, *Murder of King James I*, pp. 203, 243–4.
97 Thomas Cogswell, 'John Felton, Popular Political Culture, and the Assassination of the Duke of Buckingham', *HJ* 49:2 (2006), 357–85.
98 On early modern misogyny, see Sara Mendelson and Patricia Crawford, *Women in Early Modern England, 1550–1720* (Oxford, 1998), pp. 69–72; Tim Reinke-Williams, 'Misogyny, Jest-Books and Male Youth Culture in Seventeenth-Century England', *Gender & History* 21:2 (2009), 324–39; Sommerville, *Sex and Subjection*, pp. 9–10. For a recent theoretical account, see Kate Manne, *Down Girl: The Logic of Misogyny* (Oxford, 2018).

# 1

# Sexual satire and partisan identity, 1637–42

In a retrospective account, Edward Hyde, earl of Clarendon, argued that the spring of 1637 marked a moment when 'the whole nation' had begun 'to be so civilized that it was a jewel of great lustre in the most royal diadem'.[1] At the time, he had good reason for thinking so. A recent decree against unlicensed publishing from the royal court of Star Chamber – the harshest press regulation law yet passed in England – ensured that civility reigned in print, while even scribal libellers had slowed their pace since the onset of King Charles I's parliament-less 'personal rule' in 1629.[2] Yet destructive energies swirled beneath the kingdom's ostensible placidity. Charles's subjects, bereft of a public forum in which to air their grievances, fumed about his unwillingness to intervene in Germany's still-raging Thirty Years' War and bemoaned the mounting costs of extra-parliamentary taxation. English and Scottish puritans alike found the presence of Catholic agents at court particularly alarming.[3] When the king moved in June to enforce a new conformist prayer book on the Presbyterian Scottish kirk, therefore, it proved akin to fishing with dynamite.

That rash decision ignited a chain reaction that sent the kingdom spiralling into civil war by the summer of 1642. Alongside the collapse came two key developments in English sexual politics. First, Hyde's veneer of civility shattered as the demands of partisan conflict brought Caroline political hegemony to a sudden end and the kingdom's press licensing system disintegrated under the same pressure. Secondly, sex-talk rapidly invaded English public culture, initially in manuscript and then increasingly in unlicensed print, as partisan writers harnessed familiar post-Reformation and patriarchal arguments to stake their respective claims to political legitimacy amid the resulting chaos. Notably, however, both Charles and his parliamentarian opponents largely avoided sexual satire in their formal publications, either for fear of alienating potential supporters with overly provocative language or simply because they had not yet grasped its revolutionary polemical potential. While sexual politics had gained a tenuous foothold in print by October 1642, in other words, they did so almost exclusively in cheap, anonymous and unlicensed forms.

This chapter examines that development through the lens of partisan politicking. Between 1637 and 1642, explicit sex-writing played an essential role in the formation of partisan stereotypes on both sides of the widening political divide. Although hardly the exclusive source of those new identities, sex-talk was especially significant to their genesis for two reasons. The first was widespread contemporary agreement regarding the conflict's fundamentally confessional roots, which quickly cemented the post-Reformation polarities of anti-puritanism and anti-popery as central pillars of the resulting controversy. Second was the near-universal need, on both sides of the nascent conflict, to mobilise a reading public that preferred smut and scandal to high-minded debate. Consequently, as partisan writers crafted the satirical caricatures that soon came to dominate mid-century polemical culture – from lecherous puritan hypocrites and foppish court gallants to royalist 'cavaliers' and parliamentarian 'roundheads' – sexual politics made their inaugural foray into England's print marketplace. Unpacking the relationship between those two processes therefore can reveal much about the origins of civil war England's most enduring cultural stereotypes – a storyline that has not yet been adequately addressed by historians – while positioning us to appreciate the much more sophisticated polemical roles played by politicised sex-talk after the outbreak of civil war.[4]

## 'Conquered twice by bastards': post-Reformation sex-talk and the Bishops' Wars

On 23 July 1637, the day appointed by King Charles's advisors for the imposition of an anglicised new prayer book on the Presbyterian Scottish kirk, rioting Edinburgh churchgoers interrupted Sunday services to protest the new liturgy. Unhappy Scots across the kingdom soon followed suit, while the king's northern supporters organised to resist the nascent revolution. As Presbyterian 'Covenanter' rebels – so named for the Scottish National Covenant signed in February 1638 – squared up against their conformist opposition, headed by the Scottish bishops, both groups began issuing public appeals for support. In each camp, and eventually south of the border as well, the sexual politics of anti-popery (among Scottish Covenanters and English godly reformers) and anti-puritanism (for Charles's conformist partisans and alarmed moderates alike) took on an increasingly prominent role, as the conflict's post-Reformation roots provided plentiful opportunities for satire, libel and porno-political critique despite widespread anxieties about the propriety of public sex-talk.

Over the next several years, Covenanter partisans derided the new prayer book as a popish relic of the Catholic Whore of Babylon while the king's conformist supporters smeared their puritan enemies as seditious, hypocritical lechers. At first, these polemics circulated almost exclusively in Scottish manuscript culture, but they eventually migrated south as the conflict expanded into a full-blown insurrection against Caroline ecclesiastical authority. In turn, the Covenanters' anti-popish rhetoric was integrated into a burgeoning canon of radical English oppositional printed and manuscript texts that similarly denounced Charles's English bishops, courtiers and soldiery as popish fops and sexual predators. Two wars and a contentious parliamentary session followed, each sparking more recrimination. By the time that another parliament (the 'Long Parliament') assembled in London in November 1640, graphic sex-talk had made significant inroads into unlicensed partisan print for the first time in English history.

Scotland was a kingdom intimately familiar with post-Reformation sexual politics. The sixteenth-century reign of Charles's Catholic grandmother Mary Stuart, who had earned a reputation as an adulterous murderer among earlier generations of British Protestants, had long provided Scottish commentators with evidence of the linkage between popish and sexual corruption. Indeed, Mary's unsavoury reputation owed much to salacious Presbyterian exposés like the Scottish evangelical George Buchanan's *Detectio Mariae reginae* (1571), which had chronicled her escapades for an international audience.[5] Those accounts, in turn, drew on an older tradition of Scottish libelling, or 'flyting', in which the playful exposure of sexual foibles played a central role.[6] As such, sexual satire was already a staple of Scottish polemical culture when the troubles began in July 1637.

Northern critics of the new prayer book wasted no time in putting that tradition to use. Within weeks of the Edinburgh riots, the earl of Montrose was castigating Charles's Scottish liturgy as 'the brood of the bowels of the whore of Babel', while elsewhere Scottish ministers preached that the new prayer book 'smeld o'th whore of Babylon'. Additional sermons against the 'whoredomes and abominations' of the Babylonian strumpet appeared in print the following year, accompanied by attacks on the Scottish bishops as the playthings, pimps and panders of the whorish Roman church.[7] These apocalyptic critiques, reminiscent of the Reformation polemics of John Bale, reflected a longstanding puritan fear that papists were scheming to overthrow British Protestantism with the connivance of Charles's Catholic queen; more fundamentally, they linked the recent innovations, as well as those responsible for promulgating them, with femininity, unfaithfulness and promiscuity.[8] Such imagery would serve as a defining motif of British anti-episcopal rhetoric for years to come.

Meanwhile, the Covenanters presented an earthier case in manuscript against their local opponents. From mid-1637, scribal writers appropriated the language of courtly corruption once deployed against the duke of Buckingham to denounce Charles's Scottish allies as 'cuckold-lyke' cowards, while prominent Presbyterians scribbled acidic personal notes dismissing their enemies as 'grate Leicher[s]' and 'hooremounger[s]'.[9] By parroting this English anti-court lexicon, Covenanters presumably hoped to garner southern support for their cause. In time, they would employ similar tactics against the bishops, thereby challenging their literal chastity alongside their spiritual purity.

In response, Scottish anti-Covenanters also turned to sexual slander, albeit of a different variety. In several manuscript libels that appeared shortly after the Edinburgh riots, sceptical satirists lambasted the Covenanters as hypocritical lechers in a classic anti-puritan mode. One representative verse described a Scottish reformer who, 'thanks to the Covenant', now kept his 'whoores . . . at rest within his doores' to preserve his manufactured reputation for moral purity. It summarised this hypocrisy in the Scots' own terms: 'among all whores [they] reject not one, / except the whore of Babylone'. Given that several Scottish clergymen had recently received 'publick censure' for their 'vyle adulteries', at least according to the embarrassed Covenanter Robert Baillie, such slanders must have seemed especially apropos. (Baillie wrote that one of these offenders, 'Mr. Archibald Grahame', had been 'thought ane eunuch . . . but I chanced to be at one of his tryells in Glasgow, where so fowll practices were deponed against him, that had he bein my father, I would have subscribed to his depositione'.)[10] More importantly, they – like many of the anti-popish polemics currently being harnessed by Scottish Presbyterians – implicitly established sexual honesty as an acceptable criterion for assessing competing claims to political and spiritual legitimacy in the debates to come.

Apocalyptic sexual metaphors and more traditional sexual libels thus circulated in Scottish manuscripts, and less frequently print, from the beginning of the prayer book troubles. Yet Caroline leaders initially paid little attention to the brewing northern storm.[11] Only after mid-1638, when Covenanter propagandists tentatively began directing exculpatory scribal and printed polemic southward – carefully omitting inflammatory references to the Whore of Babylon and Caroline court immorality – did Charles's government respond. Even then, several months passed before the king issued his first formal proclamation against the Scots and their 'infamous Libels'.[12]

This was partly because the Covenanters' uprising against Caroline ecclesiastical overreach had electrified a similarly vibrant puritan opposition in England. Largely stymied from print by the 1637 Star Chamber decree, these English activists turned to foreign publishers in Amsterdam and underground London presses, from whence they began manufacturing abusive anti-episcopal satires of their own. Yet unlike the Scots, whose initial appeals to southern readers generally avoided defamatory language, English puritans favoured a bawdy anti-popish lexicon inspired by the sixteenth-century satires of Martin Marprelate and seasoned with Protestant apocalypticism. The first of their Amsterdam pamphlets, published late in 1638, thus accused the English episcopate of plotting to re-clothe the national church in 'the rags and dregs [i.e. the surplice?] of the Babilonian whore'. Robert Baillie and his fellow Scots expressed alarm at this 'beastlie' language, but worse was soon to come.[13]

In Scotland, meanwhile, the Covenanters grew more aggressive in their attacks on the Scottish episcopate: as Baillie wrote in November, 'no kinde of cryme which can be gotten proven of a Bishop will now be concealed'. The Scots proved particularly attuned to charges of sexual impropriety.[14] On 29 October, William Wilkie of Govan wrote to Walter Balcanquhall, dean of Durham and a fellow Scot, about a 'famous lybel against our Archbyshop' recently presented to the Glasgow presbytery by Covenanter partisans. By 'libel', Wilkie meant a formal indictment; and, like all such charges, it was consequently disseminated by a 'wryter boy' who 'reid it in the readers saife in church' before the laity. Among its many allegations, Wilkie was most shocked by the accusations against 'Mr Patricke [Lindsay, archbishop of Glasgow] and his [also Wilkie's] colledge . . . of incest adulterie drunkenness etc', because most sceptics 'believed that both the Bishop and we wer free of these'. Although similar accusations had proliferated in Covenanter oral and scribal culture for months, their recitation before the Glasgow presbytery was, for Wilkie, a clear sign of the kingdom's deteriorating condition.[15]

In November 1638, the Covenanters convened a General Assembly in Glasgow to formalise their platform. They also impeached the bishops, who had wisely decided against attending. When the proceedings began, attendees were treated to a libellous spectacle: one by one, the entire Scottish episcopate was named and shamed for a litany of crimes – including eye-raising charges of sexual misconduct. The bishop of Brechin was accused of 'adulterie' on the evidence of both 'a woman and child'; the bishop of Moray of 'countenancing of a vile dance of naked people in his own house' (although even Baillie believed this charge 'not sufficientlie proven'); and John Spottiswood, archbishop of St Andrews, of the particularly unsavoury trio of 'adulterie, incest, [and] sacriledge'.[16] Word of the Assembly's censures soon filtered southward. As one Englishman reported, 'the Scotts in their convocation proceeded very violentlie against the Bishops . . . [some] for grosse Crimes'.[17] It is not difficult to guess which charges he meant.

The Covenanters eventually published an account of these proceedings. In describing the bishops' impeachments, however, they conspicuously excluded the sexual allegations, perhaps because they lacked sufficient evidence to validate their most inflammatory claims.[18] Surprisingly, the Scottish bishops made an identical choice in their (printed) response. As Baillie had confirmed, the prelates knew that some Covenanter ministers, too, were guilty of sexual malfeasance; even so, they announced that they would 'forbeare to expresse' their enemies' most 'personall faults and enormities' out of 'charitie'. But this, too, was a polemical tactic. In a subsequent counter-rebuttal, the Presbyterians noted that such a damning 'generall imputation' was 'more uncharitable, then if they had designed the persons and expressed the faults in particular' – although this did not stop them from simultaneously insisting, in precisely the same manner, that the bishops had been 'slandered also for other grosser crimes, but time served not for sufficient trial'.[19] This cautious repartee, so reminiscent of the hedging of Buckingham's prosecutors in 1626, demonstrates the delicacy with which Scottish polemicists of all stripes continued to approach politicised sex-talk even they contemplated the possibility of war.

For Balcanquhall, who published a combative declaration in the king's name early in 1639, the entire episode embodied Covenanter malice. Asking whether the Presbyterians truly believed the Scottish bishops to be 'guiltie' of 'whoring . . . adulterie, incest, and what not', he answered, 'most certainly they did not'. The charges, therefore, were obviously intended 'to raise up in the people an utter abhorring of the present Bishops persons . . . and calling' rather than to cleanse the kirk of sin.[20] One reader of Balcanquhall's tract offered a similar judgement in a marginal note: this hypocritical 'practise of Scotish presbiters', it read, 'would make Turks & Infidells abhorr Christianity'.[21]

Covenanter partisans continued to slander the bishops' literal and spiritual chastity in less public forms throughout the spring. In May, an irate northerner complained that 'here Bishops are altogeather cursed . . . if one be burnt with a Scottish whore, presently a Pox upon the Bishops'. Sometime afterward, a Covenanter sympathiser in Ireland was imprisoned for accusing the conformist Scottish minister John Corbet of adultery without any proof. Archbishop William Laud was still muttering about the Covenanters' 'sacrilegious humour' towards Corbet many months later.[22] Still, none of these anti-episcopal libels appeared in print, suggesting that the prayer book controversy had not yet grown dire enough for contemporaries to risk challenging the standing moratorium on public sex-talk.

That spring, Charles marched an army northward to confront the Scots. Godly observers, mindful of the horrors unfolding in war-torn Germany, worried that a similar fate awaited England's northern counties: one Londoner moaned that the king had 'taken men for war[r]es with him who are more fitter to use such weapons as thies are' – here grabbing hold of his genitals – 'then for weapons of warr'.²³ Initially, Covenanter soldiers were largely spared from similar denunciations, perhaps because their army's published articles of conduct prescribed harsh punishments for keeping 'whoores' and 'unmaried wom[e]n'.²⁴ In fact, one scribal poet claimed that Scottish discipline would finally ensure that English 'panders [would] be punished & bawds rides in carts / and whores . . . sent upp to tiburn [London's gallows] to have their desarts'. Elsewhere, as more sceptical onlookers wondered if 'Bellum Episcopale' was soon to give way to 'Rebellio Puritanica', anti-Covenanter scribal satirists snidely equated 'Scotch sin' with the 'French fire' (i.e. syphilis) spread by common 'sluit[s]' and 'whore[s]'.²⁵ In both cases – English and Scottish alike – contemporaries drew repeated parallels between soldiering and sexual malfeasance.

Only rarely did Charles's godly critics dare to direct such language at more illustrious targets. In August 1639, however, the king learned that a Scotsman named James Bowey had made dangerous statements about his father's paternity (specifically, that 'Kinge James his greate Grand-ffather was a Bastard') and, consequently, Charles's own legitimacy (although 'in his conscience hee thought, that both Kinge James and Kinge Charles are rightfull heires to the Crowne'). Such brazen commentary on the royal succession was alarming enough, but when pressed, Bowey revealed that these 'divers undecent & unfittinge words' were also circulating among his Covenanter brethren. Charles, cognizant of the linkage between hereditary and kingly legitimacy, sentenced Bowey to 'the severest punishment, that by the lawes can be inflicted upon him'.²⁶ Whether any Scots truly were employing the Stuarts' questionable sexual history – and some of them surely knew of Mary Stuart's adulterous past – as a pretext for resisting royal authority is unclear, but the king's response suggests that he, at least, considered the possibility.

Indeed, by August, Charles was in a foul mood. Faced with the Covenanters' superior forces at the northern border, he acceded to a humiliating truce and retreated to London, where he summoned a parliament – the first in eleven years – in the hope of funding a second campaign. The new assembly convened in March 1640 amid a rising tide of puritan activism. Throughout the spring, godly militants convinced of a popish conspiracy against British Protestantism churned out manuscript libels against the bishops and foreign Catholics at court. Some – including a radical printer, Richard Overton, who revived the Martin Marprelate persona for a series of acrid anti-episcopal pamphlets – even found their way into print despite redoubled regime efforts to monitor the kingdom's presses.²⁷ The criticisms only grew louder when Charles, angered by the grievances pouring forth from parliament, promptly dissolved the assembly just weeks after it was convened. Consequently, English scribal culture – and, slowly, unlicensed print – began to heave throughout the summer of 1640 with anti-popish screeds in which Protestant apocalypticism and Marprelate-esque sexual satire featured prominently.

One familiar theme for English puritan activists was the Whore of Babylon. Both printed pamphlets and scribal satires decried the influence of 'the Scarlet whore' on the kingdom's political troubles, although the latter were usually more explicit.[28] Other scribal poets addressed their enemies directly, mocking Catholic priests who would no longer 'sipp / on Nunns Cherry Lipp' and accusing Queen Henrietta Maria's resident friars of supporting numerous 'bastards' on the kingdom's funds.[29] Even the Covenanters, who had long resisted such inflammatory language in transnational print, joined in. From mid-1640, Scottish polemicists with access to Edinburgh's comparatively unfettered presses followed London's puritan pot-poets in indicting England's ongoing liaison with 'the whore of Babel'. Charles's supporters, for their part, quickly tired of this endless chorus: what else did those 'sonnes of zeale' have to do, one joked, except to 'stay at home / & Rime to death both Antechrist & Rome'?[30]

Renewed attention to the Babylonian Whore soon implicated the English bishops as well, whom godly writers outed as the Roman strumpet's pimps and panders. In both print and manuscript, reformers described the ongoing popish intrigues against the national church as a sexual conspiracy spearheaded by Charles's seduced, corrupted episcopate. The fact that the bishops were themselves, in a common genealogical idiom, renegade 'children' in rebellion against 'the Church their mother' lent such metaphorical critiques even more force. Again scribal poets, relatively unconcerned with the threat of suppression or reprisal, proved most aggressive in detailing the bishops' 'conn[iv]ance with Babylons whore'; but as the kingdom's troubles intensified, the prelates' critics, and their London publishers, appeared increasingly willing to risk censure by broadcasting their polemics in (anonymous) print.[31] And, as had been the case since the beginning of the Anglo-Scottish troubles, many of those attacks took the form of sexual satire.

English puritans did not rely on metaphor alone when attacking the prelates. Some critics also focused on the bishops' jurisdiction over sexual crime in the kingdom's 'Antichristian' ecclesiastical courts, where it was alleged that fornication, adultery and incest were routinely forgiven for a piddling fee.[32] Meanwhile, Richard Overton reprinted one of Marprelate's sixteenth-century attacks on an infamous Elizabethan bigamist bishop, suggesting that if the prelates had once committed such blatant sins, they surely could again.[33] The bishops' literal chastity, just like their spiritual purity, thus became a running theme of anti-episcopal rhetoric. Then, weeks after the parliament's dissolution, rioting London apprentices celebrating Maytide attacked bishops' residences instead of the customary bawdy houses, indicating that the identification of episcopacy with sexual malignancy had spread from the page to the streets.³⁴ The godly effort to tar Charles's bishops as the scions of popish sexual corruption appeared to be working.

But it did not go uncontested. In response to the anti-popish fever sweeping London's godly community, alarmed English moderates took to manuscript and print during the summer of 1640 to rebut what they believed to be an impending flood of radical Protestantism. Well-versed in the longstanding anti-puritan assumption (owed, above all, to the memory of Anabaptist Munster) that sectarianism led indelibly to promiscuity, polygamy and venereal disease, these writers relied heavily on sexual satire. One pamphlet entitled *A whip for the back of a backsliding Brownist* thus argued that if the separatist 'Bretheren' did 'so much as looke upon a woman', they might succumb to their baser instincts. Like their godly opponents, moreover, anti-puritan writers also operated in a figurative register. In the *Whip*, for instance, sectarian procreation became a metaphor for the alarming recent proliferation of godly activism: 'the worlds in labour, her throwes comes so quick', it rhymed, 'that with her paine shee's growne starke lunatick'.³⁵ This familiar post-Reformation theme – that radical Protestantism, like all heresy, spread predominantly through its practitioners' uncontrollable lust – would soon grow into a prominent royalist trope.³⁶

Anti-puritan writers defending Charles from his godly critics presumably had less to fear from Caroline press licensers than did the publishers of anti-episcopal propaganda. Nevertheless, even the king's partisans remained wary of breaching public decorum. Consider a March 1640 pamphlet entitled *The epistle congratulatorie of Lysimachus Nicanor*, authored by the anti-Covenanter John Corbet. In one excerpt, the *Epistle* described Scottish puritans engaged in 'holy fornication' during secret 'night-meetings': an exercise dismissed by its practitioners, in true antinomian fashion, as 'no sin at all' if 'acted for good ends and intentions'.³⁷ Such straightforward descriptions of sectarian sexuality were still relatively rare in print during the spring of 1640, and in this respect the *Epistle* broke new ground. (At least one reader took him to task for it, too, refiguring 'Lysimachus' as 'Lies maker' on the title-page of their personal copy.)³⁸ However, Corbet published the piece under a false name, suggesting that even the king's most zealous apologists remained uneasy about openly flouting the longstanding taboo on public sex-talk.

But anonymous manuscript scribblers harboured no such concerns. One revealing springtime lampoon attacked the 'light heeled Matrons of Edinborrough' responsible for the Scottish prayer book rebellion three years prior. This tract dramatically exceeded Corbet's *Epistle* in eroticising Scottish Presbyterian worship, where it claimed the 'gift' of the 'naked spirit' routinely left 'many of our holy sisters' with 'a belli-full of devotion and hote zeal'. Moreover, following the *Whip* (albeit in much franker language), it argued facetiously that only the 'gifts' of these 'Ladyes, holy sisters and devot votaryes' could ensure that the Covenanter ministry would 'ejaculat . . . without meditation', thereby enabling the miraculous procreation of more Scottish rebels.[39] This poem, like the *Whip*, thus exemplified an early iteration of mid-century 'porno-politics': a novel polemical form for the period in which sexual activity served as a vivid metaphor for political change. We will encounter many similar descriptions in the chapters that follow, as royalist partisans turned increasingly to the language of monstrous reproduction to indict their puritan-parliamentarian enemies as a malignant family conspiracy.

In August, an English army departed London to confront the Covenanters once again. As it marched northward, godly correspondents again complained in letters and pamphlets about the 'foul misdemeanours' committed by wayward soldiers against civilian women.[40] But elsewhere, other critics took a different tack by satirising the new conscripts as randy gallants defined by their love for the 'Ladyes' of 'venus'.[41] This alternative satirical mode, which equated the English soldiery with the foppish cavalier poets who populated Charles's court in the 1630s, owed much to the rhetoric of courtly corruption that had once been marshalled against lecherous royal favourites like Buckingham and which had more recently appeared in Covenanter scribal satires. Taken together, these critiques – still circulating almost entirely in manuscript – equated the king's soldiers with a dangerous hyper-sexuality bordering on effeminacy, thereby undermining their patriarchal, moral and martial credentials in one blow.

At the same time, anti-puritan scribblers unleashed a barrage of libels at the Covenanters. Scottish military leaders came under particular fire. This was an old theme: Corbet's *Epistle*, for instance, had accused the Scottish general Alexander Leslie of having 'forsake[n] his wife, to joyne himselfe with an harlot' while on campaign. (One reader even wrote Corbet directly to praise another section that compared 'Loyola, the Captaine & founder of Jesuites, and Leslay, the Captaine of Covenanters, both bastards, soldiers, debauched in their youth . . . &c'.)[42] The abuse continued during Leslie's second campaign. One manuscript squib purportedly transcribed a speech in which Leslie promised his soldiers their 'choice of English Lasses, whereon you may gett a new & a better world'. Nor did this mock-Leslie doubt his soldiers' own lineage: 'was not theire Greate William the Conqueror a Bastard', he asked, 'and inn some things we are not inferiour to him'? Disgusted English observers would echo the sentiment months later by moaning that 'England now is conquer'd twysse by Bastards'.[43] Here, again, patriarchal legitimacy became the metric by which the Scots were held accountable – and found wanting.

Sexual satire thus suffused English scribal culture, and occasionally anonymous print, in mid-to-late 1640. One Covenanter scribbler even claimed to 'know . . . what the honest King does in his bedchamber' with 'that Papish wench' – Queen Henrietta Maria – 'that lyes by his side'. The regime discovered this squib in July, and Charles's ministers were undoubtedly horrified by its frank equivalence between the queen's sexuality and her 'whorish Religion': although English puritans had long treated Henrietta Maria with suspicion, none since William Prynne had dared to peer into the royal bedroom so brazenly.[44] Reports of other 'insolencyes', 'not fitte to be publishd in a pulpit' yet openly preached by godly ministers, soon surfaced in Bedfordshire.[45] If, as some Caroline officials surely feared, disaffected commentators were growing increasingly dismissive of royal authority, sexual politics apparently provided an effective mode of critique.

Later that summer, a scribal satire entitled 'Pigges Coranto' surfaced to lacerate the Scots and the English alike. As it narrated, both nations were guilty of profound sexual disorder, albeit in distinctive ways: 'in Scotland they frequent the Kirks all night long men & woemen togeather as it is thought to fast & pray', the libel crowed, 'but in England after Twilight is in & somtimes before they haunt Baudy houses to drinke & whore'. Its author condemned the armies gathering in the north with especial vigor. 'Pigg' claimed that 'the Covenanters [had] sent primly into England for a Catologue of all the rarest beautyes about the Court', whom they hoped to marry after slaying their husbands on the battlefield. The English soldiery, he reckoned, were even less polite. All told, 'with Kentish longtayles before, & blew bonnets behind[,] there is not a lasse has the greene sicknes nor hardly her maiden head'.[46] Ideologically ambiguous and rhetorically nuanced, 'Pigges Coranto' embodied the full range of sexual satire percolating in British manuscript culture during the fall of 1640.

By October, when Charles's generals surrendered again to the Covenanters in a treaty that inflicted crippling financial obligations on the defeated English, the archipelago's troubles had become fodder for partisan sexual politics. Primarily in manuscript but increasingly in illicit print – a medium that, in England, still technically fell under ecclesiastical supervision – eager writers dissected the fraught political moment using a vivid collection of post-Reformation sexual tropes. The ideological opacity of 'Pigges Coranto' demonstrated that these potent discourses of puritan lechery and popish corruption were not necessarily mutually exclusive; but they had undoubtedly grown more refined since the 1637 prayer book revolt. They were also being purchased, digested and debated with vigour by British readers. When Charles, desperate for funding to pay off the victorious Scots, decided to summon parliament once again, therefore, sex-talk was poised to assume an even greater role in the ensuing debates.

## 'Away for Hammersmith': evil counsellors, anti-sectarianism and the 'print explosion'

Charles's new parliament convened on 3 November 1640 in London, a city swarming with godly reformers and similarly overrun with scribal satires and illicit pamphlets.[47] The provinces, too, throbbed with anxiety: Exeter municipal leaders, for one, decided on 16 November to purchase a new cart for disciplining 'whores & such other lewde people', since such 'offences hath of late more abounded then heretofore'.[48] Those who prayed that a parliament might cure England's woes would be sorely disappointed. Instead, two factors soon rocketed the burgeoning sexual polemics of 1638–40 fully into print.

The first was political. With the Covenanters perched on the northern border, Charles was beholden to parliament for funding. But the parliament-men, flush with grievances still outstanding from the spring's short-lived session, chose to demand redress for prior ills before granting him supply. In particular, the senior Commons figure John Pym – a godly politician convinced that popish plotters infested Charles's court – recognised his king's misfortunes as an opportunity to force a full-scale reform of the national church. Yet Pym, a savvy leader, also knew that open criticisms of royal policy remained a high-risk endeavour, since contemporary reverence for the monarchy remained high despite the recent troubles. Accordingly, he turned to a different strategy to indict Caroline misgovernance more obliquely: the Tacitean trope of the evil counsellor once employed against Buckingham and other royal favourites.[49] From the session's outset, Pym and his allies blamed Charles's malignant advisors for perverting his government towards popery and tyranny. The chief malefactors, it was alleged, were Archbishop William Laud, architect of the kingdom's recent hated ('Laudian') ecclesiastical innovations, and the Deputy Lieutenant of Ireland, the earl of Strafford. Both Laud and Strafford, like other implicated regime figures, quickly discovered that the evil counsellor label effectively stripped them of the legal protections against public criticism usually afforded to royal servants. Slanders against Charles's evil counsellors soon proliferated in manuscript and print alike as godly activists called on parliament to purge the court while the king looked helplessly on.[50]

Sexual politics surfaced early in these proceedings when, four days after the session opened, the godly Irish planter Sir John Clotworthy intervened in a parliamentary debate regarding Strafford's conduct in Ireland. Clotworthy introduced the case of John Atherton, Irish bishop of Waterford and Lismore, who had recently been found 'guilty of incest & murder in England & sodomy in Ireland'. News of Atherton's 'fowle offences' had circulated widely in scandalised manuscript reports since June, but their appearance in parliament represented a new level of publicity. Moreover, when Clotworthy wondered aloud 'who commended this whorish incestuous Bishop who lay with his sister' (the answer, he knew, was Strafford), there was more at stake than the earl's head.[51] As an anonymous scribal commentator noted, 'when Bishopps shalbe condemned for the sinne of Sodomie, its time for the church to looke into and suppresse them'.[52] Atherton's sins, in other words, could be employed to justify the overthrow of English prelacy.

That sentiment was given voice just one month later, when hardline reformers petitioned the Commons for the total abolition of episcopacy, 'root and branch'. Among their grievances appeared a familiar godly complaint. Article eight indicted the prelates, who oversaw the kingdom's press licensing system, for enabling 'the swarming of lascivious, idle, and unprofitable books and pamphlets, play-books and ballads . . . in disgrace of all religion [and] to the increase of all vice'.[53] Like the Scottish Covenanters, who claimed to have discovered 'prophane Comadies . . . unworthy papers and scurvy pamphletts' in the libraries of English clergymen during their northern occupation, these petitioners drew an explicit association between England's unreformed national church and its robust culture of lascivious writing.[54] By suppressing good Protestant literature and allowing profane books to flourish instead, they argued, the bishops had hastened the kingdom's moral collapse.

Although the petition ultimately failed, its architects had a point about English literary culture. Since 1637, Caroline court poets and dramatists had published a flurry of bawdy verses in print alongside new vernacular editions of classic erotic favourites – some, like 'Ovid's "Fits of Love"', specifically identified in the 1640 petition.[55] Although sceptics scoffed that the 'gaites [i.e. 'gayeties'] of Ovid' were ludicrous as 'a motive for the extirpation of Bishops', they could not deny that sex-talk had grown more visible since the outbreak of the Scottish troubles.[56] To the root-and-branchers, at least, both phenomena signalled an urgent need for wholesale ecclesiastical reform. Meanwhile, the apparent – albeit likely untrue – fact that Charles had condoned the publication of the condemned texts went unnoted, but surely not unnoticed, by the petitioners.

Elsewhere, 'railing rimes' continued to circulate in manuscript.[57] Unlike the preceding summer's predominantly anti-popish scribal verses, however, the libels of winter 1640/41 were increasingly anti-puritan, a reaction against the undeniably godly leanings of the new parliament. Sexual satire, both literal and metaphorical, remained highly popular. Scribal writers described 'Godly Sisters' being 'ticle[d]' in secret prayer meetings until they were 'belly'ed', while others parodied the godly obsession with 'old Antichrists whore'.[58] Puritan celebrities like the 1630s martyrs John

Bastwick, Henry Burton and William Prynne also became targets: 'Prin and Burton say women, that are lewd and loose / Must weare Italian lockes for their abuse / But they will have private keyes for their owne use', rhymed one poet. As Pym and his fellow parliament-men called for a kingdom-wide moral reformation, such depictions of godly sexual hypocrisy grew correspondingly more pronounced.[59]

The second major factor that propelled sex-talk further into public view from November 1640 was the steady dissolution of Caroline press licensing. Although illicit pamphlets had circulated relatively freely since the outbreak of war with Scotland, several new parliamentary policies – including the intentional abatement of press oversight during the session's opening weeks and the establishment of a new licensing committee the following spring – sparked a revolution in the production of partisan print, which took on a new, shortened form to keep pace with political events.[60] Parliament's dissolution of the prerogative courts of Star Chamber and High Commission (historically responsible for punishing errant publishers and authors) in July 1641, combined with unrest within the Stationers' Company, proved even more decisive. Although parliamentary committees continued to monitor London's presses throughout the year, the lack of comprehensive oversight encouraged enterprising polemicists to propel sexual politics of all varieties even more decisively into print.[61]

Parliamentary apologists seized on the new milieu. No longer would reformers announce, as they had the previous spring, that 'wee know their names but hide their shames / Till time reveile their facts'; by December 1640, godly ministers were preaching instead that 'the prelates and the popish Lords were now known men in print' and thus fair game for slander.[62] The same held true in Scotland, where, in February 1641, Baillie celebrated that the Covenanters could now 'pray, preach, and print against' the bishops 'most freebie'. As provincial activists sent hundreds of petitions pouring into parliament, each enumerating the failings of local clergymen whose dubious Calvinist credentials and/or scandalous personal lives were deemed antithetical to the godly vision of a learned parish ministry, English puritans must have hoped that the kingdom's salvation was imminent.[63]

But others claimed to be horrified by the spreading plague of pamphlets. Cautionary tracts declared the 'nameless Authers . . . Of slanderous Pasquils' to be 'cankers of the State' and griped that 'true tales' could now be printed only 'under the name of lies'.[64] Preaching at court in April 1641, Robert Skinner inveighed against 'this scribbling age, when so many needlesse uselesse, senselesse pamphletts . . . come every day sweating from the presses'.[65] Similar anxieties were reflected in a 1641 pamphlet entitled *Sion's charity towards her foes in misery*, which addressed the recent profusion of 'bad language' against Charles's evil counsellors. Ultimately, the tract argued, the 'tart or bitter' style of 'such Satyricall spirits' proved counter-productive by robbing their targets of the opportunity for 'shame and repentance'.[66] It was a lesson that the author apparently hoped that English readers would take to heart.

That message certainly appeared to resonate in Whitehall and Westminster. Indeed, the necessity of suppressing unlicensed print was one of the few things on which king and parliament ostensibly agreed during the winter of 1640/41. Yet while both factions publicly denounced the flood of illicit publications, each continued to applaud, and occasionally abet, the covert production of partisan propaganda. The potential value of such material was simply too tempting to pass up, especially as the spring brought new developments – the impeachments of Strafford and Laud, deadlock between king and parliament, heightened separatist activity in London – that only encouraged partisan divisions.

Sex surfaced regularly in these proceedings. On 8 May 1641, for instance, the puritan parliament-man John White reported to the Commons on a London vicar named Edward Finch. Finch, a known Laudian whose godly parishioners had petitioned parliament for his removal, received short shrift from White, who dubbed the vicar 'a man of profane life, scandalous in his doctrine and conversation, and a hinderer of preaching'. Most strikingly, White accused Finch of committing gross sexual impropriety with several parishioners, and Sir Simonds D'Ewes, for one, subsequently dubbed Finch 'a notorious whoremaster' in his journal. After hearing White's report, the Commons voted Finch 'not fit to hold any benefice or promotion in the Church'. He was the first of many parochial clergymen censured and dispossessed by the Long Parliament.[67]

Puritan agitators had long prayed for this moment. Their ire at Laudian moral laxity was encapsulated that spring in a prolonged assault on the ecclesiastical courts, long viewed by the godly as hotbeds of 'whoredom and adultery' that tacitly licensed sexual misconduct by punishing offenders with trivial fines rather than more serious penalties. This rhetoric had a long history, but England's so-called 'bawdy courts' had faced even more complaints than usual since 1639.[68] Those grievances reached new levels of vitriol in 1641, inspired by recent criticisms of the bishops as sexually suspect and the ongoing deluge of provincial petitions against lecherous parish ministers like Finch. One representative pamphlet suggested that 'countrey wenches would sell their peticoats', or worse, rather than pay the requisite fines for adultery; court officials were happy to oblige, it continued, so long as those 'wenches ... were either willing, or rich, or handsome'. When parliament finally dissolved the ecclesiastical courts later that summer, similar jokes echoed in celebratory satires featuring London's pimps – fed up with officials whose price for protecting their whores from prosecution was always 'the best ware i'th[e] house' – as well as its prostitutes, known as the 'sisters of the scabbard', who were pleased that 'Civil Lawyers ... shall now ready pay for their venery' rather than taking it freely.[69] While outraged onlookers cried that the dissolution would only encourage sexual crime, godly apologists argued instead that it had finally cleared the way for a legitimate moral reformation.

Reformers also targeted the English soldiery, which streamed into London from the north throughout the summer of 1641. These men – dubbed the 'brothers of the blade', natural allies of the sisters of the scabbard, for their love of fighting, whoring and gambling – were said by godly reformers to be so 'experienced in the Laws of Venus' that they could not appear in public without a 'female peece of iniquity'. This association between soldiering, hyper-sexuality and courtly vice was already familiar from the work of earlier English satirists during the Bishops' Wars. It was strengthened further in 1641 by the presence of bawdy 'Poets' like Sir John Suckling within the army's ranks.[70] In one satirical pamphlet, Suckling – notorious as one of Charles's court versifiers during the 1630s – boasted that 'I that in court have made such sport / As never yet was found-a, / And tickled all both great and small / The Maides of honour round-a'; in another, his 'debaucht' followers (the 'Sucklington faction') gorged themselves on 'wine and women' in London's 'Bawdy-houses'.[71] Here, as with the mounting case against Charles's evil counsellors, hostile polemicists apparently felt confident enough to denounce Suckling's profligate sexuality directly in print: a strategy that would have been far riskier even six months earlier, before the effective collapse of Caroline press licensing.

Sexual politics also shaped the fate of another evil counsellor, Strafford, who was executed for treason in May. During his trial, the earl was asked about the disgraced Bishop Atherton, to which the earl could only answer that 'I conceived him a fitting man, though he proved otherwise'. Nor did he escape personal scrutiny: Baillie, writing to a friend, recounted a popular story that Strafford had murdered his second wife after she discovered evidence of his extramarital affairs. More broadly, the execution generated a new wave of anti-regime polemic against Charles's evil counsellors: by one contemporary estimate, over 'three hundred lying Pamphlets'. As one tract warned the still-imprisoned Laud, 'I see the multitudes of paper sheets ... sent from the Presse, and thus they cry them still, / Come buy a booke concerning little Will'.[72]

These repetitious attacks on whoremongering soldiers, lecherous royal counsellors and bastard popish bishops indicate that by mid-1641, post-Reformation sexual politics had found a home in reformist polemic, which itself had migrated decisively into print from its earlier scribal roots. Sometime that summer, for example, there appeared two anonymous pamphlets describing the recent parliamentary interrogation of a captured

Jesuit named John Browne. Browne had apparently accused several court Catholics of sexual misconduct, which both tracts duly repeated. Among the named offenders, according to one of the tracts, was the queen's confessor, Father Phillip, who was said to have 'three wives at this present all alive'.[73] Yet while the pamphlets purportedly drew on the same official report, they did not always get their stories straight. For instance: instead of accusing Father Phillip of bigamy, as the first tract had, the second pamphlet instead fingered the queen's cupbearer for this crime. (This was the correct answer, as confirmed in a clandestine printed edition of Phillip's impeachment articles later that year.)[74] Even so, the decision to level such allegations at the queen's own household in print spoke to the puritan opposition's growing comfort with sexual libel.

The bishops faced similar recrimination. Transposing a familiar idiom from earlier scribal material into print, godly publicists excoriated the prelates as both pimps and the misbegotten offspring of 'Romes Strumpet' throughout the summer of 1641. This genealogical argument proved persuasive enough that one parliamentary diarist scribbled 'the Bishops the brood of Antichrist' into his journal.[75] Additionally, individual bishops – now outed as both evil counsellors and popish malignants – were attacked directly in print for their 'Luxurie and laciviousnesse'.[76] Laud himself, a perpetual 'Batchelour', was spared from sexual slander, but others were less lucky: Matthew Wren of Ely was reported to have carried on an affair with a neighbour's 'very handsome' wife while studying at Cambridge, and another writer jested that William Piers, the 'lusty' bishop of Bath and Wells, had grown 'enamoured on every female Sexe'.[77] There was no better example of episcopal depravity than Stafford's disgraced appointee John Atherton, whose lurid history was now recounted in a detailed verse pamphlet. Announcing that 'so farre basenesse did in him prevaile, / that unto Lust he himselfe set to saile', the tract described how Atherton had 'Defloured Virgins, Marriage beds defilde [sic]', and 'Incest committed with the Sister of his wife'. Its author then begged the other bishops to 'Shun Lust, Shun Buggary, / Shun Incest, Rape, and shun Adultery'. The tract even recycled a libellous image of Laud on the frontispiece to reinforce the association between Caroline episcopacy, popery and sexual depravity.[78]

Libels against the bishops were soon joined by printed exposés of the malignant provincial clergy hauled, like Edward Finch, before parliament on the basis of petitions submitted by their indignant flocks. The printed account of Bedford vicar John Gwin's 'lascivious wenching, drunkenesse, and wanton life' – including 'hanous crime[s] of Adultery' with five different women – featured a woodcut image of a cuckoo atop a steeple to illustrate his cuckolding ways.[79] Gwin's disgrace was even more notable because of his relative obscurity. Like Charles's evil counsellors, mundane clergymen

# ARTICLES MINISTRED,
## By His
## MAJESTIES
### Commissioners.

For Causes Ecclesiasticall. Presented to the High Court of Parliament against John Gwin, Vicar of Cople in the County of *Bedford*.

*Wherein is discovered his lascivious wenching, Drunkennesse, and wanton life, and most vild, and unbecomming courses, most unfit for his Function.*

London Printed for *V. V.* 1641.

Figure 1.1 *Articles ministred . . . against John Gwin* (1641)

of all stations had become fair game for public humiliation by mid-1641. Again, sexual politics provided a compelling tool for the job.

The most distinctive clerical victim of this trend was Finch himself. Sometime in 1641, parliament's proceedings against Finch were chronicled in an anonymous pamphlet, accompanied by a lengthy editorial. Sex was a prominent theme. While only three of the original twenty-one parliamentary articles had concerned Finch's chastity, more than one third of the pamphlet's added text was devoted to his carnal sins. Finch, its author alleged, had propositioned a dying woman during her final communion; additionally, he had been a 'constant frequenter of . . . two mens wives'. The lengthiest account of the cleric's depravity came from a coachman who purportedly had transported Finch, two 'deboist Comrades of his owne Coat and condition', and three women to Hammersmith for a secret liaison. Each man choosing a partner – Finch selecting 'the fattest of the three' – they entered an inn, where the coachman later found them using 'the most vile and obscene gestures, upon beds, even to the utmost of what hands could do under their clothes'. To illustrate this story's centrality to the pamphlet's argument, its frontispiece depicted Finch boarding a coach beneath the slogan 'away for hamersmith'. All told, in this tract (which one godly reader carefully transcribed in his journal), Finch's Laudianism ceded polemical primacy to his alleged sexual malfeasance: evidence that the unknown author, or perhaps its enterprising publisher, believed the latter to be more appetising to English readers than the complicated ecclesiastical politics under debate in parliament.[80]

Faced with this humiliating account, Finch made a remarkable choice: he responded. By normal standards, this was a bizarre decision. Litigation, not retaliation, had long been the traditional recourse for aggrieved victims on those rare occasions when personal defamation found its way into print prior to 1640. But with the relevant courts dissolved or in disarray, Finch must have believed that only a rebuttal could vindicate his good name from the 'Envious Pamphlets, and scurrilous Frontispiecs' of his anonymous accuser.[81] Consequently, Finch took to print himself to contest the allegations of misbehaviour – and, in doing so, established an important precedent for litigating personal sexuality not in court, but through the unquestionably more public medium of print.

Finch's rebuttal dwelt at length on the allegations of sexual misconduct. First, the vicar announced that he 'knew not any woman I kept company withall, any waies suspected of incontinencie', and he asserted that the two women with whom he had been accused of committing adultery were his landlady (and thus someone he could 'hardly avoid') and the wife of a close friend.[82] Next, he addressed the coachman's testimony. Noting that 'it is no argument of Incontinency to ride abroad in a Coach', Finch suggested that had they 'intended any incivility', they never would have 'call[ed] up a Coachman to be witnesse of it'. 'Besides', he wrote,

> the fattest of the three was my own Sister, since dead, and . . . I hope the World wil in Charity beleeve, that God has not given me over to a reprobate sence, to be so unnaturall, as . . . to pollute and defile my own Sister.

The tract concluded with a petition for Finch's reinstatement signed by sympathetic parishioners, although the vicar offered to wait until all 'weighty Affaires of the State' were concluded.[83]

It would be a long delay. The unlicensed publication of Finch's offenses – not formally sanctioned by parliament, but probably released with John White's connivance – demonstrated just how dramatically the collapse of Caroline press licensing had catalysed English print culture by mid-1641. Even John Pym struggled to navigate the new milieu. That summer, Commons backbenchers balked when he moved to name Charles's evil counsellors in print. The king himself warned parliament on 12 July against using 'Slander . . . to deter any, that I trust . . . from giving me free Counsel'. Chastened, Pym and his allies reluctantly made an example of several puritan publishers who had proceeded too violently against the bishops, hoping thereby to prove their loyalty to church and state.[84]

Yet as parliament's hardcore reformers – among them Sir John Clotworthy, who proposed on 19 July to punish Jesuits and priests by gelding – faced more pushback from their less enthusiastic colleagues, sexual satire continued to proliferate in unlicensed pamphlets.[85] Godly activists took to the streets, too, which provoked vitriolic opposition from anti-puritan opponents who blamed zealous parliament-men like Clotworthy for the skyrocketing visibility of radical Protestantism. Soon enough, the conflict seeped into the provinces, transforming whole counties into ideological battlegrounds over England's ecclesiological future.[86]

In those debates, whether printed, scribal or face-to-face, sexual politics were never far from view. Throughout the summer of 1641, puritan polemicists produced damning accounts of Catholic 'whoredome', 'incest' and 'Sodomy', and then explained, via complicated genealogies of popish diabolism, that the national church had been infected with the same disease under the bishops' approving gaze.[87] In return, anti-sectarian writers – not all of them opposed to moderate parliamentary reforms, but nonetheless frightened by the rising profile of sectarian radicalism – denounced the hypocrisy of hyper-godly seducers that 'exercised their [sexual] talent' exclusively with their 'holy sisters' so as not to 'defile themselvs with the wicked'.[88] As parliament continued to experiment with ecclesiastical reform, its critics proved the louder chorus. Soon sympathetic contemporaries were blaming 'the present dystractions' on the 'preaching of mechanycks', and by the fall the deluge of hostile pamphlets had grown so violent that the parliament-men were allegedly 'fearefull to bee named' at all. This abuse was almost entirely the work of freelancing writers; but although Charles's ministers did not officially contribute, they took careful notes.[89]

The chief architect of the summer's anti-sectarian reaction was John Taylor, a celebrity poet with a love of bawdy humour and an equivalent regard for the national church. In nearly a dozen anonymous tracts published across 1641, Taylor ridiculed the sexual gospel of godly radicals who coupled piously for 'the encrease and multiplying' of the 'Saints'. These lurid tales of too-hot Protestants who 'love[d] their Neighbour as themselves' (assuming those neighbours were female and not 'unhandsome') resembled the crude satires marshalled by government penmen against Martin Marprelate during the later 1580s, and they provided a model for other pamphleteers who mimicked Taylor's jesting style throughout the year.[90]

Two sects in particular drew Taylor's ire: the 'Brownists', a catch-all term for English separatists derived from a sixteenth-century radical, Richard Browne; and another familiar Tudor bugbear, the 'antinomian' Family of Love. Taylor repeatedly attacked both groups as promiscuous, libertine and sexually predatory. He was especially scornful of sectarian women, both for their vulnerability to honey-tongued heterodox seducers and, increasingly, for using their feminine charms to lure gullible men into the radical fold.[91] Other pamphleteers soon joined Taylor in profiling women seduced by the Family's 'poeticall brother[s]'.[92] Brownists, too, were attacked for their 'lustfull . . . conscupiscence', which allegedly inspired their preaching and through which they converted 'chast Virgins' into 'harlots' and 'the mothers of bastards'.[93] Throughout this printed literature, patriarchalist misogyny melded with post-Reformation truisms about the 'voluptuous wantonnesse' of heterodox doctrine to cement sexual politics – and, particularly, attacks on the spiritual and sexual deficiencies of radical Protestant women – as a defining feature of mid-century anti-sectarianism. It would not be long before Taylor and his fellows expanded that platform to encompass the entire parliamentary coalition.[94]

In July, a new group of radicals appeared on Taylor's radar: the Adamites, who purportedly worshiped 'as naked as they were when they came from their mothers womb'.[95] More likely a product of fevered imaginations than an actual practicing sect, the Adamites featured in a spate of hostile tracts that summer and remained relevant in anti-sectarian print for the remainder of the year. Although sometimes portrayed as deluded innocents, they were also accused of hosting lecherous conventicles wherein the 'Plannet of Venus' made the brethren's 'flesh to rise' for 'the lively act of Generation, and propagation of the godly' with their sisters.[96] Adamite women were particularly scandalous, as shown by one caricature, 'Alice the Adamite', who 'as bare as ones naile . . . shames not her taile [i.e. clitoris]'.[97] Furthermore, several of these screeds bore woodcut frontispieces depicting naked Adamite radicals flagellating one another while others coupled in corners. Marking, as Sarah Toulalan has noted, the first appearance of such explicitly sexual images in the history of English print, they left no doubt that radical Protestantism was fundamentally defined by sexual anarchy.[98]

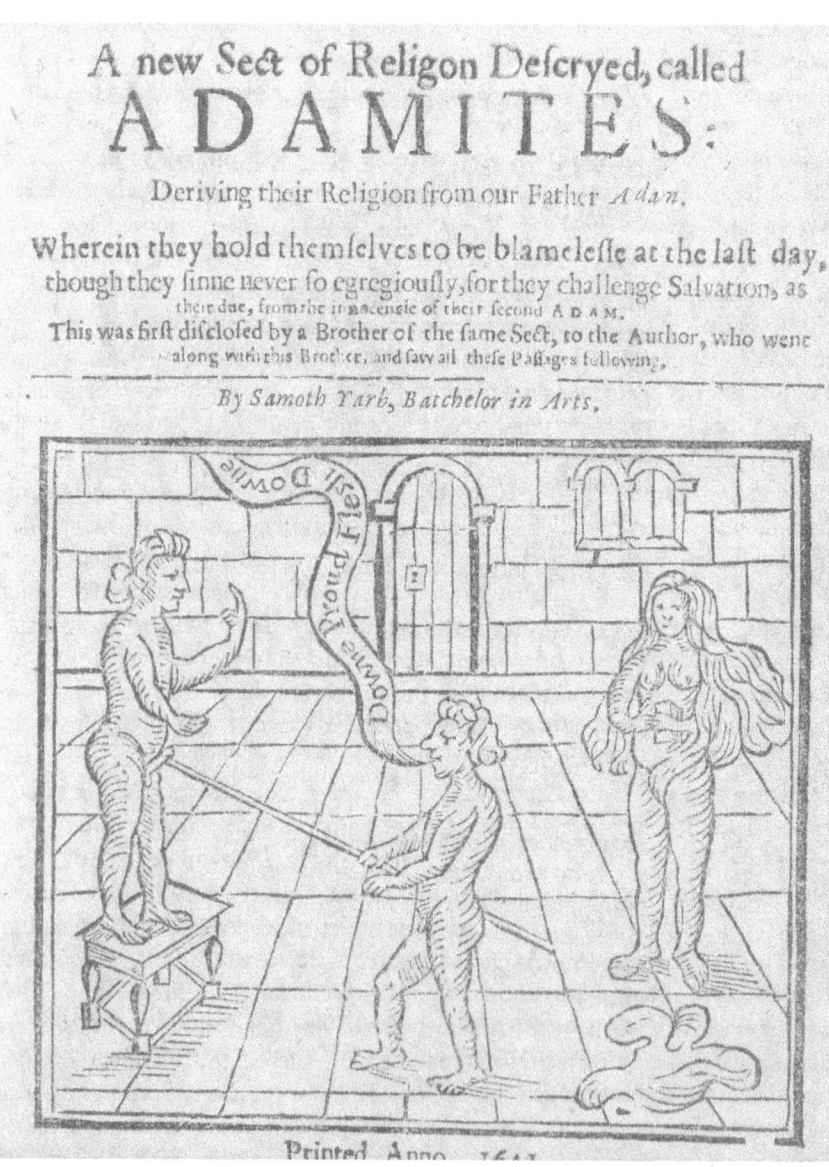

Figure 1.2 *A new sect of religion descryed* (1641)

The summer of 1641 therefore witnessed an anti-sectarian reaction in print that soon rivalled the corpus of anti-popish publications emanating from parliament's supporters. Moreover, neither group wrote in a vacuum. Instead, fractious collisions repeatedly erupted between the two burgeoning factions, often featuring accusations of unchastity. Through such exchanges, as in Edward Finch's case, personal sexuality – once the exclusive province of closed courtrooms, private exchanges and the occasional manuscript libel – was propelled ever more forcefully into the kingdom's nascent public sphere.

One such feud began with Taylor's *A swarme of sectaries and schismatiques*, a short pamphlet chronicling the sexual appetites of various London sectarians. In a series of vignettes, the tract described how 'one Sidrath Cave . . . rais'd up his maids belly' in spite of his marital vows; explained that another divine, John Howgrave, had impregnated a Rotterdam maid after fleeing abroad to escape his wife; and shared that yet another sectary had wooed Howgrave's abandoned spouse in his absence. By identifying these figures, some of whom were real-life radicals (albeit likely innocent of the crimes described in the pamphlet), Taylor broke new ground, for very few of the anti-sectarian tracts yet published had indicted specific individuals by name. Perhaps for that reason, he soon became a victim himself.[99] Months later, a pamphlet authored by the fervent puritan Henry Walker proposed to 'correct' Taylor's 'knavery' and make him 'feele the smart of his lascivious life'. But while he dismissed Taylor's lurid attacks as spurious and lewd – 'he writes of kissing, and whoring, and such ribble and rabble of his own braine', Walker sneered – the *Answer* employed precisely the same tactics, accusing Taylor of entertaining 'threescore whores in a day' when he was not busy revelling in other 'amorous actions, effeminate glances, pictures of prostitution, and Veneriall vanities'. The spat continued for months, eventually culminating in a spectacular woodcut image of the devil defecating into Taylor's open mouth. The caption read, 'such is the language of a beastly railor, / The Divels privi-house most fit for Taylor'.[100] It was a fitting summary of the current state of English public discourse.

Walker's willingness to turn Taylor's lascivious language back against his enemy signalled the growing appeal of sex-talk for even the most pious of contemporary polemicists. Granted, some checks remained on England's print marketplace by the time that Taylor and Walker published their vitriolic tracts, mostly owing to parliament's continued inability to ignore overt attacks on Charles's authority without risking royal censure. Indeed, Walker was later hauled before the Commons for lobbing a petition into Charles's coach in January 1642, while Taylor fled London shortly thereafter when his royalism put him in danger from puritan activists.[101] Even so, sexual polemic had clearly become a regular feature of unlicensed partisan print by the summer of 1641, framed predominantly through the post-Reformation polarities of anti-popery and anti-puritanism. Moreover, although the furore cooled briefly in August while parliament recessed and Charles journeyed north to Scotland, it soon came roaring back to life.

### 'Reforming on a bedside': inventing 'roundheads' and 'cavaliers'

Writing from London in November 1641, just before the king's return from his Scottish excursion, an observer despaired at 'how little Danger ther is in printinge and how great in writing'.[102] Nevertheless, during the weeks that followed, English print culture grew even more violent as news broke of a massive Catholic rebellion in Ireland. Embellished accounts of Irish Catholic atrocities, including graphic accounts of sexual assault, soon flooded into London's bookshops, and both king and parliament moved to capitalise on the hysteria.[103] The resulting exchanges – including parliament's controversial publication of a Grand Remonstrance blaming the Irish situation on Charles's misgovernance – drove partisan recrimination to new heights by sparking a formal paper war between the king's royalist coalition and his critics in Westminster.[104] By the time that Charles raised his standard at Nottingham in August 1642, both king and parliament had published dozens of declarations, proclamations and pronouncements detailing the constitutional principles over which the impending conflict would ostensibly be fought.[105]

Those materials were entirely devoid of slander, suggesting that both factions remained unwilling to sanction such language in official publications before hostilities had begun. However, neither party prevented sympathetic freelancers from deploying it on their behalf, and an independent printed literature brimming with sexual satire quickly emerged to mobilise support in decidedly earthier terms. With it arrived two era-defining stereotypes – the parliamentarian roundhead and the royalist cavalier – that calcified the relatively fluid post-Reformation positions of anti-puritanism and anti-popery into genuine partisan identities that would shape English political culture for years to follow.

Although both of these archetypes have received considerable scholarly attention, the foundational role played by sexual satire in their creation has not yet been adequately documented.[106] Following the anti-puritan precedent set by John Taylor, the proto-royalist pamphlets of 1642 defined their roundhead opponents as lascivious cuckolds whose faux godly piety masked a lustful core. Parliamentary sympathisers, meanwhile, revived the anticourt rhetoric deployed against English soldiers during the Bishops' Wars to denounce Charles's cavaliers as rapacious, popish womanisers. Sex-talk thus provided a key link between the post-Reformation slanders of 1638–41 and the partisan stereotypes of 1642. As with earlier royalist porno-political productions, its reproductive resonances also offered a unique epistemological lens for assessing the source of the kingdom's mounting tensions. One manuscript satire put it thusly: roundhead 'saints' would 'goe five miles to preach & pray, / and with a Sister lye by'th way', while the 'dam'd Cavilier' was more likely to find 'a drunken whore, / and kis[s] her 'gainst a Chamber dore'. In both cases, pregnancy usually followed – and with it, the next generation of 'roundheads' and 'cavaliers'.[107]

Both stereotypes emerged during the winter of 1641/42. When godly pressure in London sent Charles fleeing for York early in January, he left behind a city still brimming with anti-puritan sentiment. During the months that followed, local royalist sympathisers continued to bombard Pym and his allies in rude manuscript squibs. These writers specialised in libellous exposés of the parliamentary leadership, whose pious pretensions to ecclesiastical and moral reformation rendered them ripe targets for sexual slander. One recurrent victim was the earl of Essex – ridiculed as a cuckold ever since the 1613 Overbury affair, and now one of the king's chief aristocratic opponents – whom royalist scribblers depicted as a cuckold-horned 'ram'.[108] But one did not require an embarrassing sexual past to fall prey to these libellers, and they dismissed even Pym, an elderly widower, as a pox-afflicted 'true brother' of whom 'the holy sisters approve[d]' like 'none other'.[109] In both cases, sex provided a potent tool for illustrating the laughability of parliamentarian moral reform. Although *ad hominem* attacks against the parliament-men were not yet common in print (perhaps because London publishers feared reprisal if they were ever discovered), scribal libels continued to serve as a palatable alternative for Charles's supporters.

Such material likely proved popular among readers alarmed by the heightened visibility of Protestant sectarianism. One Londoner complained in January about the 'factious preaching of ill affected Ministers to the present Government of the Church & State' during 'theire unlawfull meetings in the cittie'. Weeks later, the army officer Thomas Reade reported satirically from Oxford on the local 'deformed' puritan 'sisters', whose 'nightly devotions' ostensibly included 'that religious exercise of copulation'.[110] Meanwhile, provincial anti-puritan activists drew up county petitions against the 'now so much abounding sins of Incest, Adultery, and Fornication', which they blamed on parliament's dissolution of the church courts.[111] Like Taylor, these contributors took for granted the correlation between radical puritanism, parliamentarian plotting and sexual depravity.

By early 1642, those themes had coalesced in the caricature of the 'roundhead', so named for the distinctive hairstyle worn by London apprentices. One January pamphlet, *The resolution of the round-heads*, portrayed its titular character as a hypocritical cuckold defined by his 'zealous lusting' after the puritan 'Shee-Lecturers' running amok in London's streets. Symbols of patriarchal failure abounded: this roundhead, for one, had no illusions about his own wife's fidelity, given her frequent participation in orgies of 'great love and comunity betwixt the brethren and the Sisters'.[112] Centred on sexual hypocrisy and effeminate cuckoldry, the *Resolution* repurposed the chief anti-puritan tropes of 1640–41 for an explicitly partisan attack on the parliamentarian coalition.

Meanwhile, London's presses pumped out pro-parliament propaganda.[113] Familiar targets like the English bishops – recently impeached and imprisoned on parliament's orders – continued to suffer from the attentions of hostile pamphleteers, while the Commons received a new wave of county petitions against Charles's evil counsellors as the Irish rising sent popish panics rippling across the kingdom.[114] Amid it all, parliamentary freelancers constructed a new anti-royalist archetype: the swaggering, lusty 'cavalier'. This term, originally a generic phrase for skilled horsemen, had recently been re-coined to describe the carousing ex-soldiers who maintained a constant presence around Charles during the closing months of 1641. These were menacing figures whose presence had sparked recurrent godly accusations of wanton violence, Catholic conspiracy and cannibalism.[115] But while the label surfaced prior to Charles's January departure from London, it flourished only once he and his soldiers had left the capital, bolstered thereafter by outraged reports about their escapades in the provinces.[116] Soon enough, Charles's swaggering cavaliers had become synonymous with popery, plunder and rapacity.

Within months, the nascent roundhead-cavalier binary had developed into a full-blown libellous dialogue. The *Resolution*, for instance, inspired a parliamentarian *Answer* in which the cavaliers were assailed for preferring 'Brothels in stead of Broths' and threatening the chastity of 'Cobler and Feltmakers wives'. (Some readers, like one Essex parishioner who thrust a copy of the *Answer* at his local curate and bid him to 'read you that', apparently found the response more compelling than the original.)[117] Tellingly, both terms also began to see use beyond print. 'Puritans (as they called them) grewe very odious & were called of all Round heads', noted the diarist Thomas Wyatt in April 1642; later, the earl of Pembroke indicted Oxford University for 'admitting . . . Cavaleers, & taking up Armes . . . against the Parliament'.[118] In turn, by appropriating the new partisan labels for personal use, contemporaries greatly broadened their polemical footprint.

The new stereotypes were not the only novel storyline of English sexual politics in 1642. Elsewhere, sex-talk began to infiltrate contemporary political theory. When Charles appeared at the magazine town of Hull in April, for example, the parliamentary governor Sir John Hotham ordered the gates barred before telling the king 'that he could not admit his majesty' without breaking his pledge to secure Hull 'for his Majesty's Honour, and the Kingdoms use'.[119] Here, in a novel reading of the medieval theory of the king's two bodies, Hotham was arguing that Charles's physical person lacked the authority to overrule his body politic, the metaphorical 'king-in-parliament' still resident in Westminster. The king retreated, livid, and promptly wrote to the Lords that 'the Reason of the said Denial [was] as strange to His Majesty as the Thing itself': how could Hotham bar Charles from his own armoury by invoking 'His Majesty's Honour'? Despite his anger, parliament ruled that the governor had 'done nothing but in Obedience to the Commands of both Houses of Parliament', and by August the Houses had simplified their position even further: 'all such persons as shall upon any pretence whatsoever, assist his Majesty in this war', they declared, 'are Traytors to his Majesty'.[120] Thus began a parliamentarian co-option of the king's two bodies that would only grow more pointed – and more fixated on royal sexuality – with time.

Meanwhile, Charles's supporters also continued experimenting with porno-politics. Months after the Hull debacle, one manuscript libel imagined the king's parliamentarian opposition in terms of an unnatural pregnancy that was soon to yield a monstrous, miscegenated birth. Entitled 'A True Description of the Malignant Party in England', the poem described 'a Monster', 'begott' on devilish 'Incub[i]' and 'Succuba' by the 'great Rabby pim' and the rest of 'this great parliament'. Over the next ten pages, the misshapen 'monster' – denounced variously as 'the sonn of reformation', a 'puritan of lust', and the 'Roundhead of knavery' – was anatomised and then blamed for all of the kingdom's recent troubles.[121] The 'True Description' was a clever amalgam of two familiar tropes: first, the traditional English conjugal equivalence between king/husband and parliament/wife; second, the providentialised monstrous birth narratives of prewar print culture. By combining them into a metaphorical account of parliamentary copulation and monstrous pregnancy, this unknown satirist offered a strikingly theoretical – and, again, nascently porno-political – reading of the kingdom's imploding constitution.

As partisan polemicists scribbled away, king and parliament began recruiting for war. Once again, both Pym and Charles demurred from licensing outright libels in their formal appeals to the kingdom; but unlicensed print was a different story. Consider a July 1642 pamphlet entitled *An appeale to the world*, which accused royalist leaders of forging anti-parliamentary petitions in order to exaggerate support for Charles's cause. In fact, the *Appeale*'s holier-than-thou attitude was a charade. As Thomas Wyatt noted, although the 'appeale hath no name to it', it was 'certainly made by Pym for there be in it the very same phrases that are in his speech . . . within the house Jan: 25 1641[/2]'. Of course, another writer may have simply appropriated Pym's language for his own use. But if Wyatt was correct, the Westminster junto, just like the royalist grandees indicted in the *Appeale*, was still too worried about preserving political decorum in mid-1642 to risk openly voicing its most caustic criticisms.[122] Not until after the outbreak of civil war would either regime alter its strategy.

As they equivocated, freelancing polemicists unconcerned with the maintenance of public civility continued to develop the cavalier-roundhead binary in partisan print. Parliamentarian accounts of royalist outrages in the provinces – including sexual assaults purportedly committed by Charles's soldiers against civilian wives and daughters – equated English cavaliers with Irish Catholics who had reportedly ravished Protestant women by the thousands since November. At the same time, royalist writers bolstered their anti-roundhead literature with lurid references to London sectarianism. By the fall, moreover, the sexual attributes of both caricatures were regularly appearing in private correspondence and public confrontations alike. In one case, the Londoner Elizabeth Humphries was summoned before the local quarter sessions 'for bidding the devil to take the Parliament & said that they were al cuckolds'. In another, a Westminster petitioner reported to the Lords that some royalist soldiers near York had abused one 'Mrs. Marwood' as a 'Protestant Whore, and Puritan Whore'.[123] One Cambridge man heeded these rumours so credulously that he offered to keep his brother's female relatives safe in London while 'the Cavaliers for the kinge' prowled the countryside; in the meantime, he wrote, 'I have gott you some pistolls for your defense'. Puritan preachers were no less invested, and in August, a northern minister linked the king's 'worst counsellors' with 'the whore [of Babylon]' before urging his listeners 'to burne her with fier'.[124]

The libellous back-and-forth continued throughout the fall. The roundhead's defining characteristic remained his godly 'Hypocrisie', which ensured that while he professed to 'have all things done in spirit', he was in fact obsessed with 'meere flesh'.[125] Because the 'Puritane' and the 'Roundhead' were 'termini equivalentes', he also followed the godly commandment to 'Increase and Multiply', whether it required 'teaching against the backe of a Chaire, / instructing at a Tables end, / revealing in a Basket, / exhorting over a Buttery Hatch', or 'reforming on a Bed side'.[126] In this mocking literature, chock-full of roundhead lechers hoping to 'unhors[e] the Whore of Babel, / with a Lance of Inspiration', parliamentarianism and puritan hypersexuality melded into one.[127]

Another key facet of the roundhead trope was emasculated cuckoldry. This strain of rhetoric implicated the wealthy London merchants whose financial support had underwritten parliamentarian mobilisation since 1641. There was a simple reason for that endless well of funding, royalists claimed: puritan lecturers had 'Horned' London's leadership by seducing their wives from the pulpit and then convinced those women to siphon their husbands' wealth for the cause. According to John Taylor, moreover, these illicit copulations between puritan 'Auditors' and their 'good [City] Dames' had a second consequence. 'The concupiscence of your Consciences', he warned in August, 'hath got you with child with Rebellion'.[128] This pregnancy metaphor, which mimicked the monstrous birth narrative of the 'True Description', would in time grow into a comprehensive royalist porno-political indictment of London puritanism.

For the moment, however, many of Charles's partisans were still writing secretly from the capital, where parliament's erratic press control efforts were most effective. As such, anti-parliamentarian manuscript libels continued to appear in London throughout mid-to-late 1642. These scribal satires largely mirrored their printed counterparts, mocking godly 'Roundheads' whom 'the sisters under laye' and cuckolded London 'citizens' who were forced to 'drinke in a horne / of your owne sweet wifes providing'.[129] In a poem composed by the clergyman Accepted Frewen, for instance, much was made of 'shee-zelot[s]' whose 'hungerie loyness' were satisfied only by the preaching of the godly 'grave clergie'. Another central conceit was puritan hypocrisy, showcased by roundhead apprentices who would 'beat an ould Bawd or fright poore whores' on 'shrove tewesday or May Day' only to retreat to a 'Conventickle' meeting and 'put out the light' for a rendezvous with some godly 'Cambridge women'. (In the end, the joke was on the laymen, because ultimately their 'womens sighes' were 'tunde to the teachers nose'.) Here, hypocrisy, lechery and cuckoldry once again served as defining roundhead traits, linked together by the malevolent figure of the unbridled female sectarian. Frewen's thoroughly amateur verses demonstrate how deeply those themes had permeated English political culture by the fall of 1642.[130]

Parliamentarian writers indicted Charles's rapacious cavaliers with equal vigor. As reports of royalist plundering filtered in from the provinces throughout the summer, the king's soldiers garnered a reputation for sexual violence. These accounts of 'ravisht' women – which surely reminded some godly readers of the English soldiery's predations during the Bishops' Wars – were probably exaggerated, but that made them no less terrifying. By October, parliamentarian writers regularly cajoled their readers to protect their 'wives' from 'the outragious Cavalliers'. Even London's burgeoning serial newsbook industry joined the chorus: one October issue reported on some 'Cavaleers' in Shropshire who 'did ravish the wife of a very discreete, moderate, able and godly Minister . . . whilest the Kings Majesty himselfe was in the Towne'.[131] Again, descriptions of the cavaliers' 'Sordid-Acts', including 'many Rapes and Chamber-Adulteries', intentionally mimicked accounts of the outrages ascribed to rebellious Irish Catholics, and hostile pamphleteers would soon begin making pointed comments about the 'Irish and Welsh women' said to serve the royalist armies as camp-wives, cooks and prostitutes.[132] Popish, violent and sexually insatiable, such women were perfect female analogues to Charles's cavalier soldiery.

The cavaliers' other chief characteristic in these satires was derived from the same stock depictions of popish hyper-sexuality that had been deployed against court poets like Sir John Suckling the previous year. Parliamentarian sympathisers parodied Charles's soldier-gallants as foppish crypto-Catholic lechers who had been more concerned with holding 'Cupidinean Lecture[s]' among the 'Yorkshire maid[s]' during the Bishops' Wars than with actually fighting.[133] As they described, after the Scottish conflict ended, 'Pimps and their Whores' had remained the cavaliers' closest companions; but those liaisons did not come without cost, since the ultimate fate of 'all those blades that cannot women leave' was the 'French disease'.[134] Nor were these escapades as robustly masculine as some cavaliers might have hoped. Instead, following a commonplace tenet of early modern patriarchal theory, their critics argued that such exuberant sexuality was in fact a sign of womanly lasciviousness: the royalists' pursuit of endless pleasure, in fact, was likely to leave them 'furnisht with a horne' by their frustrated wives. In this sense, Charles's cavaliers, just like their roundhead opponents, were attacked as unmanly and anti-patriarchal despite their ostensibly hyper-masculine predilections for womanising, drink and war.[135]

Notably, while all manner of royalist affiliates came under attack in this literature, the royal family remained largely immune from censure. True, a few anonymous polemicists raised the spectre of King Ahab's 'wicked Wife' Jezebel (a not-so-coded reference to Henrietta Maria) and invoked the 'lusts' of 'Tyrants' in print later in the year, although several of these texts were subsequently burned by parliamentary command.[136] Few authors proved more daring than the London preacher John Goodwin. In an October tract entitled *Anti-cavalierisme*, Goodwin railed against 'that bloody and butcherly Generation, commonly knowne by the name of Cavaliers'. His list of the royalists' crimes encompassed the full cavalier stereotype, from stealing 'the honour and chastity of . . . wives, & daughters' to generic popish 'filthinesse and uncleannesse'. (Goodwin also linked the English cavaliers' 'lusts' with those of 'their Brethren in Ireland'.) Yet he remained deferential towards the monarchy, with one major exception: a revealing section in which he considered past monarchs who had fornicated with the Whore of Babylon.[137] Goodwin did not name Charles directly, but the subtext was clear: England's current king might pay dearly for his sinful liaison with his popish wife. Post-Reformation sexual politics, in this case, could condemn Charles's behaviour without mentioning him by name.

Both the roundhead and the cavalier were thus well-established figures in partisan polemic by October 1642. But while these were ostensibly diametrically-opposed archetypes, the shared post-Reformation and patriarchal resonances of English sexual politics ensured that they shared some features in common. Both caricatures were frequently affiliated with popery and the devil, for example, in addition to their mutual connections with effeminacy and cuckoldry.[138] Indeed, this dialogic element was crucial to their construction, as sparring satirists attempted to highlight the righteousness of their cause by excoriating their enemies' failings. One parliamentarian pamphleteer thus asserted that Charles's soldiers were the true 'Roundheads' because 'the Poxe eates of their naturall haire', leaving them bald, while a loyalist response revived an earlier trope to argue that while the puritans might be 'Brothers' of schism, they were not 'of the blade; for they cannot endure our Cavaleers, yet they are lovers of the sisters of the scaberd'.[139] Other loyalists suggested that it was in fact cavalier gallants who were cuckolding City merchants by lying with their wives, since London women much preferred manly loyalists to their effeminate puritan husbands.[140] This mutually constitutive interchange of partisan polemic would continue for years to come, as contemporaries struggled to claim the moral high ground in print by viciously slandering their opposition's patriarchal and orthodox Protestant credentials.[141] Throughout, sex-talk was never far from view.

Goodwin's *Anti-cavalierisme* appeared just before the first major military engagement between royalist and parliamentarian forces at Edgehill in Warwickshire on 23 October. The outcome was indecisive, as was the king's follow-up march on London in its aftermath. Amid the unfolding drama, polemicists on both sides continued to refine the partisan cavalier-roundhead binary in print. Contemporaries soon tired of the barrage: 'their [are] now so many false reports in the diurnals & other pamphlets declarations &c that I think so many palpable lies never were knowne', Wyatt complained.[142] But the pamphlets, replete with explicit sex-talk, proliferated nonetheless.

English sexual politics made incredible strides in the five years that separated the Covenanters' 1637 pulpit declamations against episcopal chastity from the lecherous roundheads and rapacious cavaliers that dominated partisan print by mid-1642. In one telling example of that evolution, the 1640 manuscript verse 'Pigges Coranto' – which had criticised English soldiers and Scottish invaders alike as sexual miscreants during the Bishops' Wars – was printed for the first time that year.[143] Moreover, while many contemporaries still protested the rising incidence of lascivious language in print by the fall of 1642, others had adopted the new partisan lexicons for day-to-day use: while the London turner Nehemiah Wallington denounced the king's 'Cavaliers' for 'lodg[ing] their whores in others houses', his fellow

Londoner Mary Kinge was indicted in September for wishing 'a pox' upon 'these Roundheaded Rouges' who 'hinder the kinge from his Crowne'.[144] In both cases, the influence exercised by sexual politics on contemporary notions of partisan identity was readily apparent.

That process of identity formation began with the familiar post-Reformation polarities of anti-puritanism and anti-popery and ended with a much more concrete pair of political caricatures in the parliamentarian roundhead and the royalist cavalier. It is difficult to overstate the significance of this transformation. For one thing, the fundamental juxtaposition between lascivious royalists and hypocritical puritan parliamentarians would continue to shape mid-century political culture until the 1660 Restoration. Even more importantly, it cemented the sexual body, and especially women's bodies, as an acceptable rhetorical battleground through which to litigate the burgeoning struggle for political supremacy. For, despite their ideological differences, both Charles's supporters and their opponents identified the subversion of rightful masculine authority over wives and daughters – whether it came about via cavalier rapacity or roundhead cuckoldry – as a dangerous thing indeed, and therefore as a useful polemical touchstone. (The undeniable popularity of such bawdy material among most everyday English readers surely helped, too.) In short, despite fundamental disagreements about the future of church and state, by late 1642 royalists and parliamentarians had collectively established a discursive association between political truth-claims and sex-talk that would remain central to mid-century politicking for the remainder of the period.

Most of the polemics complicit in that process took the form of satire. This was, no doubt, an inheritance of the underground libel culture of early Stuart England, which had excoriated royal favourites and puffed-up puritan hypocrites alike with frank denunciations of sexual deficiencies from the relative safety of manuscript verse. But while many of those themes reappeared during the partisan debates of the early 1640s, there was now something indisputably novel about their fundamentally dialogic nature. Even disregarding Edward Finch's remarkable foray into print to defend his chastity, never before had English controversialists responded so vigorously, and so directly, to their opponents in such volume. That libellous back-and-forth – which derived much of its power from the (real or imagined) sexual histories of prominent partisan figures – heightened both the frequency and the timbre of printed satire, sexual or otherwise, while also reifying a nascent connection between sexual discourse and sexual practice that would flourish in the decades to come. In doing so, as the next chapter will demonstrate, it also provided considerable ammunition for military mobilisation.

Enough of the early Stuart reticence toward printed sex-talk remained intact in mid-to-late 1642 to convince Pym and Charles alike that underhanded propaganda methods were still preferable to openly defamatory pamphleteering, which might alienate potential supporters through its sheer vitriol. Even so, by October, only the royal family remained truly off-limits from censure; and, as John Goodwin's musings in *Anti-cavalierisme* suggested, that state of affairs was not likely to persist forever. Meanwhile, the evocative language of the royalist 'True Description', in which Charles's opposition in Westminster was reimagined as a satanic monstrous birth, indicated that parliament, too, had become susceptible to a new kind of political critique. All told, by the end of the year, sexual politics were well on their way to becoming a central element of English public culture.

## Notes

1 W. Dunn Macray (ed.), *The History of the Rebellion and Civil Wars in England* (6 vols, Oxford, 1888), i, p. 94.
2 Michael Mendle, 'De Facto Freedom, De Facto Authority: Press and Parliament, 1640-1643', *HJ* 38:2 (1995), 307–32, at 310; Alastair Bellany, 'Railing Rhymes Revisited: Libels, Scandals, and Early Stuart Politics', *History Compass* 5:4 (2007), 1136–79, at 1143.
3 Caroline Hibbard, *Charles I and the Popish Plot* (Chapel Hill, NC, 1983).
4 For important scholarship on the immediate prewar period, see Laura A.M. Stewart, *Rethinking the Scottish Revolution: Covenanted Scotland, 1637–1651* (Oxford, 2016); John Adamson, *The Noble Revolt: The Overthrow of Charles I* (London, 2007); David Cressy, *England on Edge: Crisis and Revolution, 1640–1642* (Oxford, 2006).
5 Gordon Donaldson, *The First Trial of Mary, Queen of Scots* (New York, NY, 1969).
6 Steven W. May and Alan Bryson, *Verse Libel in Renaissance England and Scotland* (Oxford, 2016).
7 Derek Hirst, *England in Conflict, 1603–1660: Kingdom, Community, Commonwealth* (London, 1999), p. 154; CUL, MS Add.22, fol. 118r; *A warning to come out of Babylon*, STC 20657 (Edinburgh, 1638), p. 1.
8 Frances E. Dolan, *Whores of Babylon: Catholicism, Gender, and Seventeenth-Century Print Culture* (Ithaca, NY, 1999); S. A. Burrell, 'The Apocalyptic Vision of the Early Covenanters', *Scottish Historical Review* 43:135 (1964), 1–24.
9 James Maidment (ed.), *A Book of Scotish Pasquils, 1568–1715* (Edinburgh, 1868), pp. 77, 105. See also Stewart, *Rethinking*, pp. 51–3.
10 *Scotish Pasquils*, pp. 40, 42; David Laing (ed.), *The Letters and Journals of Robert Baillie* (3 vols, Edinburgh, 1841–2), i, pp. 5–6.
11 Julian Goodare, 'The Rise of the Covenanters, 1637–1644', in Michael J. Braddick (ed.), *The Oxford Handbook of the English Revolution* (Oxford, 2015), pp. 43–57, at 44.
12 *A proclamation . . . of the seditious practices of some in Scotland*, STC 9135 (1639).

13 *The beast is wounded*, STC 22032 (Amsterdam, 1638), p. 9; Laing (ed.), *Baillie*, i, p. 114.
14 Ibid., p. 105.
15 NLS, MS Wodrow Fol.XXV, fol. 5r.
16 Laing (ed.), *Baillie*, i, pp. 154, 163.
17 TNA, SP 16/404, fol. 101v.
18 *The principall acts of the solemne Generall Assembly*, STC 22049 (Edinburgh, 1639), pp. 14–19.
19 *The declinator and protestation*, STC 22058 (1639), p. 11; *The declinatour and protestation…refuted*, STC 22060 (Edinburgh, 1639), pp. 33, 89.
20 [Walter Balcanquhall], *A large declaration*, STC 21906 (1639), pp. 222–3, 226. See also Sharpe, *IW*, 161–4.
21 BL, 186.c.10, p. 207.
22 TNA, SP 16/421, fol. 304r; TNA, SP 16/474, fol. 119r; HEHL, HA 15172.
23 TNA, SP 16/426, fol. 12r. See also *CSPD 1638–9*, p. 530; Ian Roy, 'England Turned Germany? The Aftermath of the Civil War in Its European Context', *TRHS*, 5:28 (1978), 127–44.
24 *Articles of militarie discipline*, STC 21904.5 (Edinburgh, 1639), p. 10. See also *Articles and ordinances of warre for…the armie of…Scotland*, STC 21914 (Edinburgh, 1640), p. 9; Barbara Donagan, *War in England, 1642–1649* (Oxford, 2008), p. 165n35.
25 Palace Green Library, Durham University, Mickleton Spearman MS 9, pp. 123, 161; HEHL, STT 1890; *Scotish Pasquils*, p. 57.
26 TNA, SP 16/427, fols 218r, 219v–20r; TNA, SP 16/428, fol. 71r. See also Bod., MS Bankes 18/19, fol. 45r.
27 David Como, 'Secret Printing, the Crisis of 1640, and the Origins of Civil War Radicalism', *P&P* 196 (2007), 37–82.
28 *Information for the ignorant*, STC 7435.5 (1640), sig. C2v. See also BRBML, Osborn MS b200, p. 272; Brotherton Library, University of Leeds, BC MS Lt 31, fol. 42r (later printed as *The subjects thankfulnesse*, STC 23416 (1640)).
29 HEHL, EL 8845b; TNA, SP 16/438, fol. 168r.
30 *Information from…Scotland*, STC 21916 (Edinburgh, 1640), p. 8; HEHL, EL 8843.
31 *The lofty bishop, the lazy Brownist*, 669.f.8[32] (1640); BRBML, Osborn MS b101, p. 88.
32 Bod., MS Ashmole 36–37, fol. 99r. See also *Englands complaint to Jesus Christ*, STC 10008 (1640), sig. F2r; *CSPD 1640*, pp. 542–3.
33 *A dialogue*, STC 6805.3 (1640), sig. B2v.
34 Cressy, *England on Edge*, pp. 114–17.
35 *A whip*, Wing W1670 (1640).
36 Marshall, *Toleration*.
37 [John Corbet], *The epistle congratulatorie of Lysimachus Nicanor*, E.203[7] (1640), pp. 73–4. See also Lloyd Bowen, 'Royalism, Print, and the Clergy in Britain, 1639–1640 and 1642', *HJ* 56:2 (2013), 297–319, at 306–7.

38 HRC, BX9081 .N53 1640.
39 TNA, SP 16/451, fols 263v, 264v, 275r. See also Folger Shakespeare Library, MS V.b.110, p. 78; [John Maxwell], *An answer by letter*, E.53[13] ([Bristol?], [4 July] 1644), p. 45.
40 *CSPD 1640*, p. 156. See also Cressy, *England on Edge*, p. 99.
41 Bod., MS Ashmole 36–37, fol. 53v.
42 Corbet, *Epistle*, p. 74; TNA, SP 16/447, fol. 177r. The reference to Loyola appears in Corbet, *Epistle*, pp. 59–61.
43 TNA, SP 16/464, fol. 115r; *Scotish Pasquils*, p. 111.
44 TNA, SP 16/460, fol. 208r.
45 Bedfordshire Archives, MS J1368.
46 Bod., MS Ashmole 1153, fols 48v, 51r–2v.
47 Cressy, *England on Edge*, p. 183.
48 Devon Heritage Centre, Exeter Chamber Act Book VIII, fol. 111v.
49 Como, *RP*, p. 131.
50 Anthony Fletcher, *The Outbreak of the English Civil War* (London, 1981), pp. 3, 43–57.
51 Bod., MS Rawlinson C 956, fol. 141r; TNA, SP 16/461, fol. 48r; Wallace Notestein (ed.), *The Journal of Sir Simonds D'Ewes* (New Haven, CT, 1923), p. 13. See also Peter Marshall, *Mother Leakey and the Bishop: A Ghost Story* (Oxford, 2007), pp. 101–3.
52 BL, Sloane MS 29, fol. 3r.
53 S. R. Gardiner (ed.), *The Constitutional Documents of the Puritan Revolution, 1625–1660*, 2nd ed. (Oxford, 1899), p. 139.
54 HEHL, EL 7742.
55 *Constitutional Documents*, p. 139. For some other offending titles named in the petition, see *The parlament of women*, STC 19306 (1640); [George Sandys], *Ovids Metamorphosis Englished*, STC 18968 (1640); Francis Beaumont, *Poems*, STC 1665 (1640).
56 *The third speech*, E.196[30] (1641), pp. 8–9.
57 Mary Anne Everett Green (ed.), *Diary of John Rous* (London, 1856), p. 109.
58 BRBML, Osborn MS fb106(1) (later printed as Francis Cole, *The prologue and epilogue to a comedie*, E.144[9] (1642), sigs A3r–4r); Bod., MS Rawl. Poet. 26, fol. 123r.
59 HEHL, EL 8848.
60 Jason Peacey, *Politicians and Pamphleteers: Propaganda During the English Civil Wars and Interregnum* (Aldershot, 2004), pp. 137–9; Jason Peacey, 'The Revolution in Print', in Braddick (ed.), *Handbook*, pp. 276–90, at 277–8; Como, *RP*, p. 88.
61 Joad Raymond, *Pamphlets and Pamphleteering in Early Modern Britain* (Cambridge, 2003), pp. 170–1. On the Stationers' Company, see Joseph Lowenstein, *The Author's Due: Printing and the Prehistory of Copyright* (Chicago, IL, 2002), pp. 160–9.
62 BRBML, Osborn MS fb106(12); ERO, D/DEb 14/1.

63 Laing (ed.), *Baillie*, i, p. 299; I. M. Green, 'The Persecution of "Scandalous" and "Malignant" Parish Clergy During the English Civil War', *EHR* 94:372 (1979), 507–31.
64 Martin Parker, *The poet's blind mans bough*, E.172[6] (1641), sig. A3r; *The liar*, E.169[8] (1641), sig. A4r.
65 BL, Add. MS 20065, fol. 123v.
66 *Sions charity towards her foes in misery*, E.158[13] (1641), pp. 2–5.
67 Maija Jansson (ed.), *Proceedings in the Opening Session of the Long Parliament: House of Commons* (7 vols, Rochester, NY, 2000–7), iv, pp. 266–7, 271. See also Jason McElligott, 'Finch, Edward', *ODNB*.
68 E.g., *CSPD 1640–1*, p. 348.
69 *The proctor and parator*, E.156[13] (1641), sigs A3v, Bv; *The pimpes prerogative*, 669.f.4[18] (1641); *The sisters of the scabards holiday*, E.168[8] (1641), p. 2. See also *Saint Pauls potion*, Wing S350 (1641), sig. A3r; *The spirituall courts epitomized*, E.157[15] (1641), p. 3.
70 *Vox borealis*, E.177[5] (1641), sig. Cv; *The Brothers of the blade*, E.238[5] (1641), p. 4; *Foure fugitives meeting*, Wing F1654 (1641), p. 1. See also Cressy, *England on Edge*, p. 106.
71 *A letter sent by Sir John Suckling*, E.160[19] (1641), p. 2; *The Sucklington faction*, 669.f.4[17] (1641). See also *A bloody masacre plotted by the papists*, E.181[9] (1641), p. 3.
72 Jansson (ed.), *Proceedings*, iii, 71; Laing (ed.), *Baillie*, i, 347; J[ohn] B[ond], *The poets knavery discovered*, E.135[11] (1642), sig. A2v; *The Deputies ghost*, Wing D1084 (1641). See also C. V. Wedgwood, *Thomas Wentworth, First Earl of Strafford, 1593–1641: A Reevaluation* (New York, NY, 1962), pp. 123–5; Terence Kilburn and Anthony Milton, 'The Public Context of the Trial and Execution of Strafford', in Julia F. Merritt (ed.), *The Political World of Thomas Wentworth, Earl of Strafford, 1621–1641* (Cambridge, 1996), pp. 230–51.
73 *The confession of John Browne*, E.173[1] (1641), sig. A2v. Browne was captured in April: BL, Add. MS 11045, fol. 138v.
74 Diocese of Westminster Archives, MS A.30, p. 104; Hibbard, *Popish Plot*, pp. 198–203, 297n7; *A discovery of...William Laud*, E.172[37] (1641), sigs A3v–4r; *The impeachment and articles...against Father Philips*, E.175[4] (1641), sig. A3r.
75 *Mercuries message*, Wing M1748 (1641), sig. A3v; Parliamentary Archives, BRY/18, fol. 1r. See also *Mercuries message defended*, E.160[13] (1641), p. 8; *The bishops manifest*, E.181[19] (1641), p. 3; *The true character of an untrue bishop*, E.173[17] (1641), p. 9.
76 *The bishops mittimus*, Wing B3030 (1641), p. 1.
77 *A true description*, E.168[9] (1641), p. 4; *Wrens anatomy*, E.166[7] (1641), p. 2; *A Shrove-Tuesday banquet*, E.135[1] (1641), p. [4].
78 *The life and death of John Atherton*, E.167[6] (1641), sigs A2r, A3r.
79 *Articles ministred...against John Gwin*, E.177[20] (1641), sigs A2r–v.
80 *The Petition and articles...against Edward Finch*, E.166[12] (1641), pp. 8–9; Richard Bentley (ed.), *Historical Notices* (2 vols, London, 1869), i, pp. 194–205. For an annotated copy, see Newberry Library, Case J 5453 .17.

81 Edward Finch, *An answer*, E.175[11] (1641), sig. A2r.
82 Ibid., pp. 8, 20.
83 Ibid., pp. 18–19, 26.
84 Fletcher, *Outbreak*, pp. 56–7; *CJ*, ii, p. 208. See for example Parliamentary Archives, HL/PO/JO/10/1/53, fols 60–1.
85 Conrad Russell, *The Fall of the British Monarchies, 1637–1642* (Oxford, 1991), p. 340.
86 Michael Braddick, 'Prayer Book and Protestation: Anti-Popery, Anti-Puritanism and the Outbreak of the English Civil War', in Charles W.A. Prior and Glenn Burgess (eds), *England's Wars of Religion, Revisited* (Surrey, 2011), pp. 125–46.
87 *The black box of Roome opened*, E.206[1] (1641), p. 16; *A dreame*, Wing D2156 (1641), p. 12. See also Thomas Herbert, *Newes newly discovered*, E.1102[3] (1641); *The Popes benediction*, E.158[15] (1641).
88 *The Brownists faith and beliefe opened*, 669.f.4[67] (1641); *The Brownist haeriesies confuted*, Wing B5189 (1641), p. 3.
89 BL, Add. MS 14827, fol. 7r; TNA, SP 16/484, f. 146v. See also Tim Harris, 'Charles I and Public Opinion on the Eve of the English Civil War', in Stephen Taylor and Grant Tapsell (eds), *The Nature of the English Revolution Revisited: Essays in Honour of John Morrill* (Woodbridge, 2013), pp. 1–25, at 18–25.
90 [John Taylor], *The Brownists conventicle*, E.164[13] (1641), p. 6; [John Taylor], *Lucifers lacky*, E.180[3] (1641), sig. A2v. See also [John Taylor], *The Brownists synagogue*, E.172[32] (1641), p. 4; Bernard Capp, *The World of John Taylor the Water-Poet, 1578–1653* (Oxford, 1994), pp. 53, 59 (attributions on p. 203).
91 Sharon Achinstein, 'Women on Top in the Pamphlet Literature of the English Revolution', *Women's Studies* 24:1–2 (1994), 131–63.
92 *A description of the . . . Familie of Love*, E.168[2] (1641), p. 4. See also *A discovery of 29 sects*, E.168[7] (1641), p. 4.
93 *The coblers end*, Wing C4783 (1641), sig. A3r; Edward Harris, *A true relation*, E.172[31] (1641), sig. A2r. See also Cressy, *England on Edge*, p. 214.
94 *The dolefull lamentation of cheap-side crosse*, E.134[9] (1641), p. 6. See also *A discoverie of six women preachers*, E.166[1] (1641); *The anatomy of et caetera*, E.169[1] (1641), p. 5.
95 *A nest of serpents discovered*, E.168[12] (1641), pp. 2–4. See also *The Humble petition of the Brownists*, E.178[10] (1641), p. 4; David Cressy, *Travesties and Transgressions in Tudor and Stuart England: Tales of Discord and Dissension* (Oxford, 2000), p. 259.
96 *A new sect of religion descryed*, Wing B4295A (1641), pp. 6–7; *The Adamites sermon*, Wing C6511 (1641), p. 8.
97 Richard Carter, *The schismatick stigmatized*, E.179[14] (1641), p. 15. See also [Joseph Hall], *A survay*, E.164[8] (1641), pp. 2–3; George Richardson, *The Irish footman's poetry*, Wing T471 (1641), p. 6.
98 Sarah Toulalan, *Imagining Sex: Pornography and Bodies in Seventeenth-Century England* (Oxford, 2007), pp. 41, 233–4.

99 John Taylor, *A swarme of sectaries, and schismatiques*, E.158[1] (1641), pp. 5–6. For Cave, see David R. Como, *Blown by the Spirit: Puritanism and the Emergence of an Antinomian Underground in Pre-Civil-War England* (Stanford, CA, 2004), p. 170n101.

100 [Henry Walker], *An answer to a foolish pamphlet*, E.160[15] (1641), pp. 2–3, 5; [Henry Walker], *Taylors physicke*, E.163[9] (1641). See also John Taylor, *A reply as true as steele*, E.160[23] (1641) (which also depicted a defecating devil); Alastair Bellany, 'Libel', in Joad Raymond (ed.), *The Oxford History of Popular Print Culture,* Volume One: *Cheap Print in Britain and Ireland to 1660* (Oxford, 2011), pp. 141–63. For similar imagery in use during the German Reformation, see R. W. Scribner, *For the Sake of Simple Folk: Popular Propaganda for the German Reformation* (Cambridge, 1981), p. 84.

101 Capp, *John Taylor*, pp. 144–6, 150–1.

102 TNA, C 115/107, N.3.8556.

103 Ethan Shagan, 'Constructing Discord: Ideology, Propaganda, and English Responses to the Irish Rebellion of 1641', *JBS* 36:1 (1997), 4–34, at 7–9; Kathleen M. Noonan, '"The Cruell Pressure of an Enraged, Barbarous People": Irish and English Identity in Seventeenth-Century Policy and Propaganda', *HJ* 41:1 (1998), 151–77; Joan Redmond, 'Memories of Violence and New English Identities in Early Modern Ireland', *Historical Research* 89:246 (2016), 708–29, at 722–8. For one representative pamphlet, see *The teares of Ireland*, Wing C6824 (1642). I thank Jane Ohlmeyer for discussing this tract with me.

104 Fletcher, *Outbreak*, pp. 189–90.

105 Braddick, *Fury*, pp. 187–8.

106 But see Purkiss, *Literature*, pp. 124–9; Jennifer Frances Cobley, 'The Construction and Use of Gender in the Pamphlet Literature of the English Civil War, 1642–1646' (PhD thesis, University of Southampton, 2010), ch. 2; Katherine E. Worley, 'Reason Sways Them: Masculinity and Political Authority in the English Civil War' (PhD dissertation, Brown University, 2008).

107 Bod., MS Ashmole 36–37, fol. 77r.

108 HEHL, EL 8744.

109 HEHL, EL 8841.

110 TNA, SP 16/488, fols 94r-v; TNA, SP 16/488, fol. 172.

111 [Thomas Aston], *A collection of sundry petitions*, Wing A4075 (1642), pp. [27–8]. See also Richard Cust and Peter Lake, *Gentry Culture and the Politics of Religion: Cheshire on the Eve of Civil War* (Manchester, 2020), pp. 332–3.

112 *The resolution of the round-heads*, E.132[39] (1642), sig. A2v.

113 George Thomason's book-buying reached a record high in January 1642: Braddick, *Fury*, p. 173.

114 Fletcher, *Outbreak*, ch. 6; Robin Clifton, 'The Popular Fear of Catholics During the English Revolution', *P&P* 52 (1971), 23–55. On the bishops' 'Letchery', see *The aprentices advice*, E.131[10] (1642), p. 2.

115 Mark Stoyle, 'The Cannibal Cavalier: Sir Thomas Lunsford and the Fashioning of the Royalist Archetype', *HJ* 59:2 (2016), 293–317.

116 For a reference predating Charles's evacuation, see *A judicious speech*, Wing M390 (1642), p. [3].
117 *The answer to the rattle-heads*, E.132[30] (1642), sigs A2v, A4r; John Walter, '"Affronts & Insolencies": The Voices of Radwinter and Popular Opposition to Laudianism', *EHR* 122:495 (2007), 35–60, at 58.
118 Bod., MS Top. Oxon. C. 378, p. 331; CUL, MS Baker Mm 1.39, fol. 218v.
119 John Rushworth, *Historical Collections of Private Passages of State* (8 vols, London, 1721), iv, p. 567.
120 *LJ*, v, pp. 16–17; *A remonstrance and declaration of the Lords and Commons*, Wing E2217 (1642), p. 1.
121 Bod., MS Rawl. Poet. 71, pp. 114–16, 123–4.
122 *An appeale to the world*, E.107[26] ([July 12], 1642), p. 3; MS Top. Oxon. C. 378, pp. 342–3. See also William White, 'Parliament, Print, and the Politics of Disinformation, 1642–3', *HR* 92:258 (2019), 720–36; Jason Peacey, '"Fiery Spirits" and Political Propaganda: Uncovering a Radical Press Campaign of 1642', *Publishing History* 55 (2004), 5–36.
123 LMA, MJ/SR/913/182; *LJ*, v, p. 302. See also LMA, MJ/SR/904/72; LMA, MJ/SR/915/202; David Underdown, *Revel, Riot, and Rebellion: Popular Politics and Culture in England, 1603–1660* (Oxford, 1985), p. 217.
124 CUL, MS Dd 3.68, fol. 34r; Durham Palace Green Library, Add MS 865, fols 55r, 59r.
125 *The diseases of the times*, E.136[6] (1642), sig. A3v; *Sir James Cambels Clarks disaster*, E.122[22] ([15 October] 1642), p. 6.
126 *A puritane set forth in his lively colours*, E.113[11] ([23 August] 1642), p. 5; *New orders, new*, E.150[27] (1642), p. 5; [John Taylor], *An honest answer*, E.154[7] (7 July 1642), title-page. See also T[homas] J[ordan], *A medicine for the times*, E.135[33] (1642), sig. A2v.
127 *A brief dialogue*, E.140[5] (1642), sig. A4r. See also [John Taylor], *A full and compleat Answer*, E.141[19] (1642), p. 6; *Square-caps turned into round-heads*, E.149[1] (1642), p. 4.
128 *The resolution of those contemners*, E.137[2] (164[2]), sig. A3v; [John Taylor], *Tom Nash his ghost*, E.110[5] ([10 August] 1642), pp. 4–6. See also *The Devil turn'd round-head*, E.136[29] (1642), sig. A3r; *The vindication of the seperate brethren*, E.135[25] (1642), pp. 1, 6. London women certainly contributed to the cause: Jordan S. Downs, *Civil War London: Mobilizing for Parliament, 1641–5* (Manchester, 2021), p. 66.
129 BRBML, Osborn MS b101, pp. 127–8; BRBML, Osborn MS b4, fol. 46r.
130 East Sussex Record Office, MS FRE 600.
131 *An abstract of some letters*, E.115[22] ([6 September] 1642), p. 4; *A Declaration of the Kings resolution*, E.123[19] ([20 October] 1642), pp. 5–6; *Speciall passages and certain informations*, E.121[31] (4–11 October 1642), p. 70.
132 *The English fortune-teller*, Wing E3084 (1642), title-page; *The debauched cavalleer*, E.240[43] ([18 October] 1642), p. 7; *A true declaration of Kingstons entertainment of the Cavaliers*, E.127[39] (22 November 1642), sig. A3r. See also Mark Stoyle, 'The Road to Farndon Field: Explaining the Massacre of the Royalist Women at Naseby', *EHR* 123:503 (2008), 895–923, at 905–10.

133 *A witty answer*, E.151[22] (1642), sig. A4r.
134 *Nocturnall occurrences*, E.117[16] ([16 September] 1642), sig. A3r; *The birth, life, death, wil, and epitaph, of Jack Puffe Gentleman*, E.150[1] (1642), p. 4.
135 *A Description of the round-head and rattle-head*, E.109[7] ([5 August] 1642), p. 1. See also Hughes, *Gender*, p. 95.
136 *A speedy post from heaven*, E.121[6] ([5 October] 1642), p. 3; *King James his judgement*, E.116[20] ([9 September] 1642), sig. A3v. See also *The Popes briefe*, E.113[4] ([20 August] 1642), p. [3]; Como, *RP*, pp. 134–7.
137 John Goodwin, *Anti-cavalierisme*, E.123[25] ([21 October] 1642), pp. 2, 32–3, 40. For a marked-up copy, see Newberry Library, Case J 5453 .352.
138 See for example *A true and certaine relation*, E.128[26] ([28 November] 1642), p. 4; *Grand Plutoes remonstrance*, E.138[11] (1642).
139 *The soundheads description of the roundhead*, E.148[7] (1642), p. 7; *The Anatomy of the separatists*, E.238[14] (1642), p. 3.
140 See for example TNA, SP 16/487, fol. 149v.
141 Peter Lake, 'From Revisionist to Royalist History; or, Was Charles I the First Whig Historian', *HLQ* 78:4 (2015), 657–81, at 677–8.
142 MS Top. Oxon. C. 378, p. 345.
143 *Pigges corantoe*, E.153[7] (1642).
144 BL, Add. MS 21935, fol. 266r; LMA, MJ/SR/915/240.

# 2

# Mobilisation, escalation and sexual polemic, 1642–46

On 13 November 1642, weeks after the battle of Edgehill, the king's army was rebuffed at Turnham Green outside London by an assembly of nearly 25,000 citizens. Outnumbered, Charles retreated to Oxford, where his troops began preparing for the coming winter. But royalists did not forget the Londoners' frantic efforts at self-defence, and they soon began circulating a ballad in commemoration of the showdown. It was entitled *Round-headed cuckolds, come dig*: an ode to the emasculated, horn-beaten parliamentarian of royalist partisan print.[1]

The ballad's title indicated just how thoroughly sex-talk had invaded English political culture since July 1637. While neither king nor parliament had yet resorted to sexual satire in their official publications, freelancing partisan apologists emboldened by the collapse of English press licensing – including independent 'para-propagandists', to borrow David Como's idiom, working with both regimes' tacit support – embraced it wholeheartedly.[2] Nor were these burgeoning sexual politics limited to print. In manuscript culture and face-to-face confrontations, too, the partisan lexicons of rapacious popish cavaliers and lecherous puritan roundheads continued to blossom, further attesting to their popular appeal. All told, with the notable exception of formal regime publications, sex-talk was firmly established in public discourse by October 1642.

This chapter focuses on military mobilisation during the first civil war in order to argue that the reticence of regime leaders in London and Oxford towards explicit sexual polemic did not survive the period intact. The historiography of early-1640s mobilisation is robust, and the parliamentarian coalition has to date received most of the attention.[3] However, this focus on parliament, especially during the critical period of mid-to-late 1643, has disguised the extent to which mobilisation was an entangled, dialogic, and mutually constitutive affair.[4] From the summer of 1642 until mid-1646, parliamentary efforts to secure the kingdom's limited resources – often accompanied by condemnations of royalist court corruption – were repeatedly met with similar campaigns from Charles's royalist press, as each side strove to outdo the other in the struggle for men, money and the moral high ground. Mobilisation thus begat mobilisation; and, with each escalation, the accompanying partisan rhetoric grew more vicious.

Sex-talk played a central role in that process. After successfully harnessing post-Reformation and patriarchal sexual politics for the purpose of partisan stereotyping during the skirmishes of the preceding spring, freelancing pamphleteers returned to them with vigour after the formal outbreak of war. It was therefore natural that the architects of mobilisation, who recognised the popularity of such language among those whose allegiance they hoped to capture, would follow suit. Moreover, as English publishers refined new tools – most notably the serial newsbook – to keep pace with political events, the resulting exchanges between royalist and parliamentarian propagandists grew more personal and more rebarbative, as feuding polemicists traded increasingly acrid blows in print. Consequently, the formal adoption of mid-century sexual politics in Oxford and London was accompanied by a concurrent intensification in its scope and timbre.

In this way, after percolating almost entirely in unlicensed, anonymous print prior to the outbreak of war, sex-talk became a routine element of official partisan print in the years following Edgehill. Remarkably, despite puritan moralists' historic antipathy towards bawdy language, parliamentarians outpaced their royalist enemies in adopting sexual satire for official usage. In contrast, Charles's distaste for public impropriety meant that the same process took far longer in Oxford. Even so, in both cases, the exigencies of wartime mobilisation proved inexorable in motivating a wholesale pivot towards libellous sexual polemic in official partisan print by mid-1644. The result was two competing campaigns of increasingly sophisticated sexual politics, replete with formal licenses and semi-professional penmen, in service to political leaders who had denounced the proliferation of such scandalous rhetoric just years earlier. Between 1642 and 1646, in other words, graphic sexual polemic was transformed from a target of regime suppression into a privileged propaganda tool.

### 'Shagpoll locust sodomites': escalation and innovation after the outbreak of war

The Turnham Green showdown led to a turbulent winter. In London, the parliament-men argued over how best to proceed against the king while citizens debated the same question in the streets.[5] Meanwhile, royalists began converting Oxford into a makeshift headquarters. Neither process heralded a pause in partisan politicking. Pamphleteers repeatedly complained about the 'infinite issue of bastards Books daily' that were apparently 'begotten even by Eunuches, and brought forth by the Barren', they were so numerous. Charles's supporters fretted especially at the 'dispersing of false and scandalous Books and Pamphlets' in London.[6] Altogether, both king and parliament remained publicly opposed to the spread of libellous, obscene and overtly inflammatory printed material throughout the winter of 1642/43.

In Westminster, it was a practical issue. Although many parliament-men believed that Charles bore some blame for the war, they feared criticising him directly for two reasons: first, because doing so might alienate English subjects who still revered the monarchy; and, secondly, because most assumed that the conflict would end in a negotiated settlement, thereby allowing Charles to punish anyone who had spoken too boldly against him during wartime. To avoid those risks, Pym and his allies instead continued to rely on the language of evil counsel to denounce royal misgovernment early in 1643.

The king's ministers faced a different dilemma. For one, Charles – who had long prized decorum as a kingly virtue – apparently harboured personal reservations about public incivility (as evidenced, for instance, by his refusal to allow women to attend Castlehaven's trial in 1631). Sex-talk, like libel, clearly fell into that category. More prosaically, the king's abrupt departure from London in January 1642 made a prolonged press offensive difficult, for his entourage had carried only two small presses along with them. Accordingly, until the court's arrival in Oxford ten months later, most royalist polemical print was still being produced secretly from the capital. Thus, while parliament set about developing a robust press machine throughout mid-to-late 1642, Charles's personal preferences, coupled with his insufficient resources, ensured that its royalist counterpart matured far more slowly.[7]

However, neither set of objections stymied the production of unlicensed partisan print, which continued at a rapid clip. As the kingdom spiralled deeper into civil war, moreover, those polemics expanded in new, imaginative directions. Consider one January 1643 production entitled *The virgins complaint*. This mock petition – probably written to satirise unmanly Londoners marching for peace with the king – ventriloquised England's virgins, who complained that the war had drawn their lovers away to be 'kild and beaten downe by multitudes' when they should have been 'beget[ting] multitudes' at home instead. The petitioners bemoaned the 'hideous and deathfull longings' of their 'stomacks beneath the waste [sic]', which had led them into rank promiscuity merely 'to ease us of that insupportable burden of our virginities'. The stakes were high. If the kingdom's 'maiden-heads' grew too 'musty' due to 'these young mens departure to these wars', the pamphlet argued, it would be 'a ruine . . . upon the Common-wealth': for 'by copulation and matrimoniall conjunction, the people of the Kingdome are increased, who are able to defend it against its enemies'.[8] Here, insatiable feminine desire became the defining feature of parliament's nascent peace movement. More broadly, in its imagery of lecherous maids clamouring for bodily satisfaction, *The virgins complaint* articulated a growing fascination with the sexual – and especially the procreative – consequences of civil war.

Elsewhere, the stereotypes of the preceding summer continued to ripen. After Edgehill, parliamentarians offered further warnings about the threat posed by 'those blaspheming and tiranous Cavaliers' to England's 'Wives and Virgins'.[9] Their denunciations were enriched by a new partisan label – the catch-all anti-royalist category of 'malignancy' – that tied the cavaliers' 'lust and filthinesse' ever more tightly to their support for Charles's cause.[10] In return, royalist apologists produced lurid descriptions of the 'family of Love' revelling 'in the obscenenesse of Conjunctions copulative' while their coreligionists in Westminster dismantled the national church.[11] Through such imagery, sectarian lechery and parliament's impending reformation became one and the same.

These freelancing pamphleteers, protected by their anonymity, also ventured further into polemical territory that grandees in London and Oxford dared not explore. For example, although parliament continued to refrain from sponsoring personal attacks on Charles's evil counsellors, sympathetic freelancers showed no such restraint. Through their efforts, direct criticisms of royal advisors past and present appeared in print during the winter of 1642/43. These included several prewar manuscript tracts that had formerly proven too scandalous for publication.[12] One, *The five years of King James*, recounted the lurid events of the 1613/14 Essex divorce, while another presented the proceedings of Castlehaven's 1631 rape and sodomy trial. By dredging up these stories of courtly immorality, no matter how weak their connection with the unfolding war, both tracts reinforced the now-common stereotype of the lecherous Caroline courtier.[13]

Chief among Charles's evil counsellors was his popish queen. As William Prynne had learned to his cost during the 1630s, Henrietta Maria had long been protected from overt public criticism. Nevertheless, the outbreak of war emboldened parliamentary para-propagandists to test the waters once more. Twice, in September 1642 and the following January, anonymous publishers printed a 1620s manuscript letter warning against Charles's impending marriage to a (different) Catholic princess on the grounds that it would allow an 'in-let' to the 'Romish Locusts' through the royal bedchamber.[14] This implicit depiction of Henrietta Maria as a popish seductress reflected longstanding puritan concerns about the royal succession: would Charles acquiesce to his sons' conversion, they wondered, if pressed by his wife? Weeks later, joking about the queen's 'absolute unlimitable power over the Kings sword and Scepter' – a bawdy reference to Charles's penis – in another anonymous tract, Henry Parker rendered similar fears about the king's sexual corruption relatively forthright in print for the first time.[15]

Meanwhile, royalist pamphleteers churned out acrid satires against the Westminster leadership, with special emphasis on godly hypocrisy. Given parliament's well-publicised plans for moral reformation, this tactic made sense: what better way to delegitimise that agenda than by showcasing the personal failings of its most self-professedly righteous promoters? The known peccadilloes of several key parliamentary figures made sexual libel especially enticing. By conflating the supposed antinomianism of radical Protestants like John Taylor's favourite targets, the Brownists, with the sober puritanism of Pym and his allies, and then buttressing those attacks with specific allegations of misconduct, freelancing royalists made great use of sexual satire during the opening months of 1643.

The anonymous author of *The complaint of the kingdom*, published sometime during the winter of 1642/43, was at the forefront of this barrage.[16] In addition to repeating familiar laments about the 'Incest, Rapes, and all Vices' left 'unpunished' after the 'suspending of all Ecclesiastical Lawes and Censures' in mid-1641, the *Complaint* targeted several prominent parliamentarians directly. One was the godly minister Cornelius Burges, whom it accused of having been 'looked upon for Adultery' by the court of High Commission during the 1630s. The author likely knew that while Burges had indeed appeared before that court, the charge had involved ecclesiastical rather than sexual misconduct; but the allegation stuck nonetheless, and several later pamphleteers echoed the *Complaint*'s depiction of Burges as a puritan lecher.[17] Of course, the rhetorical significance of this libel extended beyond mere humiliation. By contrasting Burges's apparent sexual perfidy with the rhetoric of puritan holiness, its author attacked the parliamentarian coalition at its weakest point: its claims to spiritual and moral superiority.

This tactic also worked against non-clergymen. Another of the *Complaint*'s targets was a parliament-man and military captain named John Griffith, whom it claimed had made a 'barbarous attempt upon' the 'chastity' of one Lady Sidley, only to be 'advance[d] . . . to an honourable office' in 'their Holy Army' rather than punished for the crime. Again, there was some truth to this account. Griffith had indeed been arraigned in June 1642 for the attempted rape of Elizabeth Sidley, although he was suspended from his parliamentary seat as a result.[18] Griffith's story, even more so than Burges's, thus appeared to validate royalist arguments about the intrinsic hypocrisy of godly religion. (Whether or not Griffith identified himself as a puritan is unclear.) In the process, it also countered parliamentarian descriptions of cavalier rapacity: for Griffith's case proved that roundheads, too, could be sexual predators.

*The sence of the House*, a broadside ballad published in March 1643, embodied the royalists' strategy in a pithier form. Its twenty-six verses attacked dozens of prominent parliamentarians by name, many for sexual misbehaviour. The earl of Stamford, a parliamentarian officer, was made to shout that 'if Peace come they'le reare both me, / And all my whores in pieces'; the earl of Essex, now parliament's chief general, bewailed that 'the'le call me Rebell Popular Asse, / And Cuckold to my face'; and John Hotham, who had spurned Charles at Hull the previous year, was mocked for having uxoriously 'serv'd five Wives'. Elsewhere in the tract, the parliament-man Miles Corbet feared that the 'Cavaliers will Cuckold mee, / As well as did the Round head', while the republican parliament-man Henry Marten cried, 'In the House I spake high treason, / I've sold both Land and Lease; / Nay, I shall then have but three Whores, / A pox upon this Peace'. Many of these claims, too, were based in truth: Hotham really had been married five times, while Marten was a known adulterer who had recently been censured by parliament for speaking too openly against the king.[19] All told, *The sence of the House* captured the libellous spirit of royalist sexual politics at a moment when Charles's ministers – still scrambling to establish a working press operation in Oxford – had little opportunity for sustained polemical engagement.[20]

Occasionally, however, royalist freelancers proved too clever for their own good. Tickled by the outrageous descriptions of cavalier malignancy creeping into parliamentarian print, some loyalist writers decided to lampoon that language by publishing their own tongue-in-cheek denunciations of Charles's royalists as 'shagpoll locus[t] Sodomites'.[21] Nor did these would-be satirists stop with generic stereotypes. One of their favourite faux-targets was Prince Rupert of the Rhine, Charles's German nephew and a key royalist commander, who had become a frequent target of parliamentarian polemicists for his complicity in several violent plundering episodes during the preceding fall. In February 1643, Rupert was ridiculed in two anonymous royalist satires. The first, *Observations upon Prince Ruperts white dog*, described how Rupert and his pet poodle, Boy, would 'lye perpetually in one bed, sometimes the Prince upon the Dog, and sometimes the Dog upon the Prince', sharing 'Strumpet-like' kisses with alarming intimacy. Next, *The exact description of Prince Ruperts malignant she-monkey* played on the contemporary association of monkeys with female sexual genitalia to describe an imaginary pet simian of Rupert's as his soldiers' willing sexual plaything: 'not . . . a whore', the author wrote, 'but a necessary instrument of recreation'. As Mark Stoyle has argued, these jabs were intended to parody the cavalier stereotype rather than reinforce it; presumably, readers were supposed to recognise them as farcical plays on parliamentarian credulity. However, by raising the subject of Rupert's sexuality in print, royalist writers inadvertently provided their enemies with a golden opportunity.[22]

Within weeks, the royalists' fake libels had rocketed the German prince into infamy. One representative parliamentarian satire repurposed their zoological storyline to accuse Rupert's fictional ape of sexually servicing Oxford 'Schollers and preachers' who 'love[d] to handle the Monkey better then they did their text'. More attacks against Rupert and his lascivious pets soon followed.[23] Notably, none of these rejoinders were acknowledged by the parliamentary leadership, which remained wary of direct attacks on the royal family. Even so, their appearance demonstrated just how daring some London publishers had grown since the collapse of Caroline press licensing.

Sexual satire thus flourished in unlicensed print throughout the winter of 1642/43. Nor was it limited to the page. One parliamentary committee referenced 'that Sodom, Oxford', in a March 1643 letter, suggesting that its members shared the sense of much parliamentarian polemic that profound sexual disorder had taken root in Charles's new capital. Similarly, journaling on the Isle of Wight, Sir John Oglander echoed a familiar strain of royalist propaganda by worrying that with 'no spirituall Courtes' to oversee sexual justice, 'any Notorious Mallefactor' could 'act his owne will without' fear of punishment.[24] Several Londoners even dared to tread where the most audacious pamphleteers would not. Robert Hand was summoned by Middlesex JPs in March to answer for saying that 'the King was a Traitour and his crowne was the whore of Babilon'. This statement, which morphed the generic Protestant associations between popery, promiscuity and political ruin voiced by John Goodwin six months prior into a direct attack against Charles's person, clearly troubled London's magistrates.[25] Even if they privately agreed, none of the king's opponents were willing to be quite so frank in print – at least, not yet.

### 'Midwife and nurse to a monster of rebellion': from restraint to recrimination

As Hand answered for his words, Charles and parliament prepared for the renewal of war. In search of men and money, both turned to partisan polemicists to drum up public support. Parliament gained a boost in April 1643, when news broke that Charles was negotiating to bring Irish Catholic troops to fight for him in England; but any advantage that announcement yielded was overshadowed by a series of royalist military victories in April and May. Consequently, battlefield failures prompted fiscal-military innovation in Westminster, alongside increasing levels of polemical vituperation, as parliament attempted to regain the upper hand.[26] Given the evident appeal of politicised sex-talk among English readers like Oglander, it was an obvious candidate for escalation.

Royalist pamphleteers trumpeted Charles's successes throughout the spring. John Taylor, recently arrived in Oxford from London, indicted parliamentary puritans as 'Brownists, Libertines, Hypocrites . . . [and] Cuckolds' with glee, while other writers levelled tailored allegations of unchastity at individual enemy leaders.[27] More creatively, a trio of broadsides experimented with a familiar genealogical metaphor that cast the puritan rebellion as a 'lewd' 'Monster', first 'begot' by puritans 'bigge with fanaticke thoughts' and then 'nurse[d]' in the city of London.[28] This distinctly porno-political language echoed Taylor's earlier depictions of the parliamentarian uprising as a monstrous, deformed child, and its reappearance in the single-sheet broadside format suggests that it had only grown in popularity since the outbreak of war. All told, while sexual politics were not the sole theme of these texts, sex-talk was visibly claiming a growing share of the royalists' polemical output.

In a new twist, many of these springtime tracts bore Oxford imprints. By May 1643, Oxford University printers Leonard Lichfield and Henry Hall had begun churning out explicitly royalist publications.[29] They were overseen by Sir John Berkenhead, a one-time press licenser under the Laudian regime of the 1630s who had been plucked to supervise the burgeoning propaganda effort when he arrived in town early in 1643. By mid-year, he was exercising nominal control over the king's entire press operation.[30]

The Oxford imprints adorning many of the spring's most acrid anti-parliamentarian satires appeared to suggest that Berkenhead had convinced the royalist leadership to adopt the libellous tactics of its freelancing supporters. And indeed, some of those texts – most notably the work of John Taylor – were products of the Hall and Lichfield presses. Most, however, were still the work of underground operators in London who employed false Oxford licenses to throw parliamentarian watchdogs off the scent. Tracts like *The sence of the House* were thus not necessarily part of the court's planned polemical output at all.[31] Further evidence comes from Taylor, who later wrote that Oxford's 'Presse and Printers' had been too 'full of worke of greater consequence' – namely, weightier political and theological texts – during the spring of 1643 to print his most caustic anti-puritan squibs.[32] Indeed, the relatively sober output of the Oxford presses during this period may have been intentionally designed to complement the scandalous material pouring from the capital.

Consider the popular serial newsbook *Mercurius aulicus*, published in Oxford from early 1643 with the royalist regime's express oversight. Initially authored by the cleric Peter Heylyn and later helmed by Berkenhead himself, *Aulicus*'s purpose was serious intelligence rather than antiparliamentarian slander.[33] To that end, *Aulicus* was not a highly libellous publication at its inception, and scholars have noted its polemical moderation in comparison to the work of freelancing satirists like Taylor.[34] The disparity is marked, especially considering its authors' respective propensities for graphic satire: as a youth, Heylyn enjoyed the obscene epigrams of the Roman poet Martial, while Berkenhead's own talent for lasciviousness would soon become apparent in a later string of explicit anti-sectarian publications.[35] The most believable explanation for *Aulicus*'s initial reticence towards anti-puritan satire, therefore, was an intentional decision on behalf of its editors – and, presumably, their handlers at court – to avoid overtly scandalous rhetoric.

That moderation was all the more remarkable because, in general, English serial print – itself only a recent invention – had grown increasingly partisan since the outbreak of war.[36] Some London newsbooks, for instance, began to take an interest around this time in the activities of Charles's soldiers and the salacious court lifestyle in Oxford.[37] One April issue of *Speciall passages and certain informations* thus reported that Prince Rupert's cavalrymen were 'double armed . . . with a Musket before, and behind them an Irish-Whoore'. (The editor insisted that while the claim 'seem[ed] rediculous', he spoke 'truth'.) Then, in early July, *Mercurius civicus* offered this astounding 'account of the affaires at Oxford':

> This place which should have beene the wel-spring and fountaine of learning, is now become the spring and fountaine of all profanesse and uncleannesse. Here are lewd strumpets which goe under the name of parsons, and one of them goes most comely in mans apparrell; they lie with the great Commanders sometimes with one, and sometimes with other: if the Wals of Saint Maries parish could speake, they would cry out to God for vengeance upon these and the like sodomitish actions.[38]

This was heady stuff, reeking of gross gendered disorder – leading, here, to the quintessentially popish sin of sodomy – and it reflected an increasingly dominant tendency in parliamentarian print to depict royalist malignancy as a lustful, effeminate creed. 'That Sodom, Oxford', indeed.

The contrast with *Aulicus* – which initially spent far more time refuting parliamentary slanders than it did attacking its opponents' chastity – is instructive. Throughout the spring, the royalist newsbook dismissed the rumours about Rupert's 'Irish whore[s]' and rebroadcasted royal proclamations against 'Drunkennesse, Whoredome, and all other scandalous actions' to counter the cavalier stereotype.[39] To be sure, there were occasionally exceptions. One April edition recounted John Griffith's assault on Elizabeth Sidley, noting that Griffith's 'faculty lay more in a Ladies Chamber, then in the conduct of a Warre'. But only later, in response to developments in Westminster, would sexual satire become a significant element of *Aulicus*'s strategy.[40]

For example, the earl of Essex's unfortunate sexual history had long made him a favourite royalist punching-bag. After his public cuckolding during the Overbury affair, Essex had remarried, only to watch his second wife flee to Oxford with a different lover at the outbreak of war. When she bore a child there in December 1642, royalists responded by lampooning the earl for vainly awaiting 'the Bapt[ism] of his next chylde Lawfullye begotten'. (Even solemn Charles allegedly joked that 'I think he is no more the father of it than I am'.) For a time, Essex's effectiveness as a general insulated him from serious abuse. But after a dismal spring campaign season, followed by popular agitation in London for his enforced retirement, he again fell victim to ridicule.[41]

Inspired by the possibility of unmanning the entire parliamentary war effort in one blow, freelancers turned the parliament's 'Cuckold Captains', and especially 'Essex['s] hornes', into a staple of royalist print during the summer of 1643. The campaign against parliament's 'great Cuckold' even spilled onto the battlefield, where some royalist regiments apparently marched under standards reading, 'cuckold we come'.[42] In the provinces, meanwhile, plebeian malcontents were prosecuted for repeating rude rhymes about the earl's cuckold horns.[43] Clearly the royalists' libellous message – that Essex's patriarchal failures reflected as poorly on his military prowess as it did on the masculinity of all parliamentarian rebels – resonated with their partisans.

Remarkably, however, *Aulicus* refused to address Essex's cuckoldry directly.[44] This was perhaps due in part to fears among its Oxford overseers that the story might conjure up uncomfortable reminders of Jacobean court corruption that were better left buried; but it was also undeniably a reflection of the royalist leadership's continued allergy to libellous sex-talk. As a result, whether by Charles's express command or the orders of his surrogates, sexual satire remained largely off-limits in official royalist print well into 1643.

Things were different in Westminster, where battlefield failures and factional infighting had provoked a political transformation. That summer, parliament passed a new press control ordinance intended to silence rogue royalist publishers still writing from the capital while also priming London's presses for an important role in military mobilisation. Beginning in May, sympathetic polemicists like William Prynne – by now effectively an unofficial regime apologist – unleashed a multi-part publishing effort intended to lift the coalition's flagging spirits and demonise the royalist opposition by doubling down on the interconnected discourses of Charles's evil counsellors and popish cavalier malignancy.[45] This campaign, which was legitimised by official parliamentary press licenses and advertised elsewhere in regime print,[46] was as close to a formal propaganda operation as can be imagined for the period, and royalists noted its impact: as one critic moaned, 'Mr. Prynnes books' were 'more prevalent' among parliamentarians 'than their Sermons'.[47] Modern historians, too, have paid it considerable attention; but none have yet appreciated its significance as the moment when parliamentarian leaders first established a formal program of libellous sexual politics.[48]

The parliamentary press offensive of summer 1643 drew significant inspiration from a popular puritan belief in the existence of a popish conspiracy against the national church. Several of the summer's pamphlets – some based on documents discovered during a raid on Laud's private study – traced that plot's history from the early 1620s, while others addressed more recent events. Many were interspersed with generic attacks against lascivious priests, Catholic seductresses and the Whore of Babylon.[49] But while these were all routine anti-popish tropes, their appearance in licensed publications, written by premier regime apologists with access to sensitive material drawn from parliament's evidence locker, lent them new significance.

The summer campaign also took more-or-less direct aim at the queen, who had just been impeached by the Commons in May.[50] Prynne's July tract, *The English pope*, compared 'the incestuous extractions' and 'Florentine mixtures' of the queen's French lineage with 'the nobilitie, chastitie, and beautie of the German Dames', while in August, his *Romes master-peece* described Catholic 'seducers' lurking in the 'Bedchamber, if not Bed', of the king. That same month, parliament's official *Declaration* on the 1641 Irish rebellion covertly alluded to one of the Caroline court's most caustic rumours: that Henrietta Maria was engaged in an adulterous affair with her chief household courtier, Sir Henry Jermyn. This allegation was extremely circumspect, noting only that 'what relation M. Jermin hath to the Queen is well known to the world', but the subtext was clear enough.[51] Although similar allegations had been levelled at past English queens (albeit almost never in print), the appearance of this particular accusation in a licensed parliamentarian production demonstrates the seriousness of the 1643 mobilisation effort.[52] As the parliament-men surely recognised, any imputation of queenly adultery cast suspicion on the king's patriarchal credentials as well as on the legitimacy of the royal succession. By questioning Henrietta Maria's chastity, therefore, they also undermined her husband's political authority.

The summer campaign's most magisterial production was Prynne's *The soveraigne power of parliaments*, a four-part justification of parliamentary political autonomy. Sections of this book had been published earlier in the year, but the full edition appeared for the first time in August, complete with a parliamentary press license. Running to more than 500 pages, Prynne's tome was a far cry from the short, cheap pamphlets currently flooding English bookshops. Consequently, by adopting and expanding on the more ephemeral anti-royalist material being printed elsewhere in London, it offered the most substantial guide yet to parliament's burgeoning program of sexual politics.

Accordingly, the text rehashed familiar arguments about the rapacity of Charles's 'pillaging murthering Cavaleers' and the queen's 'powerfull influence' on Charles's 'affections'.[53] But it also broke new ground in the case against Charles I by taking aim at one of the king's favourite political metaphors: the patriarchal equivalence between kingship and fatherhood, which Prynne argued could function 'onely in an improper, allegoricall, not genuine sence'. In particular, the book suggested that when a father-king's 'Tyrannie' manifested in violence – by levying war on his own subjects, for instance – the people 'cease to be . . . their Children', and instead were enabled 'by Law' to 'repulse them with open force'. This was certainly a novel reading of patriarchal monarchy, insofar as it legitimised resistance to bad kings on grounds of parental abuse, and it would eventually inspire later parliamentary apologists to follow a similar line of argument. Yet then, even more radically, Prynne inverted the entire metaphor: 'Kings are rather their Kingdoms children then Parents', he wrote, because monarchs were 'created by' the people to be 'their publike servants'.[54] This line of thinking, too – which transformed bad kings from abusive patriarchs into parricidal children – would reappear in the writings of republican theorists after the regicide.

Prynne's second innovation was more visibly transgressive. To bolster his argument for parliamentary legislative primacy, the book's final section presented a historical appendix of kingly tyranny, rapacity and malignancy. Beginning with Tarquin's 'ravishing of Lucretia' and concluding with a list of the 'tyrannies, oppressions, whoredoms, murders, rapines, and evill administrations' of Scotland's former kings – Charles's direct ancestors – this collection of exempla was nothing less than a comprehensive chronicle of monarchical vice.[55] Stories of kingly 'lusts and adulteries' abounded, from polygamous Goth rulers to the Castilian monarch 'Don Pedro the first', who abandoned 'his espoused wife within three dayes after his marriage' for 'the unchaste love' of a mistress.[56] Again, Charles himself made no appearance, and Prynne pointedly glossed over his grandmother Mary Stuart's lurid history by referring the reader instead to George Buchanan's original 1571 account. Even so, his concluding pronouncement that 'tyrannical degenerous Kings, may be justly resisted, censured, [and] deprived' could easily be read as a warning to Prynne's own embattled monarch.[57]

*The soveraigne power of parliaments* may have been a polemical bombshell, but its sheer bulk probably dissuaded many readers from cracking its considerable spine. Nor, as Charles's armies continue to triumph that fall, did it appear that the rest of the summer's polemics had made a measurable impact. Consequently, with parliament's future looking grim, Pym and his allies sealed an alliance with Presbyterian Scotland, the Solemn League and Covenant, which promised Scottish military assistance in return for vague assurances of an impending reformation in English church government. Those ambiguities would soon create considerable diplomatic friction between the two kingdoms, but in the short-term, the treaty promised to finally transform parliament's wartime fortunes.[58]

That fact was not lost on Charles's ministers, who ignored neither the treaty nor the summertime popish plot tracts. That fall, Berkenhead and his handlers engineered a countervailing royalist press campaign from Oxford, presumably intended to sway English moderates alarmed by the growing threat of British puritan hegemony. John Taylor led the van with a series of pamphlets that reduced the parliament-men to gullible, godly 'horned ... cuckolds' and their wives to sex-crazed puritan 'Sisters'.[59] A similar progression was evident in *Mercurius aulicus*, which slowly embraced sexual satire during the closing months of 1643. For example, in October, Berkenhead (now in total control of the newssheet) observed that the Salem minister Hugh Peter – recently arrived in England from the American colonies – had 'handled' a London 'Butchers wife ... better then ever he did his Text', proving that 'all those Spirituall Preachers love the flesh' despite their pretended piety. Through the end of the year, *Aulicus* accused various parliamentarian leaders of whoremongering, wife-stealing and adultery.[60] In Oxford, as in Westminster, the pressures of military mobilisation thus propelled sex-talk further into official regime print.

Parliamentary apologists responded to this new wave of royalist libels in kind. One newsbook did so with special parliamentary assistance: the London production *Mercurius Britanicus*, created specifically in late 1643 to combat the Oxford press. Marchamont Nedham, its primary editor, was a talented penman who routinely indulged in scabrous sexual satire, even to the point of occasional parliamentary censure. Nevertheless, parliamentarian grandees appreciated *Britanicus*'s value as a mobilisation tool, and they regularly squabbled for control of its content. (John Taylor later referred to the newssheet as the regime's 'learned Conduite Pipe', operated 'by your especiall favour and Command'.)[61] Nedham's incessant commentary on royalist unchastity marked another sign of the Westminster coalition's increasing comfort with libellous sex-talk during the second half of 1643.

From its earliest days, partisan sex-talk was a key element of *Britanicus*'s provocative style. The newsbook's third issue satirically accused Charles's cavaliers of 'rob[bing], and ravish[ing]' in 'defence of his Majesties person'. The following week, Nedham published a mock-letter allegedly written by a cavalier soldier, although for modesty's sake the editors 'print[ed] not the oaths, but left spaces' in their place. It read, 'Jack, we have not left one Woman ___, Lady ___ Gentlewoman Waytingmaid ___ or other honest ___ We have now some Irish ___ and Frenchwomen come to us ___ We intend not to leave till we have ___ sinned with all Nations as well as our owne'. The excised words, possibly intended to parody the cyphered royalist correspondence occasionally intercepted by parliamentarian spies, did not hinder the message's broader meaning: Charles's soldiers were nothing more than sexual predators.[62]

*Britanicus* took particular interest in courtly impropriety. In October, its editors bemoaned the 'adulteries' conducted 'behinde doores, and in [the] streetes' of Oxford by its 'Pimp[s], Players, Poets and Oyster women'. Later, the editors wondered 'how farre are ye at Oxford from Mahuimatamisme', since 'you hold the Carnall point of Polygamie as well as they, and you are for the Concubinary Doctrine too'.[63] *Britanicus* also probed at the sex-lives of individual royalists: 'who is the Lady Thin associated with, and who is Prince Rupert associated with', one issue asked, 'and divers others of your associating Lords and Ladies?'[64] Courtly promiscuity and sexual violence alike thus remained hallmarks of royalist partisan identity in the newsbook's pages.

Most egregiously, *Britanicus* accused the queen of committing adultery with Henry Jermyn. At first, Nedham played coy, noting in September that after Jermyn fled 'beyond sea' in 1641, the queen had 'staid not long after him'.[65] But then, in December, two consecutive issues referred to the queen's chief courtier as 'Jermine the Mortimer'. This was a reference to Roger Mortimer, fourteenth-century earl of March, who conducted an illicit affair with Edward II's queen and subsequently assisted her in deposing her husband. Not only did this scandalous parallel depict Jermyn as a conniving adulterer; it also figured Henrietta Maria as Isabella of France, whose lusts had led her into open rebellion against her husband. (Charles's analogue in this unflattering equivalence, Edward II, possessed a similarly troubling sexual history).[66] Even franker allegations would soon appear in *Britanicus*'s pages, illustrating yet again the Westminster grandees' developing tolerance for sexual libel.

Beyond the page, the military struggle swung slowly in parliament's favour that fall. The parliament-men celebrated with the ratification of a new Great Seal depicting an image of the House of Commons rather than the traditional visage of the king.[67] Their partisans also continued to lambast the royalists in print. In particular, the November 1643 appearance of John White's *First century of scandalous, malignant priests* confirmed parliament's full-scale adoption of sexual politics. White chaired the parliamentary Committee of Religion and oversaw Edward Finch's prosecution in early 1641; he had also personally licensed many of the summer's popish plot pamphlets. Thus, attuned as he was to the anti-royalist sexual polemics coming into vogue among parliamentarian polemicists like Nedham and Prynne, White's *Century* unsurprisingly fit the same mould.

The *Century* drew on White's experiences prosecuting royalist clergy to present the lurid personal histories of 100 such ministers recently sequestered by parliament for malignancy. Sex was a recurrent theme: the tract numbered among its subjects 'Whoremongers and Adulterers, who as fed Horses neigh after their Neighbours Wives', and 'Buggerers that change the naturall use into that which is against Nature'. To that end, its opening case described a minister who had 'divers times attempted to commit buggery' with two parishioners. Here, White had done his homework, since the offender, John Wilson, had really been accused (albeit disingenuously) of that crime during the 1630s. Not only did this equivalence between sexual and spiritual malignancy reflect the now-classic puritan position on the king's popish bishops; additionally, White argued that Wilson's vile sins reflected poorly on every one of Charles's supporters, clergyman or not. As he wrote, 'doth not their [the royalists'] affection unto . . . such uncleane beasts, abundantly evince, that they serve and prostitute themselves unto the same dung-hill Idols and filthy lusts?'[68]

White's decision to out these men in print demonstrated how thoroughly parliamentary leaders had abandoned the principles of polemical moderation that they had professed (admittedly, under some pressure from Charles) less than a year prior. The pamphlet even stirred feathers in Oxford. A contemporary anecdote related how the king, upon being exhorted by his advisors to sanction a similar 'Book of the vicious lives of some Parliament Ministers' in response to White's tract, refused outright. He offered two reasons: first, 'because recrimination is no purgation'; and, secondly, because in doing so 'the Publick enemy of the Protestant Religion [i.e. European Catholics] should make an advantage thereof'.[69] Just as parliamentarians reified their commitment to sexual satire in formal regime print, it seems, Charles could not stomach the same from his chief counsellors.

By November 1643, however, he was too late. Mobilisation was a dialogic, even mutually reinforcing, affair, and as evidenced by *Aulicus*'s gradual adoption of sexual satire, the official royalist press was already reorienting towards vicious anti-puritan polemic in response to Westminster's recent innovations. Throughout the fall, Oxford polemicists followed *Aulicus*'s lead by indicting individual parliamentarians for unchastity and offering more imaginative porno-political depictions of the Westminsterian rebellion as a miscegenated, monstrous birth.[70] That process would continue into 1644, as Berkenhead and his colleagues countered parliament's recent recruitment effort with a mobilisation campaign of their own.

English readers devoured the sexual polemics emanating from London and Oxford alike. *Aulicus* was distributed by royalist grandees to its field commanders and read even by their parliamentarian enemies, who protested at its 'lies' while nevertheless passing its issues to their friends along with other 'printed Oxford pamphlets'.[71] Similarly, *Britanicus* circulated as far afield as Scotland, and many of parliament's popish plot tracts appeared on contemporary bookshelves.[72] Some readers were even more proactive: Thomas Wyatt copied lines from a royalist pamphlet, *The discovery of mysteries* (1643), into his diary, naming 'Mr Pym' as well as Cornelius 'Burges' as 'ffamilists' and 'Adamites', both sects notorious, as we have seen, for their sexual profligacy.[73] The kingdom's streets also echoed with partisan sexual slander. In November 1643, the Devon minister John Syms recorded an encounter with a hostile parishioner who accosted him by saying, 'you puritannicall fellowes will not sweare, but you will lye & whore & be drunke'. Later that month, a Norfolk man was charged with claiming that 'there were none but whores Rogues and knaves that did follow the kinge'.[74] Both cases demonstrate that by late 1643, sexual satire had suffused English political culture, even beyond the bounds of partisan pamphleteering. Given this level of engagement, it is unsurprising that both regimes found sex-talk so compelling as a mobilisation tool – and that English publishers proved increasingly willing to produce it, despite the disapproval of scandalised commentators.

### 'Sinning with the very beasts of the field': partisan debates and serial print, 1644–45

John Pym died on 8 December 1643. While his colleagues mourned, *Aulicus* announced that the leading parliament-man had succumbed nastily, 'loaded with other diseases . . . chiefly of the Herodian visitation': in other words, the pox.[75] Pym's posthumous humiliation shows that as the new year brought new challenges – for royalists, impending Scottish military intervention; for parliamentarians, more infighting and battlefield inefficiency – both regimes continued to develop their respective polemical platforms in hopes of generating support for the forthcoming campaign season. In each case, sexual politics flourished. In London, they took the form of anti-popish attacks on courtly immorality and unmanly effeminacy, while in Oxford, anti-puritan allegations of sexual anarchy and unfettered sectarian women received extensive coverage. And, once again, escalation begat escalation, further transforming England's print marketplace into a running dialogue of partisan screeds that now bore the official symbology of formal regime approval. All the while, contemporary readers eagerly followed along.

The resulting exchanges included deeply personal disputes. In January 1644, one such feud erupted after the parliamentarian astrologer John Booker accused his royalist opposite George Wharton of counterfeiting prognostications in his most recent almanac. Weeks later, Wharton responded in an annotated edition of Booker's tract. His reply summarised Booker's astrological 'skill' by explaining that in the same year in which Booker had 'prognosticated how Salacious and wantonly disposed young women were likely to be', his own 'Sister (to fulfil your Prophesie) was happily delivered of two Bastards'.[76] More acrimony followed, fuelled by further interventions from John Taylor; but the significance of these tracts extended beyond partisan muckraking.[77] For, much like the Taylor-Walker feud of 1641, these and other similar exchanges also injected personal sexuality ever more forcefully into England's nascent public sphere.

The most vicious debates erupted between Berkenhead's *Aulicus* and Nedham's *Britanicus*. Consider *Aulicus*'s final issue of 1643, which reported that on the preceding Sunday, 'while His Majesties Forces were at Church', a parliamentarian prisoner in the royalist garrison town of Shrewsbury had been discovered 'committing Buggery on the Keepers [i.e. his jailer's] owne Mare'. Once detected, the newssheet continued, 'he openly and plainly confessed the whole fact, for which they will speedily proceed against him'. Although Berkenhead did not stop there – he also described a deformed foetus recently born to a woman 'well known to people of credit in London', leaving the 'Reader to make his inference' about what that might mean – this allegation of bestiality was the most outrageous sexual libel yet to appear in an Oxford publication.[78] Such depravity – committed on the Sabbath, no less! – illustrated the depths of parliamentarian perversity, while the royalists' swift response showcased Charles's commitment to proper sexual discipline.

*Britanicus* responded two weeks later. First, the parliamentarian newssheet insisted that 'onely barglary', not 'buggery', was the prisoner's crime, and consequently that *Aulicus*'s distortion proved 'what a lewd generation they are'. Nedham then offered a striking counter-claim:

> now they have bethought them of this kinde of impiety, you shall have them sinning with the very beasts of the field shortly, and keeping Mares for breeding Cavaliers on ... as lawfully as the Ladies of honour may keep Stallions and Monkies, and their Bishops Shee-goates and Ganimedes, for they make nothing of such prodigious fornication, they make nothing of Sodomy and Gomorrahisme, especially your Italianated Lords, and your hot privy Counsellors ... your Cathedrall men are the worst, some of your Prebends makes nothing of sinning with the little singing boyes after an Anthem; Oh! this is prodigious lust.

*Britanicus* thus rebutted *Aulicus*'s Shrewsbury story with a comprehensive anti-popish vision of royalist sexual malignancy, complete with allegations of bestiality, sodomy and paedophilia. This was 'prodigious lust' indeed, even within the parliamentarian mythos of Charles's rapacious cavaliers (and beyond, as indicated by a jesting reference to John White's 'next Century' later in the issue).[79] Here, then, we see how specific exchanges between partisan pamphleteers could heighten the pitch of mid-century sex-talk, as each contributor strove to one-up the other. As those interactions multiplied, of course, so too did the incidence of graphic sexual description in print.

Granted, partisan writers did not always respond in kind. Six weeks later, *Aulicus* returned to the Shrewsbury story. This time, rather than addressing *Britanicus* directly, Berkenhead announced that 'in a Legall Triall' the rebel had 'beene found guilty, and . . . expressed much penitence' for 'the haynousnesse of his sinnes'. He was apparently then executed without a hitch.[80] Even here, however, *Aulicus* was making an argument about the regularity and reliability of royal justice. Unlike parliamentarian predators like Captain Griffith (whose attempted rape of Elizabeth Sidley had yielded an army commission rather than a noose), Berkenhead intimated, sexual criminals in royalist territory never escaped punishment.

The weeks separating the two Shrewsbury updates were full of news. In January 1644, Charles gathered a legally dubious parliament in Oxford – later dubbed by its critics, in a tellingly porno-political idiom, a 'Mongrill Parliament' due to its bastardised constitutional heritage – in hopes of invalidating the assembly still sitting in Westminster.[81] As the new body deliberated, a Scottish Covenanter army crossed into England and besieged royalist Newcastle. Faced with an impending two-front war and desperate to recruit English moderates, royalist publishers doubled down on explicit sex-talk, perhaps believing that only the most extreme rhetoric could illustrate the dangers posed by Anglo-Scottish puritan hegemony.

That February, John Taylor's *Crop-eare curried* finally appeared in print after being delayed by royalist leaders the previous fall. Its publication signalled the beginning of a new era in Oxford, complete with a pre-publication licensing system to mirror Westminster's own. This royalist mobilisation effort has received little attention from modern scholars, but it shared many features with the parliamentarian escalation of the preceding summer, including a more intentional engagement with sexual politics.[82] From the winter of 1643/44, Berkenhead's presses began prioritising bolder, bawdier polemic after privileging hefty theological and political treatises for most of the preceding year. As a result, sexual satire surfaced consistently in royalist print throughout 1644, including in court-sponsored works that had previously avoided such scandalous content.

*Crop-eare curried* embodied the new royalist commitment to sexual politics. As its title implied, Taylor's tract was a response to William Prynne's popish plot pamphlets of the preceding summer. (Prynne's ears were cropped in the 1630s as punishment for his seditious pamphleteering.) First, Taylor went on the defensive by disparaging his opponent's appendix of 'royall and base whores' in *The soveraigne power of parliaments*: 'To what purpose' such historical figures 'should be raked up as a Testimony against Him [Charles] now', he wrote, 'is a meere Riddle to me'. But he also took shots of his own against the 'Puritan Punks [i.e. whores]' allegedly swarming in London's streets and against Prynne himself, whom Taylor accused of joining 'the Assembly of Adamites' in order to indulge in his baser desires. ('The Fornicating Brownist' John White came in for similar censure.) His most spectacular attacks were reserved for parliament's new Great Seal, 'Begotten and Borne ... [and] lick'd into fashion by Committees, Members, Votes and Ordinances'. Taylor framed the new symbol as a product of 'Adulterous Incest': adulterous, because it lacked the legitimating legislative approval of the king; incestuous, because it was the exclusive product of various parliamentary committees. This was a clear escalation of the earlier loyalist claim that puritan malcontents had 'Birth[ed]' the parliamentary 'Rebellion', and it set the tone for much royalist porno-political rhetoric to follow.[83]

*Aulicus*, having abandoned its former policy of restraint, remained the primary vehicle of royalist sexual polemic throughout the year. References to Cornelius Burges's adultery case and the rapist-soldier John Griffith appeared in January and February. Later that winter, the newssheet profiled a parliamentarian captain who had allegedly confessed that 'he had kept two young women for his owne sinfull delight' while on campaign.[84] Nor (for some royalists, at least) were these claims mere rhetoric: in March 1644, for instance, one of Prince Rupert's correspondents reported a story about the earl of Essex's 'Trumpeter' seducing the wife of a minor functionary away from her husband during an abortive peace summit earlier that spring. (The same letter-writer also referenced Essex's 'horne of plenty' in what was probably a nod to his cuckoldry.)[85] Obviously some readers believed the lascivious portrait of puritan parliamentarianism now being broadcast from Oxford's presses.

Once again, mobilisation did not go unopposed. *Aulicus* was matched by London's coterie of parliamentarian newsbooks, which slandered Charles's partisans as popish sexual malignants throughout the winter and spring. The 'carnall body of the Court' was a favourite subject of *The spie*, a new serial that wasted no time in attacking the Oxford 'Madams' for keeping a 'Troope of Stallions' – in other words, lusty royalist soldiers – 'to exercise their restife corps'. Soon, it was reporting on the 'nightly Conventicle[s]' frequented by Oxford's 'medley ... of Sexes', where royalist leaders served as emasculated 'vassalls to the female-power'.[86] Other parliamentary newsbooks declaimed against the 'loosenesse of life, adultery, yea buggery', of the royalist clergy who had received such a drubbing in White's *Century* the previous November. In this way, even more so than one-off publications, serial print helped to propagate sustained sexual narratives about parliament's malignant enemies.[87]

*Britanicus* remained *Aulicus*'s chief critic. Throughout the winter, Nedham ridiculed royalists for their 'fires of lust', exercised in 'baudy-houses' and 'brothels' across England, and resurrected stories of previous royalist embarrassments. Among them was the executed bishop John Atherton, whom *Britanicus* identified as a 'lusty brother in Ireland' who had 'commit[ted] you know what with the little boyes after Catechisme & Confirmation'. As White had done in the *Century*, Nedham then extended the charge to encompass all of Charles's royalist clergy: 'you will not beleeve', he wrote, 'what logick they would use to prove simple Fornication lawfull, and what divinity they had for illegall Copulations'.[88] The post-Reformation context remained front and centre in these slanders, as the anti-popish tropes of 1640 and 1641 continued to underwrite the cavalier stereotype that Nedham loved to ridicule.

*Britanicus*'s favourite targets included Prince Rupert, that longtime punching-bag of parliamentarian pamphleteers. One of its more inventive attacks on the 'wanton young Prince' appeared in February 1644 as a mock 'warrant' from 'Rupert the Rambler' requesting female company to attend him 'for the service of the publike'; it was followed by a note that one 'Mistris Paschall' had appeared in Rupert's rooms as ordered, only to loot them for gold in his absence. This story proved so effective that Nedham later repurposed its central conceit for another stand-alone pamphlet.[89] It was also popular among godly readers like Nehemiah Wallington, who transcribed the German prince's 'warrant for women or whores' in his diary. Later, presumably inspired by similar accounts, a puritan minister reported on Rupert's notorious sexual appetites to the Commons: evidence, again, of the impact exercised by polemical sex-writing beyond the printed page.[90]

No one was more aware of that fact than the royal family. As Henrietta Maria could attest, the escalating political crisis was rapidly dissolving the sacred protections traditionally afforded to the monarchy. Worse, royalist ministers feared that the king himself might be next. To that end, royalist writers like the poet Francis Quarles made a point of praising Charles's 'unblemisht Chastity' – all the more remarkable for 'how many would have held it a Preferment to be Attorny to His Royall Lust, or Secretary to His Bosom Sinne' – in print.[91] For the moment, such rhetoric was entirely pre-emptive, since the king's personal sexuality still remained off-limits from direct commentary even as radical parliamentarians grew more comfortable blaming him for the outbreak of war.[92] But royalist partisans continued to address the unspoken challenge nonetheless.

As the king's armies faltered against the combined Anglo-Scottish forces in the field during the summer of 1644 – culminating on 2 July with a crushing parliamentarian victory over Rupert at Marston Moor – Oxford's presses continued to pump out anti-puritan sexual satire to compensate for its soldiers' poor performances. In July, for instance, *Aulicus* identified the adulterous radical Henry Marten – previously only attacked directly in freelancing London productions like *The sence of the House* – as one of many 'religious examples' of parliamentary unchastity. (In a later issue, Berkenhead suggested that Marten had even seduced the wife of the parliamentarian general William Waller.)[93] An earlier June tract had reduced puritan hypocrisy to its essential generative imperative: 'They simply fornication think no crime / Nor you in holie place, and holie time / But wiselie to Gods glorie sanctifie / Your fornication and adulterie. / Zeale and the Spirit so work upon you then, / All at your meetings are begot new men'.[94] Elsewhere, one pamphleteer, fed up with *Britanicus*'s 'scurrilous jests', even accused Nedham – certainly no puritan, although his royalist assailant may not have known it – of 'commiting follie with an elect Sister'.[95] By mid-1644, in short, anti-puritan sexual satire had come to number among the royalists' most reliable polemical strategies.

Loyalist ministers participated from the pulpit, too. Echoing English critics of the Covenanters during the Bishops' Wars, one sermoniser announced that 'though the Scotts pretended their Coming was for maintenance of the Gospell & Liberty of the Subject, yet the End of their Coming was to take away our Estates & abuse our wives'.[96] Similarly, the bishop William Juxon inveighed against puritan zealots who used their hypocritical 'vaile of zeale' in order 'to sanctify adultery' – along with 'tyrannizing Atheisme, Sacriledge, Perjuries, Prophaness, Rebellion, Murthers, Rapes, Rapines, Lyes, and the Luciferian emulation of whosoever'.[97] But not all of Charles's clergy were so militant. Preaching in Oxford that summer, Edward Symmons deployed *Aulicus*'s Shrewsbury buggery story from January to warn his listeners about the dangers of unchecked polemic. Just 'because one of them was lately taken in the act and hang'd for the sin of Buggerie', he announced, 'if we Preachers should hereupon tell you from the Pulpits, that all these blessed Reformers . . . are . . . guiltie of that horrid sin, I believe (for my part) we should much abuse them in that particular'. This was a cogent assessment of the escalatory capacity of partisan satire – a principle proven in full by *Britanicus*'s blistering response to *Aulicus*'s initial account of the incident. But Symmons's warning not to 'inlarge the faults of some upon all', for fear that it would only spark further recrimination, came too late. Just as he predicted, 'should we but deal so with them, they would (as well they might) exclaime much upon us'.[98]

Days before Symmons's sermon appeared in print, the royalists lost at Marston Moor. The battle made a resounding impact in Westminster, but the parliament-mens' joy was short-lived. Two months later, Essex suffered a humiliating defeat near the Cornish town of Lostwithiel; then, in October, the earl failed to crush the king at Newbury. As a result, by the fall of 1644, parliament had almost entirely squandered the advantages gained at York three months prior. Essex himself, already a target of ridicule, fell even further into disgrace after these unmasculine proceedings. The royalist poet John Cleveland was still crowing in February 1645 about 'his Oxcellency', the Commons's cuckold general.[99]

At the same time, bipartisan outcries continued to mount against printed sex-talk, albeit sometimes disingenuously. A September edition of *Aulicus* inveighed against the Londoners' 'rotten talke' and 'uncleane Pamphlets' without acknowledging the irony of Berkenhead rebuking others for their abusive rhetoric. Meanwhile, a parliamentarian pamphleteer fed up with 'John Tayler' condemned the 'Ribaldry' of the 'infinite . . . pernicious Papers, the very vomit and filth of Malignant Presses' produced at 'Oxford'. Nevertheless, the setbacks at Lostwithiel and Newbury dictated that parliamentary polemicists continue their libellous campaign, encapsulated in a September pamphlet entitled *A nest of perfidious vipers*.[100] Among other slanders, the *Nest* repeated the familiar charge that Bishop Matthew Wren had 'kept another mans wife in Cambridge': an act that 'put him in minde of a brother of his in Ireland', John Atherton, 'that was hang'd for such a holy businesse'. John Finch, brother of the disgraced Edward Finch, was painted as 'another bird of the same feather' and equally 'apt a scholler . . . in the schoole of Lust'. Royalist ministers were said to 'preach against Spirituall whoredome (yet bee arrand Munkeys at the other)', and Rupert was once again indicted for defiling England's 'Virgins'.[101] By repeating such allegations *ad nauseam*, the *Nest* further institutionalised the parliamentarian canon of royalist sexual malignancy formalised since mid-1643 by Prynne, Nedham and White.

When tabulated alongside the ongoing work of anonymous pamphleteers – one of whom argued around this time that if the 'Bishop of Waterford [i.e. Atherton] had lived . . . the King had had more friends', thereby explicitly associating Charles's court with the sin of 'buggery' – the spate of parliamentarian sexual polemic printed 'according to order' appeared more akin to a flood.[102] *Britanicus*'s ongoing salvos against the king's 'obscene' cavalier soldiery – especially after Lostwithiel, where they had 'spoile[d], and ravish[ed], and deflower[ed] wives and maides' like beasts – only strengthened that impression.[103] More prominent still was Nedham's coverage of Henrietta Maria's alleged affair with 'Harry Jermin Esquire . . . of the Queens body'.[104] Eventually, *Britanicus* even suggested that Jermyn was taking turns with the royalist secretary George Digby in sneaking 'downe the backestairs [of the queen's rooms] without a candle' after 'one of Clock Consultations' while the king 'was contented to lie abed for quietnes sake': the spitting image of an emasculated cuckold.[105]

This was damning stuff indeed. But in Westminster, some polemical restraints remained intact. In December, a Norfolk man named Miles Cushion appeared before the county bench to answer for swearing that 'the king is noe king, he is a Bastard, and was crowned with a Leaden crowne'.[106] Cushion's words represented a now-familiar subversion of the period's endemic associations between genealogical, patriarchal, and political legitimacy. In voicing them so brazenly, however, he surpassed even the most daring parliamentarian pamphleteers. Although Charles's imperiousness and the tentative historicisms of regime writers like Prynne had encouraged some radicals to question the king's political authority in print by the closing months of 1644, none dared to venture beyond generalised assertions that the 'corruption of princes' might encompass 'Whoredome' as well as 'Tyrannie'.[107] For the moment, that is to say, the king's personal sexuality still remained immune from censure. Just two years after the outbreak of war, Charles was perhaps the only person left in England who retained that privilege.

### 'The base adulteries of all common eyes': contesting the *Cabinet*

On 10 January 1645, Archbishop William Laud was beheaded on Tower Hill. During his trial – spearheaded by none other than Prynne – a treason charge proved difficult to justify, leaving parliament to convict Laud via attainder, just as they had Strafford in 1641.[108] This was accomplished without much public outcry. By 1645, Laud had apparently become a relic, even among reformers who had howled for his blood five years prior.

The archbishop was an outlier in another sense as well: with only one prominent exception, the archbishop was never libelled for personal unchastity. True, some godly writers had criticised his corrupt oversight of the ecclesiastical ('bawdy') courts, and others had joked about his perpetual bachelorhood.[109] Otherwise, however, they left Laud's sex life alone, perhaps because the old cleric's well-known abstemiousness made him an unconvincing target. (Years later, one parliamentarian historian even praised Laud for 'being neither taxed of covetousness, intemperance, or incontinence'.) The sole accusation against Laud's sexual character came from Prynne in a polemical 1644 tract wherein the puritan lawyer analysed several 'scurrilous' dreams recorded in Laud's personal diary. In Prynne's eyes, the archbishop's midnight fantasies betrayed his real-life 'uncleannesse' with several (unnamed) women; but since this allegation did not make it into Prynne's published account of the trial (which included several passages from the diary), he must have eventually recognised its implausibility.[110] Laud's execution thus marked the end of an era. Thereafter, very few public figures in revolutionary England would be spared from sexual satire.

The winter of 1644/45 witnessed simultaneous drives towards war and peace in Westminster. Upset with the failures at Lostwithiel and Newbury, regime leaders set out to reform the parliamentarian military apparatus. By spring 1645, the New Model Army, led by the Yorkshireman Sir Thomas Fairfax, was ready for action. Meanwhile, a nascent peace party in parliament and the City, bolstered by the Scottish Covenanters, spearheaded a new set of treaty negotiations with Charles at Uxbridge that collapsed almost immediately after they began on 30 January. This failure was portended by the godly minister Christopher Love, who preached a sermon on the first day of the talks against royalist 'Clergie men' said to believe that 'the lives' and 'wives' of 'subjects' were forfeit to the king's 'owne will'.[111] Such a medley of cavalier rapacity, popery and (potential) tyranny was hardly a recipe for compromise.

Love's sermon soon appeared in print, where it joined a chorus of rebarbative sexual satires still ricocheting between London and Oxford. The royalist press corps indicted the amorous activities of puritan parliamentarians throughout the spring,[112] while parliamentarian apologists – *Britanicus* foremost among them – lobbed similar attacks against Charles's cavalier soldiery and the Oxford court.[113] Exasperated ministers preached against the flood of 'loose & wanton songs, & all manner of lewd & lascivious discourses' to no avail.[114] By mid-1645, they were far too late.

Both royalists and parliamentarians also experimented with less overtly libellous sexual politics. One Oxford tract employed James I's favourite marital analogy for monarchical rule to rebut the frequent parliamentarian contention that because 'the Parliament is a part of the King . . . the Parliament can do nothing [harmful] against the King'. According to the royalist response, while king and parliament ought to be as 'neer' as 'husband and . . . wife', 'it follows not . . . that it is impossible for the wife to miscarry her selfe towards her husband'. Indeed, it asked, were there not 'some untractable women in the world, that carry themselves most unchristianly towards their husbands'? Rather than proving that a wife could do her spouse no harm, therefore, marital metaphors instead provided a particularly effective framework for diagnosing political strife. The lesson was simple: 'the wife ought not to be injurious and disloyall to her husband; and . . . the Parliament ought not to be disloyall to the King'.[115] But this relatively innocuous reading carried portentous porno-political connotations.

For if the parliament-wife abandoned her husband-king for another lover – say, the puritan grandees in Westminster – what else was that but adultery?

Parliamentarians, for their part, remained demure about Charles's personal chastity in print, although their repeated salvoes against his wife's fidelity did not reflect well on his capacities as either husband or monarch. In April, however, the London bookseller George Thomason discovered an anonymous manuscript satire that laid bare the full lurid history of the king's Stuart forebearers, from James's sodomitical relationship with Buckingham to the dubious ancestry of his mother, Anne of Denmark. Similar allegations were made about Henrietta Maria: 'for them that swears that their Heirs / came from a Norman', it read, 'may sooner bee out then Hee / came from a German [i.e. Henry Jermyn]'. Even here, Charles's personal sexuality remained untarnished, save a jibe at his flirtations with the Babylonian 'whore'.[116] But no one who read the untitled satire could have missed the central argument – now apparently acceptable enough for scribal circulation – that the house of Stuart was rife with sexual disorder.

As parliament's New Model Army dominated on the battlefield that spring, worried observers noted signs of similar chaos across the kingdom. In June, a London woman confessed to Middlesex JPs that a 'Cavalier in Oxford' had 'used her there as his whoare'. More outlandish tales proliferated in print, including a report of 'hundreds of men, women, maids, and boyes' who had reportedly joined with African immigrants ('black men') to 'make sport with our English women and maids' in London's streets. Meanwhile, witchfinders rampaging through the southeast arraigned dozens of suspected witches, some accused of copulating with Satan himself.[117] Such stories, despite their sometimes questionable veracity, graphically channelled contemporary fears that civil war had unsettled English morality in addition to rattling the sociopolitical order.

Those anxieties could provoke horrific violence. After parliamentary forces crushed Charles's royalists at Naseby in Northamptonshire on 4 June, atrocity followed when Fairfax's victorious soldiers encountered a group of women who had accompanied the king's army to the battlefield. Inspired by the vicious sexual polemics broadcast by London pamphleteers since 1642 – including the dubious assertion that these royalist tagalongs, probably Welsh cooks, wives and maids, were in fact Irish prostitutes – the parliamentarians slaughtered at least 100 of the women and mutilated many more with the 'whore's mark', a slit nose. Then, in the wake of the massacre, parliamentarian publishers repeated the accusation about the women's Irish ancestry, thereby further strengthening the partisan association between royalist women, foreign invaders, and popish promiscuity.[118] Here was the most vivid illustration yet of how deadly sexual politics could prove for their (all too often female) victims.

Tragic as the Naseby killings were, their political significance was overshadowed by another surprise unfolding elsewhere on the battlefield. While some parliamentarian soldiers committed atrocities, others discovered a cache of Charles's private correspondence in the ruins of the royal coach. The letters were a bombshell: not only had the king repeatedly lied to parliament, they revealed, but he had done so on his wife's orders. After deliberating, parliamentary leaders decided to publish the letters, which appeared in July – complete with a set of damning editorial annotations – under the suggestive title *The Kings cabinet opened*. Throughout, its editors curated the captured correspondence to present the impression of profound gender trouble in the royal household.[119] Composed by Westminster's top rhetoricians (including Henry Parker, author of an earlier jibe about Charles's 'sceptre') and then 'dispersed according to direction' by troops on campaign, the *Cabinet* represented parliament's most comprehensive attempt yet to undermine its king's patriarchal, and therefore political, legitimacy.[120]

Several themes dominated the *Cabinet*'s curated correspondence. One was Charles's duplicity, long suspected by parliamentary leaders but hitherto largely unsubstantiated. Another was his uxoriousness: in the *Cabinet*'s words, the king was 'a Prince seduced out of his proper sphear' by his popish queen. That Charles's 'counsels' were 'wholly managed by the Queene' was troubling enough, but the arrangement looked even more sinister when considered alongside *Britanicus*'s campaign to discredit Henrietta Maria as a popish adulteress. If the king was in thrall to such a creature, the tract implied, what hope was there either for English Protestantism or the royal succession?[121]

Furthermore, the *Cabinet* made another brief intervention in a related sphere. One of its captured letters was addressed to Sir John Cochrane, a Scottish diplomat who had visited Denmark several times on the king's orders. As the tract revealed, Charles at one point had instructed Cochrane to warn Christian IV that parliament had 'endeavoured . . . to lay a great blemish upon his royall family' by 'endeavouring to illegitimate all derived from his Sister' – James I's queen, Anne of Denmark – 'to cut off the interest and pretensions of the whole Race'. According to Charles, this escapade had even included 'examining witnesses' about Anne's sexual history; according to the *Cabinet*'s editors, however, no such investigation had ever taken place. Instead, the pamphlet accused the king of 'stir[ring] rumours about his Mothers chastity' to solicit foreign assistance for his cause. As some royalists later noted, Nedham's ongoing campaign against Henrietta Maria's fidelity rendered such high-minded rhetoric more than a little hypocritical; but the paradox seems to have made little difference to the *Cabinet*'s editors.[122]

Royalists greeted the *Cabinet* with outrage. Several writers protested that parliamentarians had 'prostituted' the royal couple's 'chast and holy Papers' to 'the base adulteries of all common Eyes'. Others compared the pamphlet's editors to conniving literati who could 'rais[e] . . . the unchastest poems from one of the chastest'. A different tract attempted an even bolder reversal by trumpeting the captured correspondence as evidence of the royal couple's 'chast Embraces'.[123] Certainly no one could deny that the letters demonstrated Charles's affection for his wife; but given the queen's religion, not to mention her allegedly dubious chastity, that fondness hardly counted in his favor. More fundamentally, it was difficult to rebut parliamentarian polemic that merely reproduced the king's own words, and consequently none of the royalists' counter-efforts succeeded in disarming the *Cabinet*.

Even so, some of Charles's subjects shared their indignation. Readers annotated their copies about 'false' and 'fraudulent argumentacon' and protested that rather than 'tending to the justification' of the parliamentary cause, the tract had done 'rather the contrary'. The royalist earl of Bridgewater added an additional subclause after the title-page's imprint (which read, 'published by speciall Order of the Parliament'): 'the more to their shame', he scribbled, 'it being not onely a rebellious, but a Clownish action'.[124] Thomas Wyatt noted the pamphlet in his journal, while other copies appeared in contemporary library catalogues. Some readers could hardly believe that the letters were real: years later, one Thomas Sampson was arraigned for proclaiming 'that the letters that were taken in the Kings cabinett were not of the kings owne hand writings but that the State did counterfeit his hand'.[125] Such occasional inaccuracies aside, the sheer number of these hostile reactions is proof of the *Cabinet*'s impact.

Still, royalist polemicists continued to rebuke their enemies. John Taylor despaired in August 1645 that because 'civill law is turned to civill uncivill warre . . . blasphemy, atheisme, sacriledge, obscenenesse, prophanenesse, Incest, adultery, fornication, biggemy, polygamy, bastard-bearing, cuckold-making, and all sorts of beastly baudry' had become either 'generally connived at, or totally tolerated'. Elsewhere, John Griffith once again came in for ridicule: 'let not our Chast Lucretias suffer thus', one pamphlet rhymed, 'by an adulterous Griffithius'.[126] As usual, these Oxford productions were opposed by parliamentarian publishers who joked about the beleaguered royalist 'Clergy-men' who 'visit not our wives so often as they did in former time'.[127] In this way, despite parliament's crushing victory at Naseby, libellous sex-talk continued to rocket across England's print marketplace.

But the royalists' defiance could not last. The Northamptonshire disaster was soon cemented by a string of parliamentarian victories in the west and the concurrent defeat of the king's Scottish ally, the earl of Montrose. The Oxford press corps dissolved shortly afterward. Months after *Aulicus* folded in September, Charles's advisors wrote worriedly that the king could not 'possibly subsist till Midsummer next'. True to their predictions, Oxford surrendered to Fairfax in June 1646. Three months prior, the last surviving royalist weekly, *Mercurius academicus*, had published its final issue; its lead-in read, 'this is the saddest weeke we have yet knowne'.[128] Eighteen months would pass before another royalist newsbook appeared in print.

In a 1646 diary entry, Sir John Oglander complained that the 'kinges Commanders weare (or the greatests part) so deboysched, for drinkinge, hooringe, and swearing, that no mann could expect gods blessinnge on theyre actions', while 'Parliament' had taken 'all Course possible to civelise theyre Sowldieres'. Oglander had clearly imbibed at least one of the partisan sexual stereotypes that had circulated in English print since the outbreak of civil war. Nor was he alone in doing so: Edward Symmons, who had warned in 1644 about the dangers of unchecked partisan satire, would later condemn the royalist soldiery's 'blasphemy ... dissoluteness ... [and] self-seeking, lust-pleasing, and King-neglecting baseness'. Similarly, the last proclamation issued by Charles I during his lifetime, dated to 3 February 1646, inveighed against female cross-dressing and disorderly night-walking in Oxford's streets: in other words, precisely the kind of gendered and sexual chaos that had been trumpeted in London newsbooks from mid-1643. In doing so, Charles, like Oglander and Symmons, implicitly confirmed the effectiveness of parliamentarian attempts to link royalism with rampant unchastity.[129] Here, as in numerous other examples surveyed in this chapter, the value of sex-talk as a mobilisation tool becomes readily apparent. If sexual politics could motivate the king himself into action, what impact might they have exercised on other potential readers, financiers, or recruits?

This question ultimately prompted both the parliamentarian and royalist regimes to adopt sexual satire in their formal polemics after the outbreak of civil war. That process, which was tied up with the larger project of military mobilisation, differed in London and Oxford: while parliamentarian grandees proactively paved the way for sexual politics with the languages of evil counsel and cavalier malignancy during the winter of 1642/43, the royalist leadership instead allowed experienced anti-puritan freelancers like John Taylor – some writing from under parliament's nose in London – to take the lead before piling on in official publications. The turning-point came in mid-1643, when first parliamentarians and then their royalist enemies openly sanctioned the use of politicised sex-talk in official publications. By 1644, both regimes were committed fully to libellous sexual satire.

From there, pamphleteers in London and Oxford – supervised, respectively, by the parliamentary press-master John White and his royalist counterpart, Sir John Berkenhead – went to war in print. The ensuing back-and-forth provided plentiful opportunities for enterprising writers to push sexual politics in transgressive new directions. The most fruitful spaces for these innovations were serial newsbooks like Nedham's *Britanicus* and Berkenhead's *Aulicus*, which egged each other on until their victims encompassed figures as illustrious as the queen herself; but even minor exchanges, such as that between the rival astrologers John Booker and George Wharton, served to project sex-talk further into England's nascent public sphere. In the process, civil war pamphleteers reified a budding connection between public sexual discourse and personal sexual practice: true (or at least plausible) stories, like that of John Griffith and Elizabeth Sidley, were repeated *ad nauseam*, while Prynne's hard-to-believe tales about Laud's alleged trysts soon fell by the wayside. As partisan writers developed new connections between sexual polemic and political argument after the outbreak of war, in other words, they also tethered their sexual politics ever more closely to the lived experiences of engaged contemporaries.

Only Charles's personal chastity remained off-limits from public (printed) scrutiny in mid-1646; but it did so by a mere thread, as illustrated by the imputations against his patriarchal authority in *The Kings cabinet opened*. Like *Britanicus*'s attacks on Henrietta Maria, the *Cabinet* implicitly linked patriarchal, political and royal (il)legitimacy in a way that many royalists found profoundly threatening and others found equally compelling: in October 1646, for instance, one Thomas Beevers horrified a group of onlookers by insisting that 'the Queene was gone overnite to Holland to play the whore, and that all the kings issue were bastards'.[130] Meanwhile, royalists began to refine a similarly devastating critique of the parliamentary rebellion as a monstrous, miscegenated birth. That porno-political reading would pay off in the coming years, as we will see, but parliamentarians likely paid more attention to the mundane allegations of puritan sexual hypocrisy that spewed from Oxford between 1643 and 1646. This was because, behind the scenes, parliament itself was fracturing in the face of endemic religious tensions that brought the classic biblical analogue between heterodox doctrine and sexual promiscuity into sharp focus. As the next chapter will show, although civil war would soon give way to uneasy peace, sexual politics would continue to serve as a framework for contemporary debates about politics, partisanship and the national church.

## Notes

1 Angela J. McShane (ed.), *Political Broadside Ballads of Seventeenth-Century England: A Critical Bibliography* (London, 2011), p. 37.
2 Como, *RP*, p. 11.
3 See for instance Jordan S. Downs, *Civil War London: Mobilizing for Parliament, 1641–5* (Manchester, 2021); Como, *RP*; John Walter, *Covenanting Citizens: The*

*Protestation Oath and Popular Political Culture in the English Revolution* (Oxford, 2017); Thomas Leng, 'The Meanings of "Malignancy": The Language of Enmity and the Construction of the Parliamentarian Cause in the English Revolution', *JBS* 53:4 (2014), 835–58; Michael Braddick, 'Mobilisation, Anxiety and Creativity in England during the 1640s', in John Morrow and Jonathan Scott (eds), *Liberty, Authority, Formality: Political Ideas and Culture, 1600–1900* (Exeter, 2008), pp. 175–94.

4 David R. Como, 'Print, Censorship, and Ideological Escalation in the English Civil War', *JBS* 51:4 (2012), 820–57; Michael J. Braddick, 'History, Liberty, Reformation and the Cause: Parliamentarian Military and Ideological Escalation in 1643', in Michael J. Braddick and David L. Smith (eds), *The Experience of Revolution in Stuart Britain and Ireland* (Cambridge, 2011), pp. 117–34.

5 Jordan Downs, 'The Attempt on the Seven Londoners', *EHR* 135:574 (2020), 541–71; Ian Gentles, 'Parliamentary Politics and the Politics of the Street: The London Peace Campaigns of 1642–3', *Parliamentary History* 26:2 (2007), 139–59; David Wootton, 'From Rebellion to Revolution: The Crisis of the Winter of 1642/3 and the Origins of Civil War Radicalism', *EHR* 105:416 (1990), 654–69.

6 *The Clergyes bill of complaint*, E.84[44] ([12 January] 1643), p. 1; [Peter Heylyn], *The rebells catechisme*, E.35[22] (Oxford, [6 March] 1643), p. 5.

7 Tim Harris, 'Charles I and Public Opinion on the Eve of the English Civil War', in Stephen Taylor and Grant Tapsell (eds), *The Nature of the English Revolution Revisited: Essays in Honour of John Morrill* (Woodbridge, 2013), pp. 1–25, at 23–4.

8 *The virgins complaint*, E.86[38] (31 January 1643), pp. 3–6, 8. It was later reprinted: *The virgins complaint*, E.351[5] ([24 August] 1646).

9 *A most worthy speech*, E.128[30] (29 November 1642), p. 4.

10 *Boanerges*, E.88[25] ([8 February] 1643), p. 2. See also *Look about you*, E.85[35] (21 January 1643), p. 7; *The malignants conventicle*, E.245[24] ([28 January] 1643), p. 3; Leng, 'The Meanings of "Malignancy"'.

11 *Love one another*, E.85[38] ([23 January] 1643), p. 4. See also John Taylor, *The conversion, confession . . . & advice*, Wing T444 (Oxford, 1643), pp. 7–8.

12 Adam Smyth, ' "Reade in One Age and Understood I'th'next": Recycling Satire in the Mid-Seventeenth Century', *HLQ* 69:1 (2006), 67–82.

13 *The five years of King James*, E.101[14] ([10 May] 1643); *The arraignment and conviction of . . . Castlehaven*, E.84[2] ([3 January] 1643). See also Noah Millstone, *Manuscript Circulation and the Invention of Politics in Early Stuart England* (Cambridge, 2016), pp. 174–8; Cynthia B. Herrup, *A House in Gross Disorder: Sex, Law, and the 2nd Earl of Castlehaven* (Oxford, 1999), pp. 126–7.

14 *The humble advice of Thomas Aldred*, E.244[37] ([5 January] 1643), sig. A2r (quoted); *The coppie of a letter*, E.115[12] ([2 September] 1642).

15 [Henry Parker], *The contra-replicant*, E.87[5] ([31 January] 1643), p. 15.

16 Thomas Wyatt dated it to 23 November, 'or thereabout': Bod., MS Top. Oxon. C. 378, p. 368.

17 *The complaint of the kingdome*, Wing C5616 (Oxford?, 1642), pp. 32, 44; Tai Liu, 'Burges, Cornelius', *ODNB*. Anthony a Wood, *Athenae oxonienses* (2 vols, 1692), ii, pp. 235–6, seconds the adultery story, but his source is yet another royalist pamphlet that appears to be a renamed duplicate of the *Complaint*: *Sober sadnes*, E.94[28] (Oxford, [3 April] 1643), p. 32. See also *Accommodation discommended*, E.93[12] ([16 March] 1643), p. 5; John Taylor, *John Taylor being yet unhanged*, E.21[19] (Oxford, 1644), p. 8; SRO, Q/SR/258, no. 13.

18 *Complaint*, p. 3. For Griffith's punishment, see *CJ*, ii, pp. 613, 712, 804. See also Gryffith Williams, *The discovery of mysteries*, E.60[1] ([Oxford], [12 July] 1643), p. 92; *A new diurnall of passages*, Wing N631 (Oxford, 1643), sigs A2r–v; *Certain observations*, Wing C1714 (Bristol, 1643), p. 37.

19 David Scott, 'Hotham, Sir John', *ODNB*; Sarah Barber, *A Revolutionary Rogue: Henry Marten and the English Republic* (Stroud, 2000).

20 *The sence of the House*, 669.f.6[117] ([10 March] 1643). It also circulated scribally: HEHL, EL 8778.

21 *An exact description of a roundhead*, E.238[21] (1642), p. 5. For another probable parody, see *The wicked resolution of the cavaliers*, E.127[42] (22 November 1642).

22 *Observations upon Prince Rupert's white dog*, E.245[33] ([2 February] 164[3]), sig. A3r; *An exact description of Prince Ruperts malignant she-monkey*, E.90[25] ([25 February] 1643), sig. A2v. See also Mark Stoyle, *The Black Legend of Prince Rupert's Dog: Witchcraft and Propaganda During the English Civil War* (Exeter, 2011), pp. 62–8, 98–104, 133.

23 *The humerous tricks and conceits of Prince Roberts malignant she-monkey*, E.93[9] ([15 March] 1643), sig. A2v. See also *The Parliaments unspotted-bitch*, E.92[13] ([8 March] 1643), sig. A2r; and *Prince Ruperts burning love to England*, E.100[8] ([1 May] 1643), which likened Rupert's plundering to venereal disease.

24 BL, Stowe MS 184, fol. 73r; Isle of Wight Record Office, MS OG/AA/31, p. 1.

25 LMA, MJ/SR/927/4. See also Dagmar Freist, 'The King's Crown is the Whore of Babylon: Politics, Gender and Communication in Mid-Seventeenth-Century England', *Gender & History* 7:3 (1995), 457–81.

26 Braddick, 'History, Liberty, Reformation'.

27 [John Taylor], *The noble cavalier caracterised*, Wing T490 (Oxford, 1643), p. 4; *The round-heads remembrancer*, E.105[13] (Oxford, [7 June] 1643), p. 2.

28 *The publick faith*, 669.f.8[2] ([7 April] 1643); *A strange sight to be seen at Westminster*, 669.f.8[8] ([17 May] 1643); *The city*, 669.f.8[5] ([20 April] 1643).

29 Jason McElligott, *Royalism, Print, and Censorship in Revolutionary England* (Woodbridge, 2007), p. 17.

30 P. W. Thomas, *Sir John Berkenhead, 1617–1679: A Royalist Career in Politics and Polemics* (Oxford, 1969).

31 Falconer Madan (ed.), *Oxford Books: A Bibliography of Printed Works Relating to the University and City of Oxford* (3 vols, Oxford, 1895–1931), ii, p. x. For some examples, see *Pyms juncto*, 669.f.8[6] ([8 May] 1643) (for a

manuscript copy, see BL, Harley MS 393, fols 15r–16v); *The humble petition*, E.69[24] ([5 October] 1643); *The reformado*, E.95[3] (1643).
32 John Taylor, *Crop-eare curried*, E.269[24] (Oxford, [17 February] 1644), p. 40.
33 Anthony N.B. Cotton, 'London Newsbooks in the Civil War: Their Political Attitudes and Sources of Information' (DPhil thesis, Oxford University, 1971), pp. 36–45.
34 Joad Raymond, *The Invention of the Newspaper: English Newsbooks, 1641–1649* (Oxford, 1996), p. 32; Bernard Capp, *The World of John Taylor the Water-Poet, 1578–1653* (Oxford, 1994), pp. 182–3; Thomas, *Berkenhead*, p. 35.
35 BL, Add. MS 46885A, fol. 7; Anthony Milton, *Laudian and Royalist Polemic in Seventeenth-Century England: The Career and Writings of Peter Heylyn* (Manchester, 2007), p. 11.
36 Raymond, *Invention*.
37 Lloyd Bowen, 'The Bedlam Academy: Royalist Oxford in Civil War News Culture', *Media History* 23:2 (2017), 199–217; Jason Peacey, ' "Hot and Eager in Courtship": Representations of Court Life in the Parliamentarian Press, 1642–9', *Early Modern Literary Studies* 15 (2007).
38 *Speciall passages and certain informations*, E.96[2] (4–11 April 1643), p. 287; *Mercurius civicus*, E.60[9] (6–13 July 1643), p. 53.
39 [*Mercurius*] *aulicus*, E.99[22] (15 April 1643), p. 191; ibid., E.56[11] (17 June 1643), p. 316.
40 *Aulicus*, E.247[26] (19–25 March 1643), p. 150.
41 Como, *RP*, pp. 169–71; HEHL, EL 7794; Vernon F. Snow, *Essex the Rebel: The Life of Robert Devereux, the Third Earl of Essex, 1591–1646* (Lincoln, NE, 1970), p. 343. See also Ian Atherton, 'An Account of Herefordshire in the First Civil War', *Midland History* 21 (1996), 136–55, at 142. I thank Alastair Bellany for this reference.
42 *Insigma civicas*, E.251[5] ([21 October] 1643), p. 1; *The humble petition*, p. 5; *The Cambridge royallist imprisoned*, E.62[15] ([31 July] 1643), sig. A3r; Ian Gentles, 'The Iconography of Revolution: England, 1642–1649', in Ian Gentles, John Morrill and Blair Worden (eds), *Soldiers, Writers and Statesmen of the English Revolution* (Cambridge, 1998), pp. 91–113, at 101.
43 Hughes, *Gender*, pp. 102–4.
44 Jennifer Frances Cobley, 'The Construction and Use of Gender in the Pamphlet Literature of the English Civil War, 1642–1646' (PhD thesis, University of Southampton, 2010), pp. 167–9, 185.
45 Como, *RP*, p. 163.
46 E.g., *The reformed malignants*, E.250[6] (4 September 1643), p. 3.
47 *The fallacies of Mr. William Prynne*, E.253[3] ([25 March] 1644), p. 1.
48 Como, 'Ideological Escalation'; Braddick, 'History, Liberty, Reformation'; Mendle, 'De Facto Freedom'.
49 [William Prynne], *Romes master-peece*, E.249[32] ([8 August] 1643), pp. 20–4; *The English pope*, E.56[13] ([1 July] 1643), p. 21.
50 *CJ*, iii, p. 98.
51 *Romes master-peece*, p. 32; *The English pope*, p. 7; *A declaration of the Commons*, E.61[23] (25 July 1643), p. 18.

52 Andy Wood, 'The Queen is "a Goggyll Eyed Hoore"': Gender and Seditious Speech in Early Modern England', in Nicholas Tyacke (ed.), *The English Revolution c.1590–1720: Politics, Religion and Communities* (Manchester, 2007), pp. 81–94. See also Samuel Fullerton, 'Fatal Adulteries: Sexual Politics in the English Revolution', *JBS* 60:4 (2021), 793–821, at 819–20.

53 William Prynne, *The soveraigne power of parliaments*, Wing P3962 (1643), pt ii, pp. 33, 87.

54 Ibid., pt iii, p. 132. See also Kevin Killeen, *The Political Bible in Early Modern England* (Cambridge, 2017), p. 165.

55 Prynne, *Soveraigne power*, pt v, pp. 3, 100.

56 Ibid., pt v, pp. 58–9, 74.

57 Ibid., pt v, pp. 110–11, 202.

58 Braddick, *Fury*, pp. 311–12.

59 [John Taylor], *Some small and simple reasons*, E.64[14] (Oxford, [10 August] 1643), pp. 3, 5. See also [John Taylor], *A . . . new nocturnall*, E.65[1] (Oxford, [11 August] 1643), p. 16; Robert Wilcher, *The Writing of Royalism, 1628–1660* (Cambridge, 2001), p. 154.

60 *Aulicus*, E.71[9] (7 October 1643), p. 560. See also ibid., E.69[18] (23 September 1643), p. 519; ibid., E.72[1] (14 October 1643), p. 576.

61 Jo[hn] Ta[ylor], *The generall complaint*, E.300[15] (Oxford, [10 September] 1645), pp. 4–5. See also Jason Peacey, 'The Struggle for *Mercurius Britanicus*: Factional Politics and the Parliamentarian Press, 1643–46', *HLQ* 68:3 (2005), 517–43.

62 [*Mercurius*] *Britanicus*, E.67[8] (5–12 September 1643), p. 18; ibid., E.67[26] (12–19 September 1643), pp. 26, 28. The underscores, which indicate blank spaces in the printed letter, are my insertion.

63 Ibid., E.70[9] (3–10 Octo0ber 1643), p. 54; ibid., E.71[10] (10–17 October 1643), p. 57.

64 Ibid., E.77[19] (23–30 November 1643), p. 106; ibid., E.75[14] (2–9 November 1643), p. 85.

65 Ibid., E.68[5] (19–26 September 1643), p. 34.

66 Ibid., E.79[2] (14–21 December 1643), p. 131. See also ibid., E.79[20] (21–8 December 1643), p. 140; Joyce Macadam, '*Mercurius Britanicus* on Charles I: An Exercise in Civil War Journalism and High Politics, August 1643 to May 1646', *HR* 84:225 (2011), 470–92, at 475.

67 Braddick, *Fury*, pp. 320–2.

68 [John White], *The first century*, E.76[21] ([22 November] 1643), sigs A2v, A4r, p. 1. See also Samuel Fullerton, 'Licensing Libel in Seventeenth-Century England: John White's *First Century of Scandalous, Malignant Priests* in Context/s', *HR* 96:273 (2023), 331–52.

69 Thomas Fuller, *The church-history of Britain*, Wing F2417 (1656), bk xvii, p. 208.

70 [Peter Heylyn], *Lord have mercie upon us*, E.75[5] (Oxford, [7 November] 1643), pp. 14, 44; *Aulicus*, E.78[16] (2 December 1643), p. 692.

71 H. G. Tibbutt (ed.), *The Letter Books of Sir Samuel Luke* (London, 1963), pp. 23 (quoted), 57–8, 97, 239–40, 254, 259 (quoted), 268, 322, 330. For

royalist distribution, see HEHL, HA 9681; BL, Add. MS 18980, fol. 148r; *CSPD 1641–3*, p. 503.

72 NLS, MS Wodrow Fol.XXV, fol. 39r; Vernon F. Snow, 'An Inventory of the Lord General's Library, 1646', *The Library* 5:21 (1966), 115–23, at 121.
73 MS Top. Oxon. C. 378, p. 384, adapting Williams, *Discovery of mysteries*, p. 38. Pym was not mentioned in Williams's pamphlet.
74 BL, Add. MS 35297, fol. 54r; NRO, C/S 3/33 (Joseph Barnes, 10 September 1643).
75 *Aulicus*, E.79[1] (9 December 1643), p. 703. The biblical King Herod was alleged to have died from venereal disease.
76 [John Booker], *Mercurius coelicus*, E.30[8] ([25 January] 1644), title-page; George Wharton, *Mercurius coelicus-mastix*, E.35[13] (Oxford, [4 March] 1644), p. 12. Booker's original target was [George Wharton], *A new almanack*, E.1181[4] (Oxford, 1644).
77 E.g., *Mercurius vapulans*, Wing M1775 (4 March 1644), p. 3; [John Booker], *A rope for a parret*, E.253[5] (6 March 1644), p. 5; [John Taylor], *No mercurius aulicus*, E.54[12] (Oxford, [10 July] 1644); John Booker, *No mercurius aquaticus*, E.2[22] (19 July 1644); Taylor, *John Taylor being yet unhanged*; [John Booker], *A rope treble-twisted*, E.10[14] (28 September 1644). Taylor had attacked Booker in *Mercurius Aquaticus*, E.29[11] (Oxford, [18 January] 1644).
78 *Aulicus*, E.80[8] (23 December 1643), pp. 719–20. See also Mark R. Blackwell, 'Bestial Metaphors: John Berkenhead and Satiric Royalist Propaganda of the 1640s and 1650s', *Modern Language Studies* 29:1 (1999), 105–130, at 108–12.
79 *Britanicus*, E.80[9] (28 December 1643–4 January 1644), p. 146. See also *The spie*, E.33[27] (13–20 February 1644), p. 28.
80 *Aulicus*, E.33[20] (3 February 1644), p. 807.
81 *Perfect occurrences*, E.262[44] (8–15 August 1645), sig. R2v.
82 But see Jerome de Groot, *Royalist Identities* (Basingstoke, 2004), pp. 49–53; Milton, *Laudian and Royalist Polemic*, p. 142n74. For evidence of the new system at work, see Bod., MS Add. C. 209.
83 Taylor, *Crop-eare curried*, pp. 4, 19–23, 32–3.
84 *Aulicus*, E.32[17] (27 January 1644), p. 792; ibid., E.35[27] (17 February 1644), pp. 833–4; ibid., E.34[12] (10 February 1644), p. 822.
85 BL, Add. MS 18981, fol. 74r.
86 *The spie*, E.30[20] (23–30 January 1644), pp. 2, 8; ibid., E.43[13] (11–19 April 1644), p. 92; ibid., E.47[24] (8–15 May 1644), p. 121.
87 *Mercurius anti-aulicus*, E.31[22] ([8 February] 1644), p. 10. See also *Perfect occurrences*, E.254[22] (16–23 August 1644), sig. B3v; *The London post*, E.8[5] (3 September 1644), p. 3; Peacey, '"Hot and Eager in Courtship"'.
88 *Britanicus*, E.81[20] (4–11 January 1644), p. 154; ibid., E.35[28] (26 February–6 March 1644), p. 194; ibid., E.32[18] (5–12 February 1644), pp. 171–2.
89 Ibid., E.75[29] (16–23 November 1643), p. 98; ibid., E.34[13] (19–26 February 1644), pp. 186–7; *Ruperts sumpter, and private cabinet rifled*, E.2[24] ([20 July] 1644).
90 BL, Sloane MS 1457, p. 208; Stoyle, *Black Legend*, p. 133.

91 [Francis Quarles], *The loyall convert*, E.40[35] ([9 April] 1644), p. 19.
92 Como, *RP*, p. 257.
93 *Aulicus*, E.3[19] (13 July 1644), pp. 1078–9; ibid., E.9[5] (24 August 1644), p. 1134.
94 *Sampsons foxes*, E.52[6] (Oxford, [22 June] 1644), p. 5.
95 [Daniel Featley], *Sacra nemesis, the Levites scourge*, E.3[24] ([14 August] 1644), p. 60.
96 BL, Add. MS 5829, fol. 44r.
97 WACML, MS.1972.002 (unpaginated); HEHL, HAR 3(5). See also Lloyd Bowen, 'Royalism, Print, and the Clergy in Britain, 1639–1640 and 1642', *HJ* 56:2 (2013), 297–319.
98 Edward Symmons, *A militarie sermon*, E.53[19] ([5 July] 1644), p. 15.
99 John Cleveland, *The character of a London diurnall*, E.268[6] ([February] 1645), p. 5. See also Como, *RP*, p. 275.
100 *Aulicus*, E.12[18] (4 September 1644), pp. 1158–9; Booker, *A rope treble-twisted*, p. 3.
101 *A nest of perfidious vipers*, E.9[9] (21 September 1644), pp. 4–6.
102 *The souldiers language*, E.10[10] ([26 September] 1644), sig. B4v. See also *A new mercury*, E.8[17] ([9 September] 1644), sig. A4r; *The cavaliers Bible*, E.4[24] ([7 August] 1644), sigs A4r–v. This latter tract was an expanded edition of *XXXIII religions, sects, societies, and factions*, E.35[26] ([6 March] 1644).
103 *Britanicus*, E.4[13] (26 July–5 August 1644), p. 359. See also ibid., E.16[4] (28 October–4 November 1644), p. 441.
104 Ibid., E.22[19] (23–30 December 1644), p. 498.
105 Ibid., E.35[28] (26 February–6 March 1644), p. 191; ibid., E.276[19] (31 March–7 April 1645), p. 706.
106 NRO, C/S 3/34 (Miles Cushion, 10 December 1644).
107 *Englands monarch*, Wing E2997 (1644), sig. B4v; *A survey of monarchie*, E.4[8] (2 August 1644), p. 12.
108 Braddick, *Fury*, pp. 359–60.
109 See for example *A discovery of the notorious proceedings of William Laud*, E.172[37] (1641), sig. A3v; *A true description*, E.168[9] (1641), p. 4; *The cavaliers Bible*, sig. A4r.
110 Thomas May, *The history of the Parliament of England*, Wing M1410 (1647), bk i, p. 28; William Prynne, *A breviate of the life of William Laud*, Wing P3904 (1644), pp. 29–30. See also William Prynne, *Canterburies doome*, Wing P3917 (1646).
111 Christopher Love, *Englands distemper*, E.274[15] ([21 March] 1645), p. 16.
112 *A letter to a friend*, Wing C7A (1645), p. 14; John Taylor, *Rebells anathematized, and anatomized*, E.285[13] (Oxford, [25 May] 1645), pp. 3–4; *The dangers of new discipline*, Wing D199B (Oxford, 1645), pp. 20–1.
113 *Newes from Smith the Oxford jaylor*, E.27[13] ([5 February] 1645), pp. 4–5; *A character of the new Oxford libeller*, E.269[7] ([11 February] 1645), pp. 4–5; *Britanicus*, E.269[6] (3–10 February 1645), p. 547; ibid., E.270[15] (17–24 February 1645), pp. 568–9.

114 WACML, MS.1972.002 (unpaginated).
115 *Certain considerable and most materiall cases of conscience*, E.270[7] (Oxford, [20 February] 1645), pp. 2–3.
116 'A satire in verse on King James I and King Charles I', E.276[2] ([1 April 1645]).
117 LMA, MJ/SR/967/84; *Moderate intelligencer*, E.278[14] (10–17 April 1645), p. 53; Malcolm Gaskill, *Witchfinders: A Seventeenth-Century English Tragedy* (London, 2005).
118 Mark Stoyle, 'The Road to Farndon Field: Explaining the Massacre of the Royalist Women at Naseby', *EHR* 123:503 (2008), 895–923. On nose-slitting and the 'whore's mark', see Valentin Groebner, 'Losing Face, Saving Face: Noses and Honour in the Late Medieval Town', trans. Pamela Selwyn, *History Workshop Journal* 40 (1995), 1–15.
119 For recent work on the *Cabinet*, see Laura Lunger Knoppers, *Politicizing Domesticity from Henrietta Maria to Milton's Eve* (Cambridge, 2011), ch. 2; Derek Hirst, 'Reading the Royal Romance: Or, Intimacy in a King's Cabinet', *Seventeenth Century* 18:2 (2003), 211–29.
120 TNA, SP 28/139, pt 16.
121 *The Kings cabinet opened*, E.292[27] ([14 July] 1645), sig. A3r, p. 43.
122 Ibid., pp. 42–4. I have not discovered any parliamentary investigations into Anne's sexual history during the early-to-mid 1640s. The Venetian ambassador claimed in May 1641 that the parliament-men had searched Jermyn's rooms – possibly for material related to what the ambassador dubbed his 'too great an intimacy with the queen' – but I have similarly been unable to verify this claim: Allen B. Hinds (ed.), *Calendar of State Papers Relating to English Affairs in the Archives of Venice, 1640–1642* (London, 1924), pp. 149–50. On Cochrane in Denmark in 1644, see Steve Murdoch, *Britain, Denmark-Norway and the House of Stuart, 1603–1660: A Diplomatic and Military Analysis* (East Linton, 2000), pp. 125–8.
123 *A key to the Kings cabinet*, E.297[10] (Oxford, [21 August] 1645), p. 3; *Mercurius anti-britannicus*, E.296[9] (Oxford, [11 August] 1645), p. 15; *A satyr, occasioned by...The King's cabanet opened*, E.296[1] (Oxford, [8 August] 1645), 4.
124 WACML, DA400 C47 1645a; HRC, Ah C380 645k; HEHL, RB 54008.
125 MS Top. Oxon. C. 378, p. 234; Bod., MS Bodley 878, fol. 31r; LMA, MJ/SR/994/36. Charles reacted by refusing to 'blushe for any of those Papers': BL, Add. MS 78264, fol. 86r.
126 John Taylor, *A most learned and eloquent speech*, E.298[3] (Oxford[?], [25 August] 1645), p. 5; *Chartae scriptae*, E.309[19] (Oxford, [17 November] 1645), p. 5.
127 *The malignants lamentation*, E.298[8] ([25 August] 1645), p. 11.
128 John Rylands Library, University of Manchester, MS GB 133 NP/77/15; *Mercurius academicus*, E.328[6] (Oxford, 16–21 March 1646), p. 133.

129 Isle of Wight Record Office, MS OG/AA/31, p. 98; William White, *The Lord's Battle: Preaching, Print, and Royalism during the English Revolution* (Manchester, 2023), p. 59; *Stuart Royal Proclamations*, ed. James F. Larkin (2 vols, Oxford, 1983), ii, pp. 1071–2. See also Mark Stoyle, '"Give Mee a Souldier's Coat": Female Cross-Dressing During the English Civil War', *History* 103:354 (2018), 5–26, at 18–20.

130 TNA, ASSI 45/1/5/14.

# 3

# Toleration and its discontents, 1646–48

Oxford's surrender in June 1646 scattered English royalists into hiding across Europe. Charles himself fled northward in April and surrendered to the Scots, hoping for gentler treatment there than he expected from his English enemies. Instead, the Covenanters detained him and promptly notified their allies in Westminster, sparking a diplomatic imbroglio that further exacerbated ideological frictions already swirling within the Anglo-Scottish alliance. From there, as war gave way to uneasy peace, recurrent debates between parliamentary 'Independents' and their radical allies on the one hand, and parliamentary 'Presbyterians' and the Scots on the other, over the impending renovation of England's national church – and especially over the issue of religious toleration – escalated into a polemical slugfest that surpassed even the libellous press campaigns of the early 1640s in vitriol.[1] In late 1647, moreover, Charles's royalists rejoined the fight to castigate Independents, Presbyterians and parliamentary radicals alike as puritan monsters equally complicit in the kingdom's destruction. In this hyperconfessional milieu, sexual politics proved especially fecund, as partisan writers reinvigorated the post-Reformation association between spiritual and bodily corruption to argue that any who strayed from true religion – no matter their political affiliation – were bound to abandon sexual morality as well.[2]

As this chapter recounts, the onset of uneasy peace in 1646 paradoxically inspired an escalation in printed sex-talk that focused largely on the sexual consequences of religious heterodoxy. That process began during the early 1640s, as parliamentarian religious culture buckled under the stresses of impending ecclesiological reformation, but it commenced in earnest only once the military conflict started to subside. From that moment until the renewal of war in 1648, the post-Reformation took centre stage in English sexual politics. While contemporaries did not lose sight of the partisan identities constructed and subsequently reified by the press campaigns of 1642–46, the corrosion of parliamentarian unity and royalists' growing certainty that puritanism lay at the heart of the war together ensured that the sexual satire of the interwar period adhered more closely to the traditional polarities of anti-puritanism and anti-popery. In the process, those old alignments took on new configurations, as Presbyterian parliamentarians adopted longstanding anti-puritan tropes for use against their one-time Independent allies, who responded in turn with a repurposed anti-popish lexicon of their own.

Several of the storylines examined in this chapter have drawn important scholarly commentary, including work by Ann Hughes on Thomas Edwards, Nigel Smith on the language of Richard Overton's Marpriest tracts, and Jason McElligott on the royalist newsbooks.[3] No one, however, has yet attempted to package them into a single narrative, presumably because they appear to be such disparate phenomena. Yet as we will see, when viewed through the lens of post-Reformation sexual politics, the experiences of Presbyterian heresiographers, parliamentarian radicals and royalist scribblers take on a coherence that has largely evaded scholarly notice to date. In short, penmen writing across the partisan spectrum between 1646 and 1648 took religious error to be the chief source of England's ongoing discontent. Their collective choice to illustrate its evils by way of graphic sex-talk illustrates the power that sexual politics had come to exercise in the kingdom's print marketplace, even among its most ostensibly sober-minded contributors.

Alongside the renewed significance of post-Reformation prejudices, the interwar period witnessed other important developments in sexual polemic. Personal satire grew especially popular as the dissolution of the covenanted Anglo-Scottish alliance into bands of feuding ideologues led polemicists to privilege individual slanders over the broad-based stereotyping that had predominated during wartime. Simultaneously, doctrinal and political differences – not to mention publishers' growing appreciation for the selling power of graphic sex-talk – prompted its expansion into new print genres. Whereas Presbyterian writers published lengthy heresiographies linking contemporary heterodoxy with its ancient heretical antecedents, parliamentary Independents appropriated the railing style of Martin Marprelate to attack their Presbyterian enemies in bawdy cheap print that rehashed many of the anti-popish arguments of earlier godly activists. Charles's royalists, for their part, relied mostly on serial newsbooks to build collaborative libellous profiles of the parliamentarian leadership. In this sense, it can be argued that the interwar years also inaugurated a new politics of form in English sexual polemic, as partisan writers developed distinctive genres to fit their unique rhetorical needs.

In every case, the resulting polemic was far more personal and explicit than previous iterations of civil war pamphleteering: a consequence, in part, of contemporaries' war-weariness and frustration with those (like Charles) who repeatedly obstructed the road to peace. It was also more theoretically sophisticated. Indeed, by the time that the royalist press reemerged with its own revitalised catalogue of anti-puritan sexual insult late in 1647, sex-talk had become a tool for explaining, rather than merely describing, the period's most endemic controversies: in short, full-blown porno-politics.

### 'A wide door to all libertinism': sexual politics and the toleration debate, 1643–45

The short-term roots of the diplomatic collapse precipitated by Charles's 1646 surrender lay half a decade in the past, when the parliamentary coalition first fractured over England's ecclesiological future. Two basic positions, both inherited from earlier controversies within London's puritan underground, arose during those opening moments of intra-parliamentarian agitation.[4] One favoured the small, independent congregational networks that prevailed in New England and Amsterdam; the other championed a national system of Presbyterian oversight like those established in Scotland and Geneva. From this fissure would emerge the defining conflict of interwar parliamentarian politics: how to mediate a new ecclesiological settlement for the national church that would satisfy both moderate Independent congregationalists and British Presbyterians without mandating its total dissolution – although many radicals saw this, too, as an acceptable outcome.

Divines from both camps convened in November 1641 to negotiate a ceasefire. In the ensuing agreement, later known as the 'Aldermanbury accord', both nascent factions agreed to avoid publicly airing their differences in the interest of preserving a united front against Laudian episcopacy. Most godly leaders subsequently did their best to suppress intra-puritan bickering in print.[5] At first they were generally successful, aided in June 1643 by the creation of the Westminster Assembly of Divines, which served as a moderated forum for such debates; but at the end of that year, as Elliot Vernon and David Como have shown, the concord began to break down.[6] Its impending dissolution was confirmed in January 1644, when, in flagrant violation of the ceasefire, five ministers published *An apologeticall narration* laying out a hypothetical congregationalist settlement intended to find 'a middle way' between separatist 'Brownisme [and] . . . authoritative Presbyteriall Government'.[7]

Even before the *Narration*'s appearance, however, parliamentarians had sparred over crucial aspects of the impending reformation. The most inflammatory of those issues was religious toleration, or 'liberty of conscience': the question, in other words, of how the new national church would treat heterodox beliefs. Among parliamentarians, opinions ranged from Presbyterians who advocated the total suppression of dissent to radicals like the New Englander Roger Williams, who indicted any attempt to 'force the conscience of all to one Worship' as 'spirituall rape'.[8] Much was at stake on both sides of the argument: Independents feared that intolerance was a prelude to religious persecution, while Presbyterians worried that unregulated worship would usher in political and moral anarchy.

Williams's language showcased how deeply the toleration issue was embedded in the sexual politics of Christian apologetics. As John Marshall has demonstrated, exegetical authorities since Augustine had described religious heresy as adulterous, debauched and sodomitical while literally comparing its spread to an infectious venereal disease. Scriptural warnings like that offered in 2 Timothy 3:6, which condemned heterodox confessors who 'creep into houses, and lead captive silly women ... away with divers lusts', added seduction to this list of evils while implicating women in particular as both gullible victims and malicious agents of heretical recruitment. The lurid histories of Anabaptist Munster and the Family of Love only strengthened the connection between lust and religious deviance for post-Reformation polemicists. Taken in conjunction with heightened patriarchal fears about the social and moral dangers posed by (and to) unsupervised women, it made for a persuasive argument indeed.

Throughout the mid-1640s, both Presbyterians and mainstream congregationalist Independents employed that tradition to denigrate one another as heterodox seducers, tyrants and deviants while levelling similar critiques at the separatist radicals who populated the parliamentarian coalition's outer fringe.[9] Although literal chastity was not always at issue in these debates, the indelible linkage between spiritual and sexual corruption ensured that even the mildest deviation from orthodoxy could be portrayed in terms of promiscuity, adultery, or worse, depending on the seriousness of the breach. In this way, between 1644 and 1647, sex became a crucial context through which claims about religious toleration, and therefore the future of the English church, could be mediated.

One keyword for anti-tolerationist writers was 'libertinism': a catch-all descriptor for wholesale moral disorder that, in early seventeenth-century England, had become especially associated with the hedonistic freedom from God's moral law that Protestant antinomians purportedly claimed as the natural inheritance of divine election.[10] As evidenced by one 1611 dictionary that defined 'libertinage' to mean 'epicurisme, sensualitie, licentiousnesse, [and] dissolutenesse', it was also synonymous with sexual anarchy. Consequently, it was available during the 1640s for anyone wishing to highlight the spiritual and sexual dangers posed by Protestant heterodoxy and those who tolerated it.[11]

Parliamentary Independents recognised that their support for congregational autonomy – and, therefore, for some degree of ecclesiological diversity – exposed them to such accusations. Congregationalist writers therefore expended considerable energy refuting allegations of libertine beliefs and behaviours: the *Narration*, for example, disavowed all 'sin in manners and conversation . . . committed against the light of nature, or . . . Christianity'.[12] But their detractors remained unconvinced. In July 1643, the predominantly Presbyterian Westminster Assembly petitioned parliament for a day of public fasting to repent for the kingdom's sins, including both 'corrupt Doctrines . . . which open a wide doore to all Libertinisme' and 'Fornication, Adultery and Incest, which doe greatly abound, especially of late'.[13] Although this petition drew no explicit link between tolerationist ideology and sexual crime, its authors presumably saw them as related.

Anti-tolerationist critics did not wait long for evidence of a connection. That August brought the publication of John Milton's *The doctrine and discipline of divorce*. This controversial tract argued that marital separation with the possibility of remarriage – legally proscribed by contemporary jurists in all but the rarest instances – ought to be extended to encompass differences in 'tempers, thoughts, and constitutions' as well as in the case of carnal sins. Indeed, Milton suggested that expanding the divorce laws might in fact reduce extramarital sex, since marital incompatibility 'drives many to transgresse the conjugall bed, while the soule wanders after that satisfaction which it had hope to find at home'. More alarmingly, Milton's tract defended separations stemming from religious disagreements between 'beleever[s]' and 'idolatrous heretick[s]'.[14] This argument horrified both royalists and many godly moderates, who argued that if disingenuous lechers could remarry at will on the nebulous grounds of personal conscience, nothing was to stop them from partner-swapping *ad nauseam* to satiate their innate concupiscence.

In particular, Milton's tract inflamed Presbyterian parliamentarians, who feared that their Independent allies were making a play to hijack the impending ecclesiological reformation by luring gullible believers with promises of licensed promiscuity. Their counter-manoeuvre came with the signing of the Solemn League and Covenant in September 1643, which united parliamentary Presbyterians and Scottish Covenanters in a mission to impose a full-scale Presbyterian settlement on England. They were opposed in turn by an uneasy Independent alliance of domestic congregationalists, New England apologists and radical Protestants. By the time that the *Apologeticall narration* appeared in print the following January (followed, in February, by an expanded edition of Milton's *Doctrine and discipline of divorce*), London's bookshops had become ground zero in a public battle over the future of the English church.[15]

On 13 July 1644 – eleven days after Marston Moor – the London minister Thomas Edwards published a 300-page rebuttal of the *Apologeticall narration*. His book, entitled *Antapologia*, combined the learned posture of classical Christian apologetics with a medley of controversial polemical techniques previously reserved for cheap pamphlets. In so doing, Edwards inaugurated a new genre of mid-century print culture, the 'heresiography', which set out to anatomise the radical sects that had purportedly sprung up in England since the outbreak of civil war. Following the ancient connection between lust and religious license, Edwards's text repeatedly linked Independent heterodoxy, and especially arguments for liberty of conscience, with promiscuity. In this respect, *Antapologia* and the heresiographies that followed it also marked a turning-point in mid-century sexual politics, as godly parliamentarians directed the anti-puritan rhetoric beloved by royalist apologists inward for the first time since the outbreak of war.[16]

Edwards's desire to maintain (however fictitiously) the 1641 Aldermanbury accord prevented him from censuring his Independent colleagues too boldly. For this reason, *Antapologia* did not name many names. But neither did Edwards hesitate to enumerate, in brief but suggestive terms, the sexual dangers posed by liberty of conscience. Echoing 2 Timothy 3:6, *Antapologia* related how tolerationist Independents had 'seduced' England's 'common people' (especially the 'female sex') to spiritual ruin. Edwards found the alluring power of antinomian doctrine to license all forms of lust particularly alarming. 'What if men practice Polygamie', he asked (presumably thinking of Anabaptist Munster)? More dangerous still was the possibility that a tolerationist victory might allow the 'Independent Churches' to 'breed and bring forth the Monsters of Anabaptisme, Antinomianisme, Familisme', as well as their attendant doctrines of sexual liberty.[17] Edwards thus associated severe sexual consequences, both mundane and cosmic, with the campaign for liberty of conscience. In the process, he embraced a key tenet of patristic heresiographers; for, according to *Antapologia*, the success of Independent proselytising among gullible English Christians (and especially women) was predicated entirely on lust.

That said, Edwards's book devoted relatively little space to sexual politics. One reason for the omission was an absence of hard proof: Milton's divorce tracts aside, the heresiographer lacked any evidence in mid-1644 for his claims that religious toleration led to bodily corruption. However, news from New England soon provided Presbyterian writers with one valuable example. In August, partly in response to Edwards's criticisms of Bay Colony congregationalism in *Antapologia*, a New Englander named Thomas Weld published Massachusetts governor John Winthrop's account of the 1637 'antinomian controversy' in print for the first time. This was a considerable tactical error. By detailing the Bay Colony's response to the

'American Jesabel' Anne Hutchinson, Weld hoped to demonstrate how effectively the puritan colonies dealt with heterodoxy; instead, he provided anti-tolerationist writers with proof that congregationalist church government could go terribly wrong.[18] For years to follow, Presbyterians referenced Hutchinson and her associate Elizabeth Dyer (both of whom had given birth to deformed foetuses months after Hutchinson's heresy trial) as irrefutable evidence that congregationalist ecclesiology bore no fruit but monstrosity.[19] At the same time, the sad fates of Hutchinson and Dyer also illustrated another central anti-tolerationist contention: that women's innate lustfulness and spiritual weakness made them the perfect victims of, as well as weapons for, heretical proselytising.

Faced with these allegations, Independents and thoroughgoing radicals alike responded with denial. In October 1644, for example, London Baptists published a *Confession of faith* 'disclaim[ing] as notoriously untrue' the accusation that they practiced 'acts unseemly . . . not to be named amongst Christians'. Hutchinson's fate aside, it helped that relatively few certifiable cases of sectarian concupiscence had surfaced in public view by early 1645; to that end, one February tract rebutted hostile descriptions of the Anabaptists as an 'impure and carnall sect' by noting that their critics had not yet produced 'any one instance of any one act of uncleannesse of any one Anabaptist in all England'. (In private, some Independents protested more aggressively: one wrote to Prynne, a noted Presbyterian, denouncing his anti-tolerationist screeds for 'yoake[ing] the spouse of Christ & the whore of Rome together in plotte & confederacie against kinge and kingdom'.)[20] But hostile gossip proliferated nonetheless. In March 1645, the Presbyterian Sir Samuel Luke penned a letter describing the garrison town of Newport Pagnell, which he feared might go the way of 'Sodom and Gomorrah, for here women can be delivered of children without knowing men (if they belie not themselves) and men and women can take one another's words and lie together and insist it not to be adultery'. Whether or not his words accurately reflected affairs on the ground in Oxfordshire, Luke – a voracious consumer of royalist print – had clearly embraced the anti-tolerationist conflation between sectarianism and sexual corruption.[21]

Even royalist divines chimed in. In February 1645, Daniel Featley published a lengthy history of European Anabaptism entitled *The dippers dipt*. Behind a provocative frontispiece featuring maids seductively immersed in a river, Featley tabulated the full range of 'Heretiques in the latter Ages' whose doctrine stemmed from that of the original Reformation radicals. The book attributed several familiar doctrines to the sect, including wife-swapping, polygamy and other 'adulterous and incestuous copulations'. In this, according to Featley, they and their radical descendants (which included the Adamites of 1641) outshone even the papists. The book's closing pages summarised sectarian sexuality in damning terms:

> All their often washing will neither cleanse their conscience from the guilt, nor their reputation from the staine of carnall impurity. For though they tolerate not Stewes [i.e. brothels] as the Pope doth, yet they allow of plurality of wives, and most uncleane practices under the name of spirituall marriages; nay some of them have not blushed to affirme that none of their Sect can commit adultery: because adulterium, according to the Etymologie adalterum, is solly committed with another mans wife; and defiling anothers body: but all that are of their society are so knit one to the other, that they are all one body, as well as one spirit. They had no sooner instild this doctrine into the weaker Sex, but two maids at Sancto-gall, immediately after their second Baptisme, made ship-wrack of their virginity; and a third dashing at the same rock, and being called in question by the Magistrate for her incontinency, professed that shee out of her pure conscience did it; that is, playd the Whore. For the Ring-leaders of our Sect told me, said she, that it was the will of the heavenly Father, that I should deny none the debt of Spirituall matrimony.[22]

Between these descriptions of gullible women seduced into unchastity and the alluring female bodies that bedecked the book's frontispiece, it is difficult to imagine a better encapsulation of anti-tolerationist sexual politics.

To be sure, Featley admitted that most of the 'lascivious' errors professed by the Munster sectaries, including 'the plurality of wives', were 'not . . . generally owned by our Anabaptists' in England. Even so, the danger was imminent: if 'we suffer the egges of the cockatrice to remain amongst us', he warned, 'when they be hatched there will break out of them most venemous serpents'. Ultimately, Featley conceded that he would 'touch no more upon this Pitch, lest I defile my hands, and the Readers eyes therewith', but this performative modesty was undermined by the lengthy descriptions that preceded it. Readers of his oft-reprinted book would be hard-pressed to ignore both its careful conflation between radical theology and sexual error and the lurid imagery that Featley employed to make his case.[23] In this sense, just as they harnessed sexual politics to denounce Protestant sectarians for succumbing to 'the same foule birdlime of impure lust' that assailed the 'Papists', anti-tolerationist writers propelled their own graphic brand of (potentially) lust-inducing language into print.[24]

*The dippers dipt* was only one of many screeds that erupted from anti-tolerationist pens during the spring of 1645. This press offensive accompanied another unfolding storyline: parliament's impending military reforms, which soon threatened to cede the political initiative to the predominantly Independent New Model Army. Inspired by this promising development, Richard Overton – the Baptist operator of a secret London press that had dogged the Caroline authorities in 1640/41 – began producing a flurry of

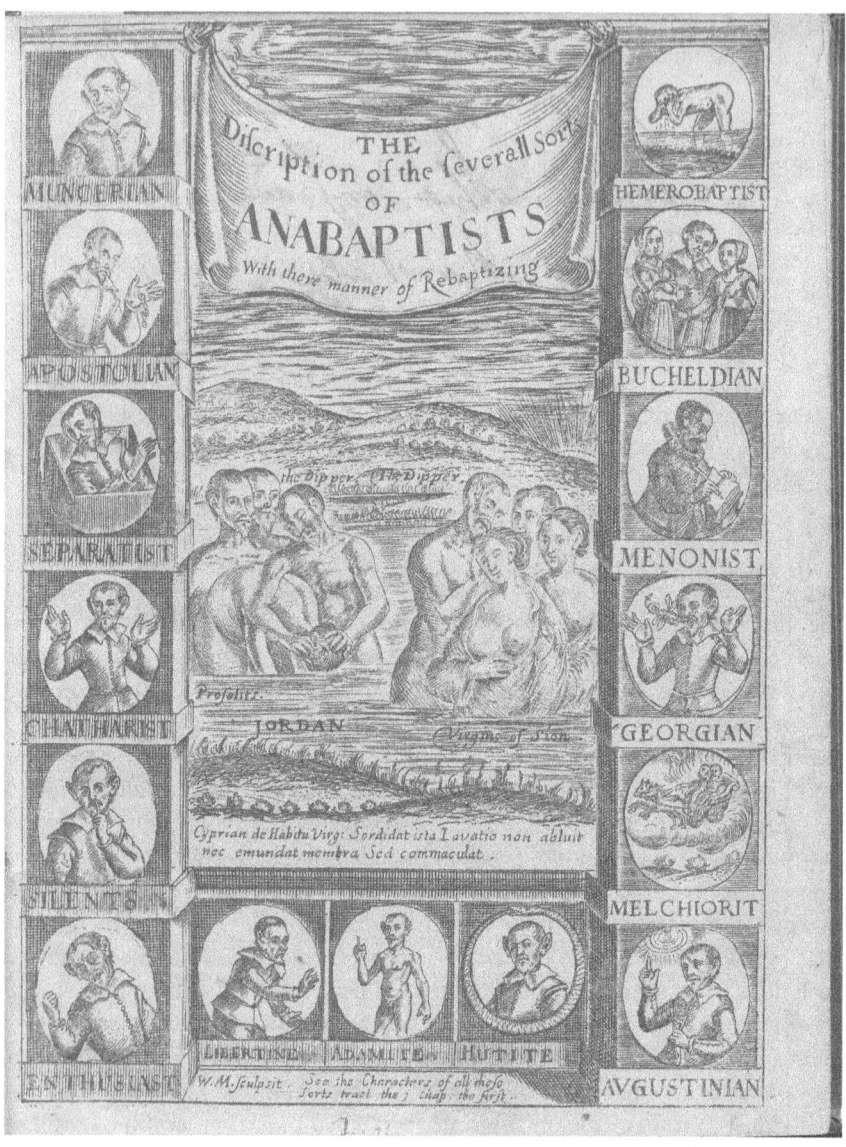

Figure 3.1 Daniel Featley, *The dippers dipt* (1645)

aggressively anti-legalist pamphlets against parliamentary Presbyterianism. The resulting polemical campaign, which hijacked the sixteenth-century persona of Martin Marprelate to condemn the Scottish-Presbyterian alliance as an imminent threat to English liberties outranked only by Charles's royalists, soon constituted another major challenge to parliamentarian unity.²⁵ And much like Marprelate's own campaign, Overton's short, cheap and militant 'Marpriest tracts' employed a distinctive style of bawdy anti-popish satire that laid considerable ground for later royalist and radical writers alike.²⁶

Overton's pamphlets abounded in sexual metaphors. His opening tract, *The araignement of Mr. Persecution* (April 1645), introduced the satirical characters of 'John Presbyter' and 'Simon Synod', who together represented the metaphorical offspring of the Presbyterians' 'toyle-some time of Deformation' inaugurated by the calling of the Westminster Assembly in mid-1643. As the *Araignement* detailed, the pair had recently emerged from the womb of that 'holy Convocation' to rail against that 'loose Libertine', 'this fellow LIBERTY-OF-CONSCIENCE'.²⁷ In subsequent pamphlets, while rebutting unsubstantiated charges of Independent sexual anarchy, Overton would argue that persecuting English Presbyterians were in fact the true sexual criminals; but his biting characterisation of the Presbyterian grandees as 'horn-mad' cuckolds enslaved by their 'Pretty sweet-fac'd lovelie Mopphets' aside, Overton's sexual politics ran far deeper than mundane slanders.²⁸

Consider *The nativity of Sir John Presbyter*, which appeared just weeks before Naseby. Addressed to the Westminster Assembly, the twelve-page tract – a far cry from Edwards's ponderous *Antapologia* – systematically inverted the anti-popish rhetoric that parliamentarians had previously directed against their royalist enemies to highlight instead the 'Sodomiticall, Papall, Prelatical, [and] whorish' nature of parliamentary Presbyterianism. Thus, in succinct but striking language, the *Nativity* described John Presbyter (from April's *Araignement*) as a 'womanish' and cuckolded 'Adulterer', fated to commit 'incest with his kindred' and 'have great quarrells and contentions about his whores', but 'scarcly ever' to 'marry' or 'have a child'.²⁹ Although framed by the same post-Reformation coupling of spiritual and sexual malignancy that infused Edwards's heresiography, Overton's slanders – inflected with Marprelate's trademark scurrility and the long tradition of English anti-popery – operated in an entirely different polemical register. Just as Edwards adopted (predominantly) royalist anti-puritan language for use against his congregationalist allies, in other words, Overton inverted the anti-popish register of generations of earlier English Protestants to denounce Presbyterian divines as disguised crypto-Catholic lechers.

The Marpriest tracts made particularly good use of reproductive imagery as an allegorical tool. Throughout the summer, Overton employed a hereditary metaphor that portrayed Presbyterian church government as the unnatural offspring of 'the Synodian Whore of Babylon' and Charles's 'late Lord Bishops'.³⁰ Later in the year, Overton expanded this dubious genealogy to include the 'litter of ugly Kubbs' that would result once 'the Presbyters committed incest with their old Beldam Mother High-Commission': namely, when (if) the Westminster Assembly succeeded in imposing a repressive, anti-tolerationist ecclesiastical settlement on the English church.[31] This was incest, presumably, because both Presbyterian legalism and the tyrannical prerogative courts of Charles's Laudian church sprang from the same popish roots; it was also porno-politics in a nutshell. In short, by employing sexual imagery to grotesquely reimagine the basic configuration of English church government – notably, using the strategy of allegorical ecclesiological embodiment that had historically undergirded Protestant diatribes against the Catholic Whore of Babylon – the Marpriest tracts transformed sexual politics into a means of explaining, rather than describing, the kingdom's fraught spiritual condition.

Overton's enemies did not sit still during this assault, for much like the royalist-parliamentarian clashes analysed in the last chapter, the intra-parliamentary toleration debate was a dialogic affair. Even before the *Nativity*'s appearance in July 1645, Presbyterian writers inspired by *Antapologia* set to work producing a new series of anti-sectarian heresiographies. Even more than Edwards's initial effort, these tracts detailed the moral perils of religious toleration at length, with particular emphasis on its seductive dangers for gullible women, children and fools.

These heresiographers saw heterodox doctrine as the source of all sectarian promiscuity. Antinomian beliefs were a particularly frightening bugbear because they effectively licensed sexual libertinism. The Covenanter Samuel Rutherford preached that if 'a justified person cannot sinne . . . the way of Grace is a wanton merry way', while the English divine Richard Byfield argued that the appeal of antinomian 'licentiousnesse', rather than any legitimate spiritual principles, had inspired the kingdom's 'Sensuall Separatists' to 'walke after their lusts'. Both agreed that any 'Gospel [that] maketh Adultery to be no sin to Believers' was fundamentally 'blasphemous'.[32] Again and again, the familiar post-Reformation refrain: sexual and spiritual corruption went hand in hand.

As Featley's *The dippers dipt* had amply demonstrated, anti-tolerationist writers could marshal a long list of historical heretics as evidence. Ephraim Pagitt's eponymous *Heresiography*, published in May, catalogued more than 100 sects both extant and extinct to illustrate the association between a misinterpreted 'sentence of Gods predestination' and 'most uncleane living'. Among his subjects were the Munster Anabaptists, who believed that 'a man should not be tyed to one wife, but to marry as many as he pleased'; the Family of Love, whose talk 'of love, and being in love, and nothing but love' masked 'shamefull villanies'; and the Adamites, known for 'pray[ing] naked' and 'promiscuous marriages' alike. English separatist congregations abroad received especially thorough coverage. For instance, Pagitt recounted how one Amsterdam Brownist attempted to 'cleare the uncleannesse of a man found a bed with another mans wife' by distinguishing 'betweene lying with a woman and in a woman'.[33] Such stories left no doubt that sexual desire was the chief driver of sectarian devotion.

To explain the appeal of radical doctrine, Presbyterian apologists turned to a scriptural analogy: the warning in 2 Corinthians 11:14 that Satan could disguise himself as an 'Angell of Light'. This was a well-worn early modern biblicism, long used by anti-puritans to denounce godly Protestants as devilish hypocrites. For anti-tolerationist parliamentarians, it also illustrated one way in which heterodox proselytisers succeeded in attracting converts. Bolstered by scriptural proof that the worst heretics might appear in the most pleasing of forms, Presbyterian writers described congregationalist ministers as alluring 'Seducers' who preached 'a faire and easie way to heaven' to tempt 'multitudes of simple men and women [to] dance after their Pipes'. Following 2 Timothy 3:6, they worried especially about the kingdom's 'silly women', who were believed to be especially vulnerable to such charmers. For example, William Prynne argued in July 1645 that by promising women the chance to preach, sectarians coerced them into 'Nocturnall Conventicles, without their Husbands, Parents, Ministers Privitie', where they were then enticed 'to propagate Christs Kingdome, and multiply the Godly Party'. (He did not acknowledge that, as modern scholars have noted, women may have joined the sects precisely because of the spiritual and personal autonomy they offered.)[34] In addition to linking toleration and promiscuity, then, militant Presbyterians theorised an Independent sexual conspiracy to literally engender godly radicalism throughout the kingdom.

Two weeks before the publication of Prynne's tract, a worried correspondent wrote to John Winthrop to express his fears that the 'common cause of religion' would fall 'together by the eares' without a shared royalist enemy.[35] As the war ground to a halt, he was proven right. Between August and December 1645, while Fairfax and the New Model Army mopped up the remaining royalist garrisons, the toleration debate continued to rage in print despite parliamentary efforts to reach a rapprochement. By the year's end, all three engaged parties – Presbyterians, Independents and sectarian radicals – had enlisted some variety of the post-Reformation equivalency between lust and heterodoxy to make their respective cases. In the process, as we have already seen, they injected increasingly lurid depictions of heterodox sexuality into England's print marketplace. The puritan campaign against 'lascivious . . . books and pamphlets' presented before parliament in December 1640 seemed a distant dream indeed.[36]

## 'A painted piece of lasciviousness and profaneness': *Gangraena* and its critics

The opening weeks of 1646 brought little immediate change in the kingdom's political climate. Yet as the Westminster Assembly of Divines deliberated in London, and as the predominantly Independent New Model army – still garrisoned across large swathes of the countryside – contested the Assembly's Presbyterian proclivities in the provinces, intra-parliamentary tensions threatened to rise even higher. Certainly London's presses showed no signs of malaise. Instead, alarmed by the army's successes, Presbyterian apologists led by Thomas Edwards redoubled their efforts to catalogue the dangers of religious toleration. Consequently, spurred on by the incipient conflict between London Presbyterianism and godly army radicalism, post-Reformation sexual politics reached new levels of acrimony in print.

The Presbyterian offensive continued on 22 January with a new edition of Robert Baillie's catalogue of congregationalist heresy, *A dissuasive from the errours of the time*. Baillie's bulky text took up several familiar heresiological themes, including a porno-political trope reminiscent of Richard Overton's Marpriest tracts: here, parliamentary Independency was figured as 'the seed and spawn of Brownisme', first 'bred and born under the wings of no other Dame then Episcopacy'.[37] 'To leave Metaphors', Baillie also proffered literal examples of radical malfeasance, including Anne Hutchinson's 'monstrous birth' in faraway New England. Now that Hutchinson's antinomian errors had been 'transplanted to Old England' via returned ministers such as Hugh Peter, he argued, similar horrors were surely forthcoming at home. As evidence, Baillie cited Milton's divorce tracts, apparently beloved by London congregationalists: 'all of them', he wrote with horror, 'maintaine, that it is lawfull for every woman to desert her husband . . . onely because he lives without that Church whereof she is become a member'.[38] Both elements of the *Dissuasive*'s recognisably anti-puritan sexual politics – its metaphorical vision of monstrous Independent ecclesiology and its literal descriptions of sectarian immorality – would resonate in Presbyterian print throughout the year.

No one did more to advance that agenda than Thomas Edwards, whose *Antapologia* had set the standard for heresiographical apologetics just two years earlier. Since then, Edwards had only grown more horrified by the rising tide of Protestant radicalism, and he soon undertook a new project intended to showcase the moral and spiritual dangers of toleration at even greater length. Early in 1646, after more than a year of work, Edwards produced the opening volume of *Gangraena*, a massive study of sectarian error that was followed by sequel volumes in May and November.

Edwards's new project diverged from other contemporary heresiographies in several respects. First, it was obsessed with the present; while most anti-tolerationist writers fixated on ancient heresies in order to typologise more recent forms of sectarianism, *Gangraena*'s focus was contemporary English, and particularly London-based, heterodoxy. This meant that Edwards's book was thoroughly anti-puritan in the classic sense, often echoing – if unintentionally – language employed by royalist partisans earlier in the decade. Moreover, to ensure accurate coverage, Edwards relied on the anonymised reports of sympathetic witnesses. This was a controversial strategy, and Edwards was repeatedly accused of using invented, unverifiable evidence to tarnish the good names of fellow Christians. Unsurprisingly, as Ann Hughes has shown, *Gangraena* therefore played a central role in the ongoing polarisation of intra-parliamentary religious and political opinion.[39]

Like *Antapologia*, *Gangraena* was deeply concerned with the sexual politics of Protestant radicalism. Although false doctrine outranked unchastity in Edwards's hierarchy of error – 'in broaching and maintaining heresies', he argued, men 'get a name and fame by them, which they do not by . . . uncleannesse' alone – the two were indelibly linked. Among the beliefs tabulated in its inaugural February volume were the antinomian principle that 'the morall law is of no use at all to beleevers', in whom 'God did see no sin' if they 'be in the state of grace'; Milton's willingness to license divorce in instances of 'indisposition, unfitnesse or contrariety of minde'; and the familiar Munsterian tenet that ''tis lawful for one man to have two wives at once'. In a familiar porno-political idiom recently deployed by Robert Baillie, *Gangraena* warned that these beliefs and more would prosper if the 'sectaries' succeeded in 'bring[ing] forth that misshapen Bastard-monster of a Toleration', which he described as 'part fish, part flesh, and part neither of both'. Moreover, if toleration were not stifled by a 'miscarrying womb', even worse horrors lay ahead: English sectaries, he wrote, would replicate the 'unheard of' sins of 'Munster' while 'run[ning] up and down naked in the streets'.[40]

Thanks to his correspondents, Edwards could marshal verifiable examples of sectarian lechery. For instance, *Gangraena* described numerous 'young maids' who were 'tempt[ed] . . . out of their fathers houses at midnight' by sectaries for illicit adult baptisms. Edwards explained how these young women were stripped 'to the naked skin', their 'secret parts' exposed to their tempters (as depicted in the frontispiece to Featley's *Dippers dipt*); but nudity was only the beginning. *Gangraena* described one notorious sectary who drew away five women at once to be 're-baptised' before picking the one he 'best liked' and marrying her 'without her Parents consent': a violation of both doctrinal orthodoxy and patriarchal authority. Furthermore, in narrating these excesses, Edwards named the alleged perpetrators, including the future Leveller William Walwyn and the radical ministers John Goodwin and John Saltmarsh. Perhaps the most infamous of his targets was a sectarian preacher, Elizabeth Attaway, who had 'run away with another womans husband' on the Miltonian grounds that marriages with nonbelievers were inherently invalid.[41] Attaway would reappear in *Gangraena*'s later volumes, as Edwards reflected on the lustful consequences of heterodox doctrine.

*Gangraena*'s first part appeared during a period of heightening Presbyterian paranoia about the growing threat of New Model sectarianism. In this polarised atmosphere, Edwards's text had a clear purpose: to unite his fellow-travellers against the menacing alliance ostensibly coalescing between the army, the sects and parliamentary Independents.[42] As the mobilisation campaigns of 1643–45 had convincingly demonstrated, sex-talk piqued contemporary interest like few other subjects could. In the context of a brewing showdown between parliamentary Presbyterians and army Independents, Edwards's emphasis on sectarian seduction – again, a restatement of the classical post-Reformation equation between lust and spiritual license – therefore made perfect polemical sense.

For the same reason, it did not take long for Edwards's victims to respond, and several of the ensuing rebuttals zeroed in on *Gangraena*'s obsession with sex. During the spring and summer, hostile critics condemned Edwards's allegations of radical promiscuity as fanciful and lurid. John Goodwin – whose *Anti-cavalierisme* had deployed similarly alarmist language against Charles's soldiers in 1642 – described *Gangraena* as a 'painted peece of lasciviousnesse and prophanenesse'. Three months later, William Walwyn compared Edwards to Machiavelli, said to believe that 'if you observe any man to be of a publique and active spirit . . . you are to give him out, to be strongly suspected of whoredom, or drunkenesse, [or] prophanesse' to discredit them. John Saltmarsh argued that *Gangraena*'s 'immodest, ridiculous Stories and Tales' had 'exceed[ed]' even 'the Oxford Aulicusses' in outrageousness and wondered what might happen if someone should 'write by your copy, and bring forth . . . the crimes of all those of your way' to public notice. Goodwin made the same threat about unveiling 'Presbyterian mistakes in the night': 'I know who hath a story of a Presbyterian Angel', he wrote, 'which doth but waite for the opening of Mr. Edwards mouth in reproaches and slanders against his Independent Brethren the second time, to clap into it, and stop it for ever'.[43] Once more, mutual recrimination was poised to propel personal sexuality into even greater public visibility.

Edwards was up to the challenge, which seemed more urgent than ever by the spring of 1646. As Fairfax's forces spread across the countryside, Presbyterians felt the noose of Independent ascendancy tightening. Granted, they had some happy news. The Westminster Assembly was inching towards a neutered form of Presbyterian church government that most moderate parliamentarians, if not their hardcore Scottish allies, found palatable enough.[44] Similarly promising was Charles's recent surrender to the Scots, which put the king in friendly Presbyterian hands. But for some onlookers, the good tidings paled in comparison to the New Model's seemingly unstoppable power and the growing boldness of London sectarians. Confronted with these bleak facts, anti-sectarian writers continued their campaign against the seductive proselytising of tolerationist ministers.

*Gangraena*'s second volume, published in May, provided a much-needed boost. This entry, too, caused Edwards's critics to bristle at his 'excrementitious filthinesse' – and for good reason.[45] Part two of *Gangraena* recounted numerous heterodox innovations for justifying extramarital sexuality, including the doctrine that sleep, like death, rendered 'the bond of matrimony . . . null' (meaning that if 'a woman should have to do with any other man, her husband being asleep, she committeth not adultery'). It also offered more stories of lecherous Independent ministers who preyed on young maidservants as well as London sectaries who 'denied that to kill a man, [or] to commit adultery . . . was sinne'.[46] Although the veracity of these rumours was questionable, they ensured that sexual libertinism remained the overarching social danger posed by tolerationist ideology throughout Edwards's sequel.

The first volume of *Gangraena* had been criticised for indicting its targets by name, but if anything the second was more aggressive. 'They that . . . serve not our Lord Jesus Christ, but their own bellies, and their own lusts', Edwards wrote, 'shall have no opportunity to wash off that durt and filth which I have cast upon them'.[47] (The references to 'bellies' and 'lust' again demonstrate how thoroughly Edwards's oeuvre was steeped in familiar anti-puritan tropes.)[48] These individual malefactors, whom he now outed with little regard for propriety, were a primary focus of *Gangraena*'s May volume. Few escaped allegations of sexual misconduct.

One such target was Samuel Oates, an itinerant Baptist minister (and later the father of the Popish Plot figurehead Titus Oates). Oates gained considerable notoriety in March 1646, when a young woman died after he baptised her in a frigid Essex river. But it was seduction, rather than murder, for which Oates was arraigned throughout *Gangraena*. As a dipper who 'traded cheifly [sic] with young women and young maids . . . in the night' (a tactic used to evade their 'husbands and Masters'), Oates was the living embodiment of every warning related by heresiographers like Featley about lecherous male baptisers. Not for nothing, Edwards suggested, was Oates 'follow[ed]' by 'notorious Whoremongers'. Later, he would relay further evidence of Oates's impropriety from 'a godly Minister' arrived in London from 'those parts in Essex, where Oats hath beene dipping', where it 'was spoken of by many... that some young women who having beene married divers yeeres, and never were with child, now since their dipping are proved with child'. For years afterward, Oates would be haunted by Edwards's exposé: proof of *Gangraena*'s libellous impact on the puritan radicals that it catalogued.[49]

The timing of Edwards's second effort was propitious. Just as the sequel appeared in booksellers' stalls, the Westminster Assembly committed to a Presbyterian church settlement. Equally providential was Richard Overton's imprisonment by the Lords in August. During his arrest, parliamentary authorities discovered a manuscript petition condemning some reformed churches as 'spirituall whore-Houses' and 'Brothell-Houses'; had they waited a few more weeks, it may have appeared as another Marpriest tract.[50] But once again, bad news accompanied the good. Plague in the countryside and a prolonged harvest crisis spoiled some of the joy that accompanied Oxford's surrender in June.[51] In particular, the looming presence of the New Model Army – which remained in arms for reasons of national security – discomfited English and Scottish Presbyterians alike. Consequently, anti-toleration apologists felt compelled to continue their printed assault on the 'Libertinisme', 'Lust', and other 'cursed carnal practises' ostensibly licensed by liberty of conscience in order to guarantee the success of the impending Presbyterian reformation.[52]

Royalist observers also expressed trepidations about the kingdom's ecclesiological divisions. One letter-writer wondered in April if the parliament's 'endeavours of Reformation' would be corrupted by 'this wild thing called Puritanisme, [which] like a Sea-breach runneth itselfe into a thousand channels, and knoweth not where to stop'. On the Isle of Wight, Oglander speculated how parliament's 'pretended... reformation inn Religion' might impact the kingdom's 'Morall businesses'.[53] Some of his fellow loyalists were even less circumspect. In his own commonplace book, Henry Oxenden scribbled short diatribes against 'a Presbyter who could not endure the Common prayer, yet Loved a Common whoore' and 'a Puritan' who 'wilt not sweare, yet... liest with an holy sister'.[54] Although they rarely stated it in print after Oxford's surrender, Charles's defeated partisans remained worried that the puritan-parliamentarian ascendancy might produce deleterious sexual consequences.

They had good reasons for doing so. Throughout the summer, anonymous writers continued to provide anti-tolerationist critics with evidence of the post-Reformation truism about the link between spiritual and sexual liberty. Take the short September pamphlet *Little non-such*, which deployed numerous biblical and historical examples to argue that laws against 'forbidden degrees in marriage' – including incest – were 'popish' inventions that ought to be abolished. The tract was apparently genuine, and its anonymous authors even defended their thesis in a follow-up pamphlet the following year (insisting, in the process, that they were neither doctrinal Independents nor sectaries).[55] Like Milton's divorce tracts, then, *Little non-such* appeared to confirm every Presbyterian assertion about the essential lustfulness of tolerationist doctrine.

Thomas Edwards was paying attention. By December 1646, roughly six months after Oxford's surrender, restless army regiments had mutinied in nearly two dozen English counties; London's Presbyterian citizens had grown agitated over the lack of a favourable settlement with the king; and negotiations between Charles, the Scots (who still held him prisoner), and the English parliament dragged on slowly.[56] It was in this fraught context that *Gangraena*'s third volume appeared, once again freighted with post-Reformation sexual polemics.

Like his Presbyterian fellow-travellers, Edwards had grown increasingly convinced of the connection between sexual license and religious toleration throughout the fall. *Gangraena*'s third volume thus presented more anecdotes of Protestant radicals who preached 'that Adultery is no Sin' and others whose love of 'dipping of naked women' was derived not from legitimate doctrine, but because it allowed them 'to feed their wanton eyes' and 'satisfie their unchast touching, by handling young women naked'. Meanwhile, Edwards claimed, Independent writers flouted God's law in 'wicked pamphlet[s]' such as '*Little Nonsuch*', which apparently reflected the beliefs of real sectarians: 'I have the names of three Independents given me out of one Country who have married incestuously', he wrote.[57] In part three of *Gangraena*, even more than in its predecessors, lust and liberty of conscience became one.

One lengthy excerpt tabulated the 'many kinds of uncleannesses' allegedly practiced by England's 'Independents and Sectaries'. The ensuing list, which was so long that Edwards had to 'reserve' some of his evidence 'for a fourth part' of *Gangraena* (which, if it existed, was never published), included 'Incest', 'entising children to marry unequally in regard of yeers', 'rapes and forcing young maidens', 'adulteries and fornications', 'handling young women naked' (while dipping), and seducing married women to 'things unseemly', alongside 'divers other instances of their uncleannesse and filthines'. Some of these reports came from provincial correspondents, while Edwards learned of others from the sectaries' own associates. One 'Sectaries wife', for instance, showed Edwards several letters that her husband's colleagues had sent 'to other mens wives ... to tempt them from their husbands' before encouraging him to request a formal parliamentary investigation of the Anabaptists' 'uncleannesses and wickednesses'. Edwards tried, but was rebuffed; according to his contact in the Commons, 'there would come little' of any such attempt because the radicals had friends who would 'obstruct it one way or other'.[58]

Again, *Gangraena* zeroed in on specific targets. One of this volume's humblest victims was Mary Abraham, a middle-aged London separatist hired as a maidservant by a widower named Thomas Clark to look after his ailing teenage son. To Clark's horror, Abraham apparently fell in love with the boy, and when her master left one day, she took advantage of his son's 'weaknesse and want of understanding' and bribed a local schoolmaster to marry them without Clark's knowledge. The outraged father had been militating ever since 'for justice against this Separatist who claims this youth for her husband'. Edwards printed Clark's story in *Gangraena* before describing how Abraham had pulled a similar trick years earlier, when she 'intangled a young youth ... and claimed a promise of marriage at his hand'. (That imbroglio had apparently only been resolved when an Independent minister – the same man who recommended Abraham to Clark – enjoined the youth to pay her ten pounds to lay off the suit.)[59] Whether Abraham's pursuit of Clark's young son stemmed from lust or simple greed, Edwards ascribed her actions to the depraved – and pointedly anti-patriarchal – morals of London's sectarian population.

None of *Gangraena*'s targets were more unsettling than the radical Baptist preacher Elizabeth Attaway. Edwards first learned of Attaway in mid-1645, after having come off badly in an exchange with another female preacher, Katherine Chidley.[60] Already convinced of the spiritual dangers posed by such women, Edwards then discovered an even more scandalous side to Attaway's story. After speaking enthusiastically of 'Master Miltons Doctrine of Divorce', she had apparently abandoned her 'unsanctified husband' for another man – one William Jenney, also married – with whom she subsequently absconded 'beyond seas' to await the Second Coming. Jenney, too, was a sectary wedded to an 'unbeleever', so by Attaway's (and, ostensibly, Milton's) logic, both separations were perfectly justifiable.[61] For Edwards, however, the pair's brazen abandonment of their marital vows embodied sectarian sexual anarchy.

For this reason, Attaway featured in all three parts of *Gangraena*. Granted, open adultery was hardly her only problematic attribute. The third volume described Attaway's unorthodox theology at length, ranging from her belief 'that she should never dye' to the conviction that she and Jenney were meant to travel to Jerusalem and usher in a new millennium. It is difficult to say how accurately these descriptions represented Attaway's beliefs, although Edwards certainly presented them as factual. Nevertheless, in *Gangraena*, Attaway's doctrine often appeared to come second to her immorality. Jenney, Edwards stressed, had been so 'perswaded' by his lover's seductive charms that he 'beleeved all Mistris Attaway told him'.[62] Elizabeth Attaway thus embodied the other side of anti-tolerationist gender politics to the gullible women of 2 Timothy 3:6 (or, say, the maids seduced by Samuel Oates): here, in other words, was womankind as an active agent of heterodox seduction.

By December, Edwards's books were the talk of England. True, *Gangraena* was only one (or rather three) of many 1646 contributions to the toleration debate. Even so, they exercised a formative impact on intra-parliamentarian discourse. Edwards's texts were read and discussed by friends and enemies alike, ensuring that they helped to construct the partisan categories that underwrote the polarisation of parliamentarian political culture by mid-decade.[63] They were also undeniably libellous, insofar as Edwards had clearly committed to the public naming and shaming of sectarian radicals after waffling in *Antapologia*. Moreover, the Presbyterian position defined in *Gangraena* was fundamentally anti-puritan in outlook, as Edwards borrowed and inverted tropes once privileged by royalist polemicists to indict parliamentarian congregationalists as honey-tongued seducers. Above all, Edwards's much-read masterwork cemented the post-Reformation association between spiritual and sexual corruption as a fundamental tenet of parliamentarian anti-tolerationist writing. It was a connection that later royalist commentators, hoping to appeal to disaffected English Presbyterians, would find exceedingly useful.

### 'Great pains and able performances': anti-popery and obscenity in the *Parliament of ladies*

On 28 December 1646, the same day that George Thomason acquired *Gangraena*'s third volume, Thomas Seaborne wrote to Sir Robert Harley with a shocking story. According to his letter, a parliamentarian soldier had outraged his commanding officers during the recent siege of Worcester by invading the home of two local women – 'one a widdowe, the other a maide' – and 'offerring to goe to bed to them both together'. Although both escaped with their 'chastetie' intact, the tale so alarmed the New Model brass that they decreed 'it should be concealed and noe more words spoken of itt'.[64] This was a wise choice, for any readers acquainted with the heresiographers' recent attacks on army radicalism might easily have attributed the trooper's proposition to Protestant sectarianism. For Presbyterians like Harley, the story's suppression by the New Model grandees likely proved doubly troubling. If they had nearly succeeded in quashing this tale, what else might the army leadership be hiding?

Similar anxieties continued to surface in Presbyterian publications as the year turned. In January 1647, Robert Baillie published a lengthy history of European Anabaptism that implicated 'most of all the Heretiques of the [present] time' – chiefly Independency, Brownism and familism – within that older sectarian tradition. Baillie's account fixated on the sexual escapades of Munster Anabaptists like John of Leiden, whose polygamist beliefs had led him to take wives 'to the number of fifteen together', and the Dutch radical David Joris (anglicised as 'David George'), for whom 'adulteries, fornications, incests, and most unspeakable villanies were so far from being any sins . . . that he did recommend them to his most perfect scholars as acts of grace and mortification'. While Baillie, like Daniel Featley before him, conceded that the English sects were not 'yet so extremely obscene' as this, worse was yet to come. The example of 'Attaway the Mistresse of all the She-preachers', as well as the fact that 'incest is [now] . . . publickly avowed in print' (i.e. *Little non-such*) proved as much. Indeed, by 'mak[ing] it lawfull for every man once a month to marry if they were thirty of his nearest kinswomen', he claimed, *Little non-such* and 'Miltons doctrine of dismissing wives' had combined to license 'a wickednesse which David George himself did never think of'.[65]

Baillie's vituperative language forecasted a broader increase in partisan recrimination – and particularly post-Reformation sexual satire – across English print culture during the spring of 1647, due in part to Charles's transfer into parliamentarian custody in February and the Scots' subsequent departure from England. Presbyterian writers, hopeful that the Scottish retreat heralded the New Model's impending dissolution, redoubled their denunciations of sectarian libertinism in print.[66] Opposing polemicists fought back despite the most difficult of personal circumstances. Richard Overton, still imprisoned by the Lords, berated his captors' wives as 'wanton retrograde Ladies' in a vituperative February tract, while an anonymous rejoinder to *Gangraena* appropriated Edwards's libellous methodology by accusing two leading (but unnamed) City Presbyterian leaders of fathering bastards on London women.[67] The case of the Presbyterian Edward King, who disrupted the Lincolnshire county sessions with a speech conflating local 'Anabaptists, Brownists, Separatist, Antinomians and Hereticks' with 'Fornicators, Idolators, Adulterers', and 'abusers of themselves with mankinde, or with beast', appeared in print in February to confirm what most observers already knew: Charles's surrender had not brought peace to England.[68]

As usual, the furore was accompanied by a flood of less overtly polemical fare. George Thomason acquired one such tract, entitled *A parliament of ladies*, on 16 April. He probably recognised it, since it had already been printed twice during the decade: first in 1640, when it was censured by the root and branch petitioners as a lascivious book, and again in 1646, when it reappeared without provoking any public opprobrium at all.[69] While the 1647 edition bore a slightly different title, its content – loosely derived from a play by the Greek dramatist Aristophanes, transposed into a Roman setting – was essentially identical.

In the tract, a collection of Roman women responded to their husbands' plans to legalise male bigamy by convening instead to 'abrogate that Law, and [vote] instead thereof, that every woman might have two husbands'.[70] The narrator then dwelt at length on the sexual fantasies of the female protagonists before concluding with the women's humiliation at the hands of their amused husbands in the senate. The message was thus comedic but also reassuring for male readers, lampooning the women's voracious lust while relegating female political agency to the realm of the absurd. Its valence in 1646/47 was muted, but suggestive; perhaps the unknown publisher was implying that the predominantly Presbyterian House of Commons was an ineffective, emasculated assembly (a reading that would fit with both royalist and radical depictions of Presbyterian parliament-men as hen-pecked cuckolds). Yet while the pamphlet was overtly sexual and deeply misogynistic, it was not libellous. There were no identifiable contemporary analogues for its Roman characters, nor was there any attempt to connect the classical context with England's current troubles. For this reason, perhaps, it received little attention.

But the kingdom's deepening strife rendered even the most innocuous tropes ripe for appropriation. Weeks later, Thomason acquired *An exact diurnall of the parliament of ladyes*, an original satire that rendered the latent political resonances of its predecessor explicitly partisan. Set in royalist Oxford and featuring a parade of real cavaliers, the *Exact diurnall* adopted a familiar parliamentarian trope – royalist women dominating their emasculated husbands – to describe the fallout after the city's recent surrender to Fairfax, as Oxford's 'Countesses and other Ladies' presided over a court in which a bevy of royalist men were arraigned for their military failures. In general, the tract limited its sexual politics to off-handed jibes about the romantic skills of 'Prince [John] Griffins' and the parliament-women's 'Inconstancy'.[71] Nevertheless, the *Exact diurnall* demonstrated that the female legislators trope could be marshalled for biting political commentary.

Because the defeated royalists were a relatively minor concern by April 1647, the *Exact diurnall* was out of step with the general thrust of English political print at the time of its appearance. Yet when tensions between the army and the Presbyterian-dominated parliament reached a fever pitch in May, leading the New Model's civilian allies (among them, the future Levellers Richard Overton and John Lilburne) to protest against their oppressors in London, its central conceit was once again repurposed for political commentary. This time, the borrower was the Berkshire republican Henry Neville, who recognised in the Parliament of Ladies a novel opportunity to ridicule the Presbyterian ascendancy that now held sway in Westminster. In the process, Neville's pamphlets – much-discussed by modern scholars,

Figure 3.2 *An exact diurnall of the parliament of ladyes* (1647)

but rarely placed in their proper political context – reached new heights of obscenity for mid-century polemical print.[72]

In May, Thomason acquired Neville's new tract, which bore the same title (*The parliament of ladies*) as the Roman-themed original. But Neville's version differed considerably from that pamphlet, as well as from April's anti-royalist *Exact diurnall*, by reporting on an imaginary London tribunal of female grandees who judged male royalists and parliamentarians alike on their deficiencies. Beyond its new setting, Neville's tract also broke with its antecedents in another key respect: in this version, graphic sex-talk was omnipresent, couched in terms familiar from the anti-popish satires directed against royalist Oxford during the first civil war and, later, Overton's 1645 Marpriest tracts.[73] In particular, *The parliament of ladies* repurposed earlier attacks on the sex-drenched Caroline court to implicate Presbyterian leaders – and even some lukewarm Independents – as equal partners with the popish royalists in an overarching plot against English liberties. In doing so, Neville, who was not known for his piety, set aside the question of religious toleration to make a political argument about (Presbyterian) parliamentary tyranny.

Descriptions of copulation, veiled only by the loosest innuendo, appeared on every page of Neville's bitter satire. During the lady parliament's ministrations, for example, the assembly commended several Presbyterian ladies for their 'great [sexual] experience in Soldery in this Kingdome' and praised the 'large talent' (i.e. penis) of 'Lord Cambaen', which had earned him 'a favourable composition at the Lady Kents'.[74] Elsewhere, familiar figures like Prince Rupert and John Griffith were parodied for their bedroom prowess, while the ladies decried the 'contagious [venereal] infection and itching humours' that had resulted from their 'present government'. Neville's range of targets was staggering, from the radical John Saltmarsh – also one of Edwards's favourite punching-bags – who was praised for his 'great pains and able performances' among the lady legislators, to the Presbyterian divine Obadiah Sedgwick, said to believe that 'if a man had been absent from his Spouse any time', he was 'obliged ... to solace her ... as often as the strength of his body will permit'. The story ended with another shocking scene, as a woman wielding a 'Dildoe' subjugated the entire assembly to her will.[75] This image of an effeminate parliament, cowed amid active collusion with the defeated royalists by an undeniably more masculine (if still ambiguously gendered) assailant, presumably reflected Neville's growing sense that only the army's intervention could prevent the rise of a combined Presbyterian-cavalier autocracy in Westminster.[76]

The pamphlet appeared remarkably prescient in the following months. On 4 June, exasperated by Presbyterian efforts to disband Fairfax's forces without issuing backpay or indemnity from wartime crimes, soldiers kidnapped Charles from parliamentary custody and relocated him to the army's headquarters. The event stimulated a rush of publication among Independents, Presbyterians, and even royalists, all of whom interpreted the soldiers' actions as a prelude to renewed civil war. Accordingly, Neville released an expanded edition of his tract on 15 July. New in this version was a lengthy libellous poem, hundreds of lines long, that accused dozens of royalist and parliamentarian leaders of unchastity. Once again, Neville did not skimp on sex-talk. The verses recalled Essex's cuckoldry ('For a Generall he had ill luck / That other men his wife should ___ [i.e. 'fuck']'); slandered prominent Presbyterian ladies ('[Lady] Alston hath got a Lord at last . . . The coward Mounson got her money, but Whertly first had got her c___ [i.e. 'cunny']'); and targeted prominent royalists like George Digby ('[Lady] Tusten she layes it one [sic] thick, / And fain would have Digbies ___ [i.e. 'prick']').[77] Neville's redactions hardly blunted the tract's lurid content, although their presence in such an otherwise already graphic piece perhaps suggests that his publisher remained reluctant to reproduce outright obscenities. In any case, they certainly did not detract from his central point about the sexual (and therefore political) malignancy of his Presbyterian and royalist enemies.

Equally interesting was Neville's choice of targets, which excluded key players in a rapidly unfolding rapprochement between the king and the Independent army leadership (embodied at this time in the figures of Fairfax and his chief lieutenant, Oliver Cromwell).[78] Indeed, Fairfax, Cromwell, Henrietta Maria and Charles, along with Neville's republican friend Henry Marten, were virtually the kingdom's only major political figures left unslandered in the new edition: a particularly remarkable fact given that Marten was probably the most infamous sexual miscreant in England at the time. For Neville, then, the upside-down world of the ladies' parliament reflected a similarly upended political landscape in which the Presbyterians, not the king, had become the greatest threat to English liberty.

For that very reason, the *Parliament of ladies* inflamed Presbyterian critics, who dubbed the expanded July edition a 'transcendant' example of libellous politicking. By the summertime, however, it was just one of many defamatory pamphlets flooding England's print marketplace.[79] The catalyst, once again, was intra-parliamentary controversy. After failing to resolve the cleavage in army-parliament relations opened by Charles's June abduction, London Presbyterians initiated a desperate gambit on 26 July by forcibly purging parliament and driving most Independent parliament-men out of the capital. However, their triumph was short-lived. One week later, New Model soldiers marched into London virtually unopposed, banished the Presbyterian leadership overseas, and restored the purged parliament-men to their seats. Sympathetic onlookers watched these proceedings with horror, while Charles's royalist partisans greeted the apparent collapse of parliamentary hegemony with glee.

The next six months witnessed a flood of printed pamphlets, broadsides and newsbooks that rivalled the initial print explosion of 1640/41 in scope.[80] Perhaps expectedly, sex-talk ran rampant, and even emboldened royalists returned to print to rebuke the Independent 'Sect of Love' and Presbyterian 'City Lechers' alike.[81] Amid the deluge appeared several tracts obviously inspired by Neville's work. For example, anonymous satirists produced three false petitions – one from London's 'maids', another from its 'shee-citizens', and a third from the 'city dames' – demanding that adultery be licensed for the good of the kingdom, which had become 'thinly inhabited, by reason of the late warres'. (Some contemporaries possibly remembered a 1643 satire, *The virgins complaint*, that anticipated precisely this concern while similarly configuring parliamentary peace-mongers as lustful women.) Their collective disdain for lecherous 'Anabaptist[s]' and 'Adamite[s]', and their celebratory descriptions of the king's 'Cavaliers . . . [who] alwaies stood stiffe' in their service, betrayed the tracts' royalist origins.[82] By replacing Neville's anti-popish language with a distinctly anti-puritan lexicon, moreover, they demonstrated that the female legislator trope, like so many other iterations of mid-century sexual politics, remained highly vulnerable to appropriation.

Neville himself produced one more satire that fall, acquired by Thomason on 13 September. Conspicuously dated to 2 August – the day of London's formal surrender to the New Model – Neville's sequel continued his practice of excoriating esteemed political figures for all varieties of sexual activity. This time, he did not spare Cromwell and Fairfax, who were applauded for their 'able performances' with two noblewomen (one, notably, the wife of a former royalist). Their inclusion possibly indicated Neville's awareness that the army grandees were soon to reject Leveller radicalism for an alliance with parliamentary moderates; certainly, he did not shy away from discussing recent events. Thus, one memorable line recalled the Presbyterians' purge of parliament: 'Lady Waller . . . was utterly incapable of sitting in Parliament', he wrote, 'for that while her Knight [William Waller, a London militia leader] with Glin, and Stapleton [both key Presbyterian grandees], were indeavouring a new war, she also was found in armes under Col. Pointz [another Presbyterian military commander]'.[83] Neville evidently disapproved of the attempted coup, but his attacks on Cromwell and Fairfax suggest that he may have been similarly unsatisfied with its abortive conclusion. Perhaps Neville had come to believe that the dildo-wielding figure who had cowed the ladies' parliament at the conclusion of his inaugural pamphlet was just another weak-willed woman after all.

The Parliament of Ladies would not reappear in print until 1650. But Neville had certainly made a mark on interwar politics by the time that he published his September 1647 sequel. By defaming Presbyterian aristocrats and royalist bishops alongside Independent parliament-men and New Model soldiers as crypto-popish lechers whose lust had propelled the kingdom to ruin, Neville's tract placed sexual disorder at the heart of England's crisis with little regard for careful ideological distinctions. Here, once again, sexual politics took on an explanatory force, as libidinousness was made to stand in for the parliament-men's apparent inability to resolve the kingdom's pressing political needs. Nor was Neville alone in linking the personal and the political late in 1647: watching from the sidelines that September, the royalist Sir Thomas Aston agreed that the two were connected. 'The whole world beeing in Combustion', he lamented to a friend, 'noe marvell the Fire takes in private Families'. Even London's separatist congregations, still under fire from anti-tolerationist writers, felt compelled in November to censure the 'lustfull inclinations, and dispositions to Fornication, Adultery', and 'other lamentable distempers' that had befallen the kingdom since the outbreak of civil war.[84] And then, as England's uneasy peace teetered on the verge of collapse, Charles's royalist press resurfaced to make the same point in even more graphic terms.

### 'Houses of disport': sexual libel and the revived royalist press

Shortly after penning his note about England's immolation, Aston received another letter raging against puritan moral hypocrisy. 'There [sic] sanctity is but a shew of holynes', it moaned, and 'if they had beene what they would seeme . . . they would not soe forgett the duetyes of morallity'.[85] By October 1647, this was a familiar refrain, undoubtedly owing in part to real-life tales of sectarian debauchery: that same month, for instance, an Essex yeoman indicted for bigamy defended himself by claiming that 'he did not beleive [sic] the scriptures but was guided by the spirite in his owne brest'. (He was accused in turn of mistaking 'liberte of conscience' for 'hellish lust'.)[86] Commentators on parliamentarian-puritan morality were not always as delicate as Aston's friend. Six months earlier, the Londoner John Doysey had been written up for denouncing the parliament-men as ungodly 'whoremasters' afflicted with 'the Pox'.[87] In his words, as in those of Aston's correspondent, can be detected the powerful post-Reformation association between spiritual and sexual incontinence that had been rehearsed endlessly against godly Protestants by royalists, and more recently Presbyterian heresiographers, since the outbreak of civil war.

When the upheavals of July 1647 sent royalist polemicists scrambling back into print, therefore, they discovered an eager reading audience – including both royalists and disaffected Presbyterians – already primed to devour anti-puritan sexual satire. Granted, this revived cavalier press corps was different than its Oxonian predecessor. Rather than working in concert under John Berkenhead's direction, its constituents operated on the margins of London's printing underground, where rogue publishers furtively produced seditious anti-parliamentarian material directly under parliament's nose. Its membership included old stalwarts like John Taylor as well as new faces – among them, one-time Presbyterians such as Samuel Sheppard as well as the former author of *Mercurius Britanicus*, Marchamont Nedham.[88] Convinced that a parliamentary implosion was imminent after the failure of the Presbyterian coup, these men set to work promoting Charles's immediate restoration as the kingdom's only hope for salvation.

While Presbyterian London squirmed under military occupation, loyalist printers, publishers and authors began stoking the fires of discontent among royalists and disaffected parliamentarians alike in cheap print, and especially serial newsbooks, that took anti-puritanism as their starting point. These, like the revolutionary mazarinades that were soon to appear across the Channel in France, were texts of action, intended to compel Charles's subjects into outraged resistance to parliamentary hegemony; and, as their royalist authors had learned during the mobilisation campaigns of the first civil war, sexual politics could serve that purpose especially well.[89]

Accordingly, godly lechers were everywhere in this fusillade, accompanied – as in many of the Presbyterian heresiographies of the preceding two years – by their 'holy sisters': 'good easy soft hearted [puritan] Women' who served their brethren as willing sexual chattel.[90] When the two groups met behind the closed doors of their puritan conventicles, the orgiastic results were predictable. In June 1648, *Mercurius melancholicus* summarised them in one of the most graphic descriptions to appear in print since the outbreak of war: 'Independent Cock-broath of the Holy Sisters owne providing'.[91] One September 1647 broadside, John Berkenhead's *The four-legg'd elder*, offered similarly frank imagery. This verse satire featured a Presbyterian maid who chose to sate her 'cupiscence' with an 'ougly Mastive Curre' rather than a man. The pair subsequently became 'Dog and Wife', although the union was cut short when the canine husband was hanged for 'Buggery'. The broadside, which next equated the couple's bestial offspring with the 'whelp' of reformed church government recently approved by the Westminster Assembly, shared more than a passing similarity with Berkenhead's earlier coverage, in *Aulicus*'s pages, of the parliamentarian prisoner in Shrewsbury caught violating a mare in 1643.[92] Four years after profiling that case as an outlandish illustration of parliamentarian deviance, Berkenhead chose in *The four-legg'd elder* to depict puritanism itself as an intrinsically bestial creed.

Berkenhead's Presbyterian villainess lived in London, itself a routine royalist target. Both the wealthy Presbyterian citizenry, long parodied by royalists as obedient cuckolds of the Westminster leadership, and their promiscuous wives were pilloried in cavalier print throughout the fall.[93] After the New Model occupied the city in August, some royalists even metaphorically figured London's defences as a 'harlot' who 'prostituted her body' to Fairfax and thereby allowed a 'Rape' to be 'committed' on the Presbyterian parliament.[94] These writers expended considerable energy exploring the capital's sexual geography. From infamous prostitution hotspots like Clerkenwell's 'Turnball-street' to entirely novel sites of lechery such as the parliament's new 'houses of disport' in 'Westminster', where MPs cavorted with their 'feminine turn-ups', royalist polemicists reimagined London as a veritable playground of parliamentarian sexual fantasies.[95]

Their chief preoccupation remained the moral failings of Charles's puritan-parliamentarian enemies.[96] Consider this passage from a November 1647 tract, *A vindication of King Charles*, authored by the royalist minister Edward Symmons:

> Yea . . . heare how some unworthy Members have attempted to ravish and defloure Ladies of Honour, and no punishment inflicted for the same; How some others neglecting their own wives, have kept divers lewd women, yea, and allowed yearely pensions to filthy Bawds to furnish them with such Commodities, for the satisfying their brutish lusts, and base appetites: How some have defloured young Virgins whose Parents (in respect of their abused Children) are unwilling to publish their dishonour to the world: How some, having committed this vile wickednesse with young Gentle-women, have used (or advised) to meanes to hinder conception, yea and to destroy the fruit in the wombe when conceived . . . How some (having undone Gentlemen of good quality . . . have taken advantage of the poverty of their Children, and allured their daughters . . . to the losse of their Honours and precious Souls for ever.[97]

Just three years earlier, preaching about the Shrewsbury buggery case, Symmons had argued against the notion 'that all these blessed Reformers . . . are . . . guiltie of that horrid sin' because, in his words, 'I believe (for my part) we should much abuse them in that particular'.[98] Apparently the recent experience of parliamentary rule had changed his mind.

In December 1647, Charles signed a military alliance with Scottish Presbyterians in return for his nominal commitment to a Presbyterian church settlement in England. Then, while the Scots gathered their forces, royalist revolts began erupting across Wales and southeastern England, fuelled by the fiscal burden of parliamentarian governance and dissatisfaction with the current Independent ascendancy. Royalist efforts to tar parliament with the brush of sectarian anarchy conceivably played a role in motivating this transnational resistance effort; certainly the Scots, like some disaffected English Presbyterians, expressed concern about the moral and spiritual dangers posed by Independent hegemony in Westminster.[99] What Charles's partisans did not expect, however, was for the threat of renewed civil war to reunite the parliamentarian coalition against its common enemy. Consequently, throughout the spring and early summer, parliament responded with surprising efficacy to the domestic upheavals while also preparing for an imminent Scottish invasion.

The political fallout in Westminster was swift. On 3 January 1648, incensed by Charles's treachery, the Independent majority in parliament passed a moratorium on all future communication with their king. This Vote of No Further Addresses effectively stripped Charles of any agency in negotiating the kingdom's post-war future, and it was accompanied by a lengthy parliamentary declaration justifying the vote through a comprehensive description of Charles's many crimes. Between its (true) allegations about the king's duplicity and more sensationalist accusations about his complicity in his father's murder, the tract made it clear that he, and no one else, was responsible for the renewal of war.[100] For the first time in formal parliamentarian print, that is to say, Charles was held personally guilty for the kingdom's sorry condition.

Enraged by parliament's presumption and inspired by the revolts erupting across England and Wales, royalist publishers redoubled their efforts to denounce the puritan enemy. Again, post-Reformation sexual satire proved contagious, as godly lechers, cuckolded City merchants and sex-crazed parliament-men filled the pages of loyalist print. Even more common were personal libels. Indeed, the (real or imagined) sex-lives of Charles's chief parliamentarian opponents became a central feature of royalist polemic during these months. This material has been examined by Jason McElligott, who rightfully argues that it functioned alongside an 'additional repertoire of rhetorical devices', including biblical and natural allusions, that complicate any attempt at privileging sexual satire above the nonsexual; but when considered in light of transformations like Edward Symmons's, described above, it is impossible not to place anti-puritan sexual politics at the heart of late-1640s royalist polemic.[101] In short: even more so than Edwards's naming-and-shaming in *Gangraena* or the obscene jests of Neville's *Parliament of ladies* tracts, the revived cavalier press of 1647–49 marked the apotheosis of mid-century sexual libel.

The royalists' most infamous victim was the republican parliament-man Henry Marten, who had long carried on an adulterous relationship with a lover in London while his wife lived in exile on his Berkshire estate.[102] Marten's adultery earned him unparalleled opprobrium from Charles's partisans, who had linked his radical politics and his unchastity in print repeatedly since 1643. Marten himself remained largely indifferent to such charges. Indeed, his private papers revealed an almost proto-modern appreciation of the distinction between public and private affairs: when it came to 'sinnes' like 'committing fornication', Marten scribbled, 'nobody besides himself was concerned in any of them'.[103] Naturally, these sentiments only bolstered his reputation as an atheistic libertine.

From late 1647, Marten was lampooned in dozens of royalist publications as an insatiable sexual predator. Royalists depicted him as a 'peticoat-diver' who pursued 'whore[s]' by the 'score', cajolingly 'perswad[ing] them as they lye on their backs to turne up the white of their eyes, and blesse the Lord';[104] accused him of lobbying for new legislation to 'keep all things in common' so that he could 'king it over his Whores' both in the London 'Suburbs' as well as his 'Empire of Barkshire';[105] and portrayed him as so afflicted by the 'Pox' and the 'clap' that he 'carrie[d] an Apothecaries shop about him' for relief.[106] Indeed, as royalist confidence grew throughout early-to-mid-1648, some writers even suggested that Marten would 'cary a score or two of honest Wenches' into New England (because there were no 'Bawdy houses in that Country') to escape Charles's retribution.[107]

As Sue Wiseman has argued, much of this abuse stemmed from Marten's republican politics; as had been the case for the Presbyterians' congregationalist targets during the toleration debates of 1644–46, his radical proclivities rendered him vulnerable to charges of sexual anarchy.[108] But Marten was only one of many parliamentarians – not all of them republicans or radical sectarians – attacked by royalist libellers in this period. Another prominent victim was the New England minister Hugh Peter. Peter had already garnered a reputation for lechery in earlier cavalier print, but his sexual exploits featured even more widely in the 1647–48 material. Alongside mundane charges of promiscuity, two stories received repeated coverage.[109] The first involved a landlord (sometimes Dutch, sometimes English) who had apparently once hosted Peter overnight, only to be repaid with cuckoldry when the New Englander 'left a point or two of consolation' with the man's wife before his departure. The second tale, already familiar to royalist readers of *Aulicus*, involved a London butcher's wife whom Peter had 'converted ... from an honest woman to a whore' through sheer 'zeal'.[110] In both cases, Peter was made to embody the lustful puritan ministers whom royalists had long accused of seducing vulnerable London women – married or otherwise – into rebellion against the king.

Meanwhile, Londoners were represented by John Warner, a City merchant and alderman who was currently serving as the capital's Lord Mayor.[111] As the elected head of London's cuckolded citizenry, Warner was endlessly libelled by royalists for his 'hornes', earned 'whil'st another rides his Wife'. Indeed, according to the revived *Mercurius aulicus*, his full title was 'the onely Acteon of the horned head, Grand Signior and Metropolitan of all the Congregationall Cuckoldryes'.[112] But royalists claimed that the Lord Mayor did not sit idly by while others dallied 'betwixt [his] Lordships Ladies thighes'. Instead, they depicted Warner perverting his legislative powers to 'command bawdy houses' while 'commit[ting] adulterie, with any well shapt woman'.[113] The 'Bastard Heires' spawned from the 'wench[es]' that Lord Mayor 'got with childe' then became another burden on the kingdom's weary population. Mocked as both cuckold and whoremonger, Warner's libellous profile encapsulated the vicious inconsistency of royalist libellers.[114]

Among loyalists, the archetypical parliamentarian cuckold was the Norfolk Independent parliament-man Miles Corbet, or 'Corbet the Couckold' for short. Corbet's wife Mary rarely made public appearances, but royalists had no doubt that she had logged numerous entries in her husband's 'horn-book'. In 1646, in fact, John Taylor had journeyed to Norfolk to investigate some of these stories, and royalists continued to repeat them in print over the next two years.[115] (Crucially, his wife's infidelity did not preclude 'Black Corbet' from enjoying 'Copulation' with 'pockey Whore[s]' of his own.) All told, with the death of Essex, 'that Honorable Stag of State', Corbet appeared destined to take up the dead earl's horned mantle.[116]

Dozens of other parliamentarian affiliates fell victim to royalist sexual satire after the fall of 1647. They included the parliamentary journalist Henry Walker, whose alleged affair with the wife of his printer, Robert Ibbitson, was a favourite topic of the royalist newsbook *Mercurius elencticus*;[117] the Presbyterian army colonel Edward Rossiter, said to have suffered a terrible injury to his 'Testicles' in combat, 'to the great greife' of the 'Holy sisters';[118] and the future regicide Thomas Scot, accused of ravishing and impregnating a young child.[119] Many more – including ministers, parliament-men, military leaders and puritan peers – received similar treatment.[120] Even the king's nephew, the Prince Elector Palatine, was lambasted for 'dally[ing]' with 'a whole Kennell of prostituted Bitches' on a parliamentary salary of 'eight thousand pounds per annum' in return for tolerating the uprising against his royal uncle.[121]

Henry Marten's republicanism therefore did not render him uniquely vulnerable to sexual libel. Instead, Presbyterians, Independents and radicals fell victim in relatively equal measure to printed allegations of unchastity, most of which emphasised the same post-Reformation themes of corruptive sexuality that shaped the intra-parliamentary toleration debates of 1644–47. Indeed, the royalist anti-puritanism of this period is perhaps best understood as an expansion of the very anti-tolerationist arguments previously deployed by Presbyterian heresiographers against radical parliamentarians to encompass all adherents of the Westminsterian cause, identifiably puritan or not. Given how desperate the king's partisans were to exacerbate intra-parliamentary tensions by appealing to Presbyterians against their Independent counterparts (and vice versa), the royalists' decision to attack both groups relatively indiscriminately certainly feels like a tactical mistake;

but perhaps they had little interest in such distinctions in the face of a comprehensive puritan rebellion. (Alternatively, the loyalists' own internal divisions during this period may simply have prevented the creation of any such overarching strategy in the first place.)[122] Absent any hard evidence, it is impossible to say for sure.

Even so, royalists retained an eager audience among English readers unsettled by parliamentary rule. Charles's partisans were urged to distribute royalist pamphlets and broadsides in tandem with the spring's revolts, and several civilians faced arrest for dispersing similar tracts in London and the provinces.[123] Thanks in part to these efforts, contemporaries from Cheshire to Hertfordshire collected, read and discussed the work of the revived royalist press with vigour, sometimes scribbling heated responses into the margins of their copies.[124] Through such exchanges and rejoinders, libellous sex-talk – particularly, but not exclusively, of the anti-puritan variety – burrowed ever further into English political culture.

Royalists' hopes of victory were crushed in August 1648, when Oliver Cromwell and the New Model defeated a combined force of Scots and English royalists near Preston in Lancashire in the final major field engagement of England's second civil war. Days later, Fairfax cowed the last remaining insurgent stronghold at Colchester. Together, these successes left Charles – imprisoned on the Isle of Wight, devoid of any remaining military prospects, and with his credit utterly ruined among parliamentary Independents and the army leadership – facing bleak circumstances indeed. The king remained hopeful only because his opponents could not agree on a fitting solution to the novel constitutional quandary engendered by his ongoing captivity.

Meanwhile, politicised sex-talk had never been more popular in English print. Ironically, the conclusion of military conflict in 1646 proved almost more effective than civil war itself in catalysing partisan polemicists. First, bereft of a common enemy, the parliamentarian coalition – members of the same godly constituency who had lobbied parliament against the proliferation of lascivious books in December 1640 – imploded in a spectacular fashion, with Presbyterian heresiographers and Independent apologists like Richard Overton warring in print over the vexed issue of religious toleration. Henry Neville fanned the flames even further in 1647 with his *Parliament of ladies* series, which offered a creatively obscene reconfiguration of conventional anti-court and anti-popish stereotypes to portray Presbyterian and royalist grandees as sex-crazed cuckolds who owed fealty to their lascivious wives. When, later that year, royalist penmen unleashed a barrage of sexual libels at targets across the spectrum of English parliamentarianism, they were building on a rich interwar tradition of sexual satire.

The key theme that united these disparate iterations of sexual politics was confessional: namely, the post-Reformation polarities of anti-popery and anti-puritanism, which were repeatedly deployed, inverted and reappropriated by partisan writers who identified religious error as the overarching evil plaguing England throughout the mid-to-late 1640s. Although the political labels of the first civil war – 'roundhead', 'cavalier' – remained relevant, they served little purpose for parliamentarians who directed their venom inward with increasing vigour from 1644 onward. As Presbyterian writers adopted the anti-puritanism of their royalist enemies for use against their Independent colleagues (who redirected a familiar set of anti-popish stereotypes against the Presbyterians in turn), therefore, the post-Reformation resumed pride of place in English sexual politics. When Charles's royalists resurfaced late in 1647, they employed a similar confessional logic to libel Presbyterians and Independents alike as two sides of the same lascivious puritan coin.

There is another, equally important, context to consider in assessing what Joad Raymond has dubbed the 'bitter and vitriolic mercurialness' that assailed England's print marketplace during the later 1640s: mundane hatred.[125] By 1648, the divisions that separated royalists from parliamentarians, and indeed Presbyterians from Independents, had hardened (with some notable exceptions) into real vitriol. It should perhaps be no surprise, then, that print reflected those heightened animosities; nor that, in a partisan context which had by now firmly identified human sexuality as a primary arena of political dispute, personal chastity should take on a correspondingly more central role as ideological divisions deepened. If, to put it another way, war-weariness and repeated disappointment were enough to transform Charles from a sovereign (if dangerously misled) king into 'that man of blood' for certain members of the parliamentarian coalition, as Patricia Crawford has shown, we should not be surprised that sexual politics underwent a similar intensification.[126]

By the time of the royalists' defeat at Preston in August, English sex-talk had grown more graphic, more public, and more politically daring than ever before. Furthermore, the inspired porno-political language of miscegenated birth beloved by interwar apologists from Richard Overton to Robert Baillie shows that the libellous polemics of the early-to-mid-1640s had expanded beyond descriptive satire into a new realm of theoretical sophistication. Nor were they alone. As contemporaries turned their attention to Westminster, where parliamentarian leaders gathered to discuss their next moves, not even the kingdom's most exalted political figures – including the soldier-statesman Oliver Cromwell and King Charles himself – would be spared from critique.

## Notes

1  For these labels, which were employed in both religious and strictly political senses, see Elliot Vernon, *London Presbyterians and the British Revolutions, 1638–64* (Manchester, 2021); Como, *RP*. The classic account remains David Underdown, *Pride's Purge: Politics in the Puritan Revolution* (Oxford, 1971).
2  John Coffey, 'A Ticklish Business: Defining Heresy and Orthodoxy in the Puritan Revolution', in David Loewenstein and John Marshall (eds), *Heresy, Literature and Politics in Early Modern English Culture* (Cambridge, 2006), pp. 108–36, at 110.
3  E.g., Ann Hughes, *Gangraena and the Struggle for the English Revolution* (Oxford, 2004); Nigel Smith, 'Richard Overton's Marpriest Tracts: Towards a History of Leveller Style', *Prose Studies* 9:2 (1986), 39–66; Jason McElligott, 'The Politics of Sexual Libel: Royalist Propaganda in the 1640s', *HLQ* 67:1 (2004), 75–99.
4  Peter Lake and David Como, '"Orthodoxy" and Its Discontents: Dispute Settlement and the Production of "Consensus" in the London (Puritan) "Underground"', *JBS* 39:1 (2000), 34–70.
5  Como, *RP*, pp. 102–5.
6  Vernon, *London Presbyterians*, chs 3–4; Como, *RP*.
7  *An apologeticall narration*, E.80[7] ([3 January] 1644), p. 24.
8  Roger Williams, *Queries of highest consideration*, E.32[8] (1644), p. 3.
9  Marshall, *Toleration*, pp. 207–8, 218–19, 244–52.
10  English Catholics could also deploy this charge against wayward members of their own confession: Peter Lake and Michael Questier, *All Hail to the Archpriest: Confessional Conflict, Toleration, and the Politics of Publicity in Post-Reformation England* (Oxford, 2019), p. 164.
11  Randle Cotgrave, *A dictionarie*, STC 5830 (1611), sig. ccc2v. See also Jean-Pierre Cavaillé, 'Libertine and Libertinism: Polemic Uses of the Terms in Sixteenth- and Seventeenth-Century English and Scottish Literature', *Journal for Early Modern Cultural Studies* 12:2 (2012), 12–36.
12  *An apologeticall narration*, p. 9.
13  *A copy of the petition of...the Assembly*, E.63[19] ([4 August] 1643), pp. 3, 5. See also *CJ*, iii, p. 173.
14  [John Milton], *The doctrine and discipline of divorce*, E.62[17] ([1 August] 1643), pp. 2, 14, 17. See also David R. Como, 'Print, Censorship, and Ideological Escalation in the English Civil War', *JBS* 51:4 (2012), 820–57, at 841–4. For a marked-up copy of Milton's 1645 reprint, see WACML, PR3570 D61 1645.
15  Thomas Kranidas, 'Milton Rewrites "The Doctrine and Discipline of Divorce"', *Studies in English Literature, 1500–1900* 53:1 (2013), 117–35. The second edition was subsequently suppressed by the Stationer's Company: *CJ*, iii, p. 606.
16  Peter Lake, 'Anti-Puritanism: The Structure of a Prejudice', in Kenneth Fincham and Peter Lake (eds), *Religious Politics in Post-Reformation England: Essays in Honour of Nicholas Tyacke* (Woodbridge, 2006), pp. 80–97, at 94.

17 Thomas Edwards, *Antapologia*, E.1[1] ([13 July] 1644), pp. 65, 86, 250, 262. For an annotated copy, see Bod., Marl. M 1.
18 [Thomas Weld], *A short story*, E.4[18] ([6 August] 1644), p. 66. See also Michael Winship, *Making Heretics: Militant Protestantism and Free Grace in Massachusetts, 1636–1641* (Princeton, NJ, 2002).
19 Valerie Pearl and Morris Pearl, 'Governor John Winthrop on the Birth of the Antinomians' "Monster": The Earliest Reports to Reach England and the Making of a Myth', *Proceedings of the Massachusetts Historical Society* 102 (1990), pp. 21–37.
20 *The confession of faith, of those . . . called Anabaptists*, E.12[24] ([16 October] 1644), sig. A2v; Samuel Richardson, *Some briefe considerations*, E.270[22] (25 February 1645), pp. 3–4; TNA, SP 16/503, fol. 65r.
21 H. G. Tibbutt (ed.), *The Letter Books of Sir Samuel Luke* (London, 1963), p. 197.
22 Daniel Featley, *The dippers dipt*, E.268[11] ([7 February] 1645), sig. B2r, pp. 202, 209.
23 Ibid., pp. 178, 210–12. For an annotated later edition, see The John Carter Brown Library, DA651 F288d.
24 Featley, *The dippers dipt*, p. 209.
25 Como, *RP*, p. 311; B. J. Gibbons, 'Overton, Richard', *ODNB*.
26 Smith, 'Richard Overton's Marpriest Tracts', pp. 61–2.
27 [Richard Overton], *The araignement of Mr. Persecution*, E.276[23] ([8 April] 1645), sig. A5r, p. 17.
28 [Richard Overton], *A sacred decretal*, E.286[15] (6 June 1645), p. 4; [Richard Overton], *Martin's eccho*, E.290[2] ([27 June] 1645), p. 19.
29 [Richard Overton], *The nativity of Sir John Presbyter*, E.290[17] ([2 July] 1645), pp. 6, 9–10.
30 [Overton], *Araignement*, pp. 22, 25; [Overton], *Sacred decretal*, p. 1.
31 [Richard Overton], *The ordinance for tythes dismounted*, E.313[27] ([29 December] 1645), p. 8.
32 Samuel Rutherford, *The tryal & triumph of faith*, E.283[4] ([12 May] 1645), pp. 24, 197; Richard Byfield, *Temple-defilers defiled*, E.278[20] ([22 April] 1645), pp. 29, 33.
33 Ephraim Pagitt, *Heresiography*, E.282[5] ([8 May], 1645), pp. 5, 53, 82, 85–6, 115.
34 Byfield, *Temple-defilers*, sig. A3v; Pagitt, *Heresiography*, sigs A2r–v (first epistle); William Prynne, *A fresh discovery of some prodigious new wandring-blasing-stars*, E.261[5] ([24 July] 1645), sig. A2r (for a marked-up copy, see The John Carter Brown Library, DA643 .P973d). On this last point, see Katharine Gillespie, *Domesticity and Dissent in the Seventeenth Century: English Women's Writing and the Public Sphere* (Cambridge, 2004).
35 *Winthrop Papers, Vol. 5: 1645–49* (Boston, MA, 1947), p. 90.
36 S. R. Gardiner (ed.), *The Constitutional Documents of the Puritan Revolution, 1625–1660*, 2nd ed. (Oxford, 1899), p. 139.

37 Robert Baillie, *A dissuasive from the errours of the time*, E.317[5] ([22 January] 1646), 7. The first, shorter edition was published the preceding November.
38 Ibid., pp. 4, 63, 90, 116.
39 Hughes, *Gangraena*, pp. v, 324–30.
40 *Gangraena I*, pp. 24–5, 34, 152, 166, 176.
41 Ibid., pp. 55, 67, 120–1 (appendix). On Elizabeth Attaway, see Jason A. Kerr, 'Elizabeth Attaway, London Preacher and Theologian, 1645–1646', *Seventeenth Century* 36:5 (2020), 733–54.
42 Hughes, *Gangraena*, p. 332.
43 John Goodwin, *Cretensis*, E.328[22] ([19 March] 1646), pp. 8, 34; William Walwyn, *An antidote against Master Edwards*, E.1184[4] ([10 June] 1646), p. 8; John Saltmarsh, *Groanes for liberty*, E.327[20] ([10 March] 1646), pp. 30–2. See also Samuel Eaton, *A just apologie*, Wing E122 (1647), sigs A3v–4r.
44 Elliot Vernon, '"They Agree Not in Opinion Among Themselves": Two-Kingdoms Theory, "Erastianism" and the Westminster Assembly Debate on Church and State, *c.* 1641–48', in Elliot Vernon and Hunter Powell (eds), *Church Polity and Politics in the British Atlantic World, c. 1635–66* (Manchester, 2020), pp. 130–54.
45 Jeremiah Burroughs, *A vindication of Mr Burroughes*, E.345[14] ([23 July] 1646), p. 3.
46 *Gangraena II*, pp. 8, 141, 145.
47 Ibid., p. 135.
48 On the puritan 'belly-god', see Kristen Poole, *Radical Religion from Shakespeare to Milton: Figures of Nonconformity in Early Modern England* (Cambridge, 2000), pp. 45–7.
49 *Gangraena II*, pp. 10, 146–7; *Gangraena III*, p. 189. Oates was eventually acquitted of the woman's death: Stephen Wright, 'Oates, Samuel', *ODNB*.
50 Como, *RP*, p. 401.
51 Steve Hindle, 'Dearth and the English Revolution: The Harvest Crisis of 1647–50', *Economic History Review* 61:1 (2008), 64–98.
52 *A relation of severall heresies*, E.358[2] ([17 October] 1646), pp. 16, 19; *Proper persecution*, 669.f.10[104] ([22 December] 1646). This latter broadside was a direct response to Overton's Marpriest tracts.
53 Clare College, Cambridge, MS CCAD/1/1/2a, no. 3; Isle of Wight Record Office, OG/AA/31, p. 9.
54 BL, Add. MS 54332, fol. 165r.
55 *Little non-such*, E.353[8] ([3 September] 1646), p. 5; *The counter buffe*, E.399[25] ([22 July] 1647), p. 14.
56 Austin Woolrych, *Soldiers and Statesmen: The General Council of the Army and its Debates, 1647–1648* (Oxford, 1987), pp. 2–3; Michael Mahoney, 'Presbyterianism in the City of London, 1645–1647', *HJ* 22:1 (1979), 93–114.
57 *Gangraena III*, pp. 3–4, 14, 261.
58 Ibid., pp. 187–90.
59 Ibid., pp. 82–3, 85. See also Hughes, *Gangraena*, p. 114.

60 Edwards addressed Chidley in *Gangraena I*, pp. 79–80.
61 Ibid., appendix 120–1; *Gangraena II*, p. 11; *Gangraena III*, p. 27.
62 Ibid., p. 26.
63 Hughes, *Gangraena*, pp. 317, 331–2. For one contemporary who owned both *Gangraena* and Pagitt's *Heresiography*, see Houghton Library, Harvard University, MS Mus 182 (unpaginated; 'a note of all my bookes', nos 109 and 110).
64 BL, Add. MS 70005, fols 188r–v.
65 Robert Baillie, *Anabaptism*, E.369[9] ([1 January] 1647), sig. b4r, pp. 9, 15, 53, 100. See also *Hell broke loose*, E.378[28] (9 March 1647), p. 5.
66 *A catalogue of the severall sects*, 669.f.10[111] ([19 January] 1647); *Reall persecution*, 669.f.10[114] ([13 February] 1647).
67 [Richard Overton], *The commoners complaint*, E.375[7] ([10 February] 1647), p. 17; *A letter to Mr. Tho. Edwards*, E.378[3] ([25 February] 1647), p. 3.
68 Edward King, *A discovery*, E.373[3] ([1 February] 1646), p. 16. See also Clive Holmes, 'Colonel King and Lincolnshire Politics, 1642–1646', *HJ* 16:3 (1973), 451–84.
69 *The parlament of women*, STC 19306 (1640); *The Parliament of women*, E.1150[5] ([14 August] 1646).
70 *A parliament of ladies*, E.384[9] ([16 April] 1647), sig. A2r.
71 *An exact diurnall of the Parliament of ladyes*, E.386[4] (6 [May] 1647), pp. 3, 5–6.
72 See, for instance, Mary Beth Norton, *Separated by Their Sex: Women in Public and Private in the Colonial Atlantic World* (Ithaca, NY, 2011), pp. 55–61; Purkiss, *Literature*, pp. 65–70; Turner, *Libertines*. For a nuanced contextual reading, see Nigel Smith, *Literature and Revolution in England, 1640–1660* (New Haven, CT, 1994), pp. 47–9.
73 [Henry Neville], *The parliament of ladies*, E.388[4] ([18 May] 1647). Modern commentators frequently attribute all of the 1647 *Parliament of ladies* pamphlets to Neville, but only this publication, its variants, and the sequel (*The ladies, a second time*, explored below) are likely his work.
74 Ibid., pp. 4, 6, 8. These excerpts include both Presbyterian and royalist women of varying political eminence.
75 Ibid., pp. 9, 12, 14. See also TNA, SP 16/487, fols 147r–v.
76 Purkiss, *Literature*, pp. 69–70.
77 [Henry Neville], *The ladies Parliament*, E.1143[1] ([15 July] 1647), sigs Gv, G3r–v. For Mary Alston, wife of the 'zealous Presbyterian' James Langham, see William Birken, 'Alston, Sir Edward', *ODNB*.
78 Michael Mendle, 'Putney's Pronouns: Identity and Indemnity in the Great Debate', in Michael Mendle (ed.), *The Putney Debates of 1647: The Army, the Levellers and the English State* (Cambridge, 2001), pp. 125–47, at 131–5.
79 *Match me these two*, E.400[9] ([29 July] 1647), p. 13.
80 Samuel Fullerton, ' "A Warre of the Pen": The Force on Parliament and English Polemic, 1646–48', *HLQ* 82:2 (2019), 221–47.

81 *A justification of…Sion Colledge*, 669.f.11[76] ([6 September] 1647); *The armies letanie*, E.408[20] ([24 September] 1647), sig. A2v. See also *Universall madnesse*, E.412[14] ([1 November] 1647), pp. 2–3.
82 *A remonstrance of the shee-citizens of London*, E.404[2] ([21 August] 1647), p. 2 (quoted); *The maids petition*, E.401[26] ([11 August] 1647); *The city-dames petition*, E.409[12] ([28 September] 1647). See also *Hey hoe, for a husband*, E.408[19] ([24 September] 1647).
83 [Henry Neville], *The ladies, a second time*, E.406[23] ([13 September] 1647), pp. 4, 7.
84 BRBML, GEN MSS 205, Box 1:25; *A declaration by Congregationall societies in . . . London*, E.416[20] ([22 November] 1647), p. 7.
85 BL, Add. MS 36914, fol. 229r.
86 Talya S. Housman, '"To Plunder All Under the Petty-Coate": Prosecuting Sexual Crime and Gendered Violence in the English Revolution' (PhD dissertation, Brown University, 2019), p. 219.
87 LMA, MJ/SR/994/19.
88 Jason McElligott, *Royalism, Print and Censorship in Revolutionary England* (Woodbridge, 2007).
89 Christian Jouhaud, *Mazarinades: la Fronde des mots* (Paris, 1985).
90 Samuel Fullerton, 'The "Holy Sister" Anatomized: Religious Polemic and Erotic Writing in England, 1640–1660', *Journal of Modern History* (forthcoming).
91 [*Mercurius*] *melancholicus*, E.448[8] (12–19 June 1648), p. 257.
92 [John Berkenhead], *The four-legg'd elder*, 669.f.11[70] ([1 September] 1647); *Aulicus*, E.80[8] (23 December 1643), pp. 719–20.
93 For London cuckolds, see [*Mercurius*] *bellicus*, E.443[39] (16–23 May 1648), p. 2; [*Mercurius*] *elencticus*, E.464[22] (13–20 September 1648), p. 343. For their wandering wives, see *Pratle your pleasure*, 669.f.11[65] ([21 August] 1647); *Mercurius poeticus*, E.442[4] (5–13 May 1648), p. 6.
94 *Articles of high-treason*, E.417[11] ([26 November] 1647), p. 2; *Mercurius anti-melanchollicus*, E.408[9] (18–24 September 1647), p. 4. See also *Melancholicus*, E.407[23] (11–17 September 1647), p. 4.
95 Samuel Sheppard, *The committee-man curried*, E.398[21] ([16 July] 1647), sig. A3v; *Melancholicus*, E.417[17] (20–9 November 1647), p. 77. See also *An outcry against the speedy hue and cry*, E.402[22] ([18 August] 1647), p. 4; *Westminster fayre*, E.407[43] (22 September 1647).
96 For some representative examples, see *The parliaments accounts cast up*, Wing P510A (1647); [*Mercurius*] *pragmaticus*, E.435[12] (4–11 April 1648), sigs Br–v; *Mercurius critticus*, E.435[23] (6–13 April 1648), p. 4; and below.
97 Edward Symmons, *A vindication of King Charles*, E.414[17] ([November] 1647), p. 131. For two contemporary owners of this book, see University of Nottingham Library, MS PwV 4, 194; HEHL, RB 147922.
98 Edward Symmons, *A militarie sermon*, E.53[19] ([5 July] 1644), p. 15.
99 See, for example, *Directions of the Generall Assembly*, E.406[6] (Edinburgh, [7 September] 1647).
100 *CJ*, v, pp. 415–16; *A declaration of the Commons…touching no farther address*, E.427[9] (15 February 1648).

101 McElligott, 'Politics of Sexual Libel', p. 89.
102 Sarah Barber, *A Revolutionary Rogue: Henry Marten and the English Republic* (Stroud, 2000).
103 BL, Add. MS 71532, fol. 24v.
104 *The second part to the same tune*, 669.f.11[96] ([13 November] 1647); *Bellicus*, E.429[15] (22–9 February 1648), sig. Er; *Aulicus*, E.461[5] (21–8 August 1648), pp. 30–1. See also *The remonstrance or declaration of Mr. Henry Martin*, E.464[37] ([25 September] 1648).
105 *Melancholicus*, E.445[12] (22–9 May 1648), p. 239; *Pragmaticus*, E.433[28] (21–8 March 1648), sig. D3v; *Melancholicus*, E.462[7] (28 August–4 September 1648), p. 163.
106 *Elencticus*, E.476[4] (5–12 December 1648), p. 529; *Pragmaticus*, E.419[12] (30 November–7 December 1647), sig. Mr; *Turn apace, turn apace*, E.449[15] ([22 June] 1648), p. 3. See also *Bellicus*, E.432[7] (7–14 March 1648), pp. 1–2; *Elencticus*, E.446[16] (31 May–7 June 1648), p. 215.
107 *Mr. Henry Martin his speech*, E.446[19] (8 June 1648), pp. 3–4. See also *Pragmaticus*, E.411[23] (19–26 October 1647), p. 46; Samuel Fullerton, 'New England in the Royalist Imagination, 1637–89', *EHR* 137:588 (2022), 1346–76.
108 Susan Wiseman, ' "Adam, the Father of all Flesh": Porno-Political Rhetoric and Political Theory in and After the English Civil War', in James Holstun (ed.), *Pamphlet Wars: Prose in the English Revolution* (London, 1992), pp. 134–57, at 143–4.
109 E.g., *The old Protestants letanie*, E.405[5] ([1 September] 1647), p. 4; *Aulicus*, E.425[8] (25 January–3 February 1648), sig. A2v.
110 *Melancholicus*, E.407[25] (11–17 September 1647), p. 17; ibid., E.416[17] (13–20 November 1647), p. 74. See also *The last will and testament of Tom Fairfax*, E.451[38] ([9 July] 1648), p. 5; *Pragmaticus*, E.464[45] (19–26 September 1648), sig. Ll2r; Alexandra Walsham, 'Phanaticus: Hugh Peter, Antipuritanism and the Afterlife of the English Revolution', *Parergon* 32:3 (2015), 65–97.
111 Valerie Pearl, *London and the Outbreak of the Puritan Revolution: City Government and National Politics, 1625–43* (Oxford, 1961), pp. 325–7.
112 *Melancholicus*, E.421[10] (18–25 December 1647), pp. 100–1; *Aulicus*, E.426[16] (3–10 February 1648), sig. B2r.
113 *The dagonizing of Bartholomew Fayre*, Wing D109 (1647); *Aulicus*, E.429[4] (17–24 February 1648), sig. D2r; *The cities X commandements*, 669.f.11[133] ([27 February] 1648).
114 *The fooles of fate*, E.453[47] ([24 July] 1648), p. 1; *Melancholicus*, E.437[26] (24 April–1 May 1648), p. 206. See also *An elegy, on . . . John Warner*, 669.f.13[43] ([17 November] 1648).
115 *Mercurius anglicus*, E.456[22] (27 July–3 August 1648), sig. A2r; *Melancholicus*, E.423[30] (22–9 January 1648), p. 129. See also *Mercurius psitacus*, E.449[28] (21–6 June 1648), p. 1. For Taylor's exposé, see [John Taylor], *A briefe relation of the idiotismes and absurdities of Miles Corbet*, Wing T434A (1646).
116 *Pragmaticus*, E.417[21] (23–30 November 1647), sig. L3v; *Elencticus*, E.465[33] (27 September–4 October 1648), sig. Xx4r; *Mercurius fidelicus*,

E.460[32] (17–24 August 1648), p. 5. Cf. *A case for Nol Cromwells nose*, E.448[9] ([17 June] 1648), p. 6, which claimed that Sir Thomas Fairfax (married to an allegedly domineering wife) had become parliament's chief cuckold in Essex's stead.

117 *Elencticus*, E.423[25] (19–26 January 164[8]), p. 65; ibid., E.463[6] (6–13 September 1648), p. 341; ibid., E.536[31] (26 December 1648–2 January 1649), p. 551.
118 *Pragmaticus*, E.453[11] (11–18 July 1648), sig. Q3v; *Elencticus*, E.459[8] (9–16 August 1648), p. 310. See also *Elencticus*, E.454[12] (19–26 July 1648), pp. 270–1.
119 McElligott, 'Politics of Sexual Libel', pp. 84–6.
120 *Pragmaticus*, E.423[2] (11–18 January 1648), sig. S3v (John Goodwin); *Melancholicus*, E.436[23] (17–24 April 1648), p. 203 (John Weaver); *Mercurius domesticus*, E.445[41] ([5 June] 1648), sig. A3r (Fairfax); *The earle of Pembroke's speech*, E.453[30] ([20 July] 1648), p. 7.
121 *Melancholicus*, E.412[32] (30 October–6 November 1647), p. 59.
122 Jason Peacey, ' "The Counterfeit Silly Curr": Money, Politics, and the Forging of Royalist Newspapers during the English Civil War', *HLQ* 67:1 (2004), 27–57.
123 See, for instance, The John Carter Brown Library, DA648 .B682b; TNA, ASSI 45/2/2, nos. 17 and 23; LMA, MJ/SR/1009/56.
124 BL, Add. MS 36914, fol. 237r; *Calendar of the Manuscripts of the Most Honourable The Marquess of Salisbury, Preserved at Hatfield House* (24 vols, London, 1976), xxiv, p. 282. See also BRBML, Z17 92c, where a hostile reader scribbled the epithet 'Lying Aulicus' into the margins of one May 1648 newsbook.
125 Joad Raymond, *The Invention of the Newspaper: English Newsbooks, 1641–1649* (Oxford, 1996), p. 52.
126 Patricia Crawford, 'Charles Stuart, That Man of Blood', *JBS* 16:2 (1977), 41–61.

# 4

# The porno-politics of regicide, 1648–51

The Scots' defeat at Preston kicked off the most consequential six-month period in English history. Between August 1648 and the following February, a radical minority in the Commons and the army grew so incensed at the efforts of parliamentary moderates to compromise with their twice-defeated king that they orchestrated a coup to bring him to justice. That process culminated with Charles's trial and execution on 30 January 1649, followed by the dissolution of the English monarchy and the establishment of a republican commonwealth in its place.

The death of King Charles, by his own account England's beloved father and husband, marked the most jarring blow to date against the kingdom's reeling body politic. Although sex barely surfaced during the trial itself, the regicide brought to a head a long-running argument between royalists and parliamentarians about the sexual politics of early modern kingship. The issue was straightforward: in a personal, hereditary monarchy, what role did royal sexuality play in good governance? Variations on this question had circulated in print since at least 1643, and it possessed far older roots in the ancient political fiction of the king's two bodies. Now, with both Charles's person and his crown on trial, it became pressingly relevant for the king's defenders and detractors alike.

A major touchstone in that debate had long been the traditional patriarchal equivalence between kingship and fatherhood. Yet both royalists and republicans found an equally fruitful canvas in the image of the early modern husband-king that had flourished in England for decades. Even before James I's 1604 declaration that 'I am the Husband, and this whole Island is my lawful Wife', Elizabeth had wedded herself to her 'husband . . . the kingdom of England'. Charles, for his part, centred his own happy marriage as a symbol of English political harmony.[1] This was a powerful political metaphor, and while its most subversive implications remained largely unvoiced before the outbreak of war, by 1648 English polemicists had grown far less squeamish about royal bodies.[2] The result was an unprecedented printed debate over monarchical sexuality, both metaphorical and literal, that raged in print during the years bracketing Charles's January 1649 execution. In these exchanges, porno-politics – meaning, again, the use of explicit sexual imagery as a theoretical tool for explaining political change – took centre stage, as partisan apologists escalated the connection between sex-talk and political truth-claims first established during the early 1640s into full-blown political theory.[3]

The regicide has long interested scholars of the politics of the early modern family.[4] Intellectual historians, too, have connected the events of January 1649 with the hyper-patriarchal arguments of royalist stalwarts like Sir Robert Filmer as well as the birth of the Hobbesian sovereign state.[5] But although many of these scholars have assessed Charles's execution through the lens of the period's patriarchal and (less commonly) marital metaphors for kingship, only rarely have they pursued those languages to their logical conclusions by unpacking the metaphysical conjugal relationship that underlay both analogies: in other words, the 'sexual contract' that Carole Pateman has identified as the fundamental legitimating act of virtually all patriarchal political systems.[6] This chapter, in contrast, takes Pateman's sexual contract as its starting point to argue that the period 1648–51 witnessed a revolution in contemporary attitudes toward kingly sexuality. Indeed, its increasingly frank debates over 'conjugal kingship', as I term it here, represented the first explicit discussions of the sexual responsibilities of contemporary monarchs ever to appear in English print.

As will be seen, those debates spun off into several different directions. For royalists, the porno-politics of conjugal kingship, combined with the equally potent political metaphors of illicit pregnancy and monstrous birth, explained England's otherwise puzzling abandonment of its rightful husband-king in a way that few other available polemical modes could. For republican apologists, meanwhile, conjugal language provided a useful tool for depicting patriarchal monarchy, and especially the Stuart dynasty, as a bastion of sexual tyranny. Eventually, international contempt for the regicide prompted Commonwealth apologists to expand this argument to encompass the dead king's personal chastity as well, thereby shattering every remaining contemporary taboo against the discussion of monarchical sexuality. Both campaigns – one focused on the sexual usurper Oliver Cromwell, the other on the husband-tyrant Charles I – exemplified the degree to which, by 1648, mid-century sex-talk had cohered into distinct partisan programs of sexual politics. And as Cromwell and the young Stuart heir, Charles II, would soon learn, no English ruler would ever again be free from them.

## 'Tyrant, traitor, murderer': Charles I on trial

By August 1648, English parliamentarianism had reached a breaking point. Despite the wishes of parliamentary Independents and army radicals to bring their duplicitous king to justice, parliamentary moderates spent the fall campaigning for renewed negotiations with Charles over the terms of his eventual return to power. In fact, on the same day that the New Model met the Scots at Preston, the Commons – now controlled by a Presbyterian majority – moved to revoke January's incendiary Vote of No Further Addresses before scheduling another round of talks with the king.[7] During those discussions, held at Newport between September and November, Charles once again secretly attempted to recruit military aid (this time from Irish Catholics) for another royalist uprising in England. Eventually, overcome by *déjà vu*, the army leadership decided to intervene, spurred on by the Commons' maddening decision on 5 December to continue negotiations with Charles despite the failure at Newport.

The next day, the parliament-men were met on the steps of St Stephen's Chapel by Colonel Thomas Pride, who proceeded to turn away any MPs who had voted in favour of continuing negotiations with the king while letting most Independents pass unmolested. Shorn of the moderates, the purged House was finally free to discipline Charles for his crimes, and weeks of wrangling followed as the parliament-men debated how best to proceed. Finally, on 1 January 1649, they voted to try him for treason. Twenty days later, a newly-minted High Court of Justice convened in Westminster Hall for the opening proceedings.

What followed was a messy affair. Never before had a sitting English monarch been tried by his subjects, and consequently the prosecution struggled to articulate a coherent case.[8] Moreover, perhaps in order to allow the king a chance to submit and thereby save his own life, the parliamentary prosecution intentionally withheld their most damning allegations from the formal indictment; but it all proved for naught when Charles refused to plead.[9] With no other choice, the parliamentary commissioners declared him guilty on 27 January. They executed the king in front of his own Banqueting House just three days later.

The next few weeks frothed with activity. In Westminster, the purged House of Commons responsible for the trial (later derisively dubbed the 'Rump Parliament') codified its new supremacy by dissolving the monarchy and the House of Lords before establishing England's first republican commonwealth. The new regime then appointed a rotating Council of State, initially dominated by New Model officers and chaired by the celebrated parliament-man and soldier Oliver Cromwell, to manage it. Those leaders soon set to work on an ambitious legislative agenda that included, among other things, a kingdom-wide reformation of manners intended to stamp out immorality and transform England into the perfect godly state. But between the threat of royalist violence, a bloody war raging in Ireland, and the international furore sparked by Charles's death, serious obstacles stood in their way.

Sex remained latent throughout most of these proceedings, apart from intermittent intrusions: during the trial, for example, an unknown woman (possibly Anne Fairfax, wife of parliament's leading general) shouted from an upper gallery to denounce the commissioners as fools and Cromwell himself as a traitor, only to be condemned by a nearby army colonel as a whore.[10] The charges themselves – that Charles had become a 'Tyrant, Traytor, Murtherer, and publike Enemy to the Common-wealth' – were suggestive, especially considering the longstanding classical equivalencies between tyranny and sexual rapaciousness.[11] But these were too generic and vague to hold any significance for Charles's personal reputation. From the view in Westminster Hall, therefore, sex hardly impinged upon the regicide at all.

Yet for anyone attuned to the still-raging pamphlet wars, the impact of Charles's execution on English sexual politics was immediately self-evident. Since late 1647, a fiery debate over conjugal kingship – again, the notion that monarchs and their subjects were joined in a metaphorical sexual bond – had inundated partisan print, informed by the porno-political language pioneered earlier in the decade by commentators as diverse as John Taylor and Richard Overton. First, royalist writers constructed an elaborate genealogical history of parliamentarian sexual excess centred on the twin figures of 'Mistress Parliament' and her lover, Oliver Cromwell. Then, soon after the regicide, republican writers transformed the pioneering anti-monarchical sexual politics of Prynne's *Soveraigne power of parliaments* (1643) into a holistic indictment of conjugal kingship while also slandering the personal chastity of both Charles and his Stuart ancestors. In each case, the sexual contract between England's husband-king and his espoused people was rendered more visible, and more explicit, than ever before.

## 'The royal progeny of Mrs Parliament': royalists write the parliamentarian family of love

According to royalist polemicists, the regicide represented the horrifying climax of a years-long parliamentarian plot to usurp Charles's position as England's loving husband-king. The general shape of this conspiracy, laid out piecemeal in many dozens of loyalist tracts during the later 1640s, was simple. All knew that the parliamentarian coalition was composed of hypocritical lechers whose pretensions to moral reformation masked insatiable sexual appetites. But alongside their literal concupiscence, royalists argued, the puritan enemy had also seduced English subjects from their rightful royal partner and into the arms of an adulterous usurper: the eminent soldier-statesman Oliver Cromwell. In this inversion of the Stuarts' beloved conjugal analogy for kingship, the allegorical figure of 'Mistress Parliament' became the willing victim of a sexual plot to pollute the kingdom's constitutional inheritance and establish an ungodly puritan polity – the adulterous parliament's bastard offspring – in its place.

This porno-political theorising suffused royalist anti-parliamentarian polemic for more than a year after the loyalist press's fall 1647 resurgence. In newsbooks, pamphlets, and single-sheet broadsides, Charles's allies produced grotesque descriptions of puritan homewreckers abusing the kingdom's constitutional body from Westminster while its rightful husband-king sat in a parliamentary prison. Nor did this material disappear after the king's defeat. Instead, for nearly a year after the regicide, royalist writers continued to publish aggressive porno-political attacks on the Commonwealth from underground London presses until the passage of new press censorship legislation in September 1649 suppressed all but the most committed loyalists from print.[12]

Two specific developments spurred this escalation in royalist sexual politics. The first was the burgeoning radicalism of parliamentary Independents and their army allies, whose attitudes towards Charles had soured so severely by 1648 that a constitutional crisis was assured if he did not emerge victorious. Secondly, royalists were bewildered by the ongoing cooperation of English subjects with their oppressors, which persisted throughout the summer of 1648 despite the loyalists' frantic efforts to document parliamentarian depravity in print. To explain the kingdom's ongoing thralldom while simultaneously accounting for the ascendancy of Independent extremists in Westminster, royalists constructed a complex porno-political reading of early modern monarchical theory that began by equating the king's political authority with the active exercise of his conjugal abilities. On this account, there was only one explanation for the kingdom's rejection of Charles's loving embrace: adultery.

Consider an anonymous six-page squib entitled *A citie-dog in a saints doublet*. Written before the defeat at Preston and thus during a period of royalist optimism, the tract presented an array of sexual libels against key parliamentarians (including, as usual, 'the Fuckster' Henry Marten). But the pamphlet also made another argument. In a sixteen-line epistolary poem, the author reimagined London itself as an adulterous wife who had abandoned her rightful husband, Charles, for 'base prostitution' with parliamentarian leaders. As a 'strumpet disloyall to thy Soveraigns Throne', the capital and its citizens were thus made into complicit participants in the ongoing rebellion, seduced by the 'Bawdes at Westminster' into abandoning 'thy husband to whom thou wert wed' to become 'to each Junto-man a common Whore'. This meant that, assured as the unknown author was of Charles's impending victory, the City's eventual punishment would fit its crime. Accordingly, the poem promised that London would 'be whipt till thy shoulders bleed', like any other 'base slut', once 'thy Paramours' had been defeated.[13] As a metaphor for Charles's betrayal by his once-loyal subjects, it was striking indeed.

Between 1647 and 1649, royalist publications employed similar porno-political language (already familiar to readers of Overton's 1645 Marpriest tracts) to portray the parliamentarian rebellion as an adulterous intrusion into the constitutional marriage between king and people. In doing so, their authors rendered explicit the conjugal metaphor that lay at the heart of early modern patriarchal kingship while also doubling down on the caustic anti-puritan language of earlier royalist productions. Importantly, this strategy also required that Charles be publicly depicted as an active sexual agent: in *A citie-dog*, for instance, he was seen having 'resolv'd nere more to bed with thee' (again, London) upon learning of the City's 'cursed sin'.[14] In order to indict their opponents for constitutional adultery, in other words, royalists also had to represent the king's own (constitutional) sexuality in unprecedentedly frank terms.

This was not entirely new ground for royalist writers. As we saw in Chapter 2, Charles's vulnerability to sexual politics – a product of his father's notorious appetites as well as his own well-documented love of marital imagery – had immediately set his partisans on guard against any allegation of kingly impropriety at the outbreak of civil war. Once parliamentarian publications like *Britanicus* began attacking Henrietta Maria's chastity during the early 1640s, and especially after the 1645 appearance of *The Kings cabinet opened*, therefore, the king's sexual probity became a running theme of royalist print. 'How kinde He [Charles] is, and yet withall, how Chast', one Oxford apologist wrote in response to the *Cabinet*, 'how full of warme expressions of Love, and yet how farre from Wanton?'[15]

Royalists continued in this vein throughout the king's parliamentary captivity. In April 1648, *Mercurius pragmaticus* raged that Charles's imprisonment had dangerously jeopardised his fecundity, since 'his Majestie is never like to kisse his Mistrisse again'. But loyalist writers were far more concerned with ongoing parliamentarian attacks against royal sexuality. They insisted that by 'slandering, scoffing and affronting His sacred Majestie', and particularly by 'call[ing] his Majestie Cuckold, the Queen Whore, and the Prince Bastard' – thereby undermining the legitimacy of the royal succession as well as Charles's patriarchal-constitutional credentials – parliamentarians would destroy England's political order.[16]

In this sense, then, monarchical sexuality had suffused loyalist print since the outbreak of war. Yet before the later 1640s, those discussions were usually defensive, intended to protect Charles against aspersions of unchastity while emphasising his role as a loving patriarch-husband. Only intermittently did royalist writers take the offensive by arguing, for example, that parliamentarians had played the role of biblical Absaloms by impinging on their king-father's sexual authority in order to usurp his political power.[17] But as tensions rose and Charles's place in the postwar polity became a matter of debate rather than a foregone conclusion, the royalist press saw a new opportunity to weaponise the language of conjugal kingship by repainting their enemies as homewrecking adulterers whose interruption of the loving bond between Charles and his people had thrown the entire kingdom askew.

To do so, loyalists needed a compelling villain. They found one in Oliver Cromwell, the obscure puritan gentleman who became successively an army commander, a leader on the new republican Council of State, and, eventually, Lord Protector of the English Commonwealth. Cromwell's meteoric rise lent him a singular status among royalist conspiracy theorists, who soon recognised 'King Cromwell' as the rebellion's leading patriarch.[18] As such, between 1647 and 1649, royalist theorists crafted the Huntingdonshire parliament-man into the perfect inversion of Charles's own husbandly self-image from the 1630s, both as an adulterous usurper into the sacred relationship between king and people as well as a straightforward tyrannical lecher.[19] Exemplified before the regicide by 'Mistress Parliament' and after it by the satirical trope of the 'Bull of Ely', anti-Cromwellian sexual satire remained the centrepiece of royalist porno-political writing until its late-1649 collapse.

Royalists first took aim at Cromwell's chastity late in 1647. As the army butted heads with parliamentary Presbyterians in July and August, Charles's resurgent press corps began experimenting with porno-political theory. Figuring the army's radical 'Agitators' as 'Whelps' of 'Cromwels own breed', royalist writers placed Cromwell – now the New Model's second-in-command – at the centre of parliamentarian radicalism with a paternal metaphor that reflected his leading position.[20] As a key military leader, influential parliament-man, and true puritan believer, as well as a literal father-figure to several New Model officers, Cromwell encapsulated the cause in a single, masculine body.[21] He was therefore the ideal patriarch for the parliamentarian rebellion.

That trope was especially effective because royalist polemicists had long portrayed the parliamentarian coalition itself as a subversive family conspiracy. To do so, Charles's press corps chose a notorious historical model: the sixteenth-century Family of Love. For nearly a century following its appearance on English shores, the perfectionist Protestant doctrine known as familism – originally based on the teachings of the Dutch mystic Hendrick Niclaes ('H.N.') – had become synonymous with debauched sectarian sexuality.[22] Among familism's recent critics were Presbyterian heresiographers like Ephraim Pagitt, whose 1645 *Heresiography* accused Niclaes of conducting sexual trysts with both his 'sister' and his 'cousin'.[23] (Needless to say, the sect's familial language provided plentiful opportunities to advance the familiar anti-tolerationist argument about incestuous sectarian sexuality.) Similarly lurid anti-familist literature continued to flourish in print until the regicide.

Royalists were responsible for much of it. Since the early 1640s, anti-puritan satirists had deployed familist imagery to mock the 'Conjunctions copulative' allegedly practiced in godly conventicles.[24] Those efforts also benefited from a broader strain of godly familial imagery that thrived both before and during the civil wars, albeit in terms certifiably distinct from those employed by H.N. Among many mainstream godly believers, for example, 'brethren' and 'sisters' (language that also inspired the royalists' beloved 'holy sisters' trope) were standard forms of address, while descriptions of the church as a family united in faith had patristical roots stretching back to Paul the Apostle.[25] Furthermore, this standard lexicon of godly piety came packaged with a metaphorical language of conception and spiritual reproduction that, as Katharine Gillespie has shown, lent female believers a special significance within radical circles.[26] Consequently, not only did puritans frequently refer to themselves as 'babes of grace' (i.e. believers reborn in Christian love), but they also extended their reproductive language to encompass England's impending rebirth as a godly nation. Printed sermons from the early 1640s thus described the Long Parliament's reforming agenda in terms of a 'child of reformation' soon to be born.[27] Given early Stuart England's longstanding anxieties about monstrosity and miscegenation, such rhetoric made an easy target for royalist satirists.[28]

And, indeed, anti-puritan libellers had long deployed the biblical commandment to 'increase and multiply' to ridicule godly sexual hypocrisy.[29] But a more potent strain of royalist discourse, first promulgated by early freelancers like John Taylor, identified the parliamentarian rebellion itself as a monstrous birth. As a 1642 pamphlet entitled *Rules to get children by* warned: 'if you chance to mingle your loves promiscuously ... as you interweave opinions, and beget monsters ... your Church may well Vie with Africk for monstrous shapes'. (Associations with non-European monstrosity were quite common in royalist polemic, although Charles's partisans soon became convinced that even 'sunburnt Affrick never had nor hath / A Monster like our English publicke Faith'.)[30] The 'Parents of this

Rebellion' were undoubtedly the parliamentarian leadership (themselves, other royalists argued in an inversion of earlier puritan anti-episcopal rhetoric, the 'sonnes' of the devil), and as their reformation proceeded, the true nature of their misshapen offspring became abundantly clear.[31] Hence the second major component of late-1640s royalist porno-political rhetoric: the claim that the Westminsterians' adulterous interruption of English sexual harmony had resulted in the birth of a deformed, devilish puritan state.

By combining anti-puritan tropes with godly familial language, then, royalists denounced the parliamentarian 'Family of Reformation' for usurping England's loving patriarch-king to become the new 'Fathers of their Countrey' in his stead. Loyalist writers summed up this new 'publike State of the Family of Love' – envisioned as a permanent world-turned-upside-down in which the hypocrisy of puritan moral reformation yielded an endless orgy of godly copulation – under a simple refrain: 'them whose Lust must be their Law'.[32] Like Niclaes's sect, the parliamentarian regime was accused of seeking sex above all else, buttressed by an antinomian logic of perfectionist freedom from sin. It was, in short, everything that royalist writers had railed against in print since the early 1640s.

At the centre of this conspiracy sat Oliver Cromwell. In 1648, as vicious printed debates gave way to renewed civil war, royalists repeatedly claimed that the 'Devills in Parliament' were mentoring 'sons . . . nurs'd up so long in rebellion', over whom Cromwell presided as the chief 'Father of all Schisme, Sedition, Heresy and Rebellion'. Thus branded as the 'master' of the parliamentarian 'Family of separation', Cromwell therefore also became the metaphorical progenitor of the entire parliamentarian cause. The implications of this argument, including the possibility that an alternative lineage of 'Saints begotten of [Cromwell's] owne body' might unseat the Stuarts forever, were articulated with increasing dismay as Charles's position weakened.[33]

For royalist writers, the reproductive metaphor explained the otherwise inexplicable durability of the parliamentarian rebellion. But it also presented a new problem: for if Cromwell was indisputably the uprising's father, who then was the mother? Loyalist polemicists initially offered several different possible answers, ranging from the mangled national church (recently 'reformed' from 'old Babels whore . . . into a new English Saint') to the 'Nation' itself, which had 'prostitute[d] her Beauty, To the unlimited and ravanous Lust / Of such who have betrayed their Countreyes Trust'.[34] As *A citie-dog* revealed, another scapegoat indicted for 'cursed Fornication' with the parliamentary 'State-Committee' was that 'strumpet' London, 'who hath too long prostituted to their lust'.[35] All of these figures, royalists argued, had 'plaid the whore these 5 yeeres with Parliament-men', and some had been got 'with child' as a result. Occasionally, loyalists explained the entire conflict in such terms: 'behold a monster borne at Geneva', one wrote in September 1647, 'fostered in Scotland, called Rebellion . . . [and] guided into England by a Scotch-man'.[36]

By mid-1648, however, most royalist writers agreed that the central adulterous partner of the Westminsterian family of love – and of Cromwell above all – was parliament itself. This formulation, too, owed a debt to the conjugal metaphor. Precisely because the pairing of 'the Kinge and his wyfe the Parliament' had been such a dominant trope in early Stuart England, parliaments had long been vested with a latent sexuality.[37] Royalists first rendered it visible after the outbreak of war in passing references to 'that painted whore / who sits at West-minster'. From there, parliamentarians had scoffed at Charles's 1643 Oxford Parliament as a 'Mongrell Parliament', and later Henry Neville reimagined the institution as a legislative hub of feminised lust in the *Parliament of ladies*.[38] But it was not until 1648, as a recognisably parliamentarian state emerged from the wreckage of civil war and Charles's continued sovereignty began to look increasingly dubious, that royalists coined a new nickname for the adulterous body upon which the Westminsterian family had fathered its rebellion: 'Mistress Parliament'.

Mistress Parliament was introduced in four short pamphlets published during the summer of 1648 by the same figures responsible for the loyalist newssheets *Mercurius melancholicus* and *The parliament-kite*.[39] Composed as dramatic dialogues, these tracts presented parliament as a living female allegory for the thousands of Charles's once-loyal subjects who had deserted him for the parliamentarian cause since the early 1640s. This was a powerful metaphor for the kingdom's betrayal, and it served a double duty by emasculating those traitors as effeminate weaklings while simultaneously implicating them as participants in the ongoing adultery at Westminster. No longer were royalist writers content to portray most of the kingdom as innocent victims of parliamentary rapacity; now, the corrupted body of Mistress Parliament rendered every subject who had not fought on Charles's behalf complicit in the conspiracy.

The play-pamphlets implied that, like most English subjects, Mistress Parliament had once served as a devoted wife to her husband. Since the outbreak of war, however, she had been transformed into a promiscuous, puritan harlot. The final tract thus wondered how

> our honourable Sister Mrs. Parliament, who was arrived to the very highest pitch of honour and said to her selfe, I sit like a Queen, and shall know no sorrow, should on the sudden become wretchedly miserable . . . in open Rebellion and Disloyalty against her head and Husband.[40]

The first pamphlet was even more abrupt. It described Mistress Parliament as 'a Whore, and no better then the arrantest Strumpet that ever went upon two shooes', who had 'imprisoned her Husband', Charles, in order to 'prostitute' her 'Members to all manner of Wickedness and Uncleanness'. Accompanied by a host of allegorical sidekicks, Mistress Parliament embodied the puritan hypocrisy of Charles's parliamentarian opposition, who had 'converted' England 'to the satisfying of your own private Lust, though pretended to be done for the publique good of the Kingdom'.[41]

Mistress Parliament's religion was arguably more influential than 'the weakness of her sex' – after all, the authors noted, 'she is not the first Woman that hath done amiss' – and throughout the first two play-pamphlets, she exhibited all the traditional signs of godly lechery. But the third tract in the series contained a surprising twist when she appeared 'in a Scarlet coloured Robe, Riding on a beast of many heads, and a Cup of Red Wine in her hand': the classic garb of the Whore of Babylon.[42] In revealing parliamentarian puritanism to be the old Catholic enemy in disguise, the royalist authors harnessed the inversionary logic of their world-turned-upside-down topos to marry traditional anti-popish porno-politics with the anti-puritan themes of the early-to-mid 1640s.[43] Their Mistress Parliament figure thus encompassed what royalists believed to be the true nature of parliamentarian reformation: monstrous popery, feminised sedition and hypocritical godly unchastity, all rolled into one.

The ultimate consequence of her perfidy was monstrous reproduction. Mistress Parliament's travails as a nursing mother to 'a most precious Babe of Grace' – 'the hopefull fruit of her seven Yeers Teeming' in rebellion, soon to 'prove [a] Monster' – provided the tracts' dominant storyline, which also featured 'mistris London' as a reluctant midwife and 'Mrs. Sedition, Mrs. Schisme, Mrs. Toleration, and Mrs. Leveller' as malevolent helpmeets. The delivery scene was especially traumatic. Mistress London, presumably unsettled by the iron grip of her New Model occupiers (holdovers from Fairfax's August 1647 intervention), interrupted Mistress Parliament's labor to chastise her for having 'brought forth the Bastard Issue of thine own Lust . . . begot in obscenity' and to wish that 'may it prove as monstrous in its birth, and as fatall to it selfe, as it hath been ominous to others'. At the narrative's climax, her premonition was proven true: Mistress Parliament's offspring appeared as a monstrous 'childe of deformation'. This 'deformed' infant – a metaphor for the antichristian national confession designed by the Westminster Assembly – captured royalists' disgust at parliament's ungodly religious reforms.[44] By harnessing the familiar language of monstrous births, they enabled virtually any English reader to draw the same conclusion.

The eponymous play-pamphlets of summer 1648 were soon bolstered by references to Mistress Parliament in other contemporaneous royalist productions, as 'the Whores tricks' of 'Mistris Parliament their beloved Concubine' became a staple of loyalist print. So, too, did the tracts' inversionary equivalence between 'the skarlet coloured whore at Westminster' and 'the Whore of Babylon'.⁴⁵ Even absent the Mistress Parliament nomenclature, many royalist writers blamed parliament (for committing 'adulterie with his Maiesties throne') and Charles's wayward subjects (for having 'divorst from your Royall King' to 'imbrace Strumpets . . . after the enjoyment of so happy an Issue, as Peace, Plenty, and all blessings whatsoever') using similar conjugal language.⁴⁶ Granted, the metaphor was not always consistent – when Thomason acquired his first Mistress Parliament tract in May 1648, he also purchased another loyalist pamphlet that glossed the Houses as a dying 'S[ir] Parliament' – but such irregularities did not significantly compromise its potency.⁴⁷

Mistress Parliament's adultery was mirrored in the sins of her monstrous 'bastard[s]' (so dubbed because they lacked the legitimising 'assent of Majesty'). The precise nature of this 'Parliamentary Progeny' remained unsubstantiated, but it was widely acknowledged to be grotesque. 'If this Monster beget Monsters', *Melancholicus* moaned, 'O then what a generation of Monsters will our Parliament Ladies shortly bring forth'.⁴⁸ One common analogue for Mistress Parliament's 'Bastard Ordinance[s]', following an earlier argument of Daniel Featley's in *The dippers dipt* (1645), was a 'Cockatrice'.⁴⁹ *Pragmaticus* was particularly taken with the figure of the parliamentarian 'man-midwife', responsible for ushering Mistress Parliament's 'monsterous Moon-Calfe' into the world before it could 'suck the teates of the Common-wealth dry'.⁵⁰ An imprisoned Exeter royalist scribbled a different take into his commonplace book in 1651, deriding 'proud Babilon' as the 'Parent' of the 'most prodigious race' of parliamentary 'Sectarye[s] & Regicide[s]'.⁵¹ In every case, the threat remained the same: a perpetual cycle of monstrous godly births, supplanting forever the rightful royal succession.

It was Cromwell's relationship with Mistress Parliament that royalists found most threatening. If 'king Cromwall' emerged victorious over Charles, they knew that the 'Rebells' would 'have no King to reigne over them except he be of the Royall Proginy of Mrs. Parliament, or the Childe of Reformation'.⁵² This danger of a 'new sanctified brood of Kings', 'beget' by Cromwell and 'the Kingdomes Army', was particularly troubling because Charles's partisans feared that the 'everlasting Parliament' might 'become hereditary' after Cromwell and his minions had 'take[n] care to make it run in a blood, from generation to generation'.⁵³ Cromwell's intrusion into the happy marriage of king and people thus threatened a world turned permanently upside down by misbegotten puritan monsters.

By arguing that all parliamentarian rebels had been made in Cromwell's image via a monstrous union with an adulterous parliament, royalists consolidated their long-running campaign against puritan-parliamentarian sexual malignancy into a single porno-political trope between late 1647 and the closing months of 1648. Not even Cromwell's brief northern sojourn to

Scotland in October and November put an end to royalist attacks against the parliamentarian family's adulterous patriarch. But then came the regicide, which obviously necessitated a change in strategy. With Charles dead at his subjects' hands, the loving union between king and people had clearly dissolved; seduction was thus no longer a useful metaphor for Cromwell's subversion of the political order. Royalists adjusted their libellous portrait accordingly by transitioning away from the potent allegorical language of the previous eighteen months and instead recasting Cromwell – now the temporary head of England's new Council of State – in the mould of the lecherous tyrant. Using similar language to that which would soon be deployed by republican writers against Charles himself, royalists refocused on the literal body of the Commonwealth's new figurehead with singular vigor after January 1649.

Of course, royalists had slandered Cromwell's chastity before the regicide, including accusations ranging from casual affairs with puritan 'Whorysisters' to sodomy.[54] Nor did they abandon porno-political metaphor after it. Throughout 1649, Cromwell remained the 'Father' of the parliament's 'blessed Family' in royalist print, siring 'Cubbs' with that 'common-Strumpet', the state, in hopes that those 'children' would ensure 'for ever and ever Parliament everlasting'.[55] In a new formulation, royalist writers also began depicting Charles's loyal subjects as 'widdowed' victims of puritan rapacity.[56] But their overwhelming focus was now Cromwell's literal sexuality, which they explored through a fictional personal history that stretched from youthful excesses in East Anglia to an alleged affair with the wife of his chief subordinate. Moreover, although most of these stories were invented, at least one remained plausible enough to significantly boost their potency.

After the regicide, then, royalists accused Cromwell of an incredible variety of sexual crimes. Alongside generic accusations of spreading the 'pox' among his puritan 'Sisters', he was also charged with 'towz[ing]' the 'back-doore[s]' of his parliamentarian colleagues.[57] Royalists famously satirised Cromwell's large nose as a pox-infected sex-toy, but in addition to lampooning his 'notable Head-piece', they also parodied 'another Piece too' – 'every inch of him'. When Cromwell left England to lead the Irish war effort in mid-1649, for instance, royalists announced that he had 'lost Lusts Instrument' when a 'brace of bullets in his Gennitals' abruptly 'shot off' his 'Main-yard' but 'missed the rest of his Tacklings'. Throughout, Cromwell's 'concupiscence' reflected his treacherous nature: his 'flesh' simply 'Rebell[ed] against the spirit', just like 'hee against the King'.[58]

These misadventures were subsumed under a moniker: the 'Town Bull of Ely'.[59] This title, derived from Cromwell's imagined escapades as an East Anglian youth, condensed his most notable sexual attributes – hyper-masculinity and effeminate cuckoldry – into a single libellous label.

In short: after a wild string of sexual conquests, royalist claimed, young Cromwell had been exiled from Ely 'for getting Bastards' with local women, but not before he was 'forced to Marry' his 'Fathers Maide' after 'having got [her] with Child'. From there, due in part to his talent for seducing a 'Shee-Saint' with a 'Town-bull trick', he relocated to London and subsequently clawed his way to political and patriarchal ascendancy. As one pamphlet put it, all parliamentarian rebels were 'Calves of this Town-Bulls begetting'.[60]

Just as bulls embodied aggressive sexuality, the most iconic element of the 'Town Bull' persona was Cromwell's alleged adulterous affair with Frances Lambert, wife of the parliamentarian general John Lambert. This accusation first appeared in a September 1648 newsbook, which claimed that Lambert's 'Pretty Spouse', 'being Ambitious to tast of the fruites of Royalty', had offered herself to King Cromwell. As royalist libellers knew, Cromwell and Frances Lambert were undeniably close friends, although probably not lovers. However, even innocent intimacy proved damning, and accounts of Cromwell 'feed[ing] upon the sweet flesh' of Mrs Lambert quickly became a staple of anti-Cromwellian royalist print.[61] Not only did graphic depictions of Cromwell 'driv[ing]' his 'Nayle' into 'Lamberts wife' indict the Commonwealth's chief political leader and its preeminent military commander as an adulterer and a cuckold, respectively; they also pointedly contradicted the new regime's professed commitment to moral reformation. When compared with Charles, England's faithful husband-king, the fictionalised Cromwell-Lambert affair made for a stark contrast.[62]

Another aspect of the 'Town Bull' persona, its horns, undermined Cromwell's masculinity even as it showcased his alarming fecundity. As gender scholars have shown (and as we have already seen with the foppish cavalier archetype), early modern moralists identified male hypersexuality with effeminacy, and even cuckoldry, on grounds that the abandonment of self-control to pursue sexual pleasure was a fundamentally feminine characteristic.[63] Accordingly, Cromwell's wife Elizabeth also featured in royalist polemic as an enthusiastic adulteress. Her rumoured paramours included parliamentary administrators and puritan divines as well as at least one 'impoverished Cavalier' with whom Cromwell's 'yeast and graynes Lady' played 'at the In and In' while her husband was away on campaign.[64] Her usual partner was the parliament-man Herbert Morley, soon to become one of Cromwell's fiercest opponents, and multiple tracts depicted Elizabeth being 'devoutly kist' by Morley while they cavorted in the parliament's 'Nurceries of Sodomy, Lust, and Uncleanness'.[65] Elizabeth's supposed infidelity obviously damaged her husband's credentials as a military and political leader; equally importantly, by trumpeting Cromwell's cuckoldry, hostile writers also challenged the legitimacy of the presumed parliamentarian succession.

All told, porno-political depictions of Cromwell as a lecherous patriarch uniquely embodied royalist interpretations of the parliamentarian rebellion as a subversion of proper sexual-political order. Charles's trial and execution presented the ultimate proof that the kingdom had become a whore to 'Crumwells lust'.[66] The result of that ungodly union, as evidenced by the subsequent birth of the English Commonwealth and the dissolution of the monarchy, was a world turned permanently upside down.

As time went on, royalists focused increasingly on Cromwell's literal activities, first as a Cambridge youth and later as a wayward husband to his promiscuous wife. That transformation paralleled Cromwell's own apparent transition from rebellious subject to upstart head of state. As the spectre of 'King Cromwell' loomed ever larger, royalists seized on the classical association between lust and tyranny to attack his personal chastity, and through it, the legitimacy of the new Commonwealth. In doing so, they crafted a debauched Cromwellian lineage – even indicting his 'great Grand Father' for allegedly 'committ[ing] Incest' with 'his own Daughter' – to argue that the entire family was sexually corrupt. Both metaphorically and literally, royalists claimed that the Commonwealth's 'Monstrous Government' was the result of a correspondingly monstrous union between Cromwell's unnatural virility and the adulterous Mistress Parliament.[67]

In general, parliamentarian writers did not engage with royalist porno-politics beyond standard denunciations of the cavaliers' 'sucking libels' and 'precious Ribaldry', which had extended even to 'vilifie the representative Body of the Kingdome' after 1647. At key moments, however, they could not resist rebutting. For one, the parliamentarian newsheet *Mercurius anti-mercurius* took exception to *Elencticus*'s 'indelible imputation cast upon the vertuous Spouse of Major Gen. Lambert, and the victorious Lieut. Gen. Crumwell', although few readers likely bought *Anti-mercurius*'s concurrent argument that such 'scandals' served only 'to make the lovely pictures of Innocence seem more excellent'.[68] There were other signs that republican writers took the royalists' charges seriously. For one, Cromwell's sexual continence became a staple of republican paeans during the early 1650s, as Commonwealth apologists set about constructing a polemical edifice of virtuous masculine patriarchy to replace the effeminate Stuart tyranny they had just overthrown. In those later productions, it is possible to detect a latent, albeit possibly incidental, repudiation of royalist porno-politics.

In any case, the new regime soon crushed any opportunities for further dialogue. Cromwell and his colleagues cracked down on printed dissent in September 1649 with a draconian press censorship act that put a stop to seditious royalist polemic – including, for the most part, direct attacks against Cromwell and Mistress Parliament.[69] But these efforts at suppression came too late to prevent readers from collecting, annotating, and distributing royalist porno-political print during the later 1640s.[70] Not even the efforts of parliamentarian press watchdogs, who arrested several hawkers for selling royalist publications beneath the regime's nose in London, could stop their illicit circulation.[71]

Proof of their popularity appeared in the seditious whispers that dogged the new republican regime from its inception. Cromwell's chastity became a topic of hostile conversation soon after his ascension to the Council of State: a drunken Yorkshire schoolmaster dubbed him 'the son of an whore' in February 1650, and a Somerset man was dragged before the local sessions court later that year after he put a cuckold's 'horne' in his hat and called it 'Crumwells Collours'.[72] The adulterous Mistress Parliament, too, received her share of abuse. One Chester local wished 'a pox ... upon the Parliament' in language that vividly recalled royalist imagery of a corrupted, monstrous parliament. In June 1650, Thomas Repwells was alleged to have said that 'the parliament hath sate on broode these seaven yearres ... & hath brought no thinke to good'. Three years later, an Essex man (ironically named John Milton) glossed all 'Parliament Rogues' as 'Cromwells Bastards'.[73] Whether or not these examples reflected royalist influence or merely the gripes of a disgruntled populace, they would continue to haunt Cromwell and his regime long after the dissolution of the royalist press.

By depicting the parliamentarian rebellion and its lecherous patriarch as a twisted inversion of the conjugal metaphor while simultaneously indicting English subjects for their seduction at the hands of Charles's enemies, royalist writers dramatically expanded the theoretical scope of mid-century porno-politics. Logical inconsistencies and troubling implications aside – by figuring Cromwell and Mistress Parliament as adulterous partners, for example, loyalists thereby also rendered Charles into a figurative cuckold – the language of conjugal kingship transformed royalists' mundane anti-puritan slanders into a powerful critique of parliamentarian rule. Even after the regicide, Cromwell's presence allowed cavalier polemicists to continue their depictions of the new regime as a lecherous godly tyranny. By that time, moreover, they had a potent example to follow in the republican attacks against Charles I that erupted into print after 30 January 1649.

## 'Distasteful to all good men': republican porno-politics and the king's two bodies

Those assaults appeared suddenly after years of pointed parliamentarian silence about Charles's personal sexuality. Given the Stuarts' collective predilection for the conjugal metaphor and the even longer history of English patriarchal monarchy, however, that moratorium was never destined to last;

and the regicide, followed by the success of Charles's posthumous memoirs and the rapid-fire formation of a new republican government in the face of continued opposition from his heir, Charles II, finally forced the issue. Soon thereafter, driven by political expediencies as well as its burgeoning self-representation as the overseer of England's moral reformation, the new Commonwealth marshalled its own take on the porno-politics of conjugal kingship into a comprehensive sexual indictment of Charles's crown, his ancestors, and, eventually, his royal person.

Parliament's complicated relationship with monarchical sexuality stemmed from Charles's unique political position during the 1640s, when he had remained ostensibly immune from public criticism even as attacks against his soldiers, advisors, and family members proliferated in print. Although those protections gradually dissipated as the conflict worsened, parliamentarian theorists struggled to condemn the king's destructive policies without alienating sympathetic readers by resorting to personal attacks. As we have seen, one favourite scapegoat was Charles's coterie of evil counsellors. Parliament's other preferred weapon, first deployed by Sir John Hotham at Hull in April 1641, was the medieval theory of the king's two bodies, which dictated that monarchical power resided simultaneously in the king's physical person (the 'body natural') as well as in his office (the 'body politic').[74] Although the king's two bodies had long been marshalled as a legitimating tool by English monarchical regimes by the time of the showdown at Hull, Hotham's reinterpretation flipped the script in dramatic fashion.

From that point onward, parliamentarians appropriated the king's two bodies to criticise Charles's politics without violating the sacred honour due to his office. In particular, the trope enabled parliamentarian leaders to disavow the most radical constitutional implications of their anti-royalist polemic by claiming to defend England's true body politic – the combined sovereign authority of the king-in-parliament – against Charles's misled body natural.[75] Many royalists found this an absurd distinction: after the king's imprisonment in 1646, for example, one pamphleteer satirised the two bodies thesis by joking that the parliament-men had 'committed him to close prison in his owne Name' by invoking his 'Politique Capacity' to lock his 'personal capacity' away.[76] For other loyalists, however, the king's two bodies were no laughing matter.

The Stuarts' long history of conjugal rhetoric rendered sex a crucial battleground in these debates. Royalists arguing for the inseparability of the king's natural and political persons did so with explicit reference to Charles's sexual attributes; and, in 1648, the king himself publicly linked his travails as an imprisoned 'Husband and Father, without the comfort of my Wife and Children' with his status as 'a King, without the least shew of

Authority or Power'.[77] Meanwhile, parliamentarians took the same argument in a markedly different direction. During the early-to-mid 1640s, Westminster polemicists printed lurid accounts of long-dead royal favourites and Charles's debauched predecessors in hopes of blackening his personal appetites by historical association. Later, parliamentarian attacks against Henrietta Maria's chastity implicated the king as an emasculated cuckold, while his slavish uxoriousness was catalogued in *The Kings cabinet opened*. Yet the reverence traditionally accorded to kingly bodies ensured that even as Charles's family and associates came under increased scrutiny, his personal chastity remained largely unchallenged (directly, at least). Nevertheless, this did not dissuade royalist writers from publicly defending Charles's sexual reputation in increasingly strident terms as the decade wore on.

Their vigilance was warranted, for the king's role in the renewal of civil war in 1648 drove his exasperated enemies to reconsider their previous moratorium on direct attacks against his person. In February, parliament finally breached that frontier in their formal declaration announcing the Vote of No Further Addresses. Among other claims, the *Declaration* revived an accusation from the *Cabinet* that Charles had once lied to the Danish king, Christian IV, about a parliamentary investigation into the sexual history of his sister, England's Queen Anne.[78] Although hardly the document's most damning charge, its reappearance signalled that some parliamentarians, at least, were thinking critically about royal sexuality early in 1648. And if Charles's Stuart predecessors were fair game, the scandalous histories of his father and grandmother offered plenty of material to choose from.

The parliament-men even possessed compromising evidence against Charles's own chastity. In January 1648, the king's jailers on the Isle of Wight informed them of a washing-woman who routinely supplied Charles with 'Intelligence' under the guise of 'bring[ing] his cleane Linnen'.[79] They did not elaborate further, but the subtext was obvious: what else might this woman be doing with Charles while she delivered his news?

It was a fair question. As Sarah Poynting has deciphered, by that summer Charles was engaged in a passionate affair with Jane Whorwood, a royalist spy who visited him periodically in prison. Granted, she may not have been the washing-woman observed by parliamentary watchmen in January. Whenever Whorwood did visit, moreover, the jailers possibly did not realise that she was Charles's lover, since the king burned most of their correspondence after learning from the *Cabinet* debacle.[80] Even so, by the libellous standards of the later 1640s, the mere presence of either the washer-woman or Jane Whorwood in Charles's chambers should have been enough to underwrite an extensive smear campaign.

By 1648, moreover, Charles's crown was equally vulnerable to sexual criticism, largely thanks to the propaganda of hostile polemicists like

William Prynne. The nature of the threat was made apparent in December by the prophetess Elizabeth Poole, who visited Charles's judges on the eve of his trial. Her address to the grandees systematically inverted the Stuarts' beloved conjugal metaphor by describing Charles as a sexually troubled 'Father and husband' to his subjects who hoped to render them 'a generation to his own pleasure', as if 'a wife for his own lusts'.[81] If the parliament-men had wished to challenge their king's self-representation as England's beloved husband-king, Poole's language demonstrates that they had several avenues of inquiry – including the possibility of constitutional 'divorce' – from which to choose.[82]

Yet, with only one prominent exception, Charles's two bodies went untarnished in print by parliamentarian polemicists before the regicide. There were several reasons for their reluctance. First, although parliamentary hardliners outnumbered their moderate opponents in the Commons during the early months of 1648 (and would again after the December purge), the opposition captured the majority that summer, when many militant parliament-men left Westminster to oversee the war effort. These peace-mongers had no interest in demeaning a king that they hoped to restore to power. In fact, some even adopted the conjugal metaphor to plead their case. 'The Parliament', one October newsbook read, '(like a loving Spouse, whose bowels yern for the distresses of her dearest Lord) after long divorce, forgetting all fore-passed injuries, desire[s] to bee inthroned in the imbraces of his Majesty'.[83] As evidenced by the graphic imagery of Charles's loving 'distresses', parliamentary moderates were clearly willing to forgive their estranged husband-king to secure peace in England. They were therefore unlikely to condone public criticism of either of his two bodies.

Another reason that anti-monarchical sexual politics rarely surfaced in parliamentarian polemic, even during the brief windows of hardliner ascendancy, was Charles's sterling moral reputation. No one who remembered the king's crackdown on courtly vice during the 1630s could have easily accepted attacks on his personal chastity; indeed, some of Charles's opponents praised his 'temperate, chast, and serious' demeanor in comparison with the 'debosheries' of his father's reign. In October 1648, a radical newsbook actually argued against the king's legitimacy by suggesting that he was too 'sober' to be James's son.[84] True, Charles's patronage of amorous court poets had inflamed godly moralists, and his uxoriousness suggested to others that he had been debauched by his popish wife. But neither fact could seriously undermine the king's near-spotless moral standing. As such, even when the parliament-men learned of his mysterious female visitor, they may have simply dismissed the possibility of infidelity outright.

Only one voice dared to question Charles's chastity before the regicide. This was the radical newsbook *The moderate*, a bastion of anti-royalist sentiment that was equally critical of parliamentary peace-mongers. One September 1648 issue, for instance, expressed disgust with Presbyterian descriptions of the king 'as a nursing father to this Nation' just months after the February *Declaration* had indicted Charles for his own father's murder.[85] Then, early in January 1649, the newsbook's editors detailed the king's undue affections for the 'handsom' 'young Ladies' who visited him in captivity. In particular, they noted his 'hot and eager' longing for a 'black Wench' who had allegedly attended him on the Isle of Wight. These claims, which cast Charles as a randy fornicator, may well have been based on parliamentarian suspicions about the king's summertime affair; they were almost certainly linked to the earlier washer-woman report.[86] Either way, it was a landmark political moment. No one had ever before claimed, in print, that Charles was sexually debauched.

Moreover, *The moderate*'s editors were persistent. In an issue published just after the regicide, the newssheet reported on an encounter between Charles and 'a Gentlewoman big with childe' during the trial's final days. According to the newsbook, the woman approached and 'pertended [sic] she longed to kiss the Kings hand', to which his guard reluctantly assented. 'After she had greedily kist his hand', it continued, 'his Majesty . . . eagerly saluted her lips, three or four times'. This odd scene was later clarified by 'some that then knew her', who reported the mysterious gentlewoman to be none other than the 'handsome Maid, that waited on him at the Isle of Wight'.[87] The implication was clear: this woman, Charles's secret lover, carried the king's bastard child in her womb. It is difficult to imagine a more effective rebuttal of his longstanding self-representation as his people's faithful husband.

Crucially, however, *The moderate* operated on the margins of parliamentarian politics. Even days before Charles's execution, no other hostile publications, least of all those close to the regime, dared to question the king's chastity. This was a pragmatic choice, for despite the impending trial, Charles's judges were not convinced that he needed to die. By pulling their most serious punches – including the shocking charges regarding James's murder – the parliament-men thus hoped to make it easier for Charles to plead guilty in exchange for a non-lethal sentence.[88] It was also a strategic decision, given the king's popularity among English subjects who had watched their long-suffering monarch endure captivity with apparent grace: why risk alienating the population further than necessary by twisting the knife?[89] Finally, the parliament-men's reticence also possibly reflected remnants of the once-widespread contemporary conviction that kings ought not to be judged by their subjects; even Elizabeth Poole, for all of her porno-political prophesying, had warned against regicide precisely because, as 'the Father and Husband of your bodyes . . . your right cannot bee without him'.⁹⁰ In any case, whatever the reason, the king's chastity remained thoroughly off-limits in most parliamentary print on the eve of the regicide.

But then, within months, cascading political calamities suddenly rendered the dead king's two bodies fair game for slander. The two most pressing crises were the publication of the king's posthumous memoir *Eikon basilike* and the outbreak of war with Scotland in 1650. In the face of these threats, the Commonwealth finally addressed kingly sexuality in print using an escalating repertoire of polemical strategies: first, by targeting the conjugal metaphor for monarchical rule; next, by rehashing the Stuart dynasty's debauched legacy; and finally, following scathing international criticism of the regicide, by adapting the generic charge of 'tyranny' levelled at Charles during his trial to transform him from England's loving husband-king into a lustful, rapacious tyrant. Much of this material has been ignored by historians, who have generally followed Kevin Sharpe's argument that 'after [the] regicide, no one cartooned Charles I's body either in images or words'. Yet a thorough reading of post-regicidal republican polemic reveals that the king's two bodies each came under sustained attack from Commonwealth polemicists by mid-1650.⁹¹ In doing so, Charles's assailants concocted a new porno-politics of monarchy – one framed predominantly around the imagery of sexual violence – with considerable implications for later Stuart monarchical self-representation.

The first catalyst was the unexpected appearance of the king's personal memoirs, entitled *Eikon basilike*, immediately after his execution. The *Eikon*, which presented Charles as a devout Christian and a loving father, proved enormously popular, running to forty-six English editions within twelve months of its appearance.⁹² Its success so troubled regime leaders that they hired John Milton, now a prominent republican apologist, to respond. Milton, for his part, recognised that the *Eikon*'s effusive descriptions of Charles as the paradigmatic early modern husband-king would require particular attention.⁹³ He eventually set to work on a rejoinder.

Meanwhile, several unrelated defences of the Commonwealth appeared in print, prompted by the efforts of the young Stuart heir, Charles II, to recruit European military support for his floundering cause. One, entitled *The tenure of kings and magistrates* and authored by Milton himself, appeared just two weeks after the regicide. Milton's tract offered a comprehensive history of tyrannical kingship while outlining the grounds on which former monarchs had been deposed by their subjects. The book made minor references to the 'rapes' and 'adulteries' committed by various historical tyrants, but it offered little else in response to the broader sexual metaphors that had suffused Charles's self-representation. One month later, the Council of State echoed Milton's language by accused the dead king of exceeding his 'Forefathers' in pursuing the 'lusts . . . of a Tyrant'.⁹⁴ Beyond this vague allusion to the classical conflation between tyranny and lechery, however, they offered nothing concrete or specific.

Not, at least, until the October publication of *Eikonoklastes*, Milton's response to the *Eikon basilike*. Although sex was not the prevailing theme of Milton's riposte, he nevertheless assailed Charles's gentlemen as 'the ragged Infantrie of Stewes and Brothels' and his 'Court Ladies' as 'not the best of Women'. Milton also attacked the 'licentious remissness' of Charles's 'Sundays Theater', long depicted by godly writers like Prynne as a hotbed of illicit sex, and questioned whether there were 'any Males' at all among the effeminate and 'dissolute rabble' of his courtiers. In each case, Milton indicted the Caroline court as inherently debauched and insufficiently masculine – a legacy that was partly 'deriv'd from the example of his Father James'. In a hereditary monarchy, lechery was apparently a potent birthright, and the implications of James's excesses for Charles's personal chastity were not difficult to divine.[95]

But Milton's more enticing target was Charles's political body, which he attacked with a novel interpretation of the conjugal metaphor. Addressing traditional monarchist depictions of parliaments as female consorts of the king's 'procreative reason' (i.e. the central conceit of the Mistress Parliament trope), *Eikonoklastes* offered a different interpretation that was already familiar to readers of Prynne's *Soveraigne power of parliaments*: 'certainly it was a Parliament that first created Kings', Milton wrote, 'and not onely made Laws before a King was in being, but those Laws especially, wherby he holds his Crown'. Therefore, 'if he count it not Male', parliament's proper female analogue was not wife or daughter, but rather 'Mother', and Charles's tyrannical pretensions were nothing less than the realisation of Nero's historic 'dream of copulation with his Mother'.[96] Alongside his attacks on Caroline courtly morality, Milton's incestuous revision of the conjugal kingship trope – not to mention his comparison of Charles with Nero, which Jamie Gianoutsos has identified as a particularly unsavoury (and intrinsically gendered) political analogy – thus challenged both of the dead king's two bodies while offering a powerful porno-political argument for parliamentary sovereignty.[97]

It was not enough. Not only did *Eikonoklastes* fail to stifle royalist dissent, which continued to fester at home and abroad throughout the fall, but the winter of 1649/50 soon brought more stressors. Fallout from the summer's Irish war, compounded by Charles II's pursuit of foreign military aid, convinced Commonwealth authorities that a more forceful campaign was necessary to justify their republican experiment to sceptical European powers who might otherwise side with the royalists. Accordingly, the republic licensed additional anti-Stuart polemics from mid-1649 into the early months of 1652, authored by a stable of regime apologists who recognised the value of sexual politics for criticising the dead king's two bodies.

As Milton had shown in *Eikonoklastes*, an obvious starting point for the republican assault on hereditary monarchy was the conjugal metaphor, which only a few critics had addressed in print before the regicide.[98] Beginning in the closing months of 1649, republican apologists built on the same classical equation between lust and tyranny that informed postregicidal royalist attacks on Cromwell to argue that kings' political misconduct was mirrored by malignant personal sexuality.[99] Political absolutism, on this reading, naturally encompassed an insatiable appetite for flesh. As Henry Marten scribbled in his commonplace book: 'whoever hates all tyrannie / A slave to his lusts will never bee'.[100]

In its most conventional form, the republican campaign simply inverted the royalists' conjugal thesis: if good kings resembled good husbands, then bad kings were accordingly adulterers, domestic abusers and rapists. In 1650, George Walker observed that 'the greatest Tyrants' were identifiable by the 'vicious and debauched' nature of 'their lewd lives'. To other republican pamphleteers, the 'Rapes and Ravishments' inflicted by previous tyrants on 'the Priviledges of this Commonwealth' were evidence enough of this equivalence between political and sexual aggression. Still others, including John Goodwin, stressed infidelity rather than rapacity by arguing that 'A King, and a Tyrant, are as specifically distinct, as a lawfull husband, and an adulterer'.[101] These arguments uniformly equated tyranny with sexual excess – most notably with sexual assault, in keeping with classical tales like that of Tarquin and Lucretia – without rejecting the conjugal metaphor outright.

A different set of theorists went even further. Instead of distinguishing between good and bad husband-kings, these apologists argued that 'fowle mistris Monarchy' (notably gendered female) intrinsically elevated the 'lusts of one man and his posteritie' over the needs of the commonwealth.[102] Along these lines, the former-royalist-turned-republican Marchamont Nedham noted that 'Cato called a King . . . a Ravenous Creature', predisposed to 'Cruelties and Rapine'. Antony Ascham rejected the conjugal thesis entirely: 'The nature of Marriage and of Government differ extreamly', he declared, because 'to take this or that woman to wife, is a thing of free choice; but it is not so alwaies with the People in relation to Kings, who have many of them committed great Rapes upon them'. Here, again, sexual assault provided the dominant motif, as Commonwealth polemicists paralleled political arguments about the importance of consent with images of violent coercion.[103] For these republican apologists, sexual license was not merely the mark of a tyrant, but an intrinsic feature of monarchical rule.

Those attuned to the unsavoury histories presented in Prynne's *Soveraigne power of parliaments* knew that the past held plentiful evidence of kingly depravity. Accordingly, Commonwealth writers deployed biblical and classical precedents to illustrate the moral superiority of republican government. One common reference-point was David's adultery with Bathsheba and his subsequent murder of her husband, Uriah. Several republican apologists followed Milton's *Tenure of kings and magistrates* in invoking this episode as proof that even the greatest of kings might commit 'scandalous and mortal offences'.[104] If King David could not resist his lusts, they asked, what hope was there for the Stuarts?

Commonwealth polemicists also turned to English history to highlight the dubious credentials of Charles's predecessors. Several reminded their readers that William the Conqueror was 'a Norman bastard' ('pardon the expression', Parker wrote in August 1650, 'its true though plain'), thereby compromising the legitimacy of all post-Conquest monarchs.[105] More recent events were also fair game. *The life and reigne of Kings Charls* (1651) dismissed Henry VIII as 'one that neither spared any man in his wrath, or woman in his lust'; similarly, one year prior, Parker described the same king as a 'very lascivious' ruler who 'delighted much in variety, and changes of Laws, as wives'. Elsewhere, in a strange adaptation of the Tudor patriarch's own sixteenth-century arguments, Henry's sexual history was made to endanger his Catholic daughter in turn: *A disingag'd survey* (1650) suggested that Mary Tudor's unsurpassed malignity was due to her 'incestuous' origins.[106] Unsurprisingly, Elizabeth's reputation remained unsullied, since her virginal purity provided a convenient foil against which to contrast the immoral Stuarts. But her father and half-sister came under repeated fire by republican writers as exemplars of monarchical immorality.

Charles's ancestors provided the most enticing targets. Since 1643, parliamentarian writers had recounted the chief scandals of James's reign in print, but those earlier accounts had only obliquely implicated Caroline morality.[107] Even Milton's *Eikonoklastes*, which suggested that Charles had inherited his father's toleration of courtly promiscuity, did not dwell too closely on James's dubious sexual history. But then came Charles II's uncomfortable alliance with Presbyterian Scotland during the spring of 1650, which Commonwealth leaders rightfully recognised as the precursor to yet another war. In response, the regime turned its polemical guns on the (Scottish) House of Stuart in order to discredit its young heir prior to the impending invasion. As a result, while neither James nor Mary Stuart had featured heavily in the anti-monarchical screeds of 1649, both were soon deeply caught up in republican porno-politics.

The most popular of these accounts was Anthony Weldon's *Court and character of King James*, published posthumously in May 1650 with the regime's collusion. While recounting such era-defining scandals as the Overbury affair, Weldon's lurid history reflected on James's 'passion of love' for male courtiers with 'young Faces, and smooth Chins'. Those desires, Weldon wrote, had led him to fondle his male favourites and demand pleasure from especially comely subjects. Male same-sex intimacy was, of course, among the most damning charges available to contemporary moralists, and while whispers of James's preferences had circulated in coded manuscript verses during the 1620s, the republican campaign of 1650 brought the charges into a more visible light than ever before. When taken alongside other familiar charges about the sexual escapades of the old king's most infamous favourites, those allegations made it clear that the Jacobean court was drenched in sex, from Buckingham's 'lacivious carriage' to the activities of another infamous courtier, 'old Sir Anthony Ashley, who never loved any but boyes'.[108] While Charles again went largely unmentioned, the implication that James's son (and, by extension, his grandson) might have inherited similar appetites remained difficult to miss. In the process, by exposing these tales for broad popular consumption – the book was expanded and reprinted in 1651 – Weldon's text invited readers into the royal bedroom like never before.[109]

Thereafter, James's 'inclination to effeminate [male] faces' surfaced recurrently in Commonwealth anti-Stuart publications, tarring the entire dynasty with the insinuation of unnatural sexuality.[110] Charles's grandmother, Mary Stuart, also attracted republican attention. Mary's adulterous history had appeared in print once before, and it was not long before an anonymous republican republished that piece, George Buchanan's *Detectio Mariae reginae* (1571), in English. Other writers employed Mary's infamous promiscuity to question James's paternity, thereby raising the possibility that the royalists' 'devotion to succession' may have led them to 'adore a Perkin-Warbeck' – an infamous fifteenth-century pretender to the English throne – 'instead of a Duke of York'.[111] When combined with generic attacks on the Scots' sexual 'uncleanness' (an attribute presumably shared by Scottish kings), these libels against Charles's Stuart ancestors allowed republicans to simultaneously challenge the legitimacy of their current royal foe as well as the moral authority of his predecessors, thereby refiguring the regicide as a providential judgement against the whole lineage.[112]

Yet while Charles's family and his crown both fell victim to sexual politics shortly after the regicide, the dead king's personal sexuality remained basically unblemished in republican print for almost a year. True, Milton indicted Charles as 'effeminate and Uxorious' in *Eikonoklastes* and hinted that 'the lukewarmness of his life' was the fault of the 'polluted trash of Romances and Arcadias', while other critics offered generalised allusions to Charles's tyrannical 'lusts'; but given how brazenly other republican productions had accused the executed king of tyranny, treason and parricide, such allegations appear tame indeed.[113] Republican penmen apparently recognised that they might do more harm than good by slandering the highly-touted chastity of a martyred king who, unlike his father, retained much favour among his former subjects. Considering that Charles had already been tried, executed and posthumously dragged through the mud, in other words, the Commonwealth arguably had nothing more to gain from peering into his bedchamber.

But their silence did not last. During the winter of 1649/50, republican authorities learned of a scandalous book, 'full of virulency and bitternesse against this Commonwealth', recently printed at Leiden and soon destined for England. That book was the *Defensio regia pro Carolo I*, a scathing Latin indictment of the regicide written by Claudius Salmasius, an internationally recognised French intellectual. Upon discovering Salmasius's book, the Commonwealth scrambled in vain to prevent it from reaching English shores.[114] Despite their best efforts, by springtime Londoners like George Thomason had their copies in hand, and the government had settled on a new strategy for countering its viperous allegations.[115]

Their champion, once again, was Milton, from whom the Council commissioned a Latin response to Salmasius in January 1650.[116] Given the *Defensio*'s international scope and its author's scholarly credentials, Milton recognised that this new threat required a more aggressive angle than the one he had presented in *Eikonoklastes*. (He would admit as much four years later, noting that while he had avoided 'insulting the departed spirit of the king' in *Eikonoklastes*, 'Salmasius then appeared'.)[117] His solution was simple: to silence the Commonwealth's critics, he needed to obliterate Charles's vaunted self-image. Consequently, with the republic under assault on the international stage from a decorated foreign academic, the dead king's personal chastity finally became an acceptable target for porno-politics.

Milton's response to the *Defensio regia*, entitled *Pro populo Anglicano defensio* ('Defense of the People of England'), appeared in February 1651. Like Salmasius's book, it was written in Latin and primarily directed towards European audiences rather than domestic readers. The book's opening pages explained its unusual vigor in terms that suggest how pervasive sex-talk had become in the vernacular partisan print of revolutionary England:

> If his [Salmasius's] present writings, composed in a kind of Latin, had been published in England in our language, I believe they would hardly have seemed to anyone worth the trouble of answering . . . now, however, when he makes his turgid pages current among foreigners who know nothing of our affairs, it is necessary that those who misunderstand our situation should be instructed, and that Salmasius, who so often yields to his great passion for calumny, should be treated himself as he treats others.[118]

Had it appeared in English, in other words, Salmasius's *Defensio* would have simply numbered one among many other such interventions into the kingdom's still-raging debate over conjugal kingship. But because he had chosen to make his case in the broader (and more learned) arena of international polemic, Milton was compelled to respond with a caustic counter-attack in which Salmasius, the Stuarts and Charles himself came under graphic personal assault.

Writing in the classical rhetorical mode of the satirical diatribe, Milton pulled no punches. The 'Defense' ridiculed Salmasius as an 'effeminate' hermaphrodite whose wife, an 'eager horse-woman', dominated her partner as if she were in fact his 'husband'. 'You are', Milton wrote, 'a foul Circean beast, a filthy pig well used to serving a woman in the lowest sort of slavery where you never had the slightest taste of manly virtue or the freedom which springs from it'.[119] He reserved equally brutal language for Salmasius's arguments, and especially his claim that 'a king may commit adultery or murder and yet govern well'. In the broadest sense, this was not necessarily controversial; the David/Bathsheba example, which Salmasius dutifully invoked – adding that Charles's case was in fact less severe, since he was not an 'adulterer and murderer' as David was – certainly seemed to confirm as much.[120] But Milton found both claims intolerable: first, that monarchs could get away with murder; and secondly, that Charles Stuart compared favourably in any sense with the king of Israel. Thus, although Milton wished to 'pass over in silence' the 'whole question' of Charles's 'crimes', Salmasius's gall in 'compar[ing] Charles with David, one full of superstitious fancies and a mere novice in the Christian faith with a king and a reverent prophet of God' left him with no choice but to 'make his [Charles's] memory repulsive and distasteful to all good men'.[121]

In part because Salmasius had saluted Charles's chastity as a particularly laudable virtue, Milton took direct aim at the dead king's sexuality. 'Can you praise the purity and continence of one who is known to have joined the Duke of Buckingham in every act of infamy?' he asked. (Readers familiar with early Stuart rumours about Buckingham's sexual misadventures would have recognised the severity of this charge.) In fact, Milton saw 'no need to investigate his more private habits and hidden retreats', since the answer was self-evident. Not only had Charles 'kisse[d] women wantonly' while 'in the theatre'; he even openly 'play[ed] with the breasts of maids and mothers'. His whole 'life', Milton summarised, had been 'passed in feasting and plays and troops of women'. Moreover, he had far worse tales yet to tell. Salmasius therefore must 'give up' his defence of the Stuart king, Milton warned, 'lest I be forced to recount stories of Charles which I would otherwise gladly pass over'.[122] But the damage was already done.

Milton's 'Defense' probably did not circulate extensively among everyday English readers during the interregnum.[123] Even so, it commemorated a crucial sea-change in republican sexual politics. Although some radicals had gestured towards Charles's (un)chastity prior to the appearance of Salmasius's book – the author of *Eikon alethine* (1649), for example, had resurrected the rumour of Henrietta Maria's adultery with Henry Jermyn in order to further discredit Charles II's dynastic legitimacy while suggesting satirically that 'the late King and she, differed a little in honesty as well as Religion' – it was not until after the publication of the *Defensio regia* that other Commonwealth apologists followed suit with a concentrated but potent assault on the martyr-king's body natural.[124]

Republican writers attacked the Charles's personal sexuality in several different pamphlets after mid-1650, each licensed by the regime. Henry Parker's *True portraiture of the kings of England* suggested that Charles II had been infected by his father's 'polluted loyns'. John Hall claimed that the dead king had been debauched since his youth, when 'King James' had participated in his son's first sexual experience by 'lay[ing] on that same bed' and 'blowing the bellowes to that fire'. (It was apparently a necessary intervention, since Hall also noted that Charles 'did not wooe like a Prince, for that he never was admitted to so much as one single conference with his first Mistris'.)[125] The astrologer William Lilly agreed that the dead king 'did not greatly Court the Ladyes' although 'he was manly and well fitted for Venerious spoarts', and he 'rarely frequented illicite Beds'. 'I do not heare', Lilly concluded, 'of above one or two naturall Children he had, or left behind him'. Elsewhere, the poet George Wither offered a different reading: Charles, he argued, had 'wasted' his 'vast Incomes' on 'his Lusts', especially 'maskings, and loose Revellings, at Court', and 'allur'd thereby' the most fetching of the court's 'wanton Students'.[126]

The campaign culminated in Edward Peyton's *Divine catastrophe of the kingly family of the house of Stuarts* (1652). Peyton was an old, embittered parliament-man whose millenarian anti-monarchism led him to chronicle the executed king's 'unsatiable desires' as proof of the regicide's providential significance. First, Peyton argued that Charles had 'bedded' Henrietta Maria 'without the ordinary religious forme of uniting', and in return she had 'horn-beaten' him by indulging in numerous affairs.[127] Indeed, the royal marriage was predicated on infidelity, since 'one had the freedome of Mistresses, and the other of Servants'. To demonstrate Charles's 'lubricity with divers Ladies', he described how one gentlewoman had so satisfied the king that Charles had sent her husband 'into the Low-countries' so that he 'might have more freedome with her' in what was clearly a spin on the David and Bathsheba story. Peyton also attacked Charles's ancestors, even arguing that James's wife Anne had 'initiated' her son Henry into 'the Court of Cupid' by 'shut[ting] him under lock and key in a chamber with a beautiful young Lady'. Finally, Peyton rejoiced that with the end of monarchy, 'there will be no beautiful Rosamonds to hinder a pious government' and 'no Mortimers to entice to his bed and lust the wives of princes', both references to historical instances of royal adultery that had undergirded *Britanicus*'s earlier attacks against Henrietta Maria.[128] By centring the sexual dangers that beset, and (on this account, anyway) eventually destroyed, the Stuarts, Peyton's libellous history therefore showcased the full run of republican porno-politics deployed against Charles, his family and his crown.

These slanders were not ignored by Charles's partisans, who continued to number chastity among his greatest attributes. While some royalists still insisted that Charles's remarkable fecundity had led to 'Progeny, as numerous as the Planets', praises of his sexual restraint became far more common after the regicide.[129] From January 1649, the martyr-king's 'Chast Honour' became a favourite theme of royalist mourners, who celebrated his 'conquest o're the Passions' and praised his 'white Continence' in printed verses throughout the early 1650s.[130] Whether this post-regicidal emphasis on the dead Stuart's 'Unbatter'd Chastity' in the face of 'millions of provocations' represented an active response to the 'lewde slanders' of republican polemicists or merely a standard feature of Christian martyrdom, it quickly overshadowed Charles's own self-representation as the kingdom's loving husband-king.[131] In the process, it also offered an implicit contrast to the immoral excesses allegedly erupting behind closed doors in Westminster.

Contemporary readers were clearly transfixed by republican anti-Stuart polemics, which they purchased, shelved, and circulated with regularity during the 1650s. Many marked up their copies in the excitement, occasionally with substantial political comment.[132] One (Catholic?) respondent to the *Disingag'd survey* (1650) thus rebutted its claims about Mary Tudor's 'incestuous' roots by scribbling that her parents' union had been 'made good'. Another contemporary dismissed Lilly's assertion that Charles had fathered several bastards, writing, 'I never could hear of any'.[133] In these reflections and repudiations, the sexual histories of England's most recent monarchs became fodder for spirited public debate in a manner that would have shocked many contemporaries before 1640.

Similar arguments ricocheted across the kingdom in other forms. Some subjects apparently bought into republican arguments about Charles's lasciviousness: in May 1649, for example, one Helen Wood was arraigned for reportedly saying that 'the late king of England would have Ravished her' in an ostensibly straightforward reference to Charles's tyrannical rapacity. Two years later, a Somerset woman similarly wished the king had 'beene beheaded before he was married', suggesting that she believed republican claims about his sexual corruption at Henrietta Maria's hands.[134] But others were less credulous. In a short eulogy penned for Charles sometime after the regicide, the Oxford diarist Thomas Wyatt described the dead king simply as 'proper of person & a virtuous & a good king'. He also celebrated the royal marriage, perhaps in reaction to the mounting republican case against Charles's chastity: 'he [Charles] married lady Mary sister to Lewes 13 king of ffrance', Wyatt wrote, '& loved her intirely & had by her much fayre issue'.[135] At least some of Charles's former subjects agreed. In September 1653, Somerset men could still be driven to fist-fights over tavern talk alleging that 'the Queene was a whore and had had two bastards'.[136]

At the climax of the English Revolution, then, republican porno-politics transformed the king's two bodies from an ancient prop of English monarchical legitimacy into an emblem of tyrannical lust and Stuart debauchery. Above all, the Commonwealth's decision after mid-1650 to attack Charles's personal chastity – a subject so taboo that it remained off-limits in republican print long after he had been formally accounted a tyrant – altered English monarchical politics for good. As Charles II would soon learn, never again would royal sexuality be immune from public commentary.

While royalists and republicans feuded over the regicide, Thomas Hobbes was in Paris, writing. The fruit of his efforts, entitled *Leviathan*, appeared in England in 1651. Hobbes's book offered a dramatic reinterpretation of monarchical sovereignty, natural law, and the eschaton, all formulated in more-or-less direct response to the crisis unfolding across the Channel. Royalists found it particularly shocking, for Hobbes's treatise appeared to endorse tacit submission to the new regime. As a result, although the minor public response to *Leviathan* initially paled in comparison to that which greeted the republican assault on Charles's two bodies, Hobbes's arguments quickly became infamous among royalists and parliamentarians alike.[137]

*Leviathan* was a formidable work. The book's much-discussed frontispiece left no doubt that Hobbes, like so many of his contemporaries, remained fixated on royal bodies.[138] Unlike the caustic polemics volleying between royalists and republicans, however, and in contrast to the hyper-patriarchal arguments of contemporary theorists like Sir Robert Filmer, *Leviathan* rarely engaged with the conjugal metaphor beyond vague allusions to monarchical 'lusts' and the difficulties of balancing a king's 'public interest' with his private 'Passions'.[139] (Although, as James William Johnson has shown, Hobbes's materialist theory of human appetites would later influence prominent Restoration libertines like the earl of Rochester.)[140]

**Figure 4.1** Thomas Hobbes, *Leviathan* (1651)

One exception to this general rule appeared in the book's second section, 'Of Commonwealth'. Discoursing on the problems of the commonalty, Hobbes wrote:

> For that Soveraign, cannot be imagined to love his People as he ought, that is not Jealous of them, but suffers them by the flattery of Popular men, to be seduced from their loyalty, as they have often been, not onely secretly, but openly, so as to proclaime Marriage with them *in facie Ecclesiae* by Preachers; and by publishing the same in the open streets: which may fitly be compared to the violation of the second of the ten Commandements.[141]

In these brief lines, Hobbes presented the same conjugal arguments that underwrote the royalists' Mistress Parliament pamphlets as a tenet of his new sovereign state theory, albeit in a significantly less imaginative form.

Whether Hobbes's musings in *Leviathan* drew any direct inspiration from royalist porno-political print is unknown, although cavalier polemics were certainly circulating among the exiled royalist enclaves in France during 1648 and 1649.[142] Even if he never saw a single reference to Mistress Parliament, however, the conjugal metaphor's deep roots in English political culture would have provided all the inspiration necessary to connect Charles's self-representation as England's loving husband-king with the malignant forces that brought him to the scaffold. As Milton and his colleagues eventually recognised, the porno-politics of conjugal kingship were simply too visible to ignore, even all the way in Paris.

Those porno-politics proved especially fecund in Britain. Charles's final days drove royalists and parliamentarians alike to proffer competing interpretations of conjugal kingship in dozens of printed pamphlets that laid out the personal sexual histories of both the martyr-king and his adulterous usurper, Oliver Cromwell, in unprecedentedly frank detail. In the latter case, royalists devised a puritan family conspiracy complex enough to rival the 'family romance' of Lynn Hunt's French Revolution, with Cromwell as its devilish patriarch; in the former, republican apologists appropriated the sacred myth of the king's two bodies to transform their defeated enemy, England's one-time husband-king Charles I, into the rapacious and womanising 'Bad Husband' of Restoration ballad literature.[143] In both cases, porno-politics provided the necessary toolbox for reducing the kingdom's most august political leaders to figures of disdain, disgust and ridicule.

Contemporary readers absorbed these libellous porno-political portraits with equal parts enthusiasm and outrage while disseminating them widely across England and beyond. Although earlier monarchs had been haunted by similarly subversive sexual rumours, never before had those accounts been so publicly available for contemporary consumption. Their popularity ensured that English rulers would never again be free from similar scrutiny. If we are looking for evidence of the 'desacralisation of monarchy' during the seventeenth century, in other words, the porno-politics of regicide make for a compelling turning-point; so, too, do republican depictions of the rapist-tyrant, which neatly anticipated the arguments of late-seventeenth-century Whig resistance theorists.[144] In both senses, and as the Commonwealth would soon learn to appreciate, a new era had begun in English sexual politics.

## Notes

1 *CJ*, i, p. 143; Leah S. Marcus, Janel Mueller, and Mary Beth Rose (eds), *Elizabeth I: Collected Works* (Chicago, IL, 2000), p. 59; Kevin Sharpe, ' "So Hard a Text"? Images of Charles I, 1612–1700', *HJ* 43:2 (2000), 383–405, at 388–9.
2 One exception was the 1620s scribal libel describing Buckingham's 'rape' of James's 'wyfe the Parliament': Bod., MS Eng. Poet. C. 50, fols 14r–15r.
3 Robert Darnton, 'Sex for Thought', *New York Review of Books* (22 December 1994).
4 Recent work includes Erin Murphy, *Familial Forms: Politics and Genealogy in Seventeenth-Century English Literature* (Newark, NJ, 2011); Laura Lunger Knoppers, *Politicizing Domesticity from Henrietta Maria to Milton's Eve* (Cambridge, 2011); Su Fang Ng, *Literature and the Politics of Family in Seventeenth-Century England* (Cambridge, 2007); Gianoutsos, *Manhood*.
5 Cesare Cuttica, *Sir Robert Filmer (1588–1653) and the Patriotic Monarch: Patriarchalism in Seventeenth-Century Political Thought* (Manchester, 2012); Margaret J.M. Ezell, *The Patriarch's Wife: Literary Evidence and the History of the Family* (Chapel Hill, NC, 1987); Gordon J. Schochet, *Patriarchalism in Political Thought* (Oxford, 1975).
6 Carole Pateman, *The Sexual Contract* (Stanford, CA, 1988).
7 *CJ*, v, pp. 673–4. See also David Underdown, *Pride's Purge: Politics in the Puritan Revolution* (Oxford, 1971), pp. 97–105.
8 Geoffrey Robertson, *The Tyrannicide Brief: The Story of the Man Who Sent Charles I to the Scaffold* (New York, NY, 2007).
9 Sean Kelsey, '*King Charls His Case*: The Intended Prosecution of Charles I', *Journal of Legal History* 39:1 (2018), 58–87.
10 C. V. Wedgwood, *The Trial of Charles I* (London, 1964), p. 155.
11 *A continuation of the narrative...concerning the tryal of the King*, E.541[21] (29 January 1649), p. 13; Gianoutsos, *Manhood*.
12 Jason McElligott, *Royalism, Print and Censorship in Revolutionary England* (Woodbridge, 2007), pp. 151, 182.
13 *A citie-dog in a saints doublet*, E.453[24] ([19 July] 1648), title-page, p. 3.
14 Ibid., title-page.

15 *A key to the Kings cabinet*, E.297[10] ([21 August] 1645), p. 52.
16 *Pragmaticus*, E.435[42] (11–18 April 1648), sig. C4r; *Melancholicus*, E.436[23] (17–24 April 1648), p. 199; *Mercurius psitacus*, E.449[8] (14–21 June 1648), p. 1.
17 See for example *A letter to a friend*, Wing C7A (1645), p. 14; *Absalom's rebellion*, E.308[26] (Oxford, [8 November] 1645); BL, Add. MS 22084, fol. 131v. The Absalom story is told in 2 Samuel 18:1–17.
18 *Pragmaticus*, E.422[17] (4–11 January 1648), sig. R4r.
19 Laura Lunger Knoppers, *Constructing Cromwell: Ceremony, Portrait, and Print, 1645–1661* (Cambridge, 2000), pp. 26, 39, 49; Jason McElligott, 'The Politics of Sexual Libel: Royalist Propaganda in the 1640s', *HLQ* 67:1 (2004), 75–99, at 83; Purkiss, *Literature*, pp. 131–49.
20 *Mercurius clericus*, E.408[21] ([25 September] 1647), p. 2. See also *Pragmaticus*, E.419[22] (7–14 December 1647), sig. N3v.
21 Purkiss, *Literature*, pp. 131–7. Several of Cromwell's daughters married soldiers.
22 Christopher Carter, 'The Family of Love and Its Enemies', *Sixteenth Century Journal* 37:3 (2006), 651–72; Marshall, *Toleration*, pp. 251–3.
23 Ephraim Pagitt, *Heresiography*, E.282[5] ([8 May] 1645), p. 82.
24 *Love one another*, E.85[38] ([23 January] 1643), p. 4.
25 Derek Hirst, *England in Conflict, 1603–1660: Kingdom, Community, Commonwealth* (London, 1999), p. 42.
26 Katharine Gillespie, *Domesticity and Dissent in the Seventeenth Century: English Women Writers and the Public Sphere* (Cambridge, 2004), pp. 32–8.
27 E.g., Stanley Gower, *Things now-a-doing: or . . . the child of reformation now-a-bearing*, E.3[25] (1644); Edmund Calamy, *Englands looking-glasse*, E.131[29] (1642), p. 18.
28 Mary E. Fissell, *Vernacular Bodies: The Politics of Reproduction in Early Modern England* (Oxford, 2004), pp. 162, 191–3; Kathryn M. Brammall, 'Monstrous Metamorphosis: Nature, Morality, and the Rhetoric of Monstrosity in Tudor England', *Sixteenth Century Journal* 27:1 (1996), 3–21.
29 Genesis 1:28. See, for example, *Religions lotterie*, E.107[34] (20 July 1642), sig. A2v; *The divisions of the Church of England*, Wing T454 (1642), sig. A2v.
30 *Rules to get children by*, E.238[11] (1642), sig. A4r; *The publick faith*, 669.f.8[2] ([7 April] 1643). See also Surekha Davies, *Renaissance Ethnography and the Invention of the Human: New Worlds, Maps and Monsters* (Cambridge, 2016).
31 *Aulicus*, E.29[9] (6 January 1644), p. 754; [George Wharton], *Grand Pluto's progresse*, E.405[16] ([2 September] 1647), p. 1. See also *Hells trienniall Parliament*, E.405[12] ([2 September] 1647), p. 1.
32 *Pragmaticus*, E.417[20] (23–30 November 1647), sig. L3r; ibid., E.464[45] (19–26 September 1648), sig. Mmv; ibid., E.538[18] (9–16 January 1649), sig. Ggg2r.
33 *Aulicus*, E.425[8] (25 January–3 February 1648), sig. Av; *The parliaments X. commandements*, 669.f.11[121] ([5 January] 1648); *Melancholicus*, E.441[5] (1–8 May 1648), p. 216. See also *Pragmaticus*, E.469[10] (24–31 October 1648), sig. Xx4r.

34 *Mercurius aulicus (for King Charls II)*, E.572[17] (28 August–4 September 1649), sig. Cr; *Mercurius veridicus*, E.436[18] (14–21 April 1648), sig. A4v.
35 *Pragmaticus*, E.445[21] (23–30 May 1648), sig. Ir; *Melancholicus*, E.452[40] (10–17 July 1648), p. 280. See also *Aulicus*, E.460[9] (22 August 1648), p. 81.
36 *Melancholicus*, E.441[5] (1–8 May 1648), p. 219; *Aulicus*, E.457[5] ([7 August] 1648), p. 1; *Melancholicus*, E.407[23] (11–17 September 1647), p. 1.
37 Bod., MS Eng. Poet. C. 50, fol. 14r.
38 *Ad populum*, E.49[2] (Oxford, [20 May] 1644), p. 16; *Perfect occurrences*, E.262[44] (8–15 August 1645), sig. R2v; [Henry Neville], *The ladies parliament*, E.1143[1] ([15 July] 1647).
39 Lois Potter, 'The *Mistress Parliament* Political Dialogues', *Analytical & Enumerative Bibliography* 1:3 (Dekalb, IL, 1987), 101–70, at 103. See also Purkiss, *Literature*, pp. 178–85.
40 *Mrs. Parliament her invitation*, E.446[7] ([6 June] 1648), p. 1.
41 *Mistris Parliament brought to bed*, E.437[24] ([29 April] 1648), pp. 4–5; *Mistris Parliament presented in her bed*, E.441[21] ([10 May] 1648), p. 5.
42 *Mistris Parliament brought to bed*, p. 4; *Mistris Parliament her gossipping*, E.443[28] ([22 May] 1648), p. 7.
43 On inversion, see David Underdown, *A Freeborn People: Politics and the Nation in Seventeenth-Century England* (Oxford, 1996).
44 *Mistris Parliament presented*, title-page; *Mistris Parliament brought to bed*, pp. 5, 8.
45 *The parliament-kite*, E.443[6] (10–16 May 1648), p. 7; *MITM*, E.579[11] (7–14 November 1649), p. 233. See also ibid., E.550[26] (16 April 1649), p. [8]; *Melancholicus*, E.450[24] (26 June–3 July 1648), p. 271.
46 *Bellicus*, E.445[16] (23–30 May 1648), p. 4; *Melancholicus*, E.434[14] (27 March–3 April 1648), p. 180. See also *Pragmaticus*, E.462[34] (5–12 September 1648), sig. Ggv.
47 *Ding dong, or Sr. Pitifull Parliament*, E.441[20] ([10 May] 1648).
48 *Aulicus*, E.425[8] (25 January–3 February 1648), sig. A4r; *Melancholicus*, E.431[24] (6–13 March 1648), p. 164.
49 *Aulicus*, E.427[13] (10–17 February 1648), sig. Cv; *Mercurius elencticus (for King Charles II)*, E.555[10] (7–14 May 1649), sigs Bv–2r. See also *The cities loyaltie*, 669.f.11[62] ([13 August] 1647).
50 *Pragmaticus*, E.414[16] (9–16 November 1647), p. 66. See also ibid., E.437[31] (25 April–2 May 1648), sig. E2r; Lisa Forman Cody, *Birthing the Nation: Sex, Science, and the Conception of Eighteenth-Century Britons* (Oxford, 2005). This use of 'Moon-Calfe' is likely pulled from Shakespeare's *The Tempest*; I thank Jonathan Koch for bringing the parallel to my attention.
51 BRBML, Osborn MS b230, fol. 59v.
52 *Mistris Parliament brought to bed*, p. 4; *The cuckoo's-nest a[t] Westminster*, E.447[19] ([15 June] 1648), p. 6.
53 *A new marriage, between Mr. King, and Mrs. Parliament*, E.526[34] ([30 November] 1648), p. 5; *Pragmaticus*, E.423[21] (18–25 January 1648), sig. Tv.

54 *Aulicus*, E.461[5] (21–28 August 1648), p. 30; *The second part to the same tune*, 669.f.11[96] ([13 November] 1647). See also *Elencticus*, E.450[2] (21–8 June 1648), p. 244.

55 [*Mercurius*] *pragmaticus (for King Charles II)*, E.552[15] (24 April–1 May 1649), p. 11; *MITM*, E.562[27] (27 June–4 July 1649), p. 102; *Elencticus*, E.562[18] (25 June–2 July 1649), p. 74; *The last will and testament of Richard Brandon*, E.561[12] ([25 June] 1649), p. 5. See also *Pragmaticus (for King Charles II)*, E.565[9] (10–17 July 1649), sigs Nr–v; *Cromwell's recall*, E.566[22] ([1 August] 1649), p. 5.

56 *Jeremias redivivus*, E.556[33] ([30 May] 1649), p. 2.

57 *Mercurius philo-monarchicus*, E.555[34] (14–21 May 1649), sig. B4r; *Pragmaticus*, E.540[15] (16–30 January 1649), sig. Hhhr; *The right picture of King Oliure*, E.587[9] ([2 January] 1650), pp. 2–3.

58 *A Bartholmew Fairing*, E.572[7] ([30 August] 1649), p. 2; *MITM*, E.578[9] (31 October–7 November 1649), pp. 227, 229; *Pragmaticus (for King Charles II)*, E.566[15] (24–31 July 1649), sig. Pv. For Cromwell's nose, see *Mercurius philo-monarchicus*, E.550[27] (10–17 April 1649), p. 6; *Pragmaticus (for King Charles II)*, E.555[13] (8–15 May 1649), sig. Dr; Purkiss, *Literature*, pp. 137–42.

59 *Melancholicus*, E.436[23] (17–24 April 1648), pp. 199–200. For an earlier, unrelated usage of 'Towne Bull' as a sexual metaphor, see *A paradox*, E.135[30] (1642), p. 4.

60 *MITM*, E.576[7] (24–31 October 1649), p. 221; *MITM*, E.552[8] (23–30 April 1649), p. 20; *A new bull-bayting*, E.568[6] ([7 August] 1649), p. 5. See also *A hue and crie after Cromwell*, E.565[24] ([24 July] 1649), p. 3.

61 *Elencticus*, E.463[6] (6–13 September 1648), pp. 341–2; *Pragmaticus (for King Charles II)*, E.562[21] (26 June–3 July 1649), sig. L3r; *The famous tragedie of King Charles I*, Wing F384 (1649), p. 32.

62 *Balaams asse*, E.564[7] ([13 July] 1649), p. 2. See also *A most learned, conscientious, and devout-exercise*, E.561[10] ([25 June] 1649), pp. 4–5; David Farr, *John Lambert, Parliamentary Soldier and Cromwellian Major-General, 1619–1684* (Woodbridge, 2003), p. 151.

63 Alexandra Shepard, *Meanings of Manhood in Early Modern England* (Oxford, 2003), pp. 27–8.

64 *MITM*, E.601[5] (10–26 April 1650), p. 391; *Pragmaticus (for King Charles II)*, E.600[6] (30 April–7 May 1650), sig. Fffv.

65 *Right picture*, p. 3; *MITM*, E.573[14] (5–12 September 1649), pp. 172 (quoted), 176. See also *A tragi-comedy called New-Market fayre*, E.560[9] ([15 June] 1649), p. 5; *The second part of...New-Market-Fayre*, E.565[6] ([16 July] 1649), pp. 7–9. For Morley, see J.T. Peacey, 'Morley, Harbert [Herbert]', *ODNB*.

66 *MITM*, E.560[2] (5–13 June 1649), p. 75.

67 *A new bull-bayting*, pp. 6–7. I have found no extant evidence to verify the accusations against Cromwell's ancestors, although his uncle Henry was also mocked for his large nose: BRBML, Osborn MS b197, p. 58.

68 *Mercurius Britanicus*, E.442[19] (16–25 May 1648), p. 2; *Mercurius anti-pragmaticus*, E.414[2] (4–11 November 1647), p. 2; *Mercurius anti-mercurius*, E.464[15] (12–19 September 1648), p. 5.
69 *A&O*, ii, pp. 245–56.
70 For some marked-up copies of *Pragmaticus*, for instance, see Bod., Ashm. F 14; Newberry Library, Case J 5454 .571.
71 TNA, ASSI 45/2/2, nos 17 and 23.
72 TNA, ASSI 45/3/2, no. 98A; SHC, Q/SR/82, no. 85.
73 Chester Archives and Local Studies, Chester, QJF 78/1, no. 40; SHC, Q/SR/82, no. 152; ERO, Q/SBa 2/91 (Richard Hubbert, 22 April 1653). See also LMA, MJ/SR/1059/67.
74 Ernst H. Kantorowicz, *The King's Two Bodies: A Study in Medieval Political Theology* (Princeton, NJ, 2016).
75 Joyce Macadam, '*Mercurius Britanicus* on Charles I: An Exercise in Civil War Journalism and High Politics, August 1643 to May 1646', *HR* 84:225 (2011), 470–92; Como, *RP*, p. 257.
76 *The sence of John Warners speech in his personall capacity*, E.442[22] ([16 May] 1648), p. 6 (note the title).
77 *The Kings declaration*, E.426[5] ([6 February] 1648), p. 1.
78 *A declaration*, E.427[9] (15 February 1648), pp. 31–3.
79 TNA, SP 21/24, fol. 1r.
80 Sarah Poynting, 'Deciphering the King: Charles I's Letters to Jane Whorwood', *Seventeenth Century* 21:1 (2006), 128–40.
81 Elizabeth Poole, *An alarum of war*, E.555[23] ([17 May] 1649), p. 3.
82 Gillespie, *Domesticity and Dissent*, p. 146.
83 *Mercurius anti-mercurius*, E.465[11] (26 September–2 October 1648), p. 3.
84 Lucy Hutchinson, *Memoirs of the Life of Colonel Hutchinson* (London, 1806), p. 65; *Mercurius militaris*, E.467[34] (10–17 October 1648), p. 5.
85 *The moderate*, E.464[17] (12–19 September 1648), p. 73.
86 Ibid., E.537[26] (2–9 January 1649), p. [248]. The next issue observed that the king had begun 'talking much of women' during his final days in prison: ibid., E.538[15] (9–16 January 1649), sig. (dd2)r.
87 Ibid., E.541[15] (30 January–6 February 1649), pp. 289–90. I have found no evidence to validate this account.
88 Sean Kelsey, 'Instrumenting the Trial of Charles I', *HR* 92:255 (2019), 118–38, at 135–7.
89 Braddick, *Fury*, pp. 474–6.
90 Poole, *An alarum*, p. 4.
91 Sharpe, *IW*, p. 542. Cf. Alastair Bellany and Thomas Cogswell, *The Murder of King James I* (Stanford, CA, 2015), pp. 479–88; Alastair Bellany, *The Politics of Court Scandal in Early Modern England: News Culture and the Overbury Affair, 1603–1660* (Cambridge, 2002), pp. 262–74; Peacey, ' "Hot and Eager in Courtship" '.
92 Edward Almack (ed.), *Eikōn Basilikē: Or, The King's Book* (London, 1904), pp. xxii–xxiii.

93 Knoppers, *Politicizing Domesticity*, p. 83.
94 John Milton, *The tenure of kings and magistrates*, E.542[12] ([13 February] 1649), p. 17; *A declaration of the parliament*, E.548[12] (22 March 1649), pp. 6, 13.
95 John Milton, *Eikonoklastes*, E.578[5] ([6 October] 1649), pp. 8, 15, 25, 97.
96 Ibid., p. 112. See also Ng, *Politics of Family*, p. 59.
97 Gianoutsos, *Manhood*, chs 3–4.
98 See for instance [Henry Parker], *Observations upon some of His Majesties late answers*, E.153[26] ([2 July] 1642), pp. 18–19.
99 Gianoutsos, *Manhood*.
100 BL, Add. MS 71532, fol. 24r.
101 G[eorge] W[alker], *Anglo-tyrannus*, E.619[1] ([3 December] 1650), p. 49; [Sydenham Cuthbert], *The false brother*, E.620[13] ([27 December] 1650), p. 40; John Goodwin, *Hybristodikai*, E.557[2] ([30 May] 1649), p. 31. See also *The resolver continued*, E.546[17] ([12 March] 1649), p. 6.
102 John Cook, *Monarchy no creature of God's making*, E.1238[1] (Waterford, [26 February] 1652), pp. 35, 101.
103 Marchamont Nedham, *The case of the Common-Wealth of England*, E.600[7] ([8 May] 1650), p. 42; Antony Ascham, *The bounds & bonds of publique obedience*, E.571[26] ([27 August] 1649), p. 20; Julia Rudolph, 'Rape and Resistance: Women and Consent in Seventeenth-Century English Legal and Political Thought', *JBS* 39:2 (2000), 157–84.
104 Milton, *Tenure*, p. 12; [Thomas Paget], *A religious scrutiny*, E.560[8] ([14 June] 1649), p. 38. See also Goodwin, *Hybristodikai*, p. 86; Cook, *Monarchy no creature*, pp. 7–8. The fact that Charles had long employed Davidic imagery himself made this line of attack all the more galling.
105 Henry Parker, *The true portraiture*, E.609[2] ([7 August] 1650), p. 15. See also Walker, *Anglo-tyrannus*, p. 35; *The life and reigne of King Charls*, E.1338[2] ([29 January] 1651), sig. A5v.
106 Ibid., sig. A6r; Parker, *True portraiture*, p. 36; *A disingag'd survey*, E.592[6] ([7 February] 1650), p. 22.
107 E.g., *The five years of King James*, E.101[14] ([10 May] 1643).
108 Anthony Weldon, *The court and character of King James*, E.1338[1] ([1 October] 1650), pp. 8, 94, 103, 112, 136, 146. See also Bellany and Cogswell, *Murder of King James*, pp. 469–70.
109 Anthony Weldon, *The court...whereunto is now added The court of King Charles*, Wing W1274 (1651).
110 Arthur Wilson, *The history of Great Britain*, Wing W2888 (1653), p. 162. See also Michael Sparke, *The narrative history of King James*, Wing S4818 (1651); BL, Add. MS 25348; Bellany, *Court Scandal*, p. 274.
111 George Buchanan, *A detection of the actions of Mary Queen of Scots*, E.1383[2] ([12 February] 1651), sig. *5v. See also John Hall, *The grounds & reasons of monarchy considered*, Wing H346 (1650), pp. 109–13; *A cat may look upon a king*, E.1408[2] ([10 January] 1652), pp. 86–8.
112 *An examination*, E.608[13] ([25 July] 1650), pp. 31–2.

113 Milton, *Eikonoklastes*, pp. 13, 64–5; *A declaration of the parliament*, p. 13.
114 TNA, SP 25/95, p. 3; *CSPD 1649–50*, p. 411.
115 [Claudius Salmasius], *Defensio regia, pro Carolo I*, E.1386[1] ([11 May] 1649 [1650?]). Thomason dated his copy to May 1649, but given the Council of State's failure to note the *Defensio*'s existence until November of that year, the correct date is probably 1650. Even if Thomason did acquire Salmasius's text in 1649, moreover, it clearly did not become a priority for the regime until later.
116 Gordon Campbell and Thomas N. Corns, *John Milton: Life, Work, and Thought* (Oxford, 2008), p. 229.
117 John Milton, 'A Second Defense of the English People', trans. Helen North, in Don M. Wolfe (ed.), *Complete Prose Works of John Milton, Volume Four: 1650–1655* (New Haven, CT, 1966), pp. 548–686, at 628.
118 John Milton, 'A Defense of the People of England', trans. Donald C. MacKenzie, in ibid., 296–546, at 306.
119 Ibid., pp. 312, 475–6, 518.
120 Ibid., pp. 408, 469.
121 Ibid., pp. 408, 519–20.
122 Ibid., pp. 408–9, 520.
123 However, it was reprinted frequently (in English translation) during the late Stuart period.
124 *Eikon alethine*, E.569[16] ([16 August] 1649), p. 40.
125 Parker, *True portraiture*, p. 15; [John Hall], *The none-such Charles*, E.1345[2] ([6 January] 1651), pp. 20–1, 195.
126 William Lilly, *Monarchy or no monarchy in England*, E.638[17] ([6 August] 1651), p. 79; George Wither, *The British appeals*, Wing W3143 (1651), pp. 13, 21.
127 Edward Peyton, *The divine catastrophe*, E.1291[1] ([24 April] 1652), pp. 5, 45, 56.
128 Ibid., pp. 12, 27, 56–7, 70, 121. Rosamund was a sixth-century Italian queen who cuckolded and then murdered her husband, King Alboin of the Lombards, with the help of a scheming lover. On Mortimer, to whom Henry Jermyn was compared in 1644, see Chapter 2.
129 *Right picture*, p. 6.
130 *A deepe groane*, E.555[19] ([16 May] 1649), p. 5; *Royall meditations*, Wing R2136A (1650), p. 5; J[ohn] B[erkenhead], *Loyalties tears flowing*, E.1244[4] ([30 January] 1650), p. 9. See also *Stipendariae lacrymae*, E.745[23] (The Hague, [14 July] 1654), p. 25.
131 *An Elegie on the meekest of men*, E.553[1] ([4 May] 1649), p. 8; *The tablet*, Wing A3738 (The Hague, 1650), p. 23; [Joseph Jane], *Eikon aklastos*, Wing J451 (1651), p. 4. See also Samuel Fullerton, 'Fatal Adulteries: Sexual Politics in the English Revolution', *JBS* 60:4 (2021), 793–821, at 816–21.
132 See for example University of Nottingham Library, MS PwV 4, p. 195 (Wilson's *History of Great Britain*); BL, G.15426 (*The court and character*); HEHL, RB 88529 (*The court and character*), RB 105648 (*The tenure of kings and magistrates*); Newberry Library, Case J 5453 .947 (*Anglo-tyrannus*).

133 Newberry Library, Case F 455 .66, no. 4; BRBML, Mellon Alchemical 100. See also University of Nottingham Library, MS Mi LM 15/1, p. 52.
134 LMA, MJ/SR/1027/46; SHC, Q/SR/83, no. 178.
135 Bod., MS Top. Oxon. C. 378, p. 241.
136 SHC, Q/SR/86, nos. 28 and 30.
137 Richard Tuck (ed.), *Leviathan* (Cambridge, 1991), pp. ix–xi, xliii; Jon Parkin, *Taming the Leviathan: The Reception of the Political and Religious Ideas of Thomas Hobbes in England, 1640–1700* (Cambridge, 2007), p. 97.
138 Quentin Skinner, 'Hobbes and the Purely Artificial Person of the State', *Journal of Political Philosophy* 7:1 (1999), 1–29.
139 Tuck (ed.), *Leviathan*, pp. 128, 131.
140 James William Johnson, *A Profane Wit: The Life of John Wilmot, Earl of Rochester* (Rochester, NY, 2004).
141 Tuck (ed.), *Leviathan*, p. 234.
142 Bod., MS Bodley 878, fols 31r–v, 36r–40r.
143 Lynn Hunt, *The Family Romance of the French Revolution* (Berkeley, CA, 1992); Paul Hammond, 'The King's Two Bodies: Representations of Charles II', in Jeremy Black and Jeremy Gregory (eds), *Culture, Politics and Society in Britain, 1660–1800* (Manchester, 1991), pp. 13–49; Ezell, *Patriarch's Wife*, pp. 101–2.
144 Rudolph, 'Rape and Resistance'. For the desacralisation of monarchy, see David Cressy, *Dangerous Talk: Scandalous, Seditious, and Treasonable Speech in Pre-Modern England* (Oxford, 2010), p. 222; Sharpe, *IW*, pp. 539–42.

# 5

# Contesting reformation, 1649–53

While Hobbes toiled away in Paris, England's new regime set to work. The republican leadership faced many challenges upon its establishment in March 1649. War raged on in Ireland, while Charles II campaigned against the Commonwealth abroad. Domestic unrest, promulgated by royalists and disappointed parliamentarian radicals alike, proved equally vexing. Given that the regime had its own ambitious agenda to pursue – above all, a long-promised national reformation of manners – these were no small obstacles.

Cromwell and his colleagues also wrestled with a deeper unease that infected English political culture after Charles's execution. Astrological prognostications published from January 1649 predicted considerable gendered and sexual disorder in England's near future. Although some supporters initially brushed aside the dire forecast – just before the regicide, the parliamentarian astrologer William Lilly assured his readers to 'expect discords . . . wars murthers . . . [and] miscarriage of women with child' alongside the forthcoming 'mutation in the Common-Wealth' – others, like one 1651 almanac that warned about an impending rise in 'femal[e] . . . lasciviousnesse', took a bleaker line. By 1652, Lilly, too, was conceding that some 'Lasciviousnesse' should not 'be thought strange' with 'so great matters' at hand in the state.[1]

The combination of post-regicidal malaise, impending reformation and both royalist and radical hostility provided fertile ground for sexual politics. This chapter explores the republican period through three frameworks: first, the criticisms levelled at the new government by its most vocal critics, from royalists and Levellers to Ranters and Diggers, and the Commonwealth's response to those attacks; second, the republic's campaign for a national reformation of manners, which included a public repudiation of its ungodly enemies; and, finally, the efforts of ex-royalists to further their anti-puritan agenda despite the watchful gaze of regime censors. As we will see, libertine Ranters, godly republicans, and dismayed cavaliers all made unique contributions to English sexual politics between the establishment of the Commonwealth in March 1649 and its 1653 demise. Often, they did so in terms that recalled the initial partisan alignments of the early civil war period. In 1650, contemporary readers therefore encountered the familiar stereotypes of the lecherous cavalier, the hypocritical puritan lecher, and the depraved Protestant sectarian. Although, in nearly every case, key divergences from those earlier tropes betrayed the impact of ten years of increasingly acrid partisanship, their persistence demonstrates once again that the haphazard sexual polemics of 1640–42 had, by the early interregnum period, transformed into coherent programs of sexual politics.

In other senses, too, this chapter is partly a story of continuities. For one thing, it reveals the degree to which post-regicidal commentators continued to centre bodies, and especially women's bodies, as an arena of political conflict: conflict that included, after the regicide, fundamental questions about political sovereignty and the right to rule. This, in turn, highlights another fundamental truth about republican political culture: namely, that despite the new regime's efforts to distance itself from the legacy of degenerative Stuart tyranny, its partisans frequently adopted familiar patriarchal (albeit distinctly godly) images of moral, masculine rule – resulting in what Jamie Gianoutsos has described as an idealised republican 'band of fathers' – to rebut its royalist and radical critics.[2] Focusing on the sexual politics of the early interregnum period, in other words, reveals just how little some things changed after Charles's execution.

But the same cannot be said for contemporary attitudes towards sex-talk, which underwent an important shift in the early 1650s. Among royalists, Levellers and regime insiders alike, some began to argue that sexual polemic deserved a legitimate place in public discourse. Others experimented with entirely new forms of sex-writing that bordered on calls for sexual revolution: Abiezer Coppe and the antinomian Ranters employed a sexualised lexicon of bodily communion to subvert the legalistic moral imperatives of interregnum puritanism, for instance, while Charles II's defeated loyalists, stymied by the imposition of Cromwellian press control, pivoted towards a radically erotic mode of anti-puritan satire in print. Both cases proved that polemic and practice had grown close indeed after nearly a decade of public sexual politics. To be sure, anxieties about the moral status of lascivious language remained widespread, embodied in one December 1649 sermon bemoaning that contemporary 'Eares' preferred 'a Romance, an Amoretto . . . [or] a Poysonous peece of sordid scurrilitie and Obscenitie' to 'the words of everlasting life'.[3] But elsewhere in republican England, graphic sex-talk was undergoing an important, if controversial, revaluation.

## 'Sweet ravishings and holy raptures': sex-talk and early interregnum radicalism

As the regicides erected their new republic in March 1649, they faced a stream of invective from embittered royalists still writing from underground London presses. In familiar newssheets such as *Mercurius elencticus* as well as novel productions like John Crouch's *The man in the moon*, loyalists condemned Charles's executioners for their usurpation of the dead king's husbandly mantle. In addition to these porno-political critiques, the prominence of controversial figures like Henry Marten in the new regime ensured that sexual libel remained an effective weapon. Thus, when the Commonwealth awarded Marten £3600 in April 1649 as repayment for an earlier loan, royalists brayed that the money would be 'spent . . . amongst Whoores and Drabs, whilest your Honest wives & children famish'.[4] Similar attacks continued to proliferate in print until the institution of a draconian new press censorship system in September.

But defeated royalists were not the republic's most disruptive opponents in 1649. Instead, that honour belonged to a diverse collection of radical activists who had diverged dramatically from their parliamentarian fellow-travellers since the later 1640s. Some of these groups, such as John Lilburne's Levellers, had dogged the parliamentarian leadership for years. Others, especially the libertine antinomian Ranters, represented truly novel embodiments of Protestant millenarian radicalism. Ideologically, they shared little in common beyond a general antipathy towards the new regime; but that common thread proved an influential one. Consequently, as the Commonwealth faced down its radical critics between 1649 and 1652, sexual politics – often meted through the same anti-puritan frameworks that royalists and conservative parliamentarians alike had previously deployed against parliamentary Independents – intruded on every one of the resulting confrontations.

The republic's chief radical adversaries were also its most familiar detractors. Since the mid-1640s, John Lilburne and his Leveller allies (including Richard Overton) had barraged parliament with calls for sweeping legislative and electoral reforms.[5] The regicide brought this combative relationship to an all-time low by convincing the Levellers that the new regime was just as tyrannical as its Caroline predecessor and, correspondingly, by sparking republican fears that the Levellers' acerbic writings might smother the Commonwealth in its infancy. When Lilburne's coalition published a new wave of 'scandalous and seditious' anti-regime pamphlets early in 1649, therefore, the Council of State responded promptly.[6]

As Ann Hughes and Melissa Mowry have illustrated, Leveller polemics had long been rooted in gender politics, and this latest offensive was no different. Between March and May, Leveller writers repeatedly presented themselves as honest householders victimised by a rapacious regime.[7] Overton's inaugural satire of the year, published in March, begged 'that you will not suffer . . . our wifes, and our servants to be imprisoned, [and] our children exposed to the wide world'. This was a pointed reference: several years prior, as the pamphlet next recounted, Overton's wife and infant child had been forcibly dragged from bed by parliamentarian authorities.[8] Other Levellers soon followed his lead in condemning the republican leadership as immoral, homewrecking tyrants.

In response, the Council of State imprisoned Lilburne, Overton and two more Levellers in the Tower on 28 March; but they could not prevent the radicals from writing. For weeks, the group continued to denounce their captors in print. Their diatribes revealed the degree to which the Levellers' longstanding propensity for domestic metaphors had grown to encompass explicitly sexual politics. The same was also true of their opponents: Overton raged that the officer responsible for his arrest had accused him (untruthfully) of hiding out in a 'Bawdy-house, and that all the women that lived in it were whores, and that he had taken me in bed with another mans Wife'. Later, the officer extended his critique to include the classic anti-sectarian allegation of a wife-swapping Leveller 'community of women'. Similar accusations haunted the Levellers well into May, when Overton's fellow prisoner William Walwyn published a tract rebutting rumours that he believed in 'Polygamie'. 'I wonder what will be next', he wrote resignedly.[9]

Walwyn's objection came too late. Two weeks earlier, Cromwell had crushed a Leveller-inspired army mutiny in Oxfordshire, sundering the movement wholesale.[10] Former allies soon published recantations of Leveller radicalism alongside increasingly critical regime polemics. Even so, Lilburne and his allies continued to militate in print. In July, Overton assailed Cromwell with a familiar bovine image:

> Catch me the great Bull of Bason by the NOSE, and make him roar . . . Hold, hold, he hath caught him by the Gennitals, stave him off, give the Bull fair play.—A pox—they have burnt my Dogs mouth . . . all at him againe, and bate him out of England into Ireland, and there the brave Royall Bandogs will tug him and tear him.[11]

In Overton's usage, the Bull of Bashan – a reference to Psalm 22:12 – was distinct from the royalists' 'Bull of Ely' trope, although loyalist writers themselves later noted the parallel.[12] Even so, his reference to the bull-Cromwell's pox-ridden 'Gennitals' may have brought the earlier cavalier satires to mind among well-informed readers.

Not everyone was pleased by the comparison. Overton returned to print weeks later to justify his words: 'it seems', he wrote, that 'many are offended ... with that figurative passage of the Bull; especially at the word Pox', which they deemed 'uncivill language ... [that] becommeth not the Gospell of Christ'. But while 'my Metaphor of the Bull, the use of the word Genitals, Pox, &c.' might be 'uncivill in the Letter', he continued, 'how uncivill' was it 'in the Morall'? If Cromwell was guilty, in other words, Overton's attacks were not incivilities, but righteous indictments. Furthermore, he wrote, considering that 'things as unserious as my last sheet' (the equally scurrilous *Araignement of Mr. Persecution* (1645)) had previously 'found a very large acceptance', his politics rather than his language were clearly the issue. Perhaps for that reason, Overton soon abandoned the world of polemical print. But his defense of explicit sex-talk as a legitimate, even laudable rhetoric mode – 'modest mirth tempered with due gravity', he wrote, 'makes the best composition' – marked an important milestone nonetheless.[13]

After crushing the Levellers, the Commonwealth turned towards a new menace. Earlier in 1649, a group of sectarian libertines had emerged from England's radical underground to terrify orthodox Protestants of every variety. These practical antinomians – 'practical', because of the experiential libertinism that they professed to live out – were dubbed 'Ranters' by hostile commentators due to their predilection for public obscenity, which they justified through a novel theological vision in which God and man merged as one in the bodies of true believers. Liberated from the repressive conventions of the moral law by this mystical union, the Ranters shattered the conventional duality between rightful and sinful behaviour by asserting that both were equally godly when undertaken by true believers. For their acolytes, this was genuine 'libertinism', in the celebratory sense of freedom from repressive puritan works righteousness.[14] By contrast, their horrified critics viewed the movement as a novel form of Protestant moral anarchy.

The Ranters embodied one of the period's most terrifying bogeymen. Since the early 1640s, fears of precisely this kind of antinomian radicalism had underwritten endless attacks on the promiscuous sectarians allegedly spurred into action by the outbreak of civil war. While those earlier diatribes had only intermittently been supported by concrete evidence, however, the Ranters' sudden appearance in 1649 appeared to belatedly confirm their hysterical predictions. English observers thus watched in horror as these new sectarians, inspired by the millenarian atmosphere of the regicide, produced a slew of transgressive theological treatises that numbered among the most sexually explicit publications of the entire era.

The personal history of Abiezer Coppe, who traversed the politico-religious spectrum of civil war England before undergoing a spiritual transformation mere weeks before Charles's execution, illustrates the wandering paths taken by many soon-to-be Ranters prior to the revolutionary winter of

1648/49.[15] Most of Coppe's fellow-travellers – including Jacob Bauthumley, Laurence Clarkson and Joseph Salmon – followed similarly winding trajectories.[16] Their intellectual convergence in 1649 was fleeting, more reminiscent of a spontaneous meeting of the minds than an organised coalition; but despite the assertions of some modern historians to the contrary, the Ranters certainly existed.[17] Nowhere is this more apparent than in their shared lexicon of explicit, spiritualist sex-talk. Indeed, it might be said that sexual politics both created and sustained Ranterism, for it was sex-writing above all that bound these disparate thinkers together. From Christmas 1648, when Coppe first began proselytising, they repeatedly intersected on the page and in parliamentary prisons alike.[18] Only after a systematic regime crackdown did the Ranter moment begin to subside.

As they traversed England during the years following Charles's execution, practicing, preaching and publishing their transgressive theology, the Ranters therefore came to embody a new, terrifying and unsettlingly popular form of radical Protestantism for the post-regicidal age; and what made them notorious, above all, was their promiscuity. Granted, the appeal of sexual liberty for writers who preached the total abolition of sin was self-evident. But sex went far deeper in Ranter thinking than the repudiation of conventional marital morality. On the contrary, a novel porno-political vision underwrote the Ranters' entire antinomian theology. Some even envisioned communion with God as a sexual act, in which the spiritualist merging of man and divine was likened to literal (heterosexual) penetration.[19]

The Ranters' foundational tenet was that true Christians, transformed by a holy union with God, had transcended the false dichotomy of good and evil preached by puritan pharisees. To the contrary: everything, including sin, was God's creation, and therefore everything (including sin) was holy. 'In respect of God', wrote Jacob Bauthumley, 'light and darkness are all one to him'. Similarly, Joseph Salmon claimed there was 'nothing but what is good in the pure sight of divine presence'.[20] In turn, by abandoning the false binary between good and evil and celebrating instead God's presence in all human experience, the believer became a 'true Libertine', 'free in all his actions, and in every performance'. The implications for traditional sexual discipline were clear, at least for Laurence Clarkson. 'What act soever is done by thee, in light and love, is light', he wrote, 'and . . . that act called Adultery, in darknesse, it is so; but in light, honesty . . . cannot defile it self'.[21] Illicit sex, in other words, was not immoral but divine for the properly liberated believer. Moreover, following the language of Galatians 4:31, both Joseph Salmon and Abiezer Coppe gendered the believer's new spiritual body female, as a 'freewoman' waiting inside every soul to join in 'union and fellowship with God'.[22] That union, too, was described in explicitly sexual terms.

Some Ranters apparently lived out their transgressive theology; indeed, Coppe and his fellows seemingly succeeded in aligning mid-century sex-talk and actual sexual practice to an unprecedented degree. Coppe bragged that he was blessed with 'concubines without number', and Clarkson would later publish a retrospective account of his 'ranting' days filled with tales of sexual escapades undertaken to prove that 'there was no man could be free'd from sin, till he had acted that so called sin, as no sin'.[23] Elsewhere, another anonymous Ranter proclaimed that 'I will now ly openly before the Sun, with many women, and yet with my own Wife', while 'plague[ing] bitterly, they that ly with any save their own Wives in the dark'. In each case, the principle was the same: 'sin' was nothing more than invention of puritan formalists who refused to recognise the transformative power of God's divine spirit. Even practical antinomians like Bauthumley who nominally supported sexual discipline argued that promiscuity was not inherently problematic. Only later, after being imprisoned by Commonwealth authorities, would Coppe publicly affirm that 'Murther, Adultery, Incest, Fornication, Uncleanness, Sodomie &c. are things sinful, shameful, wicked, impious, and abominable, in any person'.[24]

But, again, there was more to Ranter sexual politics than literal promiscuity. In contrast to parliamentarians who claimed that their victory over the king's forces had largely cleansed England of the popish Whore of Babylon, Ranters argued that the parliamentarian revolution had not redeemed the kingdom from spiritual fornication. As Coppe explained in a metaphorical idiom that echoed Richard Overton's Marpriest pamphlets, the Roman Whore of Babylon had been replaced by a 'wel-favoured Harlot, the holy Whore': a mystical, fleshly entity embodied in the formalist puritan theology of the repressive 'Presbyterian Churches' established by the Westminster Assembly. The Ranters thus swapped the Babylonian Whore for a much more sinister, and pervasive, spiritual force – puritan legalism – which Coppe then threatened with the traditional punishment meted out to suspected whores: 'we will strip off thy cloaths ... & slit thy nose thou wel-favoured Harlot', he wrote.[25] Only through such violence, it seems, could one's inner freewoman find her wings.

Like her Babylonian counterpart, the Westminster Assembly's 'wel-favoured harlot' also played an important role in seducing men to spiritual error. In fact, the Ranters argued that mundane sexual criminals were entirely innocent when compared to those who wilfully fornicated with the fleshly whore. 'Publicans and Harlots do sooner enter into the Kingdome of heaven, then you', Coppe proclaimed to the clergy of republican England's new national church. While admitting that some ministers had been 'blinded and deceived' by the new 'great whore', the Ranters spared no sympathy for those who were actively complicit. Indeed, for Coppe, such figures were 'the worst whore[s]' of all.[26]

Even God was a sexual being to these radical thinkers, and they were not shy about describing his amorous attributes. Writing from the divine perspective, James Hunt taunted pharisaical preachers who could not 'feele nor see' his 'Cunnie', that 'heavenlie berrie', while Coppe celebrated an erotic 'naked God . . . uncloathed of flesh and forme'.[27] For many Ranters, the 'Eternall God' was coterminous with 'UNIVERSALL Love', which meant not only that proper worship required 'pure Libertinisme' from his disciples, but also that God himself was 'the Whore and the Whoremaster', who 'kissest us and . . . dandlest us upon thy knees'. By sexualising the divine body, the Ranters thus created a porno-political theology of intercourse.[28]

In a radical formulation of the Christian erotic tradition derived from the Song of Songs, Ranter theorists presented the mystical union between God and the believer as a fruitful spiritual marriage. Sex – for Coppe, God's 'soul-ravishing consolations' – anchored this 'spirituall communion'. 'God lies downe in the sweet embraces, and refreshing bosome of his own love', wrote Salmon, and 'what sweet ravishings, and holy raptures is the soule carryed up in!'[29] Usually, the divine coupling resulted in a new birth, although various Ranters disagreed on what had been 'created or begotten'. Coppe, for instance, praised how 'the Man-childe Jesus is brought forth in Us', while others believed the fruits of the divine union between 'the Lamb [i.e. God] and the Lambes wive [i.e. the believer]' to be some form of the libertine 'freewoman' that rescued acolytes from the burdens of the moral law.[30] In either case, impregnated by God and destined to birth a new kind of ascended Christian spirit, the Ranters saw themselves as sexually embedded in the divine mystery of creation.

In short: not only did the Ranters reconfigure the entire Christian tradition around explicit sexuality; additionally, by identifying with the feminine 'freewoman' of Galatians 4:31 while elevating prostitutes and whoremongers above pious puritan ministers, they visibly broke with the patriarchal assumptions that traditionally undergirded early modern public discipline. For this reason as much as for their unconventional theology, Coppe and his fellows soon garnered a formidable reputation as blasphemous libertines. However, they also attracted a pile of emulators, acolytes, and hangers-on. In Andover, a millenarian rope-maker named William Franklin was inspired by Ranting tenets to abandon his wife for another woman, for instance, while several New Model soldiers faced disciplinary action for professing Ranter principles. Even John Bunyan read several of the Ranters' books.[31]

This was a problem for the republican regime, since the Ranters' very existence appeared to confirm longstanding royalist arguments about the correlation between parliamentarian ecclesiastical reforms and the rising incidence of Protestant radicalism. Consequently, to subvert the inevitable association between Ranterism and parliamentarian godliness – in the words of one republican newsbook, 'to stop the slandrous mouths of those that publish abroad such vile reports of this Common-wealth, as if they intended to countenance impious and licentious practises, under pretence of Religion and Liberty' – the regime soon set about soliciting a wide array of printed anti-Ranter polemic to reinforce the distinction between respectable godly government and antinomian moral anarchy.[32]

These writers had plenty of material to draw from. During the later 1640s, Presbyterians like the Scottish minister Samuel Rutherford had printed lengthy refutations of antinomian theology that reflected the anti-tolerationist principles enshrined by mid-1640s heresiographers.[33] (In fact, Thomas Edwards was the first to identify a future Ranter in print – the Wiltshire radical Thomas Webbe – in *Gangraena*.)[34] Identical concerns continued to echo in correspondence and sermons after the regicide: the Presbyterian Richard Baxter worried in 1651 about the 'forcefull groweth of abominations' in English Protestant circles, for example, while other ministers preached that 'an Antinomia[n] is a Ranter disguised'.[35] In nearly every case, the heresiographers' insistent linkage between religious heterodoxy and moral anarchy loomed large.

Consequently, republican anti-Ranter pamphlets published between 1650 and 1652 – many adorned with Commonwealth press licenses – took sexual libertinism as their starting point. Tracts such as *The Ranters Bible* (1650) described radicals who 'stript themselves quite naked' in Westminster's streets 'for the acting of that inhumane Theatre of carnal copulation'. Another pamphlet described a 'she Ranter' who would count 'her self a happy woman, and a superlative servant of Gods if any man would acompany with her carnally'.[36] Of course, in recounting these stories, the anti-Ranter rejoinders provided their readers with a plethora of stimulating descriptions of sectarian promiscuity. As such, even as regime apologists coopted the anti-puritan frameworks of earlier heresiographical writers for use against the Ranters, they propelled yet more graphic sexual polemic into print.

Several pamphlets included woodcut images of Ranter excesses. *The Ranters declaration* (1650), which detailed the supposedly real-life antics of London Ranter 'Brother[s]' and their 'Fellow-Female[s]', presented a four-part frontispiece depicting the Ranters at play. Two of the images were relatively innocuous. One pictured a triumphalist antinomian tub-preacher who cried, 'we have over come the Devil'; the other portrayed sectaries feasting gluttonously in the style of Ben Jonson's anti-puritan masterpiece *Bartholomew fair*.[37] The other two images were more alarming. One showed a Ranter couple entwined in a passionate embrace while two onlookers urged them to 'Increase [and] multiply'. The second depicted a collection of nude sectarians cavorting to music. Both vividly highlighted

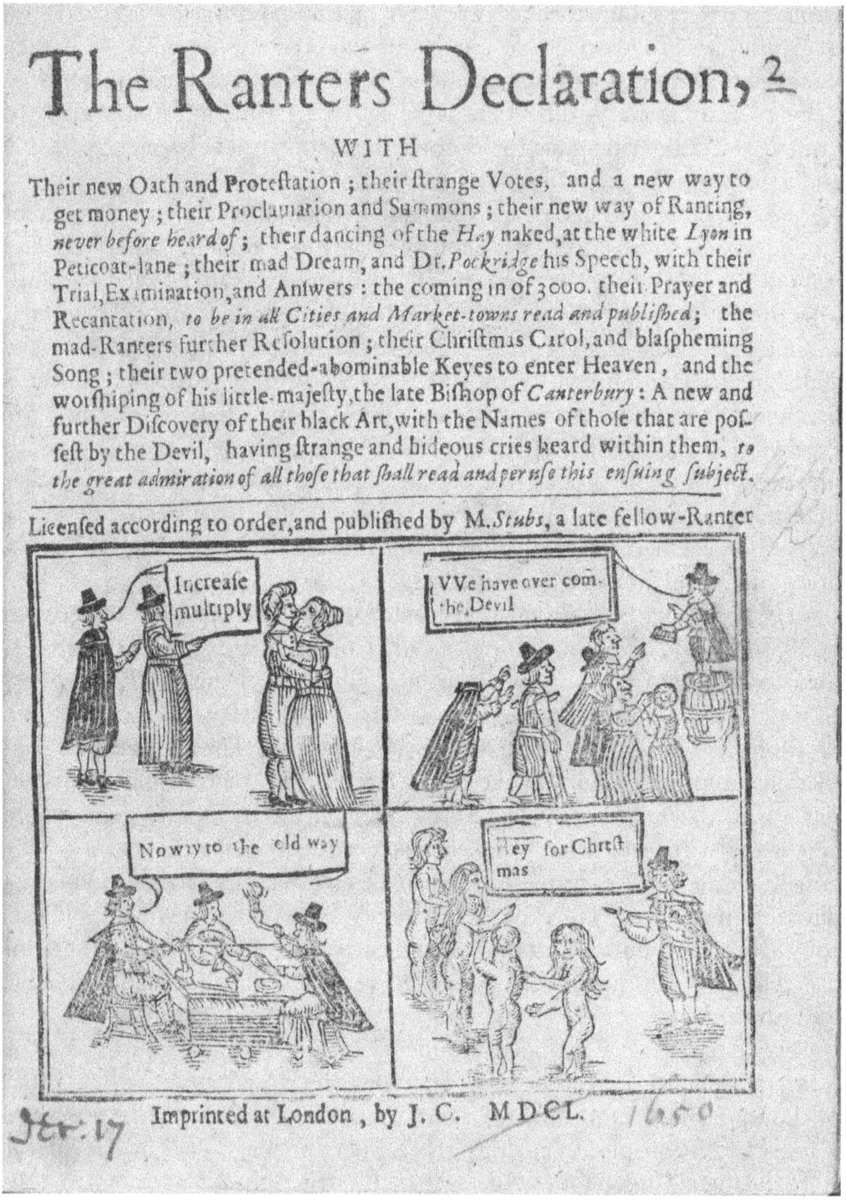

# The Ranters Declaration,

## WITH

Their new Oath and Protestation; their strange Votes, and a new way to get money; their Proclamation and Summons; their new way of Ranting, *never before heard of*; their dancing of the *Hay* naked, at the white *Lyon* in Peticoat-lane; their mad Dream, and Dr. *Pockridge* his Speech, with their Trial, Examination, and Answers: the coming in of 3000. their Prayer and Recantation, *to be in all Cities and Market-towns read and published*; the mad-Ranters further Resolution; their Christmas Carol, and blaspheming Song; their two pretended-abominable Keyes to enter Heaven, and the worshiping of his little-majesty, the late Bishop of *Canterbury*: A new and further Discovery of their black Art, with the Names of those that are possest by the Devil, having strange and hideous cries heard within them, *to the great admiration of all those that shall read and peruse this ensuing subject.*

Licensed according to order, and published by M. *Stubs*, a late fellow-Ranter

Imprinted at London, by J. C. MDCL.

Figure 5.1 *The Ranters declaration* (1650)

the text's heavy-handed association between Ranterism and promiscuity. No matter how accustomed contemporary readers had grown to encountering explicit sex-talk in print by the early 1650s, such graphic depictions of naked, writhing sectaries likely still raised eyebrows.

Some of these anti-Ranter texts were grounded in ostensibly true accounts. One series of pamphlets profiled a 'mad crew' of London Ranters who gathered to drink and sing 'filthy songs' before pairing off for ritual copulation. The first tract described one such liaison, when a female Ranter ('a true Prosolite of Cop') 'presented her self' to her partner 'naked, saying, Fellow Creature, what sayest thou to a plump leg of mutton', before 'striking her hand upon her thigh'. A few months later, a follow-up pamphlet reported on subsequent meetings of those same Ranters, 'whereat both men and women presented themselves stark naked one to the other'.[38]

The most extensive true account of Ranter-esque activity chronicled the life of the radical Wiltshire minister Thomas Webbe, who had established a libertine compact between himself, his wife and a mistress that eventually led to the arrest and trial of all three malefactors.[39] Webbe's antinomian activities were catalogued by a local magistrate named Edward Stokes in a 1652 pamphlet. Stokes had no doubt that the 'cradle of lust' nurtured in Webbe's home had been 'made after the Ranting mode', and despite occasional protestations – 'modesty', the pamphlet announced, 'commands the Author in silence to pass over many particulars of uncleannesse' – he offered effusive details of 'this famous mock-Parson, with his female fellow-Creatures . . . swimming down the stream of lust'. Because Stokes had presided over Webbe's trial, he had plentiful testimony at hand to corroborate his contention that the 'Libertine Parson Webb' embodied 'the Ranting part' in all its antinomian depravity.[40] For Stokes, at least, there was no doubt that Ranterism posed a grave threat to England's religious and moral well-being.

Between 1649 and 1652, then, the republican regime and its supporters published a slew of surprisingly graphic anti-Ranter polemics. At the same time, moreover, Coppe and his fellows also received considerable pushback from other radical groups who feared that they might suffer by association if they did not sufficiently distance themselves from the libertines. Sectarian rejoinders to the Ranters' 'most horrid abominations' (including one from Coppe's former coreligionists, the Baptists) appeared in both manuscript and print, while other congregations confronted the antinomian cancer firsthand.[41] In May 1650, for instance, two women were expelled from Norwich's Congregational church for 'lewd behaviour' possibly inspired by Coppe's *Fiery flying roll*.[42] Intimately familiar with the post-Reformation correlation between Protestant radicalism and sexual laxity, the sects attacked the Ranter menace with all the vigour of a Presbyterian heresiographer.

None were more critical than Gerrard Winstanley, leader of the egalitarian Digger community that sprang up at St George's Hill, Surrey, in April 1649. Inspired by the impending millennium and England's recent liberation from the tyrannical legacy of 'the Norman Bastard', William the Conqueror, Winstanley and his fellows colonised the local commons for a novel experiment in universalist agrarianism.[43] Responses to the Diggers were mixed: in Westminster, the Council of State viewed their escapades with bemusement; on the ground in Surrey, however, many locals reacted with violence.[44] Indeed, for these firsthand observers, Winstanley's property-usurping 'True Levellers' may have appeared just as frightening as the libertine Ranters.

A comparison between the two groups was not entirely spurious. For one, Winstanley's Diggers preached a universalist message of communal goods that ostensibly resembled the antinomian principle of collective sexual access to women first associated with Anabaptist Munster (and which had recently been attributed, falsely, to Overton and the Levellers). Yet while Winstanley trumpeted a spiritualist theology that loosely reflected the Ranters' emphasis on personal divinity, he resisted its promiscuous implications, subscribing instead to a patriarchal social vision in which sexual honesty played a defining role. When Winstanley learned that some contemporaries had equated his Diggers with Coppe's acolytes, therefore – and possibly after encountering Ranters lurking within the Digger colonies – he promptly responded in print.[45]

Winstanley's repudiation of 'the Ranting action' appeared in March 1650, just as key Ranter leaders were facing arrest or court-martial for their beliefs. His tract offered a straightforward refutation of Ranter libertinism that focused especially on the threat it posed to the patriarchal household. 'Where true Love hath united a man and woman to be Husband and Wife', he wrote, 'when this Ranting power . . . comes in, he seperates [sic] those very friends'. Winstanley supplemented this social argument with a spiritual one, writing that 'community with variety [of] women . . . is the life of the Beast'.[46] This was a strategic, as well as a moral, intervention, and by framing his rejoinder around the social dangers of sexual promiscuity, Winstanley's objections anticipated the tactics of later Protestant radicals whose spiritualist theology also appeared decidedly Ranterish from the wrong angle.

In short, galvanised by the impending millennium and the looming threat of republican (puritan), rather than royal (popish), tyranny, a disparate group of radical thinkers emerged in print during the early months of 1649 to experiment with new and alarming sexual politics which, in the case of the Ranters, included a total renovation of contemporary sexual morality. As illustrated by the vast gulf separating Winstanley's traditional patriarchalism from Coppe's libertine antinomianism, these interregnum radicals did not always reach the same conclusions. As we will see, however, the republican regime drew no such distinctions in their efforts to tar all of their critics with the brush of malignant licentiousness.

### 'Subduing lust at home': republicanism, reformation and resistance

By March 1650, sectarian promiscuity was the talk of England. Days after Winstanley's pamphlet appeared in London, for example, one letter-writer informed his father about the Andover radical William Franklin, whose adulterous lover 'laie with him constantly although he had a wife . . . and shee a husband'.[47] Again, this was unwelcome news for the republican regime, which was managing an Irish war while simultaneously policing royalist resistance in England and monitoring Charles II's recruiting efforts abroad. Atop everything else, the Commonwealth could ill afford to cultivate a reputation for indulging promiscuous Protestant radicals. That threat explained the thoroughness of the anti-Ranter response chronicled in the preceding section; but the Ranters were not the only problem confronting the new republic in 1650.

Public image concerns had haunted the regime since its inception. Beyond the criticisms of royalists and Leveller radicals, the Commonwealth also faced considerable popular disaffection that occasionally transformed Westminster itself into a hostile environment.[48] The Council of State made piecemeal attempts from March 1649 to disrupt adversarial polemicists like Lilburne and Overton, but not until May did it begin formulating a comprehensive response to 'the printing of invective & scandalous Pamphlets against the Commonwealth'. On 20 September, that effort was formalised in a draconian press control bill that empowered regime watchdogs to sniff out illicit publishing activity while punishing printers, rather than authors, for producing subversive material. The result was a strikingly competent regulatory system: England's first, in truth, since the collapse of Caroline ecclesiastical press licensing in 1640/41.[49]

Meanwhile, the Council of State set about building a distinctive republican brand. The press campaign against Charles's two bodies was one element of this broader project, which also involved redesigning the kingdom's traditional images, symbols, and discourses of sovereignty across a considerable range of public media.[50] The idealised political identity that emerged – godly, virtuous and masculine – represented a conscious effort on the new state's behalf to distance itself from the debauched legacy of Stuart tyranny by erecting an unbridgeable distinction between private desire and public duty.[51] It would prove to be no easy task.

An early formulation of the new republican ethos appeared in John Blackleach's *Endevors aiming at the glory of God*, licensed for publication in December 1649. Blackleach's defence of the Commonwealth largely derived from the scriptural history of Israel. His premise was simple: generations of Englishmen, like the Israelites, had foolishly chosen monarchy despite God's preference for rule by godly judges, with predictably disastrous results. With Charles now dead, however, there was an opportunity for redemption.

To hammer his point home, Blackleach rehearsed many of the anti-monarchical porno-politics currently proliferating elsewhere in republican print. Charles, he claimed, was 'guilty of the capital breaking of Gods Laws, in not punishing and suppressing those horrible and openly known Blasphemers, Robbers, Adulterers, [and] Whoremongers'; his forefathers, moreover, had been slaves to such 'vices' as 'Plays, Pastimes, Hawking and Hunting . . . swearing, revelling, [and] whoring'.[52] In contrast, Blackleach proffered the example of Israel's biblical judges who, unlike many historical kings, 'did not addict themselves to voluptuous pleasure, nor to build stately Palaces, not to idolatrous wives; not to many wives, not to voluptuous diet, or much wine'. The crowning sin of their eventual successor, David, provided the final test-case: 'consider', he begged, 'did Moses, Joshua, Gideon, Samuel, did they kill innocent Uriah? Did they commit Adultery with Bathsheba?'[53] Like those famous Israelites, Blackleach argued – and unlike the ungodly Stuarts – the Commonwealth's leaders were 'humble, faithful, watchful, and pious men' who would never privilege personal gain over the public weal. Ultimately merit, not genealogy, ought to be the guiding principle of English sovereignty, lest the vagaries of the royal 'succession from Father to Son' yield nothing but 'stately houses, rich gardens, [and] a thousand Wives and Concubines' after 'three or foure generations'.[54]

Yet for all his objections to Stuart patriarchalism, Blackleach invoked similarly domestic metaphors to praise the republican regime. In his telling, 'a Family . . . representeth a little common-wealth', and the state's new leaders – especially Cromwell and Fairfax – its loving 'Fathers'.[55] Blackleach was not alone in resorting to such language, either. After labouring so vigorously to link the Stuart cause with patriarchal corruption during the mid-to-late 1640s, Commonwealth activists subsequently found few convincing alternatives to buttress their own political legitimacy.[56] Rather than crafting a totally new lexicon of republican sovereignty, therefore, the Commonwealth insisted instead that its iteration of classical masculine patriarchalism was distinct from the lascivious Stuart family romance that preceded it.[57]

The key themes of Blackleach's *Endevors* – godly morality, civic masculinity and staunch anti-monarchism – echoed recurrently in regime polemics from the fall of 1649, often in tandem with suspiciously familiar domestic language.[58] In one godly 1650 elegy, for instance, the prominent parliamentarian merchant Rowland Wilson was lauded as 'the husband of the commonwealth, to which indeed he was truly married'.[59] Considered alongside Blackleach's neo-patriarchal schema, this revival of the conjugal metaphor demonstrated just how closely republican sexual politics hewed to those of their royalist enemies.

The Commonwealth's critics recognised as much. While the September press act succeeded in squelching large swathes of royalist print, some stalwarts continued to snipe in illicit pamphlets well into the following summer. One weekly newsbook entitled *The man in the moon*, produced by the royalist bookseller John Crouch, outlasted the rest. Crouch had possibly aided in the production of lurid anti-sectarian books in 1641/42, and if so, he clearly had not lost his touch for bawdy satire. Aided by his brother Edward, a printer, Crouch published fifty-seven issues of his newssheet between April 1649 and June 1650 before being captured and imprisoned by the regime.[60] *The man in the moon*'s tone was at once condemnatory, comedic and highly sexualised, peppered with scathing references to 'Harry Martins Wenches' and Cromwell's malignant 'Bull-Calfe[s]'.[61] Occasionally, it was joined by other one-off royalist publications. In January 1650, *Mercurius melancholicus* briefly resurfaced to announce that the republicans had transformed the Palace of Whitehall into a nursery of iniquity:

> wherein Sinne was corrected, it is now cherished; where Lust was condemned, it is now acted . . . the holy Vestiments, wherein the Reverend Priests did offer the Sacrifices of Righteousnesse, are sacrificed to beastly Lust, by the sonnes of Baal...these, this, to both profit and pleasure; for they have turned it into . . . a Baudy-house.[62]

In these damning terms, highly reminiscent of the loyalists' pre-regicidal polemics of 1647 and 1648, royalist scribblers pelted the regime from hiding while its soldiers hunted them through London's streets.

At the same time, radicals continued to criticise the regime from its other flank. In January, Henry Neville (now a sitting member of parliament) returned to the Parliament of Ladies in *Newes from the New Exchange*, which satirised more than 100 regime affiliates as lascivious 'Ladies Rampant' fixated entirely on sexual satisfaction. Among many targets, Elizabeth Cromwell was shown to have 'run through most of the Regiment, both Officers and Souldiers', while her husband was indicted for his ongoing adultery with 'Mrs. Lambert'. Even more so than Neville's earlier tracts, *Newes* dripped with eroticism: one victim, Lady Carlisle, was described 'being charged in the Fore-deck by Master [Denzil] Hollis, in the Poop by Master [John] Pym, whilst she clapt my Lord of Holland under hatches' in what was perhaps the period's first printed description of a foursome.[63] A later reader found the new tract so compelling that they painstakingly transcribed a lengthy poem from one of Neville's previous pamphlets into their personal copy.[64]

All told, the similarities between Crouch and Neville's lurid libels attested that in sexual politics, at least, radicals and royalists could find some common ground: a consequence of the republic's continued reliance on gendered and sexual imagery to justify its existence. For these critics, sexual satire looked especially promising when it came to the Commonwealth's plans for a national reformation of manners. This effort to remake society into the perfect image of the godly commonwealth was an old dream of English puritans, who had long militated for stricter moral regulation.[65] For this reason, Blackleach's *Endevors* had urged the Council of State to take advantage of the 'great, and glorious, or precious opportunity put into your hands of Reformation'.[66] Buoyed by such enthusiasm, England's reformation became a central project of the new regime – and, therefore, a first-rate target for its enemies.

Parliament had made several attempts at moral reform during the 1640s, only a few of which – like the forced closure of London's theatres, first enacted in 1642 and reinforced again in 1648 and 1649 – had proven successful.[67] Meanwhile, other godly efforts to reform English morality (the dissolution of the 'bawdy courts' in 1641, for instance) had arguably done more harm than good by providing high-profile ammunition for their critics. By 1648, parliamentarians had little to show for their pains beyond half-baked proposals and largely anodyne legislation. When Charles's execution appeared to signal a providential greenlight to proceed on a more comprehensive scale, therefore, godly leaders jumped at the opportunity to make good on a generations-old puritan dream.

In addition to fulfilling those old hopes, however, the reformation project also served a more immediate political purpose by providing a convenient means to collectivise and censure the regime's disparate array of domestic opponents. Just one week after the passage of the September 1649 press act, the republic published a formal declaration condemning the Levellers, the 'Cavalier and Episcopal party', and radical sectarians alike as avatars of 'Atheism and Licentiousness'.[68] Consequently, 'licentiousness' – a catch-all term for moral degeneracy – became a benchmark by which all of the regime's enemies were measured and found wanting.[69]

Royalists found the reformation project an enticing target in turn. Charles's partisans had lampooned parliamentarian efforts at moral reformation long before the regicide, and afterward they similarly dismissed the republican agenda as 'a high-way to all evil Opinions, licentious Profanenesse, illegal Marriages, Blasphemies, Schismes, Errors, and Heresies'.[70] Many assumed the campaign was a sham spun out by hypocritical puritans to hide their lascivious activities behind a veil of piety. Others insisted that it could be entirely circumvented with the right bribe: 'give them but money, you shall have May-games still, / And license too, to drink, sweare, whore, and kill', mocked Crouch's *Man in the moon*.[71] In loyalist eyes, therefore, the republican reformation encompassed venery, lechery, and godly hypocrisy all in one.

Nevertheless, urged on by cheerleaders like Blackleach, the regime began enacting waves of moralising legislation from mid-1649. Its first major intervention also became its most infamous: a May 1650 act mandating the death penalty for 'the abominable and crying sins of Incest [and] Adultery'.[72] This was a long-awaited victory for English puritans, who had spent decades praying for harsher punishments for sexual criminals; it was also a straightforwardly patriarchal one, for the law applied more strictly to women than men (who could escape the capital charge so long as their extramarital partners were themselves unmarried). In this way, the Commonwealth cemented sexual discipline as a cornerstone of its impending reformation while reaffirming its commitment to maintaining proper sexual dominion over English women.[73]

The Adultery Act was undoubtedly draconian, but it was also difficult to prosecute. A successful conviction required a daunting burden of proof: like most capital crimes, the act required two witnesses, neither of which could be the involved parties or their spouses. Moreover, probably due to the law's harshness, judges confronted with relevant cases routinely chose to forgo indictment. Consequently, the act led to very few executions, although some individuals were indeed hanged on its authority during the early 1650s.[74] Instead, the Adultery Act proved more effective as a symbol of republican moral mettle. In contrast to the sexual license championed by Coppe's Ranters or (ostensibly) Charles II's lascivious royalists, the Commonwealth staked its reputation on the systematic repression of sexual vice.

The act sparked much contemporary commentary. Several royalist writers, still convinced of their enemies' irrepressible lustfulness, took to print in May 1650 to parody the absurdity of hyper-sexual puritans outlawing their principal pastime. One loyalist pamphlet summed up their argument by describing the new act as 'but doubling our dores, and providing thick Curtains for the windowes' while republican legislators continued their amorous engagements in private. As a different scribal writer observed, the new law only made sense if parliamentarian lechers like Henry 'Martine' knew they were immune to its rules. Another royalist tract eventually gave it a fitter title: 'An Act for making Adultery Death in all persons except Representatives, for whom it shall be lawfull to have as many Women as they Represent Men'.[75] Among the most persistent of these detractors was Crouch's *Man in the moon*, which followed the new law from its earliest appearance and showered it with abuse that only let up after his June

1650 arrest. All would have agreed with an unknown contemporary who scribbled into their commonplace book around this time that 'the Devil of Rebellion dothe often come as the Angel of Reformation'. In this conventionally anti-puritan appropriation of 2 Corinthians 11:14 lay the heart of the loyalist case against the Commonwealth's moral crusade.[76]

Royalists were not alone in denouncing the Adultery Act. Even before its passage through parliament, members like Marten himself led a principled resistance against the new law that eventually spawned the evidentiary limitations which made it so difficult to prosecute.[77] Outside of Westminster, the puritan lady Lucy Hutchinson responded with even more vitriol. Writing after the attempted execution of one Anne Greene for adultery and infanticide in December 1650, Hutchinson transcribed a seething ballad into her commonplace book that opened with the lines, 'what a pittifull age is this / what cruelty reigns in this towne / to hang a poore silly wench / for using a thing of her owne'. The following stanzas wondered, in much the same tone, 'is not my body my owne / Why may I not use it then?' before concluding with a forceful quatrain: 'Be kind to a Parliament man / Lett them satisfie lust with their beasts / And sodomize when they can', it read, 'Oh revenge this cruell murther of me / committed by impotent men'. Whether Hutchinson penned this poem herself or merely recorded it from another source, its proto-feminist language and crude tone encapsulated the controversies provoked by the Adultery Act among friends and enemies of the regime alike. Even the godly could be sceptical of reformation in such a harsh form.[78]

Still, the campaign pressed on. In August 1650, the government passed a Blasphemy Act mandating steep penalties for sacrilege. This was both an expression of puritan moralism and a political response to the Ranters, whose most transgressive publications had just come to the regime's attention. The committee responsible for drafting the bill had read Laurence Clarkson's *A single eye all light*, and its denouncement of 'Adultery, Incest, Fornication, Uncleanness, Sodomy, Drunkenness, filthy and lascivious Speaking' – most of which were already outlawed by the recent Adultery Act – clearly reflected an anti-Ranter bent. Even Coppe argued in his January 1651 confession that both the Blasphemy and Adultery Acts 'were put out because of me'.[79] Here too, then, politics underwrote the Commonwealth's attempt at cultural revolution.

The Adultery and Blasphemy Acts were soon supplemented with additional moral legislation. But despite the intensity of its legislative program, the regime did not make an aggressive public case for reformation; instead, freelancing supporters were left to publicise the cause on their own in print.[80] This was a familiar arrangement for both parties. Parliament had relied on godly ministers for public support since the early 1640s, and the republic continued to do so after the regicide.[81] Across England's parishes, sympathetic preachers therefore stumped for the ongoing reformation in the pulpit and in print – sometimes, in this latter case, abetted by the regime. John Shawe's *Britannia rediviva*, published in November 1649, was one such effort. Shawe's tract began by marvelling at 'how far the glorious Gospel hath spred within these last seven yeers', even as 'devils and men . . . heightned their rage and malice against the Church'. Yet despite 'so much light of Gods Word, and so many lashes of Gods Rod', he noted, 'men are generally as unrighteous, as unjust as ever': a legacy, Shawe went on to suggest, of the late civil wars. *Britannia rediviva* offered one solution. The 'sure way to free a Land from the guilt of national sins, and destruction by National judgments', it argued, was for 'the publike Officers betrusted by that State, [to] faithfully execute justice'.[82] Only by empowering the magistrates to fully carry out their reforming mission – a project that implicitly included the destruction of the Commonwealth's various ungodly enemies – could the past be laid to rest.

Shawe's arguments were echoed in other godly publications that applauded the Commonwealth's legislative assault on 'petit treason, murthers, man-slaughters, robberies, burglaries, thefts, rapes, sodomies, buggeries, and other such things'.[83] Yet according to some commentators, enough had not yet been done to purify the kingdom. Consider a February 1650 pamphlet entitled *One blow more at Babylon*, which condemned the 'miserable poor creatures' of 'our Parish Churches' for exhibiting 'no conscience in the least of drunkenness, swearing, lying, stealing, whoredom, fornication, scoffing at, and persecuting of the Ways and People of God'. In order to finally 'dash Babels Brats against the wall', its anonymous author urged, the new regime must supplement the recent 'Act[s] against . . . swearing, incest, whoredome, [and] fornication' with more aggressive legislation. Another millenarian preacher, Jonathan Clapham, similarly cautioned a Norfolk audience in 1651 that 'Antichrist's terme is not yet exspired', advising that 'wee may exspect more shakeings' before 'the Whore of Rome can bee destroied'.[84] Like John Shawe, these bystanders worried that greater vigilance was necessary to ensure England's successful reformation.

Even so, by 1651, English readers had access to a regular supply of godly publications trumpeting the reformation's successes. 'It is easier to conquer Armies abroad, then subdue Lust at home', warned George Masterson, 'but behold, the shaking of the Earth terribly . . . ushers in the establishment of the Lords Mountain'. Hugh Peter joined Shawe and Clapham in proposing additional reforms to keep 'the sins of Sodom' at bay.[85] None denied the obstacles that lay ahead. While preaching on the 'businesse' of national reformation in July 1651, for instance, William Durham documented the efforts of 'the debauched sinner [and] the Atheistical Politician' to 'raise and foment what slanders their wits and malice can invent'. Indeed, given that they had entered 'the worlds last dayes', it was no wonder that England's parishes were 'most abounding with iniquity'; but thankfully, Durham argued, the malicious 'endeavours' of 'Papists, Atheist, Libertine, and Sectarie' would 'be in vaine'.[86] With reformation underway, God's enemies had slim hopes of triumph.

### 'Buffeted by wit': the republican campaign against British royalism

Those, like Durham, who blamed England's lethargic transformation on the Commonwealth's debauched enemies had many from which to choose. To head off their numerous critics, as we have already seen, republican writers turned to the presses to make their case against Levellers, Ranters and loyalists alike via a moralising idiom that lumped together all of their enemies as licentious, unreformed malignants. In particular, British royalists became a favourite target of Commonwealth apologists once Charles II sealed a military alliance with his northern subjects in 1650. In licensed productions like Marchamont Nedham's *Mercurius politicus*, regime writers harnessed the ongoing reformation project to depict Charles II's partisans – whether Scots, English Presbyterians, or disgruntled cavaliers – as lascivious debauchees intrinsically opposed to England's recovery.

Many English royalists remained actively opposed to Commonwealth rule after the regicide. That threat manifested most readily in print, where polemicists like John Crouch spewed sedition against the regime well into the summer of 1650; but the possibility of active rebellion proved even more alarming to republican authorities. There were certainly grounds for worrying: not only did loyalists infest England's parishes, but Charles II's network of exiled advisors continued to campaign abroad on his behalf. The threat of a royalist invasion thus haunted the Council of State throughout the early 1650s.

On 1 May 1650, Charles II signed a treaty with Scotland that promised the young king an army in exchange for his conversion to Presbyterianism. It was an uneasy alliance, for Charles's disdain for Scottish religion was matched by the northerners' discomfort about aiding another Stuart against their ostensibly godly neighbours. (Many Scots, possibly swayed by royalist and disaffected Presbyterian arguments about republican moral anarchy, consoled themselves by arguing that English puritans had grown too radical for their own good.) Reservations notwithstanding, the Scots fought two consecutive wars on Charles's behalf in 1650 and 1651. Although both campaigns were eventually crushed by Cromwell, they presented the most serious challenge yet to republican hegemony.

In response, Commonwealth apologists turned their attentions northward during the year-and-a-half preceding the Scots' final defeat at Worcester in September 1651. These writers made much of the obvious distance between Presbyterian moral discipline and the debauchery of Charles II's cavaliers.[87] Such contrasts were aided by the Scots' own unease about the dubious alliance: prior to their first defeat at Cromwell's hands in September 1650, for instance, kirk ministers forcibly purged the Scottish armies of any men they deemed too 'wicked' to fight for God's cause. Among the thousands of expelled soldiers were many battle-hardened English royalists. As one stunned observer later noted, this effort to root out wickedness also rid the Scots of 'their best soldiers'.[88] Cromwell's subsequent victory proved the truth of his words.

Elsewhere other polemicists, among them the poet George Wither, drew on older stereotypes to rebut Scottish accounts of the 'New-Heresies' (including 'the Ranters Tenents') that were apparently flourishing under the Commonwealth. Wither warned his readers to beware the Scots' 'Lousie Army . . . Nasty sluts, and Grooms', for by them 'you should see your hardly-gotten-stores, / Devour'd by loose Commanders, and their whores', and 'your Wives . . . perhaps immodestly abus'd'. One target was the Scottish general David Leslie, who led the Scottish campaigns of 1650 and 1651. Just as his predecessor Alexander Leslie (no relation) had been slandered by royalists a decade prior during the Bishops' Wars, Commonwealth apologists ridiculed Leslie for 'joviaIling up and down Yorkshire with a Gentlewoman . . . [and] leaving some fruits of his love behind him'.[89] Meanwhile, they also reiterated more traditional descriptions of the 'whoring, plundering, [and] perfidious dealings' of English royalists.[90]

The most eminent victim of republican sexual politics was Charles II himself. Like his martyred father, the 'debauched' Stuart heir came under considerable regime scrutiny during the early 1650s.[91] Unlike Charles I, however, the new king made an easy target for sexual slander. He had reportedly taken his first lover, Lucy Walter, while visiting The Hague in mid-1648, and Charles soon broadened his circle of amours even further, although he laboured to keep these affairs discreet.[92] Even so, the young king's love of 'Ladyes' – and especially his alleged affection for 'the Scotish Wenches' – quickly became a mainstay of regime polemic.[93] By 1652, when Edward Peyton suggested in *The divine catastrophe* that 'the Prince would follow the same course' of debauchery as his parents, given how 'king Charles and his mother play[ed] fast and loose so often', the young king had already garnered an outsized reputation for lechery.[94]

On multiple fronts, then, republican writers assailed Charles II and his partisans as lecherous malignants in print throughout the early 1650s. In this, as in the anti-Ranter publications surveyed above, the Council of State took a leading role. The most consistent source of official regime commentary was the state newsbook *Mercurius politicus*, brainchild of the one-time royalist and former author of *Britanicus*, Marchamont Nedham. Unsurprisingly given Nedham's background, one of *Politicus*'s hallmarks was its attacks against the sexual probity of Ranters, royalists, and Scottish interlopers alike.

This was inarguably a stylistic choice, for Nedham had long considered scurrilous satire an entirely legitimate mode of political discourse. When editing *Britanicus*, he once claimed that 'to render the wayes, and plots of the Kings party as ridiculous . . . I was pleasant on purpose, that halting my Intelligence with some sport, I might . . . jeere them out of it'. Later, in the royalist *Mercurius pragmaticus*, Nedham had crowed to see his enemies 'buffeted by wit.'[95] When he first pitched *Politicus* to regime leaders, therefore, Nedham argued that it ought to be 'written in a Jocular way' to appease the 'multitude . . . [and] make musick to the Common sence'. (He also promised to 'sayle in a middle way, between the Scylla and Charybdis of Scurrility and prophanes', in case some members of the new government remained uneasy about licentious language.)[96] The Commonwealth's approval of Nedham's prospectus later that spring suggests that finally, after a decade of denouncing the proliferation of sexual politics in print, even the soberest of contemporaries were learning to live with them.

From June 1650, Nedham set about turning *Politicus* into the regime's foremost mouthpiece. His coverage ranged across the political landscape: one October issue celebrated the recent 'Acts made by the Parl. concerning swearing, cursing, drinking . . . & other good laws' (although too 'few Magistrates see to the execution of them'), while another edition just a few weeks later described a New Model officer recently cashiered for professing the Ranter principle 'that Sin was no sinne'.[97] These announcements, interspersed with foreign news and parliamentary updates, constituted the most obvious attempt by the republic – speaking through Nedham – to intervene in the political controversies of the day. Each reflected its editor's trademark scurrility, now reinforced with a Commonwealth press license.

*Politicus* focused heavily on royalist malignancy. Nedham's newsbook derided Charles's royalists (among whom, of course, he had once numbered) for seeking solace in 'every Club and Ordinary and Alehouse' while dreaming of being 'Lord Chamberlain among the Ladies' in a restored Stuart monarchy.[98] Disaffected English Presbyterians, too, came under scrutiny. Nedham dismissed these 'lunatick Tithe-Dreamers', who by preaching against the new regime had 'prostituted things of sacred Cognisance to their own filthy Corruptions'.[99] In this case, the friendly fire was perhaps warranted: with a Scottish Presbyterian invasion imminent from the north,

Nedham and his republican employers worried that the Scots' southern coreligionists might ignite a similar uprising in London.

Nedham also targeted the Scots with the same sexual stereotypes that informed other republican anti-royalist polemics. One July 1650 issue warned readers about the outrages that would accompany a Scottish invasion, when 'your Wives, your Daughters, your Maids, your Mares, and your Hens' and 'nothing that is Female' (human or animal) would 'scape their Officers'. Another writer condemned northern clergymen who hoped to 'creep into some Conveniences again in England, and serve to say Grace, edifie the Chambermaids . . . [and] propagate Conventicles of their own'. Still more issues accused Scottish ministers of preaching so vigorously against the English heretics that Scottish women 'were made to believe they should be spitted with hot Irons . . . their Daughters undon in their Maidenheads, and themselves in their Honesty'.[100] Here, again, the slanders of earlier English anti-Covenanters were repurposed for republican use.

*Politicus* also led the charge against Charles II. In the newsbook's inaugural issue, Nedham recalled the young king's affections for 'his mothers maids of Honor, when he lay in France at Saint Germans', and indicted his English followers' 'Adulteries with the great Whore of Scotland' as yet another civil war loomed. He also cautioned royalists to 'take heed' that the new king did not seduce 'their wives', since 'they say, he hath that way an excellent faculty, as well as his Brother [i.e. the future James II]'.[101] According to *Politicus*, even loyal cavaliers were not safe from Charles's amours.

Nedham's most lasting mark against the king was a title: 'young Tarquin'. This was, of course, a reference to the infamous tyrant-rapist Sextus Tarquinius, whose rape of Lucretia had brought about the fall of the Roman monarchy and the establishment of the republic in its place. Given the ongoing attempts by other regime apologists to challenge the Stuarts' favourite conjugal metaphor, this allusion to royal sexual assault was clearly no accident. Thereafter, Charles II's identity as the rapacious 'Young Tarquin' became a republican commonplace.[102] *Politicus* employed the allusion in all but one of its first sixteen issues and continued to use it intermittently for months to follow, although the title eventually fell from regular use after Cromwell ended the young Stuart's hopes for a military restoration at Worcester.[103]

With Nedham in the van, republican polemicists took aim at Charles II's royalists for several years following the regicide. Some even attempted to merge the royalist and Ranter threats together, aided by the contemporary practice of referring to London's carousing population of gentlemen tavern-dwellers as 'Raunters'.[104] These writers, Edward Stokes among them, framed the 'new Ranting-Adamites' as debauched partisans of 'Charles the II'; after all, were not both groups primarily defined (at least according to republican leaders) by their uncontrollable sexuality? *Politicus* even reproduced a (quite possibly false) letter from one Dutch correspondent that read, 'I had thought the Ranters had been all Kings men, and spued out of your land: for, I have seen a good store of them here'.[105] By recasting Ranterism as an outgrowth of royalist debauchery rather than radical puritanism, Commonwealth apologists thus resisted the inevitable conflation between England's new godly government and the burgeoning sectarian menace. In the process, they advanced the republican campaign to reform malignant lechers of all political persuasions.

In February 1652, half a year after Worcester, the republic published an Act of Oblivion intended to effect a general reconciliation by issuing a free pardon for all outstanding criminal offenses. There were, as usual, a few exceptions. Oblivion was refused to those guilty of committing high treason against the state after 30 January 1649, which effectively meant that anyone who had taken up arms with Charles II after the regicide was ineligible. Hardcore royalists, then, were out; so too were murderers, poisoners, witches and rapists. The act exempted bigamists as well as those guilty of 'the Destestable [sic] and Abominable Vice of Buggery committed with Mankinde or Beast'.[106] In this way, nearly two years after the Adultery Act, the Commonwealth continued to broadcast its commitment to moral transformation.

But no matter how diligently the republicans pursued reformation, they could not escape their own demons. That same month, the Council of State heard troubling reports about the parliament-man and regicide, Gregory Clement. Clement, long married, had been discovered conducting an illicit relationship with his maidservant. Once parliamentary radicals learned of this news, they began clamouring for his expulsion; and, due perhaps to a genuine sense of propriety – or merely the astute assumption that Clement's transgression would reflect especially poorly on the regime's ongoing reformation project – their fellow legislators agreed. The disgraced parliament-man was discharged from the House on 11 May 1652 for conduct 'offensive and scandalous to the Parliament'.[107]

On one reading, Clement's ejection demonstrated how vigorously republican leaders stood by their commitment to moral reformation. The godly millenarian Thomas Harrison, who spearheaded the expulsion campaign, certainly believed as much.[108] But for sceptics, Clement's ejection probably raised more questions than it answered. What good was it to expel one lascivious parliament-man from the House, they might have wondered, when the adulterer-in-chief Henry Marten continued to sit at Westminster? For these critics, Clement's fate illustrated only that the republican grandees were calculating enough to sacrifice one exposed member for the new state's survival.

## 'Concupiscentiall motions': reinventing (and radicalising) royalism

By the time that parliament discovered Clement's scandalous conduct, few openly hostile critics of the republic remained active in English print. Indeed, royalist dissent had effectively dissolved with John Crouch's June 1650 imprisonment by Commonwealth press watchdogs.[109] To be sure, anti-regime sentiment continued to proliferate in more ephemeral forms: Blackleach's *Endevors* raged against the 'base language [of] Roundhead, Whores-bird, Roundhead, &c.' precisely because the early 1650s featured many such seditious outbursts against republican authority.[110] Sexual politics surfaced frequently in those encounters. In 1650, for example, a Somerset man berated local Commonwealth collaborators as 'whores birds'. Londoners proved even more virulent against the 'parliament Bastards'. One alarming 1651 case featured a City resident named Anna Watson who allegedly said that 'they that sitt att the Parliament... are all the Sonnes of Whores and Pimps, and that shee... could find find [sic] in her heart to blow them all up with Gunpowder'.[111] Verbal assaults on parliamentarian 'Whores', 'Independent divells, & Rowndheaded Rogues' continued to echo in England's streets even as the royalist press evaporated.[112]

Crouch was released from custody in September 1651 into a political situation that appeared bleaker than ever. The Commonwealth's victory over the Scots at Worcester had cemented its hegemony in England, plummeting cavalier hopes for a Stuart restoration to their lowest nadir yet. Moreover, with royalist resistance on the wane, regime leaders embarked on an aggressive campaign against the interloping traders of the Dutch Republic that soon gave way to open war. To forestall any further royalist disruptions, the Council of State continued to vigorously police the kingdom's print marketplace, convening on 18 September to discuss renewing the 1649 press act.[113] Direct attacks against the republic therefore remained largely anathema in print when Crouch regained his freedom late in 1651.

In contrast to some scholarly depictions of the interregnum as a period of royalist retreat, however, many of Charles's partisans continued to militate against the Commonwealth in less obtrusive ways.[114] In particular, it soon became apparent to some former royalists that while republican leaders responded quite harshly to overt libels against the state, they paid far less attention to milder expressions of dissent. This uneven pattern of repression likely resulted in part from the enormous pressures facing regime regulators amid multiple wars and the ongoing reformation; but it also probably owed something to the advice of Marchamont Nedham. Months before the debut of *Politicus*, the former royalist had advised the republic against cracking down too harshly on 'idle Pasquils and scandalous Pamphlets', since 'enact[ing] Lawes against such scurrilous Productions' might accidentally 'give them a kind of Reputation, and make them the more sought after'. The example of Nero, who 'by raging against the scriblers of his time ... and causing their Papers to be burnt, did but make himself the more odious, and multiply their number', was proof enough that repression only increased the potential for real unrest. Instead, Nedham argued that calculated ignorance was the better policy.[115] Evidently, the Council of State agreed, for this was precisely the strategy they employed throughout the early 1650s: direct condemnation prompted reprisal, while generic satire garnered only silence.

Crouch's arrest in June 1650 signalled that *The man in the moon* would no longer be tolerated under this new program. However, the regime's fixation on libellous language left royalist writers significant leeway to experiment with new modes of resistance. John Taylor, now in his early seventies, was among the first to test the bounds of republican forbearance with his *Epigrammes written on purpose to be read* (1651). This collection of short, playful verses was notable both for its bawdy anti-puritanism – one poem, 'Hypocrisie discovered', featured a lascivious puritan sister who waxed lyrical about the 'concupiscentiall motions' of her lover's 'whimwham' – as well as its melancholic royalism. 'Cares, griefes and sorrows, may be great', one stanza proclaimed, 'the late Kings servants have no want of those'. Yet while the royalist resonances of both themes were perfectly clear, neither proved objectionable enough to provoke a regime response. After all, the Commonwealth had recently sponsored equally lurid attacks against the Ranters, while elegiac mourning for Charles I could hardly spark rebellion on its own. In another line, Taylor clarified his position: 'my Thoughts are free, I wish my tongue were so, / then would I freely speake what I do think; / but yet my tongue too boldly shall not go, / it is more safe at injuries to wink'.[116] Here, in short, was a recipe for dissent that could satisfy both the overstretched republican grandees and their loyalist critics: generic satire and royalist melancholy tempered with a professed disavowal of seditious intent.

It was not long before Crouch joined this chorus. Although he abstained from questionable press activity for months after his release from prison – he even authored a few issues of a pro-army newsbook in January 1652, likely on the regime's orders – by the early summertime he was once again writing demonstrably anti-puritan weekly newssheets from London.[117] This time, in his new *Mercurius democritus* (later relabelled *The laughing mercury*), Crouch inaugurated an ostensibly apolitical mode of royalist sexual politics in which anti-puritan eroticism, rather than libel, reigned supreme, and which traded in the traditional patriarchalism of earlier loyalist polemicists for a novel celebration of promiscuity.[118] It proved to be a powerful, indeed transformative, formula.

Like John Taylor, Crouch was transparent about his tactics. '*Mercurius Democritus*', he declared, was the scion 'of the Family of the Jovallists, in the County of Merryford'. Jests, not jeers, were Crouch's new milieu. This was evident from the opening quatrains of one September 1652 issue of *The laughing mercury*: 'free Mirth is all I aime to write, / to laugh down Lyes and Folly', they proclaimed, 'no Law nor State do I offend, / in words, Writing or Action'. Instead, Crouch promised only to 'study Wit' and thereby 'orecome woes with gladness'.[119] This emphasis on light-hearted drollery was clearly calculated to deflect regime attention, and it worked. Commonwealth regulators would leave Crouch's newssheets unmolested for more than a year following his return to print.

In practice, the 'Lyes and Folly' that Crouch condemned were entirely the product of the new government, while his 'wit' (a word also beloved by Nedham) usually involved sex-talk. Indeed, graphic sexual descriptions were the hallmark of Crouch's post-imprisonment newsbooks, which amplified the bawdy anti-puritanism of earlier royalist print into pseudo-pornographic fantasies in which Protestant radicalism consistently begat sexual anarchy. Since none familiar with the recent Ranter controversy could refute this proposition in good faith, it was a timely intervention. To muddy the waters further, Crouch set his stories in the imaginary world of the 'Antipodes': a fantastical inverted locale in which truth became fiction and right became wrong.[120] This, too, was a political choice. For while Crouch's translocation safely removed his bawdy satire to the realm of the absurd, it also symbolised the widespread loyalist viewpoint that the regicide had literally turned the world upside down.

The very first issue of *Mercurius democritus*, which appeared right as Anglo-Dutch tensions exploded into war in April 1652, laid out Crouch's agenda in detail. It opened with an introduction to his new setting: 'perhaps you'l say these are but Lies', Crouch rhymed, 'why should I this deny, / lies are all truths ith' Andtipodes [sic], / read on, Ile tell you why'. From there, the newssheet dove into the perennial anti-puritan touchstones of illicit sex, promiscuous women and godly lasciviousness. In this single issue, *Democritus* invited 'all Citizens wives that want conception' to 'repair' to a new London office, 'where they may have full satisfaction, not withstanding any impediment'; poked fun at 'Phillip Stiff Ranter', under whom the new 'Office' was to be 'erected'; and described an Irishman discovered 'Buggering an Ele [sic] in the Town-dit[c]h, through a hole he had made in the Ice'.[121] In these lines, readers likely recognised the same language of playful bawdry that had pervaded the jesting anti-puritan polemics of early-1640s satirists like John Taylor. Now, through Crouch's practiced pen, it was refined into a scathing critique of interregnum society.[122]

A later issue of *Democritus* summarised the newsbook's central preoccupation even more neatly. 'But what is best of all, at night, / an old, but pleasant Trick', it read, 'on the green grass by two's they'l fight, / and thrust, as well as prick'. From 1652, descriptions of men, women and other creatures 'playe[ing] at In-and-In' dominated Crouch's oeuvre, often peppered with weakly-redacted obscenities.[123] (His self-censorship possibly represented another concession to Commonwealth regulators, whom he perhaps feared might use such frank language as a pretense for suppression.) Crouch's newsbooks covered the full range of conventional sexual activity, from casual fornication to masturbation – one issue described a man 'friggling himself in the green grasse' near Walthamstow village – and routinely poked fun at republican innovations like the recent 'act against Adultery'. Often, copulation ended in pregnancy. Even the masturbating Walthamstow man somehow spawned 'an innumerable company of Mandrakes', while an October 1652 issue profiled one London woman who 'was got with childe in Thames-street by eating of an Apple'.[124] Here, rather than underwriting grand porno-political theories like that of the 1648 Mistress Parliament tracts (which were assuredly a no-go after the September 1649 censorship act), early modern anxieties about monstrous births were harnessed in service to a less complicated critique of interregnum England's world-turned-upside-down. Although Crouch was not alone in equating unchecked fertility with political upheaval – a year prior, the astrologer-physician Nicholas Culpepper had published a revolutionary midwifery manual that proceeded from a similar proposition – but *Democritus*'s transgressive style rendered the metaphor of disorderly procreation particularly effective.[125]

The Walthamstow onanist aside, Crouch's preoccupation with unchecked generation ensured that his diverse cast of characters was primarily female. This, too, was entirely conventional for the early 1650s, when many royalists worried that Charles's execution had totally upended England's already mangled patriarchal order. Crouch's rags made much of this anxiety by placing nearly all the blame for the kingdom's troubles on sex-crazed, outspoken women. 'Oh Women! Monsterous Women!' *Democritus* moaned in February 1653: 'in faith *Democritus* will teach you what 'tis to rise up in rebellion against your Husbands'.[126] These women comprised a vast and varied group, from prostitutes to virgin maids.[127] Female sectarians abounded: the promiscuous holy sisters of earlier anti-puritan satires, anxious for their godly brothers' 'P[ricks] of Conscience', were joined by 'shee Ranters' whose wild lechery led them to 'increase and multiply' at an unprecedented rate.[128] The dizzying range of *Democritus*'s female malefactors was outshone only by their exuberant sexuality. Not only did Crouch describe radical sisters clamouring for 'Communion . . . in Presbyterian White-Broath' to 'warm their spirituall Wombes'; he also predicted that the kingdom's reeling condition would lead 'women [to] be more Masculine then men, taking on them to perform the Male Kinde, and be Arraigned for Buggery'.[129] In the upside-down Antipodes, the women truly were on top.[130]

The chief apostles of Crouch's fantasyland were the Ranters, whose real-life counterparts had preached and practiced the very libertine tenets that dominated the newsbooks' pages. Consequently, it was here that Crouch's publications began to feel most like legitimate coverage – even if his anti-Ranter material, too, was largely invented. In October 1652, for instance, *The laughing mercury* devoted pages to one 'Crew of Ranters' who celebrated 'Cupids Rights' with drink, sex and song. Their bawdy bacchanals included toasts 'to the best C___ [i.e. 'cunny'] in Christendom . . . [and] to the best P___ [i.e. 'prick'] that ever Pleasur'd fair Lady'. The crowning event was an orgiastic 'private exercise'.[131] In time, *Democritus* announced the appearance of 'a new Sect . . . called, The Knockers', who were said to 'exercise in More-lane, at the signe of the Instrument of Generation'. These radicals, like their Ranter colleagues, had apparently elevated sexual pleasure above all other impulses; and, as Crouch's newssheets confirmed each week, they found Antipodean England a welcome home for their debauchery.[132]

And debauchery it was. Bestiality, buggery and all other forms of illicit sex dominated Crouch's upside-down world. Accounts of monstrous copulation appeared in nearly every issue. *The laughing mercury* described how an army 'Major . . . bugger'd a Jack-a-napes in a close-bed in Southwark', while *Democritus* profiled a 'French-man' caught 'buggering a Catt'.[133] Continuing a favourite theme of late-1640s royalist newsbooks, London was imagined as a puritan dystopia, the 'new Sodome', where 'Bloomsbury Virgin[s]' were in danger of being 'ravished by a Goat'. But the capital was just one landmark in the 'mutable Strumpet World' that had been 'turn'd Bawde to each abhorred Vice' by republican rule. Like the 'Hermophrodite' described in an early edition of *The laughing mercury*, reportedly capable of pleasuring both 'Brother and Sister of the Rant, being of so good ability, as to perform both Natures', *Democritus*'s Antipodean milieu encompassed all forms of sexual depravity.[134]

Crouch produced well over 100 issues of his newssheets from April 1652. He was not the only one-time royalist still operating in the kingdom's print marketplace – indeed, his methods occasionally drew fire from exasperated former colleagues who disagreed with his tactics – but by 1653, Crouch had cornered the market on lurid anti-puritan satire.[135] Meanwhile, for hostile onlookers, this turn towards nonsensical eroticism had the effect of confirming the essential truth of the parliamentarians' decade-old cavalier stereotype. Even after Worcester, royalist lasciviousness remained a fixture for godly writers who accused English loyalists of wallowing 'in drunkennesse, whoredome, and rioting' in European exile following their defeat in Britain.

Puritan preachers, too, sermonised against those cavaliers who continued to 'drincke, & whoare, & damm, & ramm' at home and abroad.[136] In this way, Crouch's newsbooks appeared to validate godly allegations about the cavaliers' intrinsic lechery.[137]

But that might have been the point. To be sure, Crouch was as enterprising as any other early modern publisher, and his post-imprisonment pivot undoubtedly reflected a straightforward belief, bolstered since the outbreak of civil war, that sex-talk sold books. (The failure of Crouch's short-lived 1652 newsbook *Mercurius heraclitus*, which devoted most of its space to gloomy reflections on the evils of the times, probably banished any lingering doubts about this publishing truism.) His joking indictment, in an October 1652 issue of *The laughing mercury*, of Antwerp bookshops that dared to 'sell Aretines Pictures in their Shops, and make not the least scruple of Conscience in the world, so that they can but get gain thereby', indicated just how self-aware Crouch had become about the selling power of graphic sexuality in mid-century England.[138]

Yet Crouch's sex-drenched, anti-puritan merrymaking also presented a political argument. Faced with an overbearing godly regime bent on inflicting a draconian moral reformation on an unwilling populace, Crouch embraced bawdy sex-talk as a worldly antidote to puritan abstemiousness. In doing so, he broke ranks with earlier generations of moralising royalist preachers – think Edward Symmons in 1644 – who had decried the excesses of their fellow loyalists. In the process, his prolonged engagement with the comforting tropes of conviviality, drink and casual promiscuity suggested that perhaps, in comparison to the harsh discipline of godly hyper-morality, a little worldliness was not so bad after all. For other royalists dismayed by the mounting pace of republican reformation and the meagre progress of Charles II's recruitment efforts abroad, this was an increasingly inviting attitude. It also represented the opening stages of a unique form of post-regicidal royalist radicalism – one that would find its most lasting expression in the promiscuous political stylings of Charles II's Restoration court.

Crouch's efforts to lampoon the regime's reforming mission made no discernible dent in republican hegemony during the early 1650s. In any case, the Commonwealth faced more pressing dangers than cowed English loyalists. From its inception, the new government had been riven with internal debates between godly puritans, radical republicans and conservative parliamentary backbenchers. More threatening still was the longstanding antagonism between parliament and army, which only deepened throughout the period as godly officers grew increasingly disgusted by the poor conduct of legislators like Henry Marten.[139] Tensions came to a head when Cromwell entered the Commons with an escort of musketeers on 20 April 1653. In a fiery speech, he indicted the parliament-men as 'drunkards' and 'whoremasters' – the latter a reference to Marten and the now-disgraced Gregory Clement – before expelling them from the house.[140] From that moment, England's first republic was no more.

In its place Cromwell established a nominated assembly of godly enthusiasts known derisively as 'Barebone's Parliament' after one of its radical members. But despite the high hopes of some puritan onlookers who petitioned the new parliament to complete the moral reformation begun by its predecessor, the assembly collapsed just five months later in the face of intractable infighting.[141] Before it did, the assembled saints made one more stab at reformation by secularising the marriage rite; but this, too, proved unpopular.[142] Frustrated JPs reported that 'many marriages have beene and frequently are made contrary to the saide act' after its passage, and although a few pious couples claimed to 'forbeare to bedd together untill they be legally married', others were swindled by conniving ministers who forged illegitimate marriage 'certifficate[s]' for a hefty fee.[143] Much like the Adultery Act, marriage reform proved far more impactful on paper than it did in practice.

Meanwhile, the failure of Barebone's Parliament led Cromwell to assume control of the kingdom as its new 'Lord Protector' in December 1653. The sudden return to government by a single ruler after years of strident anti-monarchical propaganda placed the new Protectorate in an awkward position: was Cromwell destined to assume Charles's place as England's loving husband-father, or did he merely embody the public-serving masculine ideal that underwrote republican self-representation prior to April 1653?[144] Such questions were rendered more urgent by the fact that on this count, at least, republicans had largely followed the dead king in tying their virtuous masculine identity to their status as good fathers and husbands (whose commitment to the sexual regulation of English women, as seen by the gendered provisions of the Adultery Act, remained thoroughly intact). In this sense, the establishment of the new government seemingly pitted Cromwell against Charles II as head-to-head opponents in a contest for patriarchal supremacy – one that would be mediated, in large part, through sexual politics.

Royalists failed to make anything substantial of the transition from Commonwealth to Protectorate. Some militants probed for signs of potential weakness, but their efforts were not always elegant: in June 1653, for instance, two ex-royalist soldiers were arrested for attempting to infiltrate a parliamentarian naval vessel dressed as female prostitutes.[145] Wiser heads plotted in secret, while Crouch continued to plug away at scurrilous anti-puritan satire in print. (*Democritus* did briefly disappear from circulation in November, but the circumstances were probably economic rather than political.)[146] It may well be that many of Charles II's former partisans had finally come to accept the reality of parliamentarian hegemony in England; certainly the New Model's looming presence made the possibility of significant military resistance seem remote.

But even if that were the case, Crouch's increasingly eroticised output suggests that the new post-war reality did not necessarily mandate a retreat from politics. Instead, as the next chapter will show, ex-cavaliers marshalled a novel medley of revelry, romance and drunkenness to indict interregnum England as a benighted world-turned-upside-down. In this sense, *Democritus*'s success during the early 1650s marked the emergence of a radical royalism that embraced graphic sex-talk as a worldly remedy for puritan hyper-moralism – and which would reach its fullest form at the Restoration.

## Notes

1. William Lilly, *A peculiar prognostication*, E.537[15] ([6 January] 1649), p. 2; Samuel Thurston, *Angelus Anglicanus*, E.1343[3] ([2 July] 1651), sig. B2r; William Lilly, *Merlini Anglici ephemeris*, E.1349[5] (1652), sig. B4v. See also *The black Dutch almanack*, E.1372[1] ([4 December] 1650), sig. A4r.
2. Gianoutsos, *Manhood*, pp. 16–17.
3. HEHL, EL 6881, p. [9]. See also *New news from the Old Exchange*, E.595[6] ([16 March] 1650), and Michael Sparke, *A second beacon*, E.675[29] ([4 October] 1652), both featured in the introduction.
4. *CJ*, vi, p. 196; *Elencticus*, E.552[14] (24 April–1 May 1649), pp. 7–8. See also *Pragmaticus (for King Charles II)*, E.554[12] (1–8 May 1649), sig. C2v.
5. John Rees, *The Leveller Revolution: Radical Political Organisation in England, 1640–1650* (London, 2016).
6. BL, Add. MS 71448, fol. 49r.
7. Ann Hughes, 'Gender and Politics in Leveller Literature', in Susan D. Amussen and Mark A. Kishlansky (eds), *Political Culture and Cultural Politics in Early Modern England: Essays Presented to David Underdown* (Manchester, 1995), pp. 162–88, at 174; Melissa Mowry, *Collective Understanding, Radicalism, and Literary History, 1645–1742* (Oxford, 2021).
8. Richard Overton, *To the supream authority of England*, E.546[1] ([3 March] 1649), p. 4. See also Richard Overton, *The commoners complaint*, E.375[7] ([10 February] 1647).
9. John Lilburne, et. al., *The picture of the Councel of State*, E.550[14] ([11 April] 1649), pp. 27–9; William Walwyn, *The fountain of slaunder discovered*, E.557[4] ([30 May] 1649), p. 7.
10. Ian Gentles, *The New Model Army in England, Ireland and Scotland, 1645–1653* (Oxford, 1992), pp. 342–4.
11. Richard Overton, *Overton's defyance*, E.562[26] ([4 July] 1649), p. 6.
12. E.g., *A new bull-bayting*, E.568[6] ([7 August] 1649). This pamphlet is sometimes attributed to the Levellers, too, but it seems to me to be a royalist satire

on both Cromwell and his radical opponents. For a royalist usage of the Bull of Bashan story, see *MITM*, E.595[4] (6–13 March 1650), p. 362.
13 Richard Overton, *The baiting of the great bull of Bashan*, E.565[2] ([16 July] 1649), sigs Av–2v.
14 Smith, *CRW*, p. 8; Jean-Pierre Cavaillé, 'Libertine and Libertinism: Polemic Uses of the Terms in Sixteenth- and Seventeenth-Century English and Scottish Literature', *Journal for Early Modern Cultural Studies* 12:2 (2012), 12–36, at 28–33.
15 Ariel Hessayon, 'The Making of Abiezer Coppe', *Journal of Ecclesiastical History* 62:1 (2011), 38–58. See also Richard Thomas Bell, 'The Minister, the Millenarian, and the Madman: The Puritan Lives of William Sedgwick, ca. 1609–1664', *HLQ* 81:1 (2018), 29–61.
16 Ariel Hessayon, 'Abiezer Coppe and the Ranters', in Laura Lunger Knoppers (ed.), *The Oxford Handbook of Literature and the English Revolution* (Oxford, 2012), pp. 346–70.
17 For the debate, see J. C. Davis, *Fear, Myth and History: The Ranters and the Historians* (Cambridge, 1986); G. E. Aylmer, 'Did the Ranters Exist?', *P&P* 117 (1987), 208–19; Christopher Hill, 'The Lost Ranters? A Critique of J. C. Davis', *History Workshop* 24 (1987), 134–40; J. C. Davis, 'Fear, Myth and Furore: Reappraising the "Ranters"', *P&P* 129 (1990), 79–103; J. F. McGregor, Bernard Capp, Nigel Smith, and B. J. Gibbons, 'Fear, Myth and Furore: Reappraising the "Ranters"', and J. C. Davis, 'Fear, Myth and Furore: Reappraising the "Ranters": Reply', *P&P* 140 (1993), 155–210.
18 Smith, *CRW*, p. 15.
19 Christopher Hill, *The World Turned Upside Down: Radical Ideas during the English Revolution* (London, 1975), p. 313; Smith, *CRW*, p. 30.
20 Jacob Bauthumley, *The light and dark sides of God*, E.1353[2] ([20 November] 1650), in Smith, *CRW*, p. 229; Joseph Salmon, *Divinity anatomized* (1649), in ibid., p. 194. I have cited the editions in Smith's collection wherever possible while also providing full bibliographical references.
21 Ibid., p. 197; Laurence Clarkson, *A single eye all light, no darkness*, E.614[1] ([4 October] 1650), in Smith, *CRW*, p. 123.
22 Abiezer Coppe, *Some sweet sips, of some spiritual wine*, Wing C6093 (1649), in Smith, *CRW*, p. 48; Salmon, *Divinity anatomized*, p. 179. Galatians 4:31 reads, 'So then, brethren, we are not children of the bondwoman, but of the free'.
23 Abiezer Coppe, *A second fiery flying roule*, E.587[14] ([4 January] 1650), in Smith, *CRW*, p. 100; Laurence Clarkson, *The lost sheep found*, Wing C4580 (1660), in Smith, *CRW*, pp. 133–4.
24 *A justification of the mad crew*, E.609[18] ([21 August] 1650), in Smith, *CRW*, p. 157; Abiezer Coppe, *A remonstrance…of Abiezer Coppe*, E.621[5] ([3 January] 1651), p. 4. See also McGregor, et. al., 'Fear, Myth and Furore', pp. 167, 170.
25 Coppe, *A second…roule*, pp. 91, 97, 104.
26 Coppe, *Fiery flying roll*, p. 89; Coppe, *Some sweet sips*, 67. See also James Hunt, *The spirituall verses*, E.476[38] ([19 December] 1648), p. 4; and Coppe's

kindly reference to the 'poore pure' London prostitute Mrs Seney in Smith, *CRW*, p. 108.
27 Hunt, *Spirituall verses*, p. 7; Coppe, *Some sweet sips*, p. 43.
28 Coppe, *Fiery flying roll*, p. 78; *Justification of the mad crew*, p. 143. See also Joseph Salmon, *A rout, a rout*, E.542[5] ([10 February] 1649), in Smith, *CRW*, p. 163.
29 Coppe, *Some sweet sips*, p. 56; Salmon, *Divinity anatomized*, pp. 190–1. See also Smith, *CRW*, p. ix.
30 Salmon, *Divinity anatomized*, p. 179; Coppe, *Fiery flying roll*, p. 58; *Justification of the mad crew*, p. 150.
31 Bernard Capp, *The Fifth Monarchy Men: A Study in Seventeenth-Century English Millenarianism* (London, 2008), pp. 42–3; Hessayon, 'Coppe and the Ranters', pp. 352–5.
32 [*Mercurius*] *politicus*, E.613[17] (26 September–3 October 1650), pp. 286–7.
33 Samuel Rutherford, *A survey of the spirituall antichrist*, Wing R2394 (1648); Samuel Rutherford, *A free disputation*, E.567[2] ([6 August] 1649).
34 Smith, *CRW*, p. 12.
35 DWL, DWL/RB/2/1.260; WACML, MS.1951.011, second sequence (unpaginated; sermon on Romans 7:7). See also BL, Add. MS 4929, fols 151r–v, for a preacher's plea that 'the doctrine of free grace . . . gives noe dispensation to sin nor exemption from Morall Dutys'.
36 *The Ranters Bible*, E.619[6] ([9 December] 1650), p. 2; *The arraignment and tryall*, E.620[3] ([17 December] 1650), p. 3. See also *The Ranters monster*, E.658[6] ([30 March] 1652).
37 *The Ranters declaration*, E.620[2] ([17 December] 1650), p. 2.
38 [John Reading?], *The Ranters ranting*, E.618[8] ([2 December] 1650), pp. 3, 5; *Strange newes from Newgate*, E.622[3] ([21 January] 1651), p. 4. See also *Hell broke loose*, Wing H1379 (1651).
39 J. F. McGregor, 'Webbe, Thomas', *ODNB*.
40 Edward Stokes, *The Wiltshire rant*, E.669[5] ([2 July] 1652), pp. 4, 6, 9, 69, 82.
41 *Heart-bleedings for professors abominations*, E.594[13] ([28 February] 1650), p. 7. See also Capp, *Fifth Monarchy Men*, pp. 182–3.
42 NRO, MS FC 19/1, unfoliated entries for May 1650. I owe this reference to Joel Halcomb.
43 *The true Levellers standard advanced*, E.552[5] ([26 April] 1649), p. 14.
44 J. C. Davis and J. D. Alsop, 'Winstanley, Gerrard', *ODNB*.
45 McGregor, et. al., 'Fear, Myth and Furore', p. 193; Hughes, *Gender*, pp. 107–8.
46 Gerrard Winstanley, *A vindication of those...called Diggers*, E.1365[1] ([20 March] 1650), sigs Gv–2r. Winstanley was the first to coin 'Ranter' as a pejorative: Hessayon, 'Coppe and the Ranters', p. 352.
47 Worcester College, Oxford, MS Clarke XVIII, fol. 28r. See also a 1652 New England petition that numbered 'ffamilists, Adamites, [and] Raunters' among recent English 'heresie[s]': HRC, HRC 157.
48 Caroline Boswell, *Disaffection and Everyday Life in Interregnum England* (Woodbridge, 2017).

49 TNA, SP 25/62, p. 294; A&O, ii, pp. 245–56. See also Jason McElligott, *Royalism, Print and Censorship in Revolutionary England* (Woodbridge, 2007), p. 151.
50 Sean Kelsey, *Inventing a Republic: The Political Culture of the English Commonwealth, 1649–1653* (Stanford, CA, 1997).
51 Ann Hughes, 'Men, the "Public" and the "Private" in the English Revolution', in Peter Lake and Steven Pincus (eds), *The Politics of the Public Sphere in Early Modern England* (Manchester, 2007), pp. 191–212; Sharpe, *IW*, pp. 449–50.
52 John Blackleach, *Endevors aiming at the glory of God*, E.590[5] ([28 January] 1650), pp. 8, 43.
53 Ibid., pp. 8, 96.
54 Ibid., pp. 127, 153.
55 Ibid., pp. 87, 130.
56 Kevin Sharpe, '"An Image Doting Rabble": The Failure of Republican Culture in Seventeenth-Century England', in Kevin Sharpe and Steven N. Zwicker (eds), *Refiguring Revolutions: Aesthetics and Politics from the English Revolution to the Romantic Revolution* (Berkeley, CA, 1998), pp. 25–56.
57 Gianoutsos, *Manhood*.
58 Capp, *Culture Wars*, ch. 4.
59 Ann Hughes, 'A "Lunatick Revolter from Loyalty": The Death of Rowland Wilson and the English Revolution', *History Workshop Journal* 61 (2006), 192–204, at 198.
60 Jason McElligott, 'John Crouch: A Royalist Journalist in Cromwellian England', *Media History* 10:3 (2004), 139–55; David Underdown, *A Freeborn People: Politics and the Nation in Seventeenth-Century England* (Oxford, 1996), ch. 5; Sarah Toulalan, *Imagining Sex: Pornography and Bodies in Seventeenth-Century England* (Oxford, 2007), p. 41.
61 *MITM*, E.594[21] (27 February–6 March 1650), p. 354; ibid., E.589[15] (9–16 January 1650), p. 304.
62 *Melancholicus*, E.536[27] (25 December 1649–1 January 1650), p. 2.
63 [Henry Neville], *Newes from the New Exchange*, E.590[10] ([30 January] 1650), pp. 2–3, 10, 19. Holles was a committed Presbyterian, while Holland was a turncoat royalist recently executed for treason. Lady Carlisle, a onetime intimate of Henrietta Maria and a former paramour of the duke of Buckingham, had long suffered from similarly sexual gossip: Roy E. Schreiber, 'Hay [*née* Percy], Lucy, countess of Carlisle', *ODNB*.
64 BL, RB G.16567, derived from [Henry Neville], *The ladies Parliament*, E.1143[1] ([15 July] 1647), sigs Gr–4v.
65 Martin Ingram, 'Reformation of Manners in Early Modern England', in Paul Griffiths, Adam Fox, and Steve Hindle (eds), *The Experience of Authority in Early Modern England* (Basingstoke, 1996), pp. 47–88. On English republicanism and moral reformation, see Jonathan Scott, *Commonwealth Principles: Republican Writing of the English Revolution* (Cambridge, 2004).
66 Blackleach, *Endevors*, pp. 64, 87.
67 Capp, *Culture Wars*, pp. 196–8.

68 *A declaration of the parliament*, E.575[9] (27 September 1649), pp. 11, 21.
69 'Licentiousness', *OED Online*, www.oed.com/view/Entry/107961 (accessed 12 May 2023).
70 *MITM*, E.589[8] (2–9 January 1650), p. 294.
71 Ibid., E.600[11] (1–9 May 1650), p. 404.
72 *A&O*, ii, pp. 387–9.
73 Keith Thomas, 'The Puritans and Adultery: The Act of 1650 Reconsidered', in Donald Pennington and Keith Thomas (eds), *Puritans and Revolutionaries: Essays in Seventeenth-Century History Presented to Christopher Hill* (Oxford, 1978), pp. 257–82.
74 Ibid., p. 258; Bernard Capp, 'Republican Reformation: Family, Community and the State in the Interregnum Middlesex, 1649–60', in Helen Berry and Elizabeth Foyster (eds), *The Family in Early Modern England* (Cambridge, 2007), pp. 40–66, at 49–55; Stephen Roberts, 'Fornication and Bastardy in Mid-Seventeenth Century Devon: How was the Act of 1650 Enforced?', in John Rule (ed.), *Outside the Law: Studies in Crime and Order, 1650–1850* (Exeter, 1982), pp. 1–20.
75 *A dialogue*, E.607[13] ([11 July] 1650), p. 5; HRC, Thomas Killigrew Miscellany, fol. 97r; *Paul's church-yard*, E.637[15] ([24 July] 1651), sig. A2r. See also *Pragmaticus (for King Charles II)*, E.600[6] (30 April–7 May 1650), sig. Fff3v.
76 Houghton Library, Harvard University, MS Eng 625. For Crouch's coverage, see for example *MITM*, E.602[2] (8–23 May 1650), p. 414; ibid., E.602[24] (29 May–5 June 1650), p. 427.
77 Thomas, 'The Puritans and Adultery', p. 278.
78 Nottinghamshire Record Office, DD/HU/1, pp. 239–41.
79 *A&O*, ii, pp. 409–12; Abiezer Coppe, *A remonstrance of...Abiezer Coppe*, E.621[5] ([3 January] 1651), p. 1. See also McGregor, et. al., 'Fear, Myth and Furore', p. 157; cf. Davis, 'Reply', p. 198.
80 Capp, *Culture Wars*, p. 72.
81 Barbara Donagan, 'Did Ministers Matter? War and Religion in England, 1642–49', *JBS* 33:2 (1994), 119–56; Ann Hughes, 'Preachers and Hearers in Revolutionary London: Contextualising Parliamentary Fast Sermons', *TRHS* 6:24 (2014), 57–77.
82 John Shawe, *Britannia rediviva*, E.584[1] ([28 November] 1649), pp. 3, 5, 8, 22.
83 Thomas Edgar, *Two charges*, E.578[6] ([7 November] 1649), p. 8.
84 *One blow more at Babylon*, E.623[16] ([15 February] 1650), sig. A2r, pp. 8, 34; Jonathan Clapham, *The stone smiting the image*, E.633[8] ([4 July] 1651), pp. 24, 26–7.
85 George Masterson, *Anthrōpasthenez, a good ground to cease*, Wing M1072 (1651), sig. A2v, p. 8; Hugh Peter, *Good work for a good magistrate*, E.1364[2] ([17 June] 1651), p. 12.
86 William Durham, *Maran-atha, the second advent*, E.665[23] ([2 June] 1652), sig. A3r, p. 34.

87 See, for instance, *An examination*, E.608[13] ([25 July] 1650), pp. 22, 31.
88 TNA, SP 18/9, fol. 220r. See also David Stevenson, *Revolution and Counter-Revolution in Scotland, 1644–1651* (London, 1977), pp. 174–5.
89 George Wither, *The British appeals*, Wing W3143 (1651), pp. 26, 30; [Sydenham Cuthbert], *The false brother*, E.620[13] ([27 December] 1650), p. 62.
90 Blackleach, *Endevors*, p. 37.
91 [Henry Parker], *The true portraiture*, E.609[2] ([7 August] 1650), p. 42.
92 Ronald Hutton, *Charles the Second: King of England, Scotland, and Ireland* (Oxford, 1989), pp. 25–6, 77–8.
93 *The true manner of the crowning of Charles the Second*, 669.f.15[81] ([27 February] 1651); William Lilly, *Monarchy or no monarchy in England*, E.638[17] ([6 August] 1651), p. 9.
94 Edward Peyton, *The divine catastrophe*, E.1291[1] ([24 April] 1652), pp. 128–31.
95 *Britanicus*, E.4[13] (29 July–5 August 1644), p. 361; *Mercurius pragmaticus (for King Charles II)*, E.560[20] (12–19 June 1649), p. 69. See also Blair Worden, '"Wit in a Roundhead": The Dilemma of Marchamont Nedham', in Amussen and Kishlansky (eds), *Political Culture and Cultural Politics*, pp. 301–37, at 306–9.
96 TNA, SP 46/95, fol. 281r.
97 *Politicus*, E.615[6] (17–24 October 1650), p. 327; ibid., E.616[1] (7–14 November 1650), p. 375. For one slightly later reader of Nedham's newsbook, see WACML, MS 1970.004, heading 'F'.
98 *Politicus*, E.609[13] (8–15 August 1650), p. [160]; ibid., E.607[12] (4–11 July 1650), p. 65.
99 Ibid., E.604[8] (20–7 June 1650), p. 33.
100 Ibid., E.607[4] (27 June–4 July 1650), p. 60; ibid., E.603[13] (13–20 June 1650), p. 28; ibid., E.608[18] (25 July–1 August 1650), p. 126.
101 Ibid., E.603[6] (6–13 June 1650), pp. 8–9, 14.
102 E.g., ibid., E.610[7] (22–9 August 1650), p. 178.
103 Benjamin Woodford, 'From Tyrant to Unfit Monarch: Marchamont Nedham's Representation of Charles Stuart and Royalists during the Interregnum', *History* 100:339 (2015), 1–20, at 9–11.
104 Smith, *CRW*, p. 8.
105 Samuel Tilbury, *Bloudy newse from the north*, E.622[1] ([20 January] 1651), p. 1; *Politicus*, E.622[8] (16–23 January 1651), p. 546. Cf. Samuel Sheppard, *The joviall crew*, E.621[7] ([6 January] 1651).
106 *A&O*, ii, pp. 568–9.
107 J. T. Peacey, 'Clements, Gregory', *ODNB*; *CJ*, vii, p. 131.
108 Ian J. Gentles, 'Harrison, Thomas', *ODNB*.
109 McElligott, 'Royalist Journalist', p. 144.
110 Blackleach, *Endevors*, p. 18. See also Lloyd Bowen, 'Seditious Speech and Popular Royalism, 1649–60', in Jason McElligott and David L. Smith (eds), *Royalists and Royalism During the Interregnum* (Manchester, 2010), pp. 44–66, at 51.

111 SHC, Q/SR/82, no. 189; LMA, CLA/047/LJ/01/110/34; LMA, MJ/SR/1066/41.
112 SHC, Q/SR/83, no. 123; SHC, Q/SR/82, no. 133. See also LRO, QSR 46 (Robert Dawson, 6 April 1652).
113 *CSPD 1651*, p. 438.
114 James Loxley, *Royalism and Poetry in the English Civil Wars: The Drawn Sword* (Basingstoke, 1997), p. 202.
115 Marchamont Nedham, *Certain considerations*, Wing N381 (1649), pp. 9–10.
116 [John Taylor], *Epigrammes*, Wing T457 (1651), pp. 22, 24.
117 McElligott, 'Royalist Journalist', pp. 144–5.
118 Lois Potter, *Secret Rites and Secret Writing: Royalist Literature, 1641–1660* (Cambridge, 1989), p. 22.
119 [John Crouch], *Mercurius democritus, his last will and testament*, E.675[7] ([16 September] 1652), p. 3; *The laughing mercury*, E.674[29] (25 August–8 September 1652), p. 169.
120 For an earlier use of this trope, see *Newes, true newes*, E.144[3] (1642), p. 3.
121 [*Mercurius*] *democritus*, E.659[13] (8 April 1652), pp. 1, 6.
122 Underdown, *A Freeborn People*, pp. 97–8.
123 *Democritus*, E.667[4] (1–9 June 1652), p. 73; ibid., E.669[17] (30 June–8 July 1652), p. 112.
124 *Democritus*, E.668[12] (16–23 June 1652), p. 93; *Laughing mercury*, E.678[24] (20–7 October 1652), p. 232; ibid., E.678[6] (6–12 October 1652), p. 213.
125 Mary E. Fissell, *Vernacular Bodies: The Politics of Reproduction in Early Modern England* (Oxford, 2004), ch. 5.
126 *Democritus*, E.686[9] (2–9 February 1653), pp. 337–8.
127 E.g., ibid., E.661[4] (20–8 April 1652), p. 32; ibid., E.689[6] (23 February–2 March 1653), p. 362.
128 Ibid., E.705[13] (6–13 July 1653), p. 500; *Laughing mercury*, E.675[17] (15–22 September 1652), p. 190; *Democritus*, E.662[8] (27 April–5 May 1652), p. 39.
129 Ibid., E.687[6] (9–16 February 1653), pp. 350–1.
130 Sharon Achinstein, 'Women on Top in the Pamphlet Literature of the English Revolution', *Women's Studies* 24:1–2 (1994), 131–63.
131 *Laughing mercury*, E.678[18] (12–20 October 1652), pp. 220–1. See also ibid., E.675[25] (22–9 September 1652), pp. 199–200.
132 *Democritus*, E.665[2] (11–19 May 1653), p. 52; ibid., E.665[12] (18–26 May 1652), p. 63.
133 Ibid., E.675[9] (8–16 September 1652), p. 182; *Democritus*, E.659[25] (7–14 April 1652), p. 13. See also ibid., E.688[6] (16–23 February 1653), p. 359; ibid., E.693[8] (20–7 April 1653), p. 420.
134 Ibid., E.694[2] (27 April–4 May 1653), p. 432; ibid., E.698[15] (25 May–1 June 1653), pp. 449–50; *Laughing mercury*, E.678[1] (29 September–6 October 1652), p. 202.
135 See for instance Samuel Sheppard, *The weepers*, E.674[34] ([13 September] 1652), p. 10.
136 *The cavaliers jubilee*, E.655[25] ([8 March] 1652), p. 2; BRBML, Osborn MS b15, p. 46.

137 See also Angela McShane, 'The Extraordinary Case of the Blood-Drinking and Flesh-Eating Cavaliers', in Angela McShane and Garthine Walker (eds), *The Extraordinary and the Everyday in Early Modern England: Essays in Celebration of the Work of Bernard Capp* (Basingstoke, 2004), pp. 192–210.
138 *Laughing mercury*, E.679[5] (27 October–3 November 1652), p. 239.
139 Blair Worden, *The Rump Parliament, 1648–1653* (Cambridge, 1974), pp. 12, 73, 170, 261.
140 Ibid., p. 1.
141 E.g., M.R., *Twelve humble proposals*, Wing R51 (1653).
142 *A&O*, ii, pp. 715–18; Hughes, *Gender*, p. 136.
143 LRO, QSP/115/5; NRO, C/S 3/41A (Edward Reynolds, 26 December 1654); SHC, Q/SR/91, no. 45. See also Christopher Durston, *The Family in the English Revolution* (Oxford, 1999), pp. 69–71.
144 Sharpe, *IW*, p. 467. See also David Norbrook, *Writing the English Republic: Poetry, Rhetoric and Politics, 1627–1660* (Cambridge, 1999), p. 310.
145 *The moderate publisher*, E.213[32] (3–10 June 1653), p. 1088.
146 McElligott, 'Royalist Journalist', p. 147.

# 6

# Discipline and debauchery, 1654–59

In December 1653, the soldier and Baptist Edmund Chillenden published a tell-all exposé detailing how, years prior, the 'baits and allurements' of fleshly lust had caused him to forsake his marital bed for his maidservant's. Worse yet, he had failed to disclose his offense while continuing to lead his London congregation as if nothing were amiss. 'You are known to be a great professor of religion', he had cautioned himself, 'and if you make it known, you are utterly lost in the hearts of all that are godly'. For the same reason, Chillenden had also worried that his shameful story would give 'the enemies without' – scoffing royalists – 'occasion to blaspheme'. The whole episode, he knew, rendered him 'not worthy . . . to be reckoned amongst the godly'. Chillenden therefore offered up his book as a belated confession.[1]

The ashamed minister may not have had much choice in the matter. In a personal letter to Cromwell appended to the pamphlet's final pages, he thanked England's new Lord Protector for 'appoint[ing]' some 'Officers . . . to examine my business'.[2] Chillenden did not elaborate further, but his language suggested some measure of outward coercion. If, like Gregory Clement's affair, his adultery had caught the attention of regime reformers, he may have been pressured into confessing his sins before an enterprising critic could do so for him. Ultimately, his candour did not save him: Chillenden lost both his army commission and (temporarily) his church after the tract's appearance.[3] Even so, by taking the matter into his own hands, he helped to blunt a potential public relations debacle for the Cromwellian state.

The Wiltshire minister Thomas Chaffin would have been unsurprised at Chillenden's revelation. Sometime during the early 1650s, Chaffin scribbled a satirical catechism parodying the 'proud, factious, Covetuous, sensorious, malisious, Revengefull, desembling, lying lecherouse' puritan clergy currently ascendant in England's parishes. Although the piece did not ignore the 'nonsence . . . and Blasphemy' of godly 'Doctrin', it was the moral improprieties that accompanied their 'Convintackell howrs' which Chaffin found most compelling. For one thing, he delighted in the holy 'sisterhood', with whom the saints were commanded to 'shrift and prick all thou canst'.

Indeed, because 'the sisterhood are meeke & gentell and reddy to rayse up seed to the Church', he awarded them with a striking biblical moniker: 'the order of Mary Magdelin'. Described as 'very demure in the streets, but ranters within dores', these whorish godly women represented, for Chaffin, the heights of puritan moral hypocrisy.[4] He surely would have numbered Chillenden's unfortunate maidservant among them.

As this chapter argues, Chillenden's self-flagellating account and Chaffin's scabrous poem captured two divergent trends of English sexual politics, and of interregnum political culture more broadly, during the mid-to-late 1650s. In Westminster, Cromwell's installation as Lord Protector inaugurated renewed regime attention to moral reform. Now shorn of foot-dragging moderates, the Protectorate presented itself as a godly instrument bent on rooting out popery, irreligion and profaneness – including radical Protestant sectarianism, for Cromwell and his allies could not risk the public embarrassment of another Ranter controversy – both at home and abroad. Consequently, offenders from mundane English rabble-rousers to Charles II himself fell victim to Cromwellian moralising polemics throughout the period, as did the radical Quaker movement of the later 1650s. Even more so than its republican predecessor, the Protectorate placed a premium on sexual discipline.

Its cavalier critics, on the other hand, veered towards debauchery. With the Stuart court still in exile abroad, royalist poets and dramatists consolidated a distinctive cavalier aesthetic informed both by the traditions of fellowship and frivolity embraced by earlier Caroline court poets as well as the familiar tenets of English anti-puritanism. In a variety of printed texts published between 1654 and 1656, these writers constructed a profane vision of English communal culture that celebrated dancing, drink and promiscuity as inescapable human foibles rather than soul-damning sins. Unlike the acrid anti-puritan libels that continued to proliferate in private royalist manuscript collections, their printed drolleries and satirical newsbooks rarely called for active resistance to the regime. Instead, they subverted Cromwellian moralism by embracing bawdy obscenity while revelling in their puritan enemies' accusations of blasphemy and hedonism as badges of honour. This was, in its own way, a form of radical royalism – one that conspicuously subverted the patriarchal principles of sober, marital chastity upon which Charles I's own personal brand had been based – and it was predicated almost entirely on sexual politics.

The struggle between Cromwellian discipline and royalist jollity (or, as some republican partisans would frame it, virginal English liberty and monarchist whoredom) represented the culmination of two long-percolating trends in mid-century sexual politics first inaugurated in the early-1640s debates between 'roundheads' and 'cavaliers'. It also played a defining role in the political culture of Protectoral England. At first, the regime succeeded in quashing dissent among both royalist exiles abroad and disaffected malcontents at home. But cracks soon appeared in the Cromwellian edifice, spurred on by royalist gadflies and militant republicans appalled at the dictatorial measures instituted by the Lord Protector to advance his moralising agenda. No disruption proved more destabilising than the surging Quaker movement of the mid-1650s, which marshalled a graphic spiritualist lexicon of divine insemination to draw converts in the thousands across the kingdom. Alarmed contemporaries responded by recasting the Quakers as libertine antinomians who exceeded even the Ranters in depravity, initiating a bipartisan campaign of abuse that included, by 1659, graphic descriptions of bestiality. As cavaliers, Cromwellians and Quakers competed in print for England's moral soul, therefore – and a battle it was, no matter how ostensibly quiescent the kingdom's print marketplace might have appeared – sexual politics became the defining motif of interregnum political culture.

### 'To the mad merry people in the land of darkness': royalists confront the Protectorate

The Protectorate pursued two goals from its inception: one, the kingdom's wholesale moral reformation; the other, its settlement under stable godly government. Initially, the new regime outperformed its predecessor on both counts, passing dozens of draft ordinances and rapidly bringing the Dutch war to an end.[5] Granted, these accomplishments did not prevent Cromwell's republican critics from wondering if the new Lord Protector, like Charles I, would once more render 'Israels Common-wealth' into a 'Harlot'.[6] Yet with English royalism apparently dormant and peace settled abroad, many contemporaries hoped that England's troubles were finally ended.

At least one ex-royalist seemed content enough. After taking a hiatus from *Democritus* late in 1653, John Crouch revived the title briefly in January before launching a new serial, *Mercurius fumigosus*, later that summer. Much like its precursor, *Fumigosus* presented itself as apolitical satire, forswearing royalist plotting and abstaining from direct critiques of the Cromwellian leadership.[7] In exchange, the regime again left Crouch unmolested. Between June 1654 and September 1655, he published seventy issues of the new newssheet. And each week, in this latest rag – directed to 'the Mad Merry PEOPLE in the Land of Darkness' – Crouch continued to produce a flood of obscene anti-sectarian drollery that repudiated the Protectorate's moralising agenda by its very nature.

*Fumigosus* rehearsed many of *Democritus*'s favourite themes. The newsbook featured voracious women, from 'shee-Ranters' to London prostitutes known as the 'Sodom Ladies';[8] celebrated the full cycle of human sexuality, from lost 'Maiden-heads' to the 'swelling[s]' of (often monstrous) pregnancy;[9] and recounted alarming tales of bestiality, sodomy and rape.[10] Importantly, however, *Fumigosus* surpassed its predecessor in crassness. Abandoning *Democritus*'s careful redactions, one 1654 issue thus rebranded Norfolk as 'Norfuck'. Another described a 'young Gallant . . . sadoming [sic] the well' of his (female) lover at a 'depth whereof, few men could yet ever finde'.[11] *Fumigosus* also included snippets of 'true news', including some heartfelt denunciations of anti-regime plotting; but the scurrilous far outweighed the serious. As such, Crouch's oeuvre continued to represent the most aggressively anti-puritan – if not directly anti-Cromwellian – publication on the market.

*Fumogisus* also reached new heights of eroticism. Consider a lurid song presented in one August 1654 edition: 'dear Sisters', it pleaded,

> When you meet lusty men of strength,
> That will not bate a jot of length,
> Oh hugg them hard, and suck them in,
> Untill they even do burst your skin,
> Spread forth the crannyes of those Rocks
> That lie beneath your Holland smocks;
> Strech out your limbs, sigh, heave and straine,
> Till you have opened every veine:
> That so Loves gentle juice but flowes
> Like Dewie Nectar, out of those
> That press you down may run a tilt,
> Into your wombs, and not be spilt
> Do this (dear Sisters) and hereby
> You shall increase and multiply.

In these proto-pornographic musings, as elsewhere in *Fumogisus*'s pages, sexual pleasure seemed to have become Crouch's central theme.[12] Nowhere was this trend more evident than in its effusive descriptions of London's prostitutes, who had 'mightily increased their breeds' in recent years. (Eventually, Crouch even promised his readers 'a List ere long of their Names and dwelling'.)[13] Although still freighted with anti-puritan satire, the newsbook's growing resemblance to classic early modern whore-narratives – 'Aretine' productions that Crouch continued to jokingly decry – suggested that royalist anti-puritanism and straightforward eroticism had grown intertwined indeed by the mid-1650s.[14]

And yet the Protectorate ignored *Fumigosus* for the first fifteen months of its existence. So long as Crouch did not libel regime authorities or actively foment unrest, his newssheet apparently remained too inconsequential for censure. This was hardly a sign of laxity; on the contrary, Cromwell's chief press regulator, John Thurloe, ranked among interregnum England's most capable operators. But Thurloe, like Marchamont Nedham, recognised that full-blown censorship was best reserved for actively seditious and/or heretical texts. It was thus through Crouch's careful self-positioning, rather than regime neglect, that *Fumigosus* was left in peace.[15]

On the other hand, Thurloe's efficiency ensured that truly seditious material circulated almost exclusively in manuscript during the mid-to-late 1650s. Stymied from print by Commonwealth regulators, royalist malcontents like Thomas Chaffin instead compiled vicious anti-puritan libels against the Cromwellian leadership in commonplace books and private papers.[16] One contributor to this milieu was Edward Conway, second viscount of Conway and Killultagh, who served Charles during the civil wars before settling into a restless retirement after the regicide. Despite his withdrawal from public affairs, Conway retained strong feelings about the new Commonwealth regimes: 'nothing could be more pleasing to all degrees of men', he wrote to his son in 1653, 'than the dissolution of the Parliament men'.[17] Powerless to resist Cromwellian hegemony, Conway resorted to venting his frustrations in private.

When the viscount was not fuming against puritan tyranny, he was discussing books. A bibliophile with a substantial personal library, Conway had an especial love for classical Ovidian satire and risqué verse, and at least one correspondent applauded his taste in 'burlesque poems'.[18] Generally, these materials were far removed from interregnum politics, but Conway's printed collections were not entirely representative of his tastes. For the viscount, like many contemporaries, reserved his most sensitive material for manuscript; and in Protectoral England, few topics were more delicate than defamatory anti-puritan verse.

Conway collected many such poems in scribal copy prior to his death in 1655. His favourites were invariably bawdy, irreverent and libellous: precisely the kinds of political poetry that had thrived in royalist print prior to the reimposition of press control in September 1649. Rather than allowing that rich anti-puritan canon to evaporate after the regicide, collectors like Conway ensured its survival by preserving it in manuscript. In doing so, they continued to discretely resist Cromwellian rule without risking their livelihoods in active defiance.

Conway kept his illicit verses in large bound volumes. One of those collections, labelled with the anachronistic title of 'Rump Songs' by a later owner and now preserved in the Huntington Library, is particularly revealing of his tastes. Many of its eighty-three poems rehashed familiar anti-puritan themes, from the beloved 'holy Sister[s]' to their bastard offspring, the 'Babes of grace'.[19] Several of its most recognisable satires, such as the libellous 'Pim's Juncto', had appeared in printed broadside form during the early 1640s. When they resurfaced in Conway's manuscript, however, they occasionally contained additional stanzas.[20] In this way, royalist collectors reified and expanded a corpus of anti-puritan satire which, considering the notorious frailty of the broadside format, might not otherwise have survived the revolutionary period intact.

To that point, Conway's miscellany contains some entirely unique productions that may well have begun life as now-lost verses from the early 1640s. One, written in the style of *The virgins complaint* (1643), was a faux-petition to parliament from the 'infants babes & sucklings of the Citty of London' conceived when London's 'women' had 'la[id] themselves open to the members of this honorable Assembly'. This piece played on longstanding royalist suspicions about the sexual voraciousness of London women, and especially their connivance with the parliamentarian coalition, to indict Charles's opponents as harbingers of godly copulation run amok.[21] Several more of the volume's unique rhymes mocked the earl of Essex's 'horned pate', including a sixty-line account of his second wife's illegitimate child born at Oxford during the civil war. These attacks joined other Essex libels dotting the miscellany's pages, all of which played on his cuckold's horns – here, the dead earl became an 'Oxx' and the 'Erle of Ewe' – in a harsh, jesting style reminiscent of many earlier royalist polemics.[22]

Conway's miscellany contained more than just libels, however. Other poems (one set 'to the tune of the Reformation') celebrated the joys of 'sack' and 'smale beere' in language that mirrored John Crouch's recent pivot towards drink, amorous poetry and promiscuity.[23] These verses placed Conway's miscellany squarely within a burgeoning tradition of radical royalist worldliness, similarly embodied in *Fumigosus*'s unrepentant eroticism, even as it preserved earlier anti-puritan polemics from censorship. Indeed, Conway's manuscript collection demonstrates that Crouch's celebration of pleasure and jollity was intruding into even the most personal corners of royalist literary production during the 1650s, as Cromwellian hegemony sparked a counter-cultural, and intrinsically political, backlash of cavalier excess.

All of this material, whether printed or scribal, profited immensely from the regime's overloaded political agenda. By 1654, Cromwell had his eye on the Caribbean, long identified by godly Protestants as a source of enormous wealth as well as a stronghold of popish diabolism. That summer, emboldened by its recent victory against the Dutch, the regime began planning a naval invasion of Spanish Hispaniola.[24] When the fleet finally launched in December 1654, it represented the Commonwealth's most ambitious attempt yet to realise their providential destiny purportedly heralded by the regicide; but that optimism was soon dashed. A premature dissolution of Cromwell's first parliament in January 1655 was compounded by a domestic royalist uprising in March which, while ultimately unsuccessful, reminded regime leaders that an enemy fifth column still lurked within their borders.[25] Finally, in July, word arrived that the naval assault on Hispaniola had failed miserably. Cromwell, like many English puritans, struggled to process the devastating news.[26] Was he being tested by God, or rebuked?

Stricken with penitent piety and renewed fears of royalist unrest, the Protectorate recalibrated its priorities accordingly. One beneficiary was the project for national reformation, which received considerable attention from regime authorities after mid-1655. In August, Cromwell issued a proclamation mandating stricter enforcement of the Adultery Act.[27] Meanwhile, the regime traded its conciliatory attitude towards royalist dissent for straightforward repression, even in cases which involved no active sedition. 'Forbearance from outward action will not avail . . . if yet there be malice and revenge in the heart', Cromwell proclaimed in October 1655. For 'such men', he continued, 'nothing but the Sword will restrain them from blood'.[28]

Godly onlookers watched with approval. The unknown sermon-goer who scribbled that 'men committ contemplative adultery in seeing stage plays' into his notes sometime in 1655 was presumably delighted when Cromwellian soldiers raided London's Red Bull Theatre twice that year.[29] The reinvigorated reformation effort culminated with the creation of a new political office: the Cromwellian 'major-general'. Ten of these figures were appointed across England during the fall of 1655, and they soon set about reinforcing moral discipline and policing royalists with vigor. Ultimately (and unsurprisingly, given their penchant for closing local alehouses), the major-generals proved widely unpopular, and the entire program was shuttered after only fifteen months when Cromwell's second parliament refused to fund it further. In the interim, however, the major-generals exemplified the Protectorate's renewed commitment to moral reformation in the wake of its Caribbean disaster.[30]

The rekindled threat of royalist unrest also inspired a change in regime attitudes towards the press. In August, the Council of State issued a new mandate against the 'writing and publishing' of 'dangerous, seditious, and blasphemous books and papers', followed in September by a complete ban on the printing of public news without express regime approval.[31] Although primarily intended to stifle bad press about the Caribbean venture, these pronouncements immediately transformed England's print marketplace; Crouch's *Fumigosus*, for one, was killed almost immediately. Abroad, royalist exiles took note. The decision to 'strictly prohibi[t] the printing of newes' was a 'sure signe that Cromwell finds his affaires att home . . . [and] abroad, goe not well', wrote Sir Edward Nicholas from Cologne.[32] This was not technically the case: practically speaking, Cromwellian hegemony appeared as secure as ever when Nicholas penned his note. But that sobering truth did not prevent a vigorous wave of royalist verse, drama and drollery from filling the merry void left by *Fumigosus* in the months that followed.

### 'Our wenches and our wine': the cavalier literary renaissance

Roughly around the time of *Fumigosus*'s suppression, the poet Abraham Cowley was released from prison. Cowley had served in Charles's Oxford press corps during the early-to-mid 1640s before absconding to France as the royalist war effort began to falter. He remained abroad for nearly a decade, working as an agent for the Stuart cause and writing lurid love poetry of the kind that had once thrived, albeit in manuscript, at court during the 1630s. Then, shortly after returning to England, he was arrested – wrongly, although not without cause – on suspicions related to the March 1655 uprisings. Cowley spent his time in captivity compiling old verses for a printed collection that appeared the following year.[33]

Cowley's *Poems* was not an exhaustive compilation. As the preface explained, the poet had omitted 'all such pieces as I wrote during the time of the late troubles', including an in-progress verse epic on the civil wars themselves. This decision was purely pragmatic. Having 'submitted to the conditions of the Conqueror', Cowley wrote,

> we ought not ... to revive the remembrance of those times and actions for which we have received a General Amnestie, as a favor from the Victor ... which has made me not onely abstain from printing any things of this kinde, but to burn the very copies, and inflict a severer punishment on them my self, then perhaps the most rigid Officer of State would have thought they deserved.[34]

He would struggle to explain these lines to angry loyalists after the Restoration, but they made perfect sense in 1656. By pre-empting the Cromwellian authorities with his own self-censorship, Cowley protected himself from regime harassment without risking condemnation from the decimated ranks of English loyalists. As for any 'supercilious Readers' who objected to the collection's casual eroticism – of which there was plenty – he offered a simple rebuttal: 'much Excess is to be allowed in Love, and even more in Poetry', he wrote, so long as outright 'Obscenity and Prophaneness' were avoided.[35] By the mid-1650s, abandoning royalism apparently did not entail disavowing bawdy sex-talk.

Cowley's attempt to decouple his racy oeuvre from his royalist past is a reminder that not all one-time cavaliers followed John Crouch in equating lewd poetry with opposition to the Cromwellian state. However, his careful positioning was also likely intended to take advantage of the recent publishing success of a spate of similarly eroticised print publications, most authored by former royalists, that appeared throughout the mid-1650s. Like Crouch's newssheets, these literary productions almost never called for active resistance to the Protectoral regime; indeed, only a few invoked the recent troubles directly. Instead, by drawing on the controversial literary oeuvre of the prewar Caroline court – a tradition defined by the work of poets like John Suckling, William Davenant and Robert Herrick, who had celebrated drink, swearing and casual promiscuity as natural human pleasures rather than the depraved sins of fallen man – they remained firmly embedded in the past. Their authors therefore hoped that Thurloe and his lackeys would leave them unmolested.

This cavalier literary revival reached its peak in 1655 and 1656, just after the failed March 1655 uprisings appeared to signal the death of royalist resistance in Britain. It is possible to detect in some of the resulting publications an intimation of retreat from political life into a quiet retirement, and for some authors, including Cowley, the sentiment was probably genuine. Yet for others like Sir John Mennes, who had first begun writing burlesque verse in the 1630s and was still employed by the exiled Stuarts in 1655, the royalist literary renaissance was no act of political submission.[36] On the contrary, Mennes's bawdy productions of 1655–56 were hand-crafted to subvert the Protectorate's reformation project by shredding the façade of hypocritical Cromwellian moralism to reveal its worldly, profane roots.[37] Eventually, the regime would crack down on Mennes and his colleagues, just as they had on royalist publishers in September 1649. But first, cavalier literati successfully engineered a revival of explicit sex-talk in print that would continue to shape English culture long after the Cromwellian reformation came to an end.

These publications took several generic forms, of which the simplest was the jestbook. Like their early Stuart predecessors, interregnum jestbooks were extremely bawdy, filled with vulgar sexual allusions and misogynistic braggadocio.[38] A paradigmatic example was *Wit revived* (1655), authored by a one-time royalist soldier, Edmund Gayton. Gayton's tract did not advertise his former affiliation, although its mild anti-puritanism certainly suggested royalist sympathies. More telling were its crude jokes, which contrasted jarringly with Cromwellian moral rhetoric: 'Q. Why are many young gallants said to be like ferrets? A. Because they creepe so much into Cony-holes', read one crass pun on female genitalia. To be sure, Gayton's jests were tame in comparison with the obscenities that pervaded Crouch's *Fumigosus*. Even so, they captured interregnum royalism's essential argument: 'Q. What may be said of carnall and worldly men? A. That they make heaven descend to earth'.[39]

Another genre with robust cavalier roots was the romance.[40] Although most of the interregnum's published prose romances reflected the genre's French origins, they left considerable space for royalist drollery. The 'mock poem' *The loves of Hero and Leander* (1653), for instance, adapted a classic Greek myth into a bawdy narrative rife with sex-talk. Its readers encountered both crass metaphors for intercourse ('Guide thou the Rudder with thy hand, / And in my Poop fear not to stand', it urged, until 'the money white . . . issue out') and outright obscenity ('Quoth one, to Sea I shall him hunt, / Speak if I shall, with that the Cunt'). At one point, the narrator even assumes the perspective of Leander's penis: 'Leander rais'd 'gainst tree to piss, / He plucks me streight his Drabler out'.[41] In case the short anti-puritan satires presented in its closing pages did not do the trick, these graphic descriptors rendered *Hero and Leander*'s political commitments readily apparent.

It is difficult to overstate the degree to which *Hero and Leander* exceeded even the most obscene productions of the 1640s. Even Neville's initial *Parliament of ladies* tracts had redacted their most obvious profanities, presumably in deference to potentially uneasy publishers. In contrast, the printers responsible for the cavalier renaissance of 1655–56 – like the Cromwellian authorities themselves, who had seemingly abandoned the one-time godly commitment to suppressing lewd language enshrined in the 1640 root and branch petition – were apparently far less worried about explicit sex-talk than their predecessors. The distinction is a telling one. To be sure, interregnum publishers were likely motivated by the potential selling power of such graphic material (and many of these texts sold well indeed). But they may also have followed royalist authors in making an ideological choice to link loyalism and sex-talk in ways that would have astonished, for instance, the Oxford grandees (and, indeed, Charles I) responsible for throttling *Mercurius aulicus*'s engagement with sexual politics prior to the winter of 1643/44. What texts like *Hero and Leander* represented, in other words, was a new, radical royalism – one that was equally evident in the pioneering eroticism of John Crouch – in which explicit sexual polemic played a defining role. Ultimately, whether motivated by politics or profit, it was a development that interregnum publishers were happy to take advantage of.

Other similarly eroticised 'Mock-Romance[s]' appeared in print during 1655 and 1656.[42] Robert Cox's dramatic narrative *Acteon and Diana* (1656) traded *Hero and Leander*'s obscenity for casual amorousness. In an homage to the Ovidian source material (also the origin-story of much English cuckoldry humour), Cox's pamphlet chronicled maids who prayed for well-endowed lovers as well as sex-crazed wives who cuckolded their husbands with two men at once.[43] Cox was also fond of scatological jokes – another staple of interregnum royalist literature – and his characters reflected as much. 'O must I bumfiddle her under her Chamber window', one figure moaned; 'well, I will go wash my hands, and starch my face, because I may be sure to go cleanly about my businesse'. Crudity was apparently no bar to popularity, for the pamphlet was reprinted at least once, and Cox also briefly staged his production in London until the playhouse was shuttered by soldiers.[44] Both in print and onstage, *Acteon and Diana* provided English readers with a bawdy escape from godly moral tyranny.

By far the period's most important cavalier literary production was the printed miscellany, or 'drollery', a genre first invented in 1640 but not widely popularised until the interregnum. Eleven new miscellanies were published between 1653 and 1658. Each contained a medley of poems, many previously unpublished, on subjects ranging from medicine to drink to death. Invariably, the most common topic was love: generally erotic, often bawdy, and occasionally obscene. These publications circulated widely across England and even overseas to the exiled Stuart courts, which welcomed their unique blend of nostalgia, festivity and wit. It was in these texts, therefore, that the royalist literary renaissance of the mid-1650s found its most popular and enduring – and, again, intrinsically political – voice.[45]

Like *Hero and Leander*, the drolleries were unprecedently scurrilous for the medium, even given the effusive printed sexual polemics of the preceding decade-and-a-half. Echoing Cox's scatological fixation, some verses from *Wit and drollery* (1656) concluded, 'thus kindly and in Courtesie, / these few lines I have written, / and now O love come kisse mine ___ [i.e. 'cunny'] / for I am all beshitten'.[46] Copulation was a running theme. One of *Choyce drollery*'s (1656) poems described an overweight cardinal who, too heavy to undertake 'the strong act of Love' without assistance, constructed a mechanical 'engine' to aid him in 'steer[ing] the Prow of the pensile Galleasse ... Over the Chains, & 'tween the double Fort' of his mistress's 'incastled knees, which guard the Port'. Another collection featured the reports of an anthropomorphised louse embedded in an Italian prostitute's 'leacherous passages': 'the use of the Dildo they had without measure, / behind and before, they have it at pleasure', ran one stanza, 'all Aretines wayes, they practice with labour'. Arguably even more transgressive was a poem in John Cotgrave's *Wits interpreter* (1655) entitled, 'One falling in Love with his [biological] Sister'.[47]

Much of this material was recycled from the scribal canon of early Stuart England. Several Jacobean satires against the sodomitical 'swiving' of Buckingham and his 'lustie kindred', for instance, appeared here in print for the first time. These newly published verses were often only incidentally political, such as Richard Corbett's 'Journey into France' (which contained an unflattering portrait of Henry IV's 'little pretty Wench' of a queen and 'her incestuous House') or the famous 'Parliament Fart' poem.[48] Others, including the Buckingham pieces, even reflected an anti-Stuart sentiment.

But those verses, too, served the royalists' purposes. For, as Adam Smyth has argued, when stripped from their original contexts and redeployed in juxtaposition with the ongoing Cromwellian moral reformation, these ostensibly problematic texts became something else entirely: namely, episodes of scandalous bawdry for royalists to shove in the faces of their godly enemies.[49]

Much like Cowley's *Poems*, the drolleries defended the literary value of graphic sex-talk. 'Nor be so sowre, some wanton words to blame, / they are the language of an Epigramme', one volume explained.[50] Unlike Cowley's collection, however, they rarely disavowed their (latent) royalism. Many miscellanies featured early Stuart (and therefore safely non-topical) anti-puritan satire. Even more popular were poetic celebrations of former English monarchs, and especially wistful reflections on royal returns. In such verses, royalist publishers revealed their political preferences without actively challenging Cromwellian rule.[51]

Two drolleries of 1656 can serve as exemplars of the genre. One, a February production entitled *Sportive wit*, presented the collective output of an anonymous 'club of sparkling wits'. This miscellany had it all, from lewd verses on prostitution and the Jacobean court to anti-puritan attacks on godly tub-preachers. One poem reimagined the Narcissus myth as a nigh-pornographic epic in which the titular character's penis – 'a live thing that had little sense; / But yet . . . could lustily stand' – was mobbed by lusty women who 'shak'd it . . . stroak'd it . . . [and] kiss'd it' in equal measure. Another poem beckoned to a potential lover, rhyming, 'Leave off whining, / Let's be sw___ [i.e. 'swiving'] / Sweet, agree, agree'. (The weak redaction here suggests that not all loyalist authors, or perhaps their publishers, felt equally at home with explicit sex-talk.)[52] Still more verses, all antithetical to Cromwellian moral reformation, featured rampant obscenity and grotesque humour alongside poetic invocations of drink, tobacco and excrement. Considering also its occasional paeans to 'good Queen Mary . . . and . . . King Charles her husband', the miscellany's royalist credentials could hardly be doubted.[53]

Even so, *Sportive wit* did not openly announce its ideological leanings. In fact, its epistle assured readers that 'the publishers had no designes beyond thy pleasure [and] their owne reputation'. One of the volume's poems made the same point in verse:

> For my part let me be
> But quiet and free,
> Ile drink Sack and obey,
> Let the great ones sway,
> That spend their whole time in thinking;
> Ile nere busie my pate
> With secrets of State.[54]

Here, ostensibly, was post-regicidal royalist defeatism at its most pure, disavowing 'secrets of state' (and, later, promising to 'burn all ... Newes books' and 'Diurnall[s]') for a life of drunken fellowship. But even if one fell for the charade, the inherent royalism of those pleasures – some of which, of course, Cromwell's major-generals were currently working to suppress – made it difficult to ensure that the compromise would hold.

*Sportive wit* also offered two interesting clues about royalism's interregnum evolution. One was a word, 'lampoon', that adorned several of its poems. Lampooning, roughly synonymous with casual libelling (or, more accurately, Scottish flyting), would eventually become a popular activity at the Restoration, when Charles II's court wits excoriated one another in verse for sport. Before then, however, the word rarely appeared in contemporary parlance; in fact, it had only recently been coined in English.[55] Notably, *Sportive wit* was responsible for several of those pre-1660 usages by affixing the label to at least one Jacobean poem previously identified as a conventional libel. In this sense, the miscellany anticipated, by some years, a prominent late Stuart subgenre of court satire that also shared many thematic links with the interregnum cavalier tradition.

The second clue appeared in a poem entitled 'The Libertine', written from the perspective of a disillusioned lover who swore off monogamy for the life of an amorous playboy. 'The unconfined Bee, we see his power / to kisse and feele each Flower, / nor are his pleasures limited, / to the ruines of one Maiden-head', the narrator sighed before asking, 'why should he have more privilege than I?'[56] In language premonitory of John Dryden's opening lines in *Absalom and Achitophel* (1681), 'The Libertine' elevated sexual pleasure over marital fidelity in a teasing, tongue-in-cheek mode. By figuring libertinism as secular sexual freedom, the poem signalled a change of pace from earlier royalist polemics that had deployed the term almost exclusively against radical Protestant antinomianism; it also implicitly challenged the patriarchal principles of marital chastity that had undergirded them. To be sure, as scholars of French and Dutch erotic culture can attest, the equation of libertinism and worldliness was hardly new in 1656. But by shifting the dominant (English) royalist reading of the term from its original antipuritan context into one that celebrated, even quietly, male sexual liberty, the miscellany once again anticipated later Restoration trends.[57]

If *Sportive wit* looked towards the future, a different 1656 miscellany situated itself squarely in the past. On 15 April, Thomason purchased Abraham Wright's *Parnassus biceps*, another compilation of early Stuart verses. Wright, a royalist minister, Latinist and poet, did not hide his partisanship: the miscellany's epistle explicitly positioned its 'ravishing expressions and extasies of amorous Composures and Love Songs' against the 'blasphemous familiarity of our new-enlightned and inspired men', whose work in 'our late Parliaments' had brought 'Catastrophe' to the kingdom.[58] Peppered with odes to royalist culture in addition to erotic love-poetry and anti-puritan satire, *Parnassus biceps* encapsulated the cavalier literary renaissance's potent amalgamation of romance, scurrility and nostalgia.[59]

Many of the collection's poems were familiar from other miscellanies, although Wright steered clear of truly graphic content; perhaps, as a clergyman, he retained the same moral reservations about outright obscenity that still prevailed in certain godly circles. Particularly notable were the miscellany's anti-puritan verses. One representative poem described a godly 'Brother and Sister' so aroused by the biblical story of 'David and Uriahs lovely wife' that they decided to 'sit down and so act out the Text' beneath a nearby 'hedge'. Later stanzas explained what happened in puritan conventicles when 'the lights go out': 'no voyce is heard, no tongue does go / Unlesse a tender Sister shreek or so'. Ultimately, sex became a political tool, as the godly 'labour[ed] all . . . to have regenerate babes spring from our loyns' to join their 'faction mighty'.[60] Here, as in so much previous royalist porno-political writing, godly lechery took on a dark purpose: the overthrow of England's church and state by legions of puritan bastards.

Still, some of these reprinted poems read significantly differently in the mid-1650s than they had in prior decades. Consider one of the miscellany's closing verses, entitled simply 'A Song'. Written just before Edgehill, it condemned the 'seditious times' of the early 1640s, when 'puritans [bore] all the sway' and rioting 'Apprentices' had become 'Parliament men'. The poem went on to accuse the godly martyrs Burton, Bastwick and Prynne of ordering 'lewd and loose' women to 'wear Italian locks for their abuse' while secretly keeping 'private keys for their own use'. Finally, it celebrated Charles I and his wife: 'God blesse the King, and Queen also, / And all true Subjects from high and low'. This homage to the halcyon days of the personal rule probably rang truer than ever for nostalgic royalists mourning the kingdom's 'Antipodian state' during the mid-1650s.[61]

But some old allusions held up better than others. For instance, while the poem's anti-puritan tone remained as relevant as ever, the attacks on Burton, Bastwick and Prynne seemed remarkably old hat by 1656. Of the three, only Prynne was still alive when *Parnassus biceps* was published. Moreover, he was hardly an ideal royalist target, having spent years imprisoned by the Commonwealth for his opposition to the regicide. Equally jarring was the paean to the royal couple. Of course, it was probably obvious to readers that Charles I, rather than his son, was the intended addressee. But given the new Stuart king's brewing reputation as an inveterate womaniser, the reference may well have reminded some contemporaries of Charles II's ongoing bachelorhood in a decidedly unflattering sense. In both cases, then, Wright's decision to republish old verses enabled new – and not always positive – readings of once-familiar royalist themes. But, perhaps more importantly, they also provided him with a veneer of political irrelevance that would serve him well if the regime ever decided to crack down on the drolleries.

Wright's strategy paid off. Days after Thomason acquired *Parnassus biceps*, the Protectorate came for the royalist miscellanies – specifically, *Sportive wit*, which one of Thurloe's informants had encountered in a London stationer's shop and immediately deemed too 'scandalous' for public dissemination. London JPs interrogated the offending stationer, who revealed that most of the miscellany's original 1000-copy run had already sold around the capital. When pressed about the poems' authors, he dismissed the question, describing the miscellany's contents as 'only the collection of sundry papers . . . procured of several persons'. But he grudgingly identified the man responsible for its epistle: John Phillips.[62]

The authorities knew Phillips well. He was John Milton's nephew, in fact, and he had even briefly worked for Thurloe earlier in the decade. Tellingly, Phillips had just published an inflammatory attack on English Presbyterianism rife with the same bawdy anti-puritanism that pervaded *Sportive wit*. (One line read, 'But in th' originall it ends in Ock / For that deare sisters calls him have-a-Cock. / And truly I suppose I need not feare / But that there are many have a cocks here'.)[63] Upon learning his identity, Thurloe and his colleagues set to work.

On 25 April, the Council of State censured *Sportive wit* for its 'scandalous, lascivious, scurrilous and profane matter'. It ordered all extant copies seized and destroyed, while Phillips, the stationer and the printer were arrested and fined. Five days later, on Cromwell's personal command, *Sportive wit* was burnt in front of London's Old Exchange. Soon thereafter, the same fate was decreed for *Choyce drollery*, another miscellany published earlier that year, and with which Phillips may also have been involved. It, too, was dismissed as 'a book stuffed with profane and obscene matter, tending to the corruption of manners', and it, too, was ordered to be burnt in a public ceremony.[64]

The ritual destruction of *Sportive wit* and *Choyce drollery* indicated a sea-change in Cromwellian attitudes towards cavalier print. After many months of calculated ignorance, the combination of bawdy obscenity and not-so-latent loyalism had apparently grown too overt for the regime to stomach. It remains unclear why other drolleries did not receive the same harsh treatment; given the moral fervour currently percolating in Westminster and the provinces under the watchful gaze of Cromwell's major-generals, it certainly was not for a lack of godly antagonism. But perhaps the Protectorate's intentions were merely to indicate, via a precision strike, that even the quiet literary resistance of John Mennes and his colleagues would no longer be tolerated by regime leaders.

Whatever their internal logic, these events soon put a temporary end to cavalier drolling in print. Yet the practice did not disappear altogether: instead, royalist ribaldry retreated back into manuscript, where it circulated within the same intimate coterie networks that had sustained Viscount Conway earlier in the decade. Another participant in that milieu was the royalist poet Thomas Jordan, who compiled a large bound collection of original verses during the 1650s brimming with the central themes of interregnum cavalierism. Its anti-puritan credentials were evident: Jordan's poems derided godly malcontents who said 'Amen to every factious prayer', taking particular aim at plotting 'Parliament Men' and 'Roundhead[s]' with a candour that never would have survived in print. Similarly, he attacked puritan 'sisters', or rather 'Strumpets', in terms that rendered the rebellion itself into a feminine conspiracy. 'Com females of each degree', he wrote, 'stretch out your throats / bring in yo[u]r votes / to make good the Anarchy'.[65] Even more so than Crouch's brutal newssheets, therefore, Jordan blamed England's recent troubles entirely on the predations of malignant godly women.

Alongside the satirical material, Jordan's miscellany also echoed the bawdy, bibulous humour of the printed miscellanies (although many of Jordan's own poems predated the 1655–56 cavalier renaissance).[66] Like much melancholic royalist verse, these poems embraced drunkenness and promiscuity as partisan acts of resistance to stuffy puritan hyper-moralism. Throughout, casual sex featured second only to drink. Jordan's narrators pleaded with local 'Mayd[s]' caught up in 'Love-fitt[s]' to 'let all pleasures be free' and 'nere thinke of honor' and described their lovers' 'brests of delight' as 'two bottles of white' and their 'Eyes' as 'two Cupps of Canary'. The threat of Cromwellian censorship was ever-present: as one characteristic stanza trumpeted, 'we will drinke like English men / ffor every pottle bring upp ten', before adding, 'I hope this is no Treason'. Only Charles II's restoration, it was implied, would compel Jordan's protagonists to 'leave our wenches and our wyne'; but his descriptions of that hallowed day – 'When we see this royall spring / wee'l have Ladyes by the belly / and a snatch at t'other thing' – suggested that neither would be wanting once the Stuarts returned. In both its anti-puritan satires and its casual eroticism, Jordan's miscellany exemplified the radical sexual politics of interregnum royalism.[67]

Jordan's poems thus marked one pole of the widening mid-1650s divide between royalist debauchery and godly discipline that Bernard Capp has dubbed the interregnum 'culture wars'.[68] Yet some contemporaries found themselves more in tune with Cromwell's moralising major-generals than with disaffected cavaliers. One godly minister preached in 1656 that 'England is yet in the myre and filth of her sinnes', including 'fornication, adultry, and incest'. Months later, English music professors petitioned the government for the creation of a formal 'Colledge of Musitians' to 'regulate the profession' and 'suppress the singing of obscene scandalous and defamatory Songs and Ballads': a category that presumably included the lurid verses collected in the royalist drolleries.[69] Similarly, the Quaker leader George Fox pleaded in December 1653 that 'no Ballads nor jesting books be suffered to be printed, for they stir up lightness and wantonness'. Some royalists even joined the chorus. The diarist John Evelyn despaired in July 1655 that in 'these looser tymes . . . who can stop the malicious reproches of men; or the pencil of a licentious Aretine!'[70] Small wonder, then, that the Protectorate pressed forward with its reformation project: in some quarters, at least, it clearly resonated.

There was also a political logic at work. Since 1649, John Thurloe had tracked Charles II's exiled court across Europe, noting the young king's apparently single-minded pursuit of pleasure despite the cautions of his exasperated advisors. Dispatches from Thurloe's spies relayed a consistent tone of scandalised incredulity. 'C. Stewart' would rather 'staie here and danse' (his 'daily and nightly practice') than campaign for aid, wrote one agent in August 1654. 'I think I may truly say, that greater abominations were never practised among people, than . . . at Charles Stuart's court', another spy observed two years later: 'fornication, drunkenness, and adultery, are esteemed no sins amongst them'.[71] By proclaiming itself as a paragon of moral virtue, therefore, the Cromwellian regime also repudiated the excesses of its Stuart enemies.

Republican accounts of Charles's debaucherous court may well have been exaggerated, and they are somewhat belied by the energy with which the king attempted to mask his sexual affairs. Even so, his servants worried about the potential propaganda value of such stories. Writing from The Hague in 1655, a royalist captain mulled on 'how apt the Rebells are to instill that poysonous doctrine into our party that his Majesty is only devoted to his pleasure, and how greedily it hath bin reed by many'.[72] Having watched the republican excoriation of Charles I after the regicide, royalists presumably had no doubts that the same strategies would prove even more effective against his heir.

Their fears were realised in June 1656, when the Cromwellian regime learned that Lucy Walter had just arrived in London from Europe. Thurloe and his agents knew that Walter was a special woman: she was Charles II's first mistress, in fact, and she had borne him a son in 1649. Consequently, Thurloe wasted no time in arresting Walter and her companions. During the subsequent interrogations, Walter attempted to protect the king by falsely claiming that their child had died several years prior; she had only returned home, she insisted, to check on a pending inheritance. Unfortunately for Lucy, her maid was more forthcoming. She revealed that the royal bastard was still living and asserted that her mistress's commitment to the cause was stronger than ever. Furthermore, she produced written evidence of a generous pension awarded to Walter by the king himself.[73] This was more than enough for Thurloe, who immediately ordered the prisoner shipped back to Flanders.[74] Meanwhile, he alerted Marchamont Nedham.

Two weeks later, *Mercurius politicus* ran a story on Walter's surreptitious visit. In addition to reprinting the pension document in full, Nedham elucidated her former role at court. 'She passeth under the Character of Charls Stuart's Wife or Mistres, and hath a young Son, whom she openly declareth to bee his', he wrote, adding that the king's paternity was 'generally beleeved' to be true, 'the Boy being very like him'. *Politicus* then offered a damning interpretation of the episode: 'By this those that hanker after him may see . . . what a pious charitable Prince they have for their Master, and how well he disposeth of the Collections and Contributions which they make for him here, towards the maintenance of his Concubines and Royal Issue'. Nedham therefore placed Charles in the role of the lustful playboy whose addiction to his 'Lady of Pleasure' dwarfed the rest of his royal responsibilities.[75] This was exactly what loyalist partisans meant by 'instill[ing] that poysonous doctrine into our party': using Charles's vices to dissuade other royalists, rather than Commonwealth sympathisers, of his unreliability. For any of the latter familiar with the republican jeremiads against Charles I, of course, the new king's parallels with his lascivious Stuart ancestors would have been all too evident.

In fact, up-to-date readers would have recognised several parallels with another recent publication by Nedham himself. That piece was *The excellencie of a free-state*, a collation of Nedham's epistles from *Politicus* consolidated into a lengthy defence of republican government. Buoyed by the example of the classical tyrant Tarquin (again, Nedham's favourite historical analogue for Charles II), under whom Roman luxury had 'dissolved into Debauchery', Nedham laid out a comprehensive history of monarchical corruption that harnessed the sexual themes of earlier Commonwealth polemic to argue that 'Freedom is a Virgin that every one seeks to deflower'. As such, he continued, 'like a Virgin, it must be kept from any other Form, or else (so great is the Lust of mankinde after dominion) there follows a rape upon the first opportunity'.[76] Furthering this association between sexual violence and tyranny, Nedham went on to paint 'the brutish Principles of Monarchy' as the chief perpetrators of the 'Rapes of Usurpation' that had been historically acted upon 'Commonwealths'. All told, Nedham's exposition of the 'Adulterous Wiles and Rapes' that England could expect from 'any projecting Sophisters that may arise hereafter' masterfully summed up the republican case against single-person rule. And once news broke of the Walter affair, it seemed more plausible than ever that the return of monarchy would herald precisely the tyrannical dissoluteness described in Nedham's book.[77]

Certainly the Presbyterian Richard Baxter thought as much. Six months later, writing to a friend, Baxter posed a hypothetical question: 'whether ... that the kinge was an absolute simple monarke, & the Parliament had not part in it, it be not lawfull for a private person to resist defensively in some cases?' He illustrated his point with a striking example. 'E.g.', he wrote, was it lawful 'for the women of the Nation to resist the kings soldiers (yea or his person) if he commanded them to yield themselves to be deflowred, [since] Passive obedience to every one of the K. soldiers ... were but actuall whoredome'? Baxter's follow-up query – 'whether the 7th comandement do any strictlyer command them to save their chastity, then the 6th (or the law of nature) doth to save their lives?' – revealed that his interest lay just as much in the moral quandary of the female victims as it did the hypothetical soldiers' horrific actions.[78] More to the point, his decision to frame tyranny in such overtly conjugal terms, combined with Baxter's reliance on a Nedham-esque dichotomy between sexual purity and whoredom, suggested that the themes that underwrote earlier republican screeds against Charles I's two bodies were still resonating with contemporaries seven years later.

Baxter's letter made it clear that he was thinking about the past rather than the present. A similar sense of retrospection surfaced about this time in James Harrington's *The commonwealth of Oceana*, which reflected briefly on Elizabeth I's success in 'converting her reign through the perpetual love tricks that passed between her and her people into a kind of romance'.[79] Yet the winter of 1656/57 was a conspicuous time for resurrecting anti-monarchical sexual politics of any vintage, for it was at this moment that certain members of the Protectoral establishment began seriously entertaining the idea of offering Cromwell the crown. This was, unsurprisingly, a controversial subject. Royalist polemicists had feared the establishment of a Cromwellian monarchy since the 'King Cromwell' days of 1647, and by the later 1650s they were joined by die-hard republicans who were convinced that Cromwell wished desperately to be king. Indeed, that possibility was one inspiration for Nedham's *Excellencie of a free-state*, which did not explicitly identify Cromwell as a target but nevertheless left little doubt that the Stuarts were not the only imminent danger to England's virgin liberty. Other critics proved equally adept at modifying anti-monarchical sexual politics for anti-Protectoral ends: the radical tract *Killing noe murder* (1657), for instance, raged against the 'pimpes of [Cromwellian] Tyranny, who are only Imployed to draw In the people to prostitut theyre Liberty'.[80] Royalist malcontents, for their part, continued to indict Cromwell in more conventional terms, shouting in alehouses and bars that 'the Lord Protector was either a yonger brother or a Bastard'.[81]

Cromwell declined the crown in May 1657 after much deliberation. Beyond his own providentialist logic – namely, that the regicide had proven

God's antipathy to monarchy in England – there were also prosaic reasons for his choice, including a desire to conciliate anti-monarchist spirits in the New Model.[82] Among them may also have been a tacit recognition that, by assuming the throne, Cromwell would have opened himself up to even more vociferous personal criticisms than he faced as Lord Protector.[83] In Cromwell's dilemma, as in the widening cultural gap between Protectoral moral discipline on the one hand and royalist debauchery on the other – or, to put it in Nedham's terms, virginal republicanism and loyalist whoredom – sexual politics continued to exercise a profound influence on contemporary affairs.

## 'A mare's as good as a madam': sexual politics and the (anti-)Quaker movement

Westminster was not the only site of political drama during the winter of 1656/57. On 24 October, a former New Model soldier named James Nayler processed into Bristol on horseback while fawning associates threw palm fronds at his feet. The spectacle replicated Christ's biblical entrance into Jerusalem on Palm Sunday, and to many observers, it represented blasphemy of the highest order. Nayler was consequently arrested and forced to stand trial before parliament, which prosecuted him under the 1650 Blasphemy Act. Fortunately for the prisoner, the regime's commitment to limited religious toleration spared him from death. Instead, parliament condemned Nayler to be whipped, pilloried, mutilated and branded before being imprisoned indefinitely in London's Bridewell. Years would pass before he once again set foot outside the prison's walls.

As his persecutors knew, Nayler represented a much larger threat currently sweeping southward from northern England. This was the Society of Friends, or 'Quakers': a new Protestant movement led by the Leicestershire itinerant George Fox. By 1656, the Quakers – who drew their name from the enthusiastic quivering that accompanied their worship – had developed into the most visible radical group in interregnum England.[84] As proselytes of a spiritualist theology that shared frightening characteristics with earlier antinomian sects, they were also profoundly disruptive. Accordingly, hostile controversialists took to the presses in droves to attack the Quaker menace during the mid-to-late 1650s. And, in the tradition of much previous anti-sectarian writing, those pamphlets and broadsides inflected the most scurrilous themes of post-Reformation sexual polemic.

Unlike many of their radical predecessors, however, Quaker activists fought back against their persecutors in print. In hundreds of densely argued tracts, the Friends propounded their mystical theology and militated for the kingdom's further reformation while simultaneously rebutting their enemies' scurrilous claims with a familiar apocalyptic lexicon. The resulting give-and-take ranked among the most vibrant polemical exchanges of the entire revolutionary period; it also likely motivated some of the many horrific acts of violence visited upon proselytising Friends by angry onlookers. (It was probably due in part to such rhetoric, for example, that two women were stripped, whipped and slandered as 'whores' by Cambridge magistrates in December 1653.)[85] As such, the 1650s debate over Quakerism neatly encapsulated the ongoing potency of post-Reformation sexual politics as they coalesced in print during the interregnum's final years.

For several reasons, Fox and his allies made easy targets for sexual libel. Theologically, the Friends were radical spiritualists who imagined the personal relationship between God and believer in terms of a divine 'inner light' that true proselytes welcomed into their hearts. By this logic, anyone gifted with God's presence could achieve moral and spiritual perfection; and, unsurprisingly, many contemporaries thus compared it with Ranter libertine antinomianism.[86] That parallel was facilitated further by the eroticised language of some Quaker activists. Fox himself depicted the process of conversion using the generative metaphor of the 'Seed of God', which he described as a 'harvest white . . . lying thick in the ground, as ever did wheat that was sown outwardly'. (Nayler, another frequent user of such language, pled at his trial that it was simply borrowed from the Song of Songs.)[87] Less esteemed Quaker activists also followed suit: in April 1658, for instance, a Lancashire woman accused her local minister of being 'a Murtherer of the seede of god' in much the same spirit.[88] The similarities between this sexual lexicon of divine procreation and Abiezer Coppe's blasphemous descriptions of spiritual copulation did not escape contemporary notice.

Meanwhile, other factors – namely, the prominence of women preachers within the movement and the propensity of some Friends to walk naked in public to signal their disdain for worldly social conventions – also rendered Fox's sect vulnerable to accusations of gender inversion and promiscuity. Most alarmingly of all, these beliefs were not the product of a few idiosyncratic extremists, but the foundation of a thousands-strong movement that had invaded nearly every corner of the kingdom by 1655. Confronted by these radical millenarians who appeared to champion alarmingly Ranteresque beliefs while professing a permissive attitude towards female spirituality, sexual satire became the natural choice for anti-Quaker activists who hoped to exclude Fox and his coreligionists from the limited toleration guaranteed by the Cromwellian church by demonstrating their utter depravity. Apart from the work of Kate Peters, however (and despite much important scholarship on Quakerism and gender), this scurrilous aspect of the interregnum Quaker debate has rarely been examined by modern historians in detail.[89] As a result, scholars have missed the degree to which the Friends' sexual (im)morality was made to signify their spiritualist creed's doctrinal (im)purity – demonstrating, in turn, the continued vitality of post-Reformation sexual politics on the very eve of the Restoration.

Although Nayler's October 1656 procession intensified the Quaker hysteria in Westminster, it was well underway by the time that he marched on Bristol. Anti-Quaker attacks appeared in print as early as 1653, when Fox and his followers first trickled down from the north. Some were the work of royalists like John Crouch, whose rotating cast of female sectarians intermittently featured 'Sister Quakers'. Others were penned by parliamentary Presbyterians who considered 'Ranters, Quakers, Seekers, and Blasphemers' equally culpable for the 'sad and fearfull Blasphemies' currently assailing the kingdom.[90]

Despite the ideological diversity of these early commentators, they shared a fascination with the scurrilous, demonic and sexual connotations of Quaker theology. Their argument was familiar from the toleration debates of the mid-1640s: namely that, under the antinomian promise of their 'inner light', the Friends sanctioned sexual anarchy while seducing gullible nonbelievers to ruin with the guarantee of licensed libertinism.[91] Accordingly, in one 1653 account, Fox's sect was insinuated to follow earlier Protestant radicals in licensing the old familist practice of 'men lying with other mens wives'. This same pamphlet suggested that the Friends justified other 'abominable wicked practises' as 'perfectly sanctity [sic]' so long as they reflected 'the will of the Father'. Ultimately, it charged that the Quakers' divine inspiration came not from God but from Satan, 'the Father of uncleanenesse and impurity'. Like many sectarians before them – including the polygamist 'Anabaptists' of Munster – the Friends were thus branded as literal spawn of the devil.[92]

Some early accounts of Quaker diabolism appeared in the form of personal testimonials from their one-time victims. In July 1653, a Westmoreland man named John Gilpin published one such narrative under the title of *The Quakers shaken*. Gilpin's fourteen-page tract catalogued his experiences while caught in the 'snare' of 'Quaking' in his hometown of Kendal, complete with the physical episodes of 'quaking and trembling' that the Friends identified with the (orgasmic?) experience of spiritual communion. Notably, Gilpin did not attempt to discount Quakerism as exaggerated or bogus. Instead, he claimed to have truly experienced a 'spirituall Marriage and Union' when 'something entered into [his] body' during a prayer meeting – but as he revealed, it was Satan, not God, who next assumed control of his faculties.[93] Gilpin recounted the diabolical frenzy that followed, as he 'pla[yed] topsie turvie from one bed to another' in a secluded room in town. Only by God's grace, he concluded, were his senses restored and the devil cast out. Lest any sceptics doubt the story, he finished off his account with a list of local witnesses who could 'testifie the probabilitie . . . of the truth of it'.[94]

Gilpin's invitation to check his sources was soon taken up. In September, a Kendal Quaker named Christopher Atkinson produced a printed rebuttal denouncing *The Quakers shaken* as a hack job and Gilpin himself as a lying drunkard. Fronted by a short epistle in which another local Friend, Edward Burrough, lashed out at Gilpin and his testators as patrons of the Babylonian 'Whore' and her 'cup of Fornication', Atkinson's tract proceeded on the principle that the best defence was good offense. First, he outed Gilpin as a profane heathen whose favourite practice was to 'feedest [his] lust with . . . strong drink'. Next, Atkinson claimed that Gilpin was actually a stooge for the town's puritan clergy, who had connived with his other witnesses to slander the local Quaker community.[95] Finally, he inverted Gilpin's claims of diabolical possession by insisting instead that the former convert's recent relapse into drunken oblivion was surely Satan's handiwork. All told, Atkinson's rebuttal was almost as libellous as its anti-Quaker target; it was also apparently effective, for no response from Gilpin or his fellows surfaced for the remainder of the year. More importantly, Atkinson's vociferous defence of the cause modelled a polemical strategy that other Friends would soon adopt for themselves.

But the Gilpin story had not yet run its course. Two years later, an expanded version of *The Quakers shaken* appeared in print. This edition included a supplementary collection of more recent Quaker outrages, the most damning of which involved a Cumbrian Quaker named Hugh Brisbowne. According to the pamphlet, Brisbowne had been spotted by two local observers while 'committing the detestable sin of Buggery with a Mare'. To prove this deeply serious charge, Gilpin laid out all the relevant evidence. He identified the location of the crime ('a Common in the Parish of Warton near Silver-dale') and the two witnesses ('Unica Banke, and the Wife of Rich[ard] Clarke') as well as the peculiar demeanour of the beast itself, which 'stood' unnaturally 'quietly without the least motion' while Brisbowne performed the 'vild [sic] act'. With these facts in mind, Gilpin delivered his verdict: 'had he [i.e. Brisbrowne] not been acted by that [Quaker] power', he wrote, 'he had never been carried out to such abominable filthinesse'.[96]

Why bestiality, though? The Quakers' most infamous tenets – spiritualist perfectionism and unnatural gender parity – did not lend themselves to allegations of monstrous miscegenation; far more likely, one would think, were straightforward charges of antinomian promiscuity. But the bestiality charge instead stemmed from a different element of anti-Quaker polemic: namely, the popular allegation that Fox's sectarians practiced witchcraft, as evidenced (at least according to hostile commentators like Gilpin) by their supernatural bodily contortions. The connections between witchcraft and bestiality were far more established: according to much contemporary mythologising, witches routinely copulated with their animal familiars, and some even claimed under torture to have slept with Satan himself in the form of a great black beast. (Similar allegations had flourished during the East Anglian witch-craze of the mid-1640s.)[97] If Quakers truly were witches in disguise, therefore, bestiality was not so far-fetched a crime after all.

Later that year, another Quaker response to Gilpin's revised *The Quakers shaken* appeared in print. This one was authored by a former mayor of Kendal, Gervase Benson. Even more so than Atkinson, Benson's objective was damage control, and he devoted nearly three full pages to contesting Gilpin's account of the Brisbrowne affair. Notably, Benson did not refute the story's basic facts: indeed, he corroborated the identity of the offender and acknowledged Brisbrowne's attendance at a local Quaker meeting prior to the incident. But Benson denied that 'the man . . . who did that beastly act' had ever truly practiced Quakerism and insisted instead that several local Friends had warned Brisbrowne that he was headed for spiritual ruin. Instead, by claiming to Gilpin that Brisbrowne was 'one of your own', the tract reversed his allegation to argue that 'all such beasts and beastly acts' were in fact the purview of the Quakers' profane persecutors.[98]

Benson's pamphlet closed with a challenge. To those 'who hath slandered those that thou calls Quakers . . . with the thing called Buggerie', he wrote, 'I command thee . . . if thou canst not prove it, acknowledge thy selfe to be a slanderer, a back-biter, a tale bearer, and a busie-body'.[99] Here he echoed a now-common refrain. By 1655, Quaker polemicists were accustomed to hostile allegations of immoral conduct, usually informed by the real-life comradery shared between male and female Quakers. Some of those claims were fantastical: Fox, for example, was accused in 1654 of seducing his fellow activist Margaret Fell by tying a magical 'Ribbon' around her wrist. Others were all too believable. Christopher Atkinson, Gilpin's primary antagonist in the Kendal dispute, was excoriated in a different 1654 pamphlet for practicing a 'very immodest familiarity with . . . a woman of his way'. In this instance, as his horrified associates later discovered, the rumour was true, and Atkinson was ejected from the movement as a result.[100]

In many cases, the sexual accusations levelled at English Quakers were drawn straight from the heresiographical playbook first perfected by Thomas Edwards. Among the lurid beliefs ascribed to the Friends were (following the Brisbrowne case) 'all shamelesse and unparalel'd Bestiality'; seducing 'silly women' with 'divers lusts', after the proscription in 2 Timothy 3:6; and, in classic anti-sectarian muckraking fashion, the 'Opinion and Practice' of the polygamous Munster Anabaptists.[101] Indeed, it was widely claimed that Quaker doctrine resembled that of other 'Antinomians', including both 'Familists' and 'Libertines', in establishing that 'the pure seed of God' rendered the 'Saints, perfect, and without sin'.[102]

For many commentators, the closest analogue to Fox's sect was the Ranter movement. Several tracts discussed the antinomian 'parentage' shared by 'that uncomfortable Fraternity of Quakers and Ranters', while in the fifth edition of Ephraim Pagitt's *Heresiography* (1654), 'Quakers' and 'Ranters' were catalogued adjacent to one another for precisely this reason.[103] Having 'given themselves over to lasciviousness', yet another pamphlet argued, 'all ye Quakers, Shakers, and Ranters' had doomed themselves to eternal damnation.[104] Notably, such language was not limited to non-Friends, and the Ranter comparison was utilised by Quakers themselves during several internal disputes of the later 1650s. Again, none knew better than the Friends just how vulnerable they were to allegations of antinomian libertinism.

One publisher took advantage of this equivalence in a particularly straightforward fashion. The frontispiece of *The Quakers dream* (1655) reproduced a woodcut from a 1650 anti-Ranter tract, *The Ranters declaration*, in which prancing sectarians cavorted nude and exchanged kisses before an eager audience. To accommodate the rebrand, the author carefully revised the speech-bubble language that accompanied each image: 'increase and multiply' in *The Ranters declaration* thus became 'free-will' in the new pamphlet, while the original 'Hey for Christmas' (a textbook elision between Ranter frivolity and royalist festive culture) was replaced with a more generically antinomian paean, 'above ordinances'. Although the revised blurbs were no less damning of Quaker excesses than the originals had been of Ranterism, the alterations themselves signalled a surprising attentiveness to theological nuance on the part of the unknown author.[105]

However, hostile writers hoping to parallel Quakerism with Ranterism faced a challenge: the Quakers' visible commitment to moral purity. Fox's Friends presented themselves as paragons of sexual virtue, often contrasting their probity with that of the literal and spiritual adulterers they believed to populate the Cromwellian church. To make this case, the Quakers adopted the apocalyptic language once employed by early-1640s critics of Charles I's popish bishops (and, later, by commentators as diverse as Richard Overton and Abiezer Coppe). In 1656, for instance, Edward Burrough contrasted his coreligionists – described as the 'pure and undefiled' inheritors of the 'Seed Elect' – with beneficed English clergy whose 'cup is full of fornication, and of the wine of Whoredomes and Idolatry'.[106] Some observers apparently found this self-representation convincing, for as early as 1653, onlookers commented favourably on Quaker morality.[107] Moreover, when Friends

Figure 6.1 *The Quakers dream* (1655)

like Atkinson did slip up, they were publicly censured by their coreligionists. Indeed, several Friends were expelled from Quaker meetings during the 1650s for crimes ranging from casual fornication to Ranterism.[108] Like Gerrard Winstanley and the Diggers, therefore, Fox's sect stridently denied the sexual connotations of their spiritualist theology.

The Quakers' moral probity mattered little to some critics who continued to pepper them with sexual satire despite a general lack of hard evidence. Yet for more thoughtful antagonists, the discrepancy needed explaining: if the Friends truly were as depraved as their doctrine suggested, why did they appear to be so virtuous? Several writers found an answer in a familiar anti-sectarian scriptural text, 2 Corinthians 11:14, by asserting that the impossibly moral Quakers represented proof positive that 'the hour is comming and now is, that Satan in a more than ordinary manner doth transform himself into an Angel of Light'. In this quasi-eschatological framework, Quakerism and Ranterism became related but distinct heresies, both offspring of 'the old Whore of Rome', whose 'Doctrines' manifested in different 'terms' but shared the same 'nature'. As such, despite appearing 'temperate, just, and sober in morall things', the Quakers were merely subtler proselytes of libertine antinomianism – and there was no guarantee that, after 'having attained perfection', they might not eventually 'turn Ranters' anyway.[109] Like the seductive figure of Antichrist, the Quakers' ostensible moralism was purely a ruse to draw Christians away from the true faith.

Again, these reproaches inspired a steady stream of Quaker rejoinders. Because Fox and his allies recognised their vulnerability to sexual polemic, they often paid particular attention to allegations of unchastity. The newsmonger who insinuated an improper sexual liaison between Fox and Margaret Fell in 1654 was refuted in an eight-page pamphlet that appeared just months later. 'We demaund of thee', announced a different Quaker rebuttal, 'what they bee, that hold community of women, and other folks wives, and what women they be, and what mens wives they are, mention the names of them, and where they live, and let the Law take hold upon them'.[110] Other Friends followed a similar strategy. Upon hearing the rumours of Atkinson's incontinence early in 1654, for example, both Edward Burrough and Atkinson himself responded by requesting more evidence: 'if ye know more, why doe you not speake the truth, but slander in secret?' asked Burrough. 'I challenge thee', Atkinson followed, 'to prove what you have spoken against me and not onely so, but against all the Church of God, who doth suffer by you'.[111]

This was a novel tactic, and although it backfired in Atkinson's case, Quaker authors continued to meet sexual slander with similar requests for proof. In doing so, they illustrated just how dramatically the mid-century upheavals had transformed English sex-talk into a truly public phenomenon. For Quaker polemicists – many of whom had come of age after 1640 – sex, like nearly everything else, was apparently fair game for open debate.[112] The stifling self-censorship of the early Stuart period exercised no hold over these young activists, whose candour ensured that Quaker sexuality received more than its fair share of coverage in print.

There was good reason for this counter-offensive. As Fox himself well knew, few things would be more damning for the cause than sexual scandal, as evidenced by Atkinson's disgraceful carriage with his maidservant: a story that received an update in 1656 when it was alleged that, after repenting for his 'filthinesse and leudnesse', Atkinson had then 'f[allen] in love with a [different] young girle' while whoremongering in Norwich.[113] But even this lurid sequel paled in comparison with James Nayler's spectacle at Bristol that October. Indeed, to Fox's despair, Nayler's blasphemous procession – during which he was feted by a mixed-gender group of disciples led by the notorious female Friend Martha Simmonds – quickly assumed pride of place in English anti-Quaker polemic.

Simmonds's presence ensured that the Nayler case remained anchored in sexual politics.[114] 'I suppose tis noe newes to you that of one Naylor a Quaker in England that pretended to be the Messiah, & carry'd about with him 12 Apostles, & two sinfull Magdalens', a traveling Englishman – unwittingly imitating the anti-puritan language of the Wiltshire minister Thomas Chaffin – penned to a correspondent in January 1657. By that time, similar themes had surfaced in print. Simmonds was tarred as an 'unclean spirit' both in the press and in despairing Quaker correspondence, although commentators disagreed on whether she had seduced Nayler to ruin or vice versa. Nor did hostile writers neglect the other female participants, who were said to have 'pant[ed]' after their leader in lust.[115] For critics of these real-life Quaker 'holy sisters', only unrestrained desire could explain their abhorrent behaviour.

As the chief seducer responsible for his female disciples' corruption, Nayler also became the target of scurrilous stories. One, which came up at his trial and then was repeated in at least four pamphlets, involved a married woman named Mistress Roper allegedly seduced by Nayler on a visit to London while his own wife remained in Yorkshire. Their union had purportedly yielded a bastard child, attributed to Nayler because Roper's 'husband had been absent seven and fourty weeks' prior to the birth. When presented with the story before parliament, Nayler vigorously denied any 'lewdness' (although he acknowledged that they may have 'kissed' in fellowship, since 'it was our manner'); even so, it spread quickly.[116] Other writers charged Nayler with attempting the chastity of another Quaker maid, Rebecca Purnell, who 'refused him' only to then allow 'another Quaker' to 'doe it' at a later time.[117] Viewed through these tales, the Quakers' visionary leader was nothing more than a bumbling sexual predator.

Nayler's downfall thus became a focal point for anti-Quaker sexual politics. In February 1657, John Deacon published a full-scale libellous biography of Nayler, the 'grand Seducer', that included several allegations of 'inconstancy and adulteries'. Again, readers were treated to the full Mistress

Roper story, from the 'dandling, imbracing and kissing' that began in her husband's absence to the resulting bastard child. Deacon also included an additional detail, present in some of the earlier accounts, that Nayler had been confronted by his fellow Quakers about his infidelity in a private meeting and had responded only with 'silence, which gives consent'. Nor did the author spare 'Martha Symons and the other two Sisters in iniquity' from censure, evidence as they were of the Friends' comprehensive patriarchal failings.[118]

The Bristol incident was not Deacon's only subject. Packaged alongside the scandalous details of Nayler's life were more stories of Quaker sexual impropriety. Ranter-esque libertinism featured heavily in these accounts, as in the case of one Friend who allegedly proclaimed that his wife 'was freely to be a Whore, as he was a Whoremaster', or that of the Yorkshire 'woman of this quaking sect' who 'came naked from her own bed to another womans husband . . . and bid him open his bed, for the Father had sent her unto him'. Another section described more Yorkshire Quakers guilty of conducting an orgy after a prayer-meeting, when 'they all very lovingly (like swine in a stye) went to bed together in the straw stark naked'. Most damningly, in an episode reminiscent of the Hugh Brisbrowne case, the pamphlet described 'another in the North, whose name I think was Birch, who was seen in the act committing Buggery with a mare'.[119] Whether the author intended to reference the Brisbrowne incident or meant a different (alleged) case of Quaker bestiality altogether, this story's inclusion alongside the more conventional allegations of antinomian libertinism further anchored the spectre of inhuman copulation within the broader arc of anti-Quaker sexual politics.

Throughout the following year, Fox and his brethren scrambled to salvage the movement's reputation from the shadow cast by Nayler's blasphemy. Nevertheless, criticism continued to mount. New pamphlets recounted the Nayler-Roper story and Atkinson's notorious 'act of Fornication' alongside general complaints about Quaker women like Simmonds, who 'being seduced themselves did contribute their utmost Indeavours to seduce others' (again, a familiar anti-sectarian refrain).[120] Meanwhile, Scottish Presbyterians prayed for a time 'when schismaticks shall be as detestable to all good men, as whores and thievs'. The earl of Lauderdale wrote to Richard Baxter about the vulnerability of such 'pretended new lights' to older 'Doctrines of Devills', such as those that taught men 'to lye promiscuously with one anothers wife'.[121] Lauderdale may have been partly inspired by the recent appearance, between 1656 and 1658, of a spate of tracts advocating for the legalisation of polygamy on the basis of biblical precedent; but given the prominence of wife-swapping in anti-Quaker polemic (of which Baxter, at least, was a vigorous consumer), he was very possibly thinking of Fox's sect, too.[122]

The sectarian threat appeared to grow even more serious as Cromwell's health flagged later in the decade. During 1658 and 1659, rumours of Quaker plots against the state circulated in regime-sponsored print and among royalist exiles alike, supplemented by yet more hostile pamphlets and godly pulpit-lectures.[123] Tracts recounted how female Friends walked about 'exposing [their] nakednesse to the view of all' to prove that when it came to 'moral honesty', Quakers ranked alongside the Ranters as 'the worst Sect in the world'.[124] Meanwhile, ministers preached that the kingdom was soon to be 'transformed into a Munster' at the Quakers' hands – a theme taken up in print by commentators who worried that things would soon 'grow to a Munster business', polygamous liaisons included, if the Friends were allowed to pursue their 'filthy lusts' unchallenged.[125]

Quaker witchcraft also continued to make headlines. In Cambridge, a woman named Mary Philips reportedly underwent a harrowing ordeal at the hands of the local Quaker meeting, where she was 'bewitched . . . into the perfect shape of a Mare'. The story proved popular enough that the Quakers published a response repudiating it as libel.[126] The possibility of bewitchment was chilling enough, but Philips's fate may have especially frightened any contemporaries familiar with the stories of Quaker bestiality: in light of those accounts, she received far more lenient treatment at the Quakers' hands than had several other horses in recent memory. Similar alarm may have greeted a subsequent pamphlet, *A gagg for the Quakers*, that described two female Friends who confessed to 'Actuall copulation' with 'the Divel' in 'sundry shapes'.[127]

In Cambridge, the Quaker panic came to a head in August 1659. Fox and several other Friends had arrived in town to preach against the 'fleshly, filthy, lustfull Beasts' who inhabited this corner of the English 'Sodom' when a local scholar named Thomas Smith grew fed up with the disruption. As Smith explained in his printed account, he challenged the Friends to a public dispute and then proceeded to humiliate them in front of a crowd. (His motivations, Smith explained in an ode to 2 Timothy 3:6, were entirely altruistic, 'considering how apt silly Women were to be led away captive by such deceivers'.) Thoroughly cowed – in Smith's telling, at least – Fox and his allies slunk away in defeat, although per usual a Quaker refutation soon appeared in print.[128]

Smith was not alone in publicising the August debate. That fall, an enterprising polemicist named Richard Blome produced a supplementary pamphlet challenging Smith's opponents with further set of fifty-five queries. Several of these additional interrogatories made predictable recourse to sexual politics. 'Do you think that Fornication in a Quaker is sin?' one read, recalling Ranter libertinism; 'how do you know that Fornication is a sin in one that is a Quaker, but by the Law and the Gospell?' the next question clarified. Elsewhere, Blome inquired whether the Friends practiced wife-sharing and asked that, if true believers were intended to follow the light within, as Fox claimed, a 'lascivious man' was vindicated in submitting to his 'wanton spirit'. Finally, the tract resurrected the story of 'Hugh Brisbroune, who committed buggery with a Mare', to inquire whether he 'did sin or not sin in so doing' – since Brisbrowne, too, was presumably just following his inner light.[129] For Blome, as for so many other hostile writers, the Quakers' radical spiritualism necessarily imputed sexual anarchy.

The degree to which Blome's tract drew from a select but potent corpus of anti-Quaker sexual politics was evidenced in an expanded edition acquired by Thomason later in the year. This iteration of Blome's pamphlet included the Quakers' answers to the original questions – either replicated from a now-lost reply to the original text or entirely invented – and Blome's replies to those answers in turn. In doing so, it directed readers to tracts such as John Gilpin's *The Quakers shaken* and rehearsed the story of Atkinson's sexual escapades in Norwich, now with even more juicy details. Finally, the pamphlet's closing queries wondered whether England was indeed due for 'a Munster business' under the baleful direction of Quaker sectaries.[130] Tellingly, none of these subjects had appeared in Smith's original account of the Cambridge dispute. Presumably, Blome had intentionally chosen them to appeal to a reading public that had grown hungry for printed accounts of sectarian promiscuity.

Blome returned to Brisbrowne's case once more in the expanded tract's final pages, when he asked whether it was 'not a sin in your brother Green at Colchester as in Hu[gh] Bisbroun neer Beethom to commit buggery with a mare'.[131] While Brisbrowne's story was familiar to readers of *The Quakers shaken*, this Colchester reference had a more recent vintage: in this case, a broadside ballad authored in the spring of 1659 by the royalist poet Sir John Denham. Entitled *A relation of a Quaker, that . . . attempted to bugger a mare near Colchester*, Denham's tract transformed the period's intermittent references to Quaker bestiality into a full-blown parody of sectarian promiscuity. Its verses described a liaison between an Essex Quaker named Ralph Green and a horse whom Green apparently 'mounted' while high on the 'spirituall Collation' preached by his fellows 'Fox, and Nailor'. Unlike many censorious godly accounts of Quaker depravity, Denham's tone was joyfully raucous, as he juxtaposed Green's 'impulse of Spirit' with the 'weapon carnal' with which 'he took her by force . . . [and] us'd her like a Sister'. Even so, he did not lose sight of the fundamental theological point. 'For if no respect of persons', the tract rehearsed in a passable spoof of Quaker doctrine, 'Be due 'mongst the sons of Adam / In a large extent / Then may it be meant / That a Mare's as good as a Madam'.[132]

Denham's poem was reminiscent of a satirical broadside penned a decade prior by his friend Sir John Berkenhead, *The four-legg'd elder* (1647), which lampooned London Presbyterians by describing a monstrous assignation between a Presbyterian maid and a dog.[133] But while Denham was surely aware of that piece, he had access to a more up-to-date version: 'The Four-Legg'd Quaker', a poem written by Berkenhead sometime in mid-to-late 1659 that discussed the Green incident at length. In addition to explaining the crime in similarly vulgar language to Denham's own ('in Horsley Fields neer Colchester / a Quaker would turn Trooper; / he caught a Foal and mounted her / (O base!) below the Crupper'), Berkenhead's verses described how Green had been caught in the act by witnesses – shades of Hugh Brisbrowne – and eventually punished. Again like Denham, Berkenhead broadened Green's bestial crime to encompass his entire sect: "Tis now reveal'd why Quakers meet / In Meadows, Woods, and Pastures', he teased; it was to beget 'Hors-men' and 'Mare-men' with their poor 'four-legg'd Sister[s]'.[134] Although Ralph Green was probably not a real person – more likely, Berkenhead and Denham conceived the story together and wrote their verses in friendly competition – it is difficult to imagine a more damning portrait of Protestant radicalism gone wrong.[135]

Ralph Green's bestial liaison simmered in the English anti-puritan imagination long after 1659. Several manuscript copies of Denham's piece remain extant in commonplace books and personal miscellanies.[136] Both poems later reappeared in print, while new publications incorporated one-line references to 'the Courtship past between / She-filly and the Quaker' in winking allusions to the original tracts.[137] As the popularity of such jokes attested, even amid the collapse of Cromwellian hegemony, the post-Reformation association between lust and lechery had clearly survived the civil wars intact.[138] It would continue to shape English political and religious culture long into the late Stuart period.

Considered alongside the other developments in English sexual polemic documented in this chapter, the Quakers' travails at the hands of hostile polemicists cemented the mid-to-late 1650s as the high-water mark of mid-century sexual politics. Not only had graphic sex-talk invaded large swathes of English print culture with the help of loyalist activists like John Crouch, but regime polemicists like Marchamont Nedham had rendered Charles II's sex life into a public phenomenon that would haunt the young monarch until his death. Meanwhile, a generation of young Quaker activists took the boldest step of all by meeting the sexual slanders of their critics not with silence or legal injunctions, but requests for more evidence. In their efforts to requisition proof and rebut their accusers in print – a practice first attempted by the sequestered Laudian minister Edward Finch in 1641 – it can be seen just how deeply sex-talk had permeated English public discourse by 1659.

In the process, interregnum polemicists consolidated a decades-long debate about partisan identity, religious radicalism and moral reformation into competing ideological positions framed, by some republican activists, in terms of a battle between virginal republican virtue and royalist debauchery. On this view, Cromwellian moral reformation represented an attempt to make good on the reformist platform of the early 1640s; the royalist drolleries marked the culmination of a transformation, and indeed radicalisation, of earlier loyalist anti-puritan polemic from straightforward satire into an eroticised repudiation of godly hypocrisy (and, equally importantly, the abandonment of traditional marital morality for a celebration of hypermasculine promiscuity); and bipartisan assaults on the Quakers brought the toleration debates of the mid-1640s to their natural conclusion while highlighting the continuing vitality of post-Reformation politicking on the doorstep of the Restoration. In every case, the sexual politics of the interregnum encapsulated both the dynamism and the coherence of mid-century polemical culture. As the book's final sections will demonstrate, they also played a fundamental role in shaping the political life of late Stuart England.

## Notes

1. Edmund Chillenden, *Nathans parable*, E.723[3] ([December] 1653), sigs A3r–v, A4v, p. 9.
2. Ibid., sig. Dr.
3. P. R. S. Baker, 'Chillenden, Edmund', *ODNB*.
4. Wiltshire & Swindon History Centre, MS 865/587. Jesus's companion Mary Magdalene was often portrayed as a former prostitute.
5. Barry Coward, *The Cromwellian Protectorate* (Manchester, 2002), pp. 31–41.
6. *The grand catastrophe*, E.726[12] ([18 January] 1654), p. 2.
7. Jason McElligott, 'Crouch, John', *ODNB*.
8. [*Mercurius*] *fumigosus*, E.809[3] (16–23 August 1654), p. 113; ibid., E.821[15] (27 December 1654–3 January 1655), p. 247.
9. Ibid., E.744[5] (14–21 June 1654), p. 19; ibid., E.809[23] (30 August–6 September 1654), p. 130.
10. E.g., ibid., E.745[4] (21–8 June 1654), p. 32; ibid., E.806[3] (19–26 July 1654), p. 78; ibid., E.745[11] (28 June–5 July 1654), p. 35.
11. Ibid., E.813[17] (11 September–18 October 1654), p. 174; ibid., E.853[4] (5–12 September 1655), p. 534.
12. Ibid., E.808[5] (2–9 August 1654), pp. 94–5. See also ibid., E.808[15] (9–16 August 1654), pp. 104–5.
13. Ibid., E.826[26] (7–14 February 1655), p. 294; ibid., E.831[4] (28 March–4 April 1655), p. 249.
14. Ibid., E.809[11] (23–30 August 1654), p. 120. See also Turner, *Libertines*, pp. xii–xiii.

15 Jason Peacey, 'Cromwellian England: A Propaganda State?', *History* 91:2 (2006), 176–99, at 184–5.
16 Sarah Ward Clavier, '"Round-head Knaves": The Ballad of Wrexham and the Subversive Political Culture of Interregnum North-East Wales', *HR* 91:251 (2018), 39–60.
17 TNA, SP 18/35, fol. 339r. See also BL, Add. MS 70006, fol. 224r.
18 *CSPD 1651*, pp. 498–9.
19 'Rump Songs', pp. 20, 65. A collection of royalist poems in the Bodleian shares an identical binding: Bod., MS Firth C.1.
20 E.g., 'Rump Songs', pp. 17–18, 37–42. 'The Sense of the House' (pp. 30–5), for example, contained an additional stanza not included in the printed edition of 1643: *The sence of the House*, 669.f.6[117] ([10 March] 1643).
21 'Rump Songs', p. 107.
22 Ibid., pp. 88–9, 129, 156.
23 Ibid., pp. 9–10.
24 Carla Gardina Pestana, *The English Conquest of Jamaica: Oliver Cromwell's Bid for Empire* (Cambridge, MA, 2017). See also Jorge Cañizares-Esguerra, *Puritan Conquistadors: Iberianizing the Atlantic, 1550–1700* (Stanford, CA, 2006).
25 David Underdown, *Royalist Conspiracy in England, 1649–1660* (New Haven, CT, 1960), ch. 7.
26 Pestana, *English Conquest*, pp. 93–5.
27 Capp, *Culture Wars*, p. 135.
28 *A declaration of his Highnes*, E.857[3] (31 October 1655), p. 13.
29 Brotherton Library, University of Leeds, BC Ms Lt 57, fol. 31r.
30 Christopher Durston, *Cromwell's Major-Generals: Godly Government During the English Revolution* (Manchester, 2001).
31 *CSPD 1655*, pp. 300, 318–19. See also Peacey, 'Cromwellian England', p. 186.
32 TNA, SP 18/101, fol. 92v.
33 Alexander Lindsay, 'Cowley, Abraham', *ODNB*.
34 Abraham Cowley, *Poems*, Wing C6683 (1656), sigs a4r–v.
35 Ibid., sig. Br. See also Thomas N. Corns, *Uncloistered Virtue: English Political Literature, 1640–1660* (Oxford, 1992), p. 256.
36 Timothy Raylor, *Cavaliers, Clubs, and Literary Culture: Sir John Mennes, James Smith, and the Order of the Fancy* (Newark, DE, 1994).
37 Capp, *Culture Wars*, pp. 77–80.
38 Tim Reinke-Williams, 'Misogyny, Jest-Books and Male Youth Culture in Seventeenth-Century England', *Gender & History* 21:2 (2009), 324–39.
39 [Edmund Gayton], *Wit revived*, E.1703[1] ([27 November] 1655), pp. 12, 34–5.
40 Nigel Smith, *Literature and Revolution in England, 1640–1660* (New Haven, CT, 1994), p. 11.
41 *The loves of Hero and Leander*, Wing L3278 (1653), pp. 3, 6, 19.
42 E.g., *Wit and fancy in a maze*, Wing H2445 (1656), 57: 'Let's laugh, and leave this world behind, / And procreate till we are blind, / That Gods may view, / With a Dildo-doe, / What we bake, and what we brew, / Yet our intrinsick fervour never find'.

43 Robert Cox, *Acteon & Diana*, Wing C6711 (1656), pp. 5–6 (first section), 11–13 (second section).
44 Ibid., p. 3 (first section). See also Capp, *Culture Wars*, pp. 79, 196–8.
45 Adam Smyth, *"Profit and Delight": Printed Miscellanies in England, 1640–1682* (Detroit, MI, 2004), pp. 3, 136–40.
46 J[ohn] M[ennes] and Ja[mes] S[mith], *Wit and drollery*, E.1617[1] ([18 January] 1656), p. 30.
47 *Choyce drollery*, Wing C3916 (1656), pp. 17–19; J[ohn] M[ennes] and Ja[mes] S[mith], *Musarum deliciæ*, E.1672[1] ([28 August] 1655), pp. 30–1; [John Cotgrave], *Wits interpreter*, E.1448[1] ([7 May] 1655), pp. 75–6 (second pagination).
48 *Sportive wit*, Wing P2113 (1656), i, p. 21; Mennes and Smith, *Musarum deliciae*, p. 22. See also Michelle O'Callaghan, 'Performing Politics: The Circulation of the "Parliament Fart"', *HLQ* 69:1 (2006), 121–38, at 138.
49 Adam Smyth, '"Reade in One Age and Understood I'th'next": Recycling Satire in the Mid-Seventeenth Century', *HLQ* 69:1 (2006), 67–82, at 71–3.
50 *Recreation for ingenious head-peeces*, Wing M1714 (1654), sig. A4r.
51 Smyth, *"Profit and Delight"*, ch. 4.
52 *Sportive wit*, sigs C5r, C8r.
53 Ibid., i, p. 9.
54 Ibid., sig. A3v, ii, p. 34.
55 E.g., ibid., i, pp. 9–10, 18–22, 32–3; 'lampoon', *OED Online*, www.oed.com/view/Entry/105378 (accessed 7 May 2021).
56 *Sportive wit*, ii, pp. 40–1.
57 James Grantham Turner, *Schooling Sex: Libertine Literature and Erotic Education in Italy, France, and England, 1534–1685* (Oxford, 2003).
58 [Abraham Wright], *Parnassus biceps*, E.1679[1] ([April 15], 1656), sigs A3r–A4r, A8r. See also James Loxley, *Royalism and Poetry in the English Civil Wars: The Drawn Sword* (Basingstoke, 1997), pp. 4–6.
59 [Wright], *Parnassus biceps*, pp. 54–5, 107–10.
60 Ibid., pp. 20–1.
61 Ibid., pp. 159–60. This poem is discussed briefly in Chapter 1.
62 Thomas Birch (ed.), *A Collection of the State Papers of John Thurloe* (7 vols, London, 1742), iv, pp. 717–18.
63 Gordon Campbell, 'Phillips, John', *ODNB*; [John Phillips], *A satyr against hypocrites*, E.851[19] ([7 August] 1655), p. 13.
64 *CSPD, 1655–6*, pp. 298, 314.
65 University of Nottingham Library, MS PwV 18, pp. 2, 20, 24, 30, 32, 103.
66 Lynn Hulse, '"Musick & Poetry, Mixed": Thomas Jordan's Manuscript Collection', *Early Music* 24:1 (1996), 7–24.
67 University of Nottingham Library, MS PwV 18, pp. 39, 43, 47, 58. See also Angela McShane, 'Roaring Royalists and Ranting Brewers: The Politicization of Drink and Drunkenness in Political Broadside Ballads from 1640 to 1689', in Adam Smyth (ed), *A Pleasing Sinne: Drink and Conviviality in Seventeenth-Century England* (Cambridge, 2004), pp. 69–87, at 73–4.

68 Capp, *Culture Wars*.
69 WACML, MS.1951.011, second series, p. 157; TNA, SP 18/153, fol. 253r.
70 George Fox, *Newes coming up out of the north*, E.725[5] ([21 December] 1653), p. 23; BL, Add. MS 78298, fol. 61r.
71 Birch (ed.), *State Papers of John Thurloe*, ii, p. 502; v, p. 645.
72 G. F. Warner (ed.), *The Nicholas Papers* (5 vols, London, 1886–97), iii, p. 92. See also Ronald Hutton, *Charles the Second: King of England, Scotland, and Ireland* (Oxford, 1989), p. 78.
73 Nicole Greenspan, 'Charles II, Lucy Walter, and the Stuart Courts in Exile', *EHR* 131:553 (2016), 1386–414, at 1407–10.
74 *CSPD 1656–7*, p. 4.
75 *Politicus*, E.494[13] (10–17 July 1656), p. [7108].
76 [Marchamont Nedham], *The excellencie of a free-state*, E.1676[1] ([29 June] 1656), pp. 45–6, 52.
77 Ibid., pp. 75, 81, 85, 161. See also Gianoutsos, *Manhood*, ch. 6.
78 DWL, DWL/RB/2/3.119, fol. 120r.
79 J. G. A. Pocock (ed.), *The Commonwealth of Oceana and A System of Politics* (Cambridge, 1992), p. 56.
80 [Edward Sexby], *Killing noe murder*, E.501[4] ([June] 1657), p. 12.
81 TNA, ASSI 45/5/4, no. 45.
82 Coward, *The Cromwellian Protectorate*, pp. 89–91.
83 Sharpe, *IW*, p. 527.
84 Barry Reay, *The Quakers and the English Revolution* (New York, NY, 1985), p. 11.
85 Thomas Firmin, *The first new persecution*, E.725[19] ([4 January] 1654), pp. 4–5. See also *Something further laid open*, E.863[7] ([16 January] 1656), p. 6; Barry Reay, 'Popular Hostility Towards Quakers in Mid-Seventeenth-Century England', *Social History* 5:3 (1980), 387–407.
86 Christopher Hill, *The World Turned Upside Down: Radical Ideas During the English Revolution* (London, 1975), p. 232.
87 John L. Nickalls (ed.), *The Journal of George Fox* (Cambridge, 1952), p. 21; Leo Damrosch, *The Sorrows of the Quaker Jesus: James Nayler and the Puritan Crackdown on the Free Spirit* (Cambridge, MA, 1996), p. 126.
88 LRO, QSR 52 (Jane [Walne?], 25 April 1658). See also Nigel Smith, *Perfection Proclaimed: Language and Literature in English Radical Religion, 1640–1660* (Oxford, 1989), pp. 25, 174, 181.
89 Kate Peters, *Print Culture and the Early Quakers* (Cambridge, 2005), pp. 183–4. On Quakerism and gender, see for example Phyllis Mack, *Visionary Women: Ecstatic Prophecy in Seventeenth-Century England* (Berkeley, CA, 1992).
90 *Fumigosus*, E.821[8] (20–7 December 1654), p. 240; *A list of some of the grand blasphemers*, 669.f.17[80] ([23 March] 1654).
91 Hill, *World Turned Upside Down*, pp. 236–8.
92 *The querers and quakers cause*, E.697[14] ([20 May] 1653), pp. 24–6, 34.
93 John Gilpin, *The Quakers shaken*, E.216[2] ([4 July] 1653), pp. 2–5.
94 Ibid., pp. 9, 14.

95 Christopher Atkinson, *The standard of the Lord lifted up*, E.715[7] ([21 October] 1653), sig. A4r, pp. 17, 24, 32.
96 John Gilpin [?], *The Quakers shaken*, 2nd ed., E.831[25] ([13 April] 1655), pp. 20–1.
97 Malcolm Gaskill, *Witchfinders: A Seventeenth-Century English Tragedy* (London, 2005), pp. 47–50, 113.
98 Gervase Benson, *An answer to John Gilpin's book*, Wing B1899 (1655), pp. 5–7.
99 Ibid., p. 7.
100 *The faithful scout*, E.481[10] (23 February–2 March 1655), p. 1724; Thomas Weld, *The perfect pharise*, E.726[7] ([14 January] 1654), p. 49.
101 *The quacking mountebanck*, E.840[4] ([24 May] 1655), p. 16; William Prynne, *The Quakers unmasked*, E.828[1] ([19 February] 1655), p. 1; *Quakers are inchanters and dangerous seducers*, Wing Q13 ([21 July] 1655), p. 8.
102 Thomas Winterton, *The Quaking prophets*, Wing W3093 (1655), p. 4; *The Quakers terrible vision*, E.835[10] ([4 May] 1655), title-page, p. 3.
103 *The Quakers fiery beacon*, E.844[13] ([24 June] 1655), p. 3; Ephraim Pagitt, *Heresiography*, Wing P180, 5th ed. (1654) p. 143. Pagitt's ordering was not merely alphabetical, either, since the 'Ranters' section was immediately followed by 'Papists'.
104 *The devil turned Quaker*, Wing D1222 (1656), sigs A[3]v, A8r.
105 *The Quakers dream*, E.833[14] (1655); *The Ranters declaration*, E.620[2] ([17 December] 1650). See also Tom Webster, 'On Shaky Ground: Quakers, Puritans, Possession and High Spirits', in Michael J. Braddick and David L. Smith (eds), *The Experience of Revolution in Stuart Britain and Ireland* (Cambridge, 2011), pp. 172–89, at 185n30.
106 Edward Burrough, *A trumpet of the Lord sounded out of Sion*, E.875[3] ([12 April] 1656), pp. 12, 36. See also George Fox, *A word from the Lord*, E.809[6] ([25 August] 1654), p. 9.
107 Hugh Barbour, *The Quakers in Puritan England* (New Haven, CT, 1964), pp. 48–9. See also Mack, *Visionary Women*, pp. 227–8.
108 Peters, *Print Culture*, pp. 25, 148–9.
109 Matthew Caffyn, *The deceived, and deceiving Quakers discovered*, E.873[2] ([3 April] 1656), sig. A2r; Thomas Winterton, *The chasing the young quaking harlot out of the city*, Wing W3092 (1656), pp. 5, 16; James Brown, *Antichrist (in spirit) unmasked*, Wing B5022A (Edinburgh, 1657), pp. 16, 40–1. See also *Perfect proceedings of state-affaires*, E.833[4] (12–19 April 1655), pp. 4604–5.
110 Thomas Aldam, *The searching out the deceit*, Wing A894C (1655); *A Declaration from the children of light*, E.838[11] ([14 May] 1655), pp. 2–3.
111 James Nayler, et. al., *An answer to…The perfect Pharisee*, E.735[2] ([9 May] 1654), pp. 27–8.
112 Peters, *Print Culture*, p. 254.
113 Jonathan Clapham, *A full discovery and confutation of…the Quakers*, E.498[7] ([12 December] 1656), p. 51. Later accounts claimed that Atkinson was jailed in Norwich after being 'indited, arraigned and found guilty of adultery' at the local sessions, but it seems that Atkinson was already imprisoned on different

charges when the maidservant story went public: John Deacon, *An exact history of the life of James Naylor*, E.903[2] ([12 February] 1657), p. 48; Richard Hubberthorn, et. al., *The testimony of the everlasting gospel*, E.818[23] ([13 December] 1654).
114 Peters, *Print Culture*, ch. 8.
115 TNA, SP 18/153, fol. 65r; Patricia Crawford, *Women and Religion in England, 1500–1720* (London, 1993), p. 171; *The Quakers quaking*, E.1641[3] ([9 December] 1656), p. 12.
116 John Deacon, *The grand impostor examined*, E.896[2] ([2 December] 1656), pp. 41–5; John Towill Rutt (ed.), *The Diary of Thomas Burton, Esq.: Volume One: July 1653–April 1657* (London, 1828), p. 46. See also Ralph Farmer, *Sathan inthron'd in his chair of pestilence*, E.897[2] ([18 December] 1656), pp. 30–1; *The Quakers quaking*, p. 4.
117 *A True relation of the life...of James Naylor*, E.1645[4] ([20 December] 1656), pp. 5–6.
118 John Deacon, *An exact history*, pp. 3, 8, 16, 49.
119 Ibid., pp. 20, 31–2, 41 [mispaginated as 49], 42.
120 John Stalham, *The reviler rebuked*, E.914[1] ([6 June] 1657), p. 167; *A Sad caveat to all Quakers*, E.1645[5] ([3 March] 1657), p. 10. See also William Grigge, *The Quaker's Jesus*, E.942[2] ([30 April] 1658), pp. 2, 22; Ralph Farmer, *The imposter dethron'd*, Wing F441A (1658), p. 29.
121 NLS, MS Wodrow Fol.XXVI, fol. 24r; DWL, DWL/RB/2/3.54.
122 Christopher Durston, *The Family in the English Revolution* (Oxford, 1999), pp. 17–18. One of these books (*A remedy for uncleanness*, E.948[3] ([14 June] 1658)) was dedicated to Cromwell, which may explain the Council of State's discussion of a 'book lately published concerning polygamy' on 22 June 1658: *CSPD 1658-9*, p. 71.
123 See for example *Politicus*, E.766[23] (21–8 July 1659), pp. 617–18; *CSPD 1659-60*, pp. 155–6.
124 Thomas Danson, *The Quakers wisdom descendeth not from above*, E.2255[4] (1659), pp. 4–5 (second pagination); Thomas Smith, *The Quaker disarm'd*, Wing S4227 (1659), sig. C3v.
125 Barry Reay, 'The Quakers, 1659, and the Restoration of the Monarchy', *History* 63:208 (1978), 193–213, at 205; [Viscount Saye and Sele], *Folly and madness made manifest*, Wing S788 ([Oxford], 1659), pp. 2–3; J[oshua] S[cotton], *Johannes Becoldus redivivus*, E.2137[3] ([26 May] 1659), pp. 24–7. Saye also repeated the story about the Quaker woman who committed adultery because 'the Father had commanded her': *Folly and madness*, p. 7.
126 *Strange and terrible newes from Cambridge*, Wing S5827 (1659), p. 4; *A lying wonder discovered*, Wing B3075 (1659). See also *The loyall scout*, E.993[3] (22–9 July 1659), p. 106.
127 *A gagg for the Quakers*, E.764[2] ([3 November] 1659), 'A Memorable Advertisement'.
128 *A discovery of... the scholars of Cambridge*, Wing S537 (1659), p. 10; Smith, *The Quaker disarm'd*, sig. A2v. See also Henry Denne, *The Quaker no papist*, E.1000[13] ([16 October] 1659).

129 R[ichard] B[lome], *Questions propounded to George Whitehead and George Fox*, Wing B3219 (1659), pp. 5, 8.
130 R[ichard] B[lome], *Questions . . . With the summe of their answer, and his reply*, E.764[3] (1659), pp. 3, 6, 23–4.
131 Ibid., p. 23.
132 [John Denham], *A relation of a Quaker*, 669.f.21[35] ([20 May] 1659).
133 [John Berkenhead], *The four-legg'd elder*, 669.f.11[70] ([1 September] 1647).
134 [Alexander Brome], *Ratts rhimed to death*, E.1761[2] ([November?] 1660), pp. 73, 76, 78. Denham's piece reappeared in this collection too (pp. 69–73). Thomason's annotation appears to indicate a publication date of November 1659, but because this edition includes a piece dated to March 1660 (pp. 85–9), that identification is questionable. For a copy purchased in July 1660, see Bod., Wood 326 (1).
135 Mark R. Blackwell, 'Bestial Metaphors: John Berkenhead and Satiric Royalist Propaganda of the 1640s and 1650s', *Modern Language Studies* 29:1 (1999), 105–30, at 123.
136 E.g., BL, Harley MS 3991, fols 49v–51r; Bod., MS Ashmole 36–37, fols 88r–9r; HRC, Thomas Killigrew Miscellany, fols 114r–v.
137 *Bloody news from Chelmsford*, Wing B3263 (Oxford, 1663). See also *The four-legg'd Quaker*, Wing F1661 (1664?); Marshall, *Toleration*, pp. 455–7.
138 Roger Thompson, *Unfit for Modest Ears* (Totowa, NJ, 1979), p. 52.

# 7

# The Restoration and beyond

On 3 September 1658, Oliver Cromwell died in his bed. The old patriarch's loss proved too much for a regime already reeling from both the surging Quaker menace as well as perennial Presbyterian, royalist and republican unrest. Seven months later, coerced by radical leaders in the army, Cromwell's son and successor, Richard Cromwell, surrendered his authority to the so-called 'Rump Parliament' that had ruled the English Republic between December 1648 and April 1653. More turmoil soon followed, precipitated by ideological splintering within the New Model and the renewed threat of royalist activism. Finally, in December 1659, General George Monck marched south to London and set in motion Charles II's return to the throne. When the young Stuart heir arrived in the capital in May 1660, he was met with applause and adoration. After eleven long years, monarchy had returned to England.

The road to Charles's Restoration was accompanied at every turn by graphic sex-talk. It largely came at the expense of Commonwealth leaders, as emboldened royalists resurrected their most libellous anti-puritan tropes of the later 1640s in print to accompany their sovereign's return. From the winter of 1659/60 – the Protectorate's efforts to stifle 'Dangerous Libells and other treasonable seditious & scandalous papers & pamphletts' notwithstanding – every week brought new printed attacks against the Cromwells, the parliament-men and interregnum puritanism.[1] Meanwhile, in a familiar porno-political idiom, resurgent royalists lambasted the Rump Parliament itself with all manner of procreative and non-procreative sexual imagery. By the time of Charles II's arrival in England, Rump satires had become an entire genre of their own. They continued to proliferate in print well into the early 1660s, as the celebrated sexual culture of the Restoration period – not to mention the moralising repudiations of its godly critics – developed in the shadow of mid-century sexual politics.

Restoration political culture has garnered significant scholarly attention. Kevin Sharpe's important work on Charles II's revolutionary politics of pleasure has yet to be eclipsed, while many more historians and literary scholars have documented the sexual criticisms that assailed the Restoration court during the mid-to-late 1660s.[2] Repeatedly, however, these accounts have missed the crucial point that nearly every facet of Restoration sexual politics stemmed from the same source: their mid-century predecessors. In this way, even those scholars of seventeenth-century political pornography who begin their stories (rightly) in the 1640s and 1650s have failed to recognise that the revolutionary period bequeathed an entire political language, rather than a few significant genres, to late Stuart England.[3]

In that spirit, this short chapter chronicles the role played by explicit sex-talk in the death of revolutionary England and the subsequent establishment of Charles II's Restoration regime. Focusing first on the Rump satires of 1659/60 and then turning to the early years of Charles's reign, it demonstrates that fundamental continuities linked the effusive sexual polemics of the English Revolution with the triumphant sexual culture of the late Stuart period. Rendering the discursive connection between sex-writing and sexual practice into its most explicit formulation yet, the new king parlayed his partisans' radical interregnum medley of women, wine and frivolity into a novel formula for monarchical rule, while defeated republicans repurposed their moral reformation campaign into a potent tool for critiquing Charles's promiscuous political style. In this sense, the dichotomy between virginal republican purity and debauched royalist whoredom championed in Nedham's *Excellencie of a free-state* was willed into reality by both parties simultaneously during the early 1660s. In short, the defining tropes of Restoration political culture owed their origins entirely to the sexual politics of revolutionary England.

## 'Queen Dick' and 'Mistress Rump': sex-talk and the fall of the Protectorate

When Richard Cromwell became Lord Protector in September 1658, he was utterly unprepared for the job.[4] Considering the magnitude of the problems that confronted him – disgruntled army leaders, a supreme budget deficit and a new parliament stocked with hostile faces, among others – his failure to perform was therefore unsurprising. Unlike his father, whose singular personality had enabled him to navigate similar minefields with relative success, Richard lacked the charisma or the political acumen to rule. Consequently, in April 1659, under enormous pressure from a radical faction in the New Model, the second Lord Protector abdicated. Weeks later, the army made a public pronouncement: the parliament of 1649–53 was to be restored to power. England would be a true republic once more.

Amid the ensuing political turmoil, English print culture was overrun with anti-Protectorate polemics. Indeed, the republican tract *Margery goodcow*, acquired by Thomason on 30 May, explicitly associated the 'liberty of Printing' with the return to a 'true Commonwealth' after six years of Cromwell's 'Vices and Enormities'.[5] Royalists, too, sprang back into print, although few were yet optimistic enough to hope that a Stuart restoration was imminent. Instead of publishing anticipatory odes to Charles II, therefore, most stuck with generic anti-puritan satires and wine-drenched eroticism: in other words, precisely the same crypto-royalist material that had flourished during the early-to-mid 1650s. It was at this time that John Denham published his obscene verses on Ralph Green, for instance, while elsewhere other familiar cavalier writers returned to print after years of inactivity.

One of those returners was John Crouch, whose fortunes had fallen since *Fumigosus*'s 1655 demise. In May 1659, emboldened by the recent turmoil, Crouch produced a new issue of *Mercurius democritus* that featured a medley of the week's news alongside its familiar 'merry pranks' about 'Big-Belly'd Maidens' and bumbling cuckolds.[6] Twelve more issues followed between May and August, all set in the world-turned-upside-down of the English Antipodes. But while the revived *Democritus* was as obscene as always (some of the 1659 material, in fact, was reprinted from previous issues), it remained mute on the kingdom's tenuous future. Crouch would not risk open support for the Stuart cause without hard proof of Charles II's impending return.[7]

A few loyalist publishers were more adventurous. Some even took aim at the deposed Lord Protector, presumably hoping that the army leaders responsible for Richard's abdication would not object to his embarrassment in print. Fortunately for them, this was a safe bet. Even better, Richard – long reputed to be an indolent layabout – made an easy target.[8]

The former Lord Protector, sometimes derided as 'Queen Dick', came under fire from royalists in print within weeks of his abdication. Libellers contrasted Richard's effeminacy (and, some whispered, his homosexuality) with his hated father's hyper-masculinity.[9] In fact, the pair seemed so different that some commentators wondered if all of Cromwell's 'degenerous Posterity' were actually 'Bastards' of other, weaker loins (a claim that benefited from earlier royalist depictions of Elizabeth Cromwell as a whore). Meanwhile, another June pamphlet inquired 'whether R[ichard] C[romwell] might not get favour amongst the Ladies, though he hath lost himself amongst the People, if he had but his Fathers Long Instrument'. In this formulation, Oliver's penis became a symbol of sexual tyranny to which Richard could literally never measure up.[10]

Richard was succeeded by the 'Rump Parliament', so dubbed because Pride's Purge of December 1648 had butchered the Long Parliament's carcass and left only its soiled backside behind. As the Rump's enemies soon realised, this nickname provided extraordinary opportunities for satire, both scatological (by depicting the Rump as the source of the metaphorical excrement that had mired England since 1649) and sexual.[11] But most dissidents, still fearful of reprisal, forbore from printing such jokes during the summer of 1659. It was not until the following January, when the New Model general George Monck began marching south from Scotland to crush an army rebellion led by Cromwell's former right-hand man, John Lambert, that royalists dared to hope that England's long nightmare was finally over.

From the early months of 1660, dissident printers published scurrilous broadside ballads against the Rump in which the personified parliament became a central character.[12] In these libels, Rump affiliates like 'Pimp [Hugh] Peters' and the notorious whoremongers '[Henry] Martin and [Thomas] Scot' were joined by 'Gen[eral] Ram', the deceased earl of Essex, and Oliver Cromwell, still the brunt of jokes about his tryst with 'Lady Lambert'.[13] Other familiar targets included the London citizens' 'wives', who longed for the romantic attentions of royalist men: 'Although in her heart a Roundhead she were, / in her belly she wisht a Cavalier', one ballad joked.[14]

Nor was libellous satire the only recognisable mode of royalist sexual polemic to reappear in the ballads. In a familiar porno-political construction, some writers discussed the Rump in terms of 'lineal descent, / as the undoubted Heir, and excrement, / of the yet perpetual Parliament': in other words, Mistress Parliament. Other royalist balladeers described how, because the recent upheavals had put the Rump 'all in a pucker', its godly advocates 'humbly implore[d] the soft, and tender hands, of your fair, and pittifull Dames, to stroke it, and smooth it out'.[15] One ballad focused specifically on the Rump's chief lover, General Lambert, who 'did the Rump bestride', only (hopefully) to soon 'be try'd / for Treason, and Buggerie'.[16] In yet other ballads, 'Mistress Rump' was 'brought to Bed' with a monstrous 'Babe of Reformation' in a callback to the initial Mistress Parliament play-pamphlets of 1648. At least one writer hoped that 'Midwife Monck' would ensure that the 'heir apparent' of the Rump might in fact be Charles II himself: a happy conclusion to twenty years of monstrous, miscegenated rule.[17]

In February, Monck restored the original Long Parliament of 1640–48, which wasted no time in calling for the election of a new parliament before dissolving itself after nearly twenty years of intermittent sitting. The new assembly – the 'Convention Parliament' – met for the first time on 25 April. Two weeks later, its members formally invited Charles II to take up his father's crown. As this news spread, the Rump trope migrated from broadside ballads into other forms of polemical print. John Crouch now invoked 'tayl[s], Rump[s], [and] stump[s]' in a revived *Mercurius fumigosus*. Elsewhere, the life-story of Mistress Rump (described in one pamphlet as 'the Whore of Babylon with her Arse upwards') received tract-length attention for the first time.[18] Still other tracts alternated between chastising and ventriloquising the Rump's leading figures for their 'rapacious', 'rammish', and 'venerous' behavior.[19] The English playwright John Tatham wrote a satirical history of the Rump's fall that proved popular enough to receive another edition the following year. His narrative centred on a fictional rivalry between Elizabeth Cromwell and Frances Lambert over Oliver's sexual affections, and it reimagined the Rump as a reinvigorated Parliament of Ladies under Frances's direction.[20] Weighing in at nearly seventy pages, Tatham's comedy was a far cry from the single-sheet satires of the previous summer: proof that the anti-Rump canon was setting down roots amid the ongoing political turmoil.

The most substantial pre-Restoration Rump production was *Ratts rhimed to death*, which 'bound together' many of the recently published 'loose sheets' into a comprehensive 'Picture of the said Rump assembled, and stinking in Consort'. This collection was the work of the royalist poet Alexander Brome, whose oeuvre included bawdy drinking songs and antipuritan satire alike.[21] Alongside more than a dozen reprinted anti-Rump verses, Brome's anthology also featured both Denham's and Berkenhead's scabrous poems on Ralph Green the Quaker, thereby neatly packaging the various strands of late interregnum royalist sexual politics into a more durable, synthetic form. Yet, for supporters of the republican project, worse was still to come: as John Milton put it, the 'wicked words' spewing from the 'infernal pamphlets' of 'these tigers of Bacchus' signalled that yet 'more wicked deeds' would surely accompany Charles II's impending accession.[22]

## Constructing the 'Merry Monarch': the sexual politics of Restoration royalism

Milton was right. Dramatic changes to English political life followed Charles's triumphant arrival in London on 29 May 1660. At court, the new king's well-documented (thanks to Thurloe and Nedham) appetite for pleasure inculcated an ethos of similar frivolity among his courtiers, many of whom were anxious to make up for hard times suffered during the 1650s. Often, he led by example, publicly parading his mistresses and embracing the libertine literature and drama – some imported from continental publishers, others produced domestically – that emerged in step with the excesses of the Restoration court. Meanwhile, printed screeds against the defeated parliamentarian enemy continued to proliferate, replete with their own scurrilous brand of anti-puritan sexual satire. In each case, the influence of mid-century sexual politics was abundantly clear.

Promiscuity was the Restoration regime's premier public mode. In stark contrast with the sombre moralism of both his father and Oliver Cromwell, Charles adopted his abundant personal sexuality as a political symbol by equating his romantic prowess with his sovereignty. As Kevin Sharpe and others have argued, by crafting a clever cultural politics of provocative art, published romances and unprecedented access to the royal person, the king rendered every facet of his sexuality into a public message about his ability to provide for his subjects as abundantly as he did his many lovers.[23] Some, at least, found the new milieu exhilarating: Samuel Pepys, for one, recorded discussions about his monarch's penis and dreams about his mistresses.[24] The sexualised royal bodies – formerly a tool of republican porno-politics – thus once again became a fixture of late Stuart public discourse.[25]

Charles's subjects may not have been terribly surprised at this development; after all, his playboy reputation had been well established by republican polemicists during the interregnum. But the king's promiscuous public conduct after 1660 was not necessarily an intrinsic part of his character. Not only does that narrative fail to square with Charles's previous efforts to keep his amours hidden; it also downplays his political acumen.[26] The king knew of his lurid reputation – 'they have done me to much honore in assigning me so many faire laydies', he joked in a 1659 letter, 'as if I were able to satisfie the halfe' – and he was certainly savvy enough to use it.[27] Charles's public promiscuity may therefore have been designed, at least in part, to capitalise on the kingdom's new sexual politics of monarchy. If his subjects were going to obsess over the royal body anyway, in other words, why not give them something to talk about?

The king's apparent predilections led many of his hangers-on – most infamously John Wilmot, earl of Rochester – to follow suit, lending the Restoration court a lecherous cast unparalleled in recent history. Enterprising publishers, emboldened by the new milieu and cognizant of the impressive sales achieved by the royalist drolleries five years prior, followed suit. In the decade that followed, London's bookshops began to carry foreign pornographic novels like *L'escole des filles* (which Pepys purchased and subsequently employed as a masturbatory tool in 1668) and domestic prostitution narratives like John Garfield's Aretine *Wandring whore* series.[28] Crouch, too, returned to the fray with a revived version of *The man in the moon*, in which guides to London whoring 'School[s]' jostled with obscene descriptions of human copulation.[29] Not even periodic attempts to suppress the most blatantly erotic of these publications – Garfield was imprisoned briefly in May 1661– could stem the tide.[30] Meanwhile, bawdy anti-puritan comedies dominated London's reopened theatres, which now regularly featured female actors for the first time. By 1662, English public culture was inundated once more with explicit sex-talk.

Although some of these late Stuart productions proved even more obscene than their mid-century predecessors, the bawdy literature of the Restoration owed a clear debt to interregnum royalism. In printed miscellanies and ribald mock-dramas like *Hero and Leander*, and especially in the case of *Sportive wit*, which anticipated the very language of Restoration court culture by nearly half a decade, cavalier writers had crafted the radical royalist synthesis of anti-puritanism, eroticism and frivolity that eventually came to prevail in Charles II's England. The most visible example of these continuities was John Crouch, whose work grew more overtly political but no less vulgar after 1660 than it had been during the preceding decade. In this sense, while Charles II's personal behaviour legitimised the sexual politics of Restoration royalism, they possessed far deeper roots in the revolutionary upheavals that preceded it.

To that point – and as Crouch's newssheets attested – much post-1660 printed sex-talk was packaged within a larger cultural project inaugurated by Charles II's coronation: the repudiation of interregnum puritanism. The anti-Rump polemics of the immediate pre-Restoration period continued to proliferate for years to follow, long after the new king promised indemnity for all former parliamentarians that had not officially signed his father's death warrant. The 1660 trials of the regicides, combined with the fears of godly unrest engendered by events such as the Fifth Monarchist Thomas Venner's bloody attempt to overthrow the new government in January 1661, only strengthened the demand for anti-puritan satire. Thereafter, many polemicists redoubled their printed campaigns against the sexual predations of godly seducers and their holy sisters, while others rehearsed the lurid personal histories of parliamentarian luminaries like Cromwell and Hugh Peter in full-scale libellous biographies.[31] Samuel Butler's mock-epic *Hudibras* (1663), which narrated the bumbling escapades of a Presbyterian knight-errant during the civil wars, epitomised this revitalised tradition. In Hudibras's 'amorous battels', as in many other anti-puritan screeds published during the early 1660s, the figure of the hypocritical godly lecher found new life.[32]

Here, the links with the polemics of the preceding two decades were self-evident. Consider Alexander Brome's 1662 anthology *Rump*, an expanded version of his 1660 miscellany *Ratts rhimed to death*, which ran to nearly 500 pages. Like its predecessor, the bulk of the collection was comprised of 'Songs . . . which were never before in Print', although some had indeed been published in cheap broadside form during the early 1640s. An even greater proportion had appeared in Lord Conway's interregnum manuscript miscellany, demonstrating even more clearly the connection between the underground royalist libels of the interregnum and those that thrived after the Restoration.[33] Brome's short epistolary introduction laid bare the anthology's mid-century roots. 'Now (thanks be to God)', he announced in a revealing passage,

> there is no Cavalier, because there is nothing else, and 'tis wondrous happy to see how many are His Majesties Faithfull Subjects who were ready to hang the Authors of these Ballads. But he that does not blot out all that's past, and frankly embrace their New Allegiance, or remembers ought but what shall preserve Universal Peace and Charity, let him be Anathema.[34]

In these lines, Brome argued for the institution of royalist polemic, with all its attendant sexual politics, as the predominant discursive mode of Restoration England by insisting that the return of the monarchy had rendered the entire kingdom cavalier. It made for a compelling, if not entirely convincing, argument.

### 'Ten thousand maids': repudiating the Restoration court

Brome's plea for peace may have represented a genuine desire to put the recent past to rest. But considering the brutal libels memorialised in the 1662 *Rump* collection, it seems more likely that he had another, partisan objective in mind: namely, forestalling the return of the anti-monarchical discourses of the early 1650s. The pleasure-seeking Charles II certainly made a more compelling target for such attacks than his solemn father, and considerable godly resentment still simmered beneath the surface of Restoration merrymaking. Despite Brome's efforts to cajole his enemies into silence, sexual politics would haunt the newest Stuart king until the end of his reign.

It began during the months surrounding Charles's May 1660 accession. In whispered conversations and drunken outbursts, sceptical subjects returned to a familiar lexicon to express their frustration at the Stuarts' return. Even before the coronation, the new king was denounced as a whoremonger and the son of a whore (this meaning Henrietta Maria, recently returned to England after nearly fifteen years in France) whose promiscuous appetites could only lead the kingdom into crisis. Often these attacks were framed in the tradition of post-Reformation anti-Catholicism, since Charles's time abroad had sparked worries about his Protestant credentials; in several instances, in fact, hostile commentators even contrasted Charles's popish lechery with the godly chastity of Oliver Cromwell.[35] (In another callback to the revolutionary period, one rabblerouser faced charges after referring to the queen mother as 'Jermans whore'.)[36] While these claims circulated almost exclusively in oral form during the decade's opening years, they reflected a broader cultural reaction to Charles's promiscuous political style that heralded much trouble ahead for the new regime.

None were more cognizant of that fact than the king and his ministers, who wasted little time in cracking down on dissent in a series of repressive laws that included specific prohibitions on several republican anti-monarchical polemics of the 1650s. (The ban so frightened one contemporary that he hid his copy of John Goodwin's republican *Hybristodikai* (1649) in the roof of his stable.)[37] The most sweeping piece of legislation targeted the kingdom's presses. The Licensing Act of 1662 invoked the seditious and scandalous polemics of the preceding two decades to justify unprecedented governmental oversight of English print. Doing so was vital, wrote Charles's pressmaster Sir Roger L'Estrange in 1663, to ensure that 'the same Arguments, Pretences, Wayes, and Instruments, that Ruin'd Your Royal, and Blessed Father' – including, presumably, the post-regicidal assaults on Charles's two bodies – did not also destroy his son.[38]

The Licensing Act largely succeeded in suppressing most overt anti-Stuart polemic from print. But the vibrant public culture of Restoration England, fuelled by a surging professional manuscript industry and the rise of new conversational hubs like the coffeehouse, ensured that such materials circulated widely even when confined to oral and scribal forms.[39] As Charles's subjects amassed more grievances against their new king, the libels proliferated with greater frequency. A major turning point came in 1666 and 1667, when the combined horrors of a devastating plague season, the Great Fire of London, and a Dutch incursion straight up the Thames sparked new heights of vituperation. Thereafter, courtly promiscuity became the subject of scathing criticism, as Charles's subjects blamed the recent disasters on his relentless appetites. Ministers preaching before the king dared to ruminate on the sinfulness of sexual immorality, while Easter week 1668 saw thousands of rioting London apprentices lead attacks on the city's brothels to protest the debauchery that reigned in Whitehall. This same dissatisfaction was also made apparent in print: the 1668 riots were accompanied by broadsides in which Charles's favourite mistress, Lady Castlemaine, was ventriloquised as a whorish affiliate of the afflicted bawdy houses. Perhaps most famously, the poet Andrew Marvell satirised the king as a depraved lecher and the font of England's libertine plague in 'The Last Instructions to a Painter', a lyrical epic that circulated widely in manuscript despite its profoundly subversive content. Still darker verses revelled in descriptions of 'ten thousand maids . . . all C—nts [i.e. 'cunts'] of honor, some of Queenly Breed / that come to be anointed with thy royal seed'.[40]

These discourses had an obvious precedent in interregnum republican polemic. Charles and his court were excoriated for their sexual profligacy and the kingdom's worsening condition, but the scurrilous satires that proliferated in manuscript and (occasionally) print after 1667 were also about religion: in particular, the government's recent efforts to prosecute nonconformists while Catholic courtiers and their wives – occasionally also the king's mistresses – strolled through London with impunity. This ongoing post-Reformation context ensured that many of the links between tyranny, lasciviousness and popery that characterised anti-court sexual slanders during the later 1660s directly recalled the republican attacks levelled against Charles I in the wake of the regicide (and, before that, parliamentarian critiques of his bishops, his soldiers and his queen). As the decade went on and Charles II's affinities with the Catholic French King Louis XIV became even more evident, those connections – between sexual assault and political absolutism, between Catholicism and debauchery, and between the king's penis and his sceptre – would draw increasingly obscene commentary from disillusioned contemporaries, albeit still in predominantly scribal forms.[41] Only after the revolution of 1688/89, when William III sought to distance his new regime from the debauched legacy of Stuart tyranny, would those satires enter print, where they became yet another lurid reference-point in a new cycle of sexual politics that continued to reflect the tropes, themes and caricatures of the 1640s.[42]

All the while – and even after the celebratory excesses of the early Restoration gave way to the culture wars of the 1670s and 1680s – new genres brimming with explicit sex-talk appeared across the spectrum of late Stuart print culture, despite the efforts of later Stuart moral authorities to bury the new milieu beneath a reconstructed edifice of cultural 'politeness'.[43] The most graphic of these texts were the new vernacular pornographies (some, such as *The parliament of women* (1684), owing clear debts to earlier mid-century productions), that appeared regularly in London bookshops during the second half of Charles II's reign, but many less overtly arousing books also surfaced to render English sexuality more visible than ever before. Printed periodicals rehearsing scandalous real-life tales of infidelity, cuckoldry and adultery became standard fare from the 1690s. The popular medical advice book *Aristotle's masterpiece* (1684) retooled the specialised sexual health literature of Renaissance doctors for a plebeian audience; some eighteenth-century readers, and probably their seventeenth-century predecessors, found it arousing enough for masturbation.[44] In these and other decidedly non-political contexts, explicit sex-talk proliferated in print until the end of the century and beyond: a testament to the lessons learned by writers and publishers alike during the English Revolution about the selling power of lascivious language, as well as to the seemingly permanent failure of the generations-long puritan campaign to suppress it.

Meanwhile, late Stuart political culture – still, as historians have convincingly shown, mired in the memory of the English Revolution – provided plenty of additional source material for lurid accounts of popish (royal) sexual depravity and hypocritical godly promiscuity among Whigs and

Figure 7.1 [Roger L'Estrange], *The committee* (1680)

Tories alike, especially during the Popish Plot scare of 1678–81.[45] This was readily apparent in Roger L'Estrange's anti-Dissenter print *The committee* (1680), which featured numerous allusions to the civil war period. Here, mid-century anti-puritanism and anti-popery alike lived on, complete with references to controversial figures like James Nayler as well as libertine sects like the Ranters and the Adamites. Both Ralph Green (plus his equine lover) and Berkenhead's four-legged Presbyterian elder made a pointed appearance in the print's central tableau, while in its bottom-right corner a puritan holy sister tended to her ailing brethren.[46] All told, these vivid reimaginings of revolutionary England's contentious sexual politics spoke to their continued potency long after the Restoration. They would shape English public culture for many decades to follow.

## Notes

1 TNA, SP 25/99, fol. 43r.
2 Kevin Sharpe, ' "Thy Longing Country's Darling and Desire" ': Aesthetics, Sex, and Politics in the England of Charles II', in Julia Marciari-Alexander and Catharine MacLeod (eds), *Politics, Transgression, and Representation at the*

*Court of Charles II* (New Haven, CT, 2007), pp. 1–32; Tim Harris, "'There is None that Loves Him but Drunk Whores and Whoremongers': Popular Criticisms of the Restoration Court," in ibid., pp. 35–58; Tim Harris, 'The Bawdy House Riots of 1668', *HJ* 29:3 (1986), 537–56; Stephen N. Zwicker, 'Virgins and Whores: The Politics of Sexual Misconduct in the 1660s', in Conal Condren and Anthony D. Cousins (eds). *The Political Identity of Andrew Marvell* (Aldershot, 1990), pp. 85–110.

3 For this literature, see the introduction.
4 Barry Coward, *The Cromwellian Protectorate* (Manchester, 2002), p. 103.
5 *Margery good-cow*, E.984[9] ([30 May] 1659), pp. 2–3.
6 *Mercurius democritus*, E.979[2] (26 April–3 May 1659), p. 1.
7 Jason McElligott, 'Crouch, John', *ODNB*.
8 Ronald Hutton, *The Restoration: A Political and Religious History of England and Wales, 1658–1667* (Oxford, 1985), p. 18.
9 Antonia Fraser, *Cromwell: Our Chief of Men* (London, 2008), p. 728; Sharpe, *IW*, p. 533.
10 *The court career death shaddow'd to life*, E.989[26] ([16 July] 1659), p. 9; *The Lord Henry Cromwels speech in the House*, E.1001[15] ([31 October] 1659), p. 4; *Fourty four queries to the life of Queen Dick*, E.986[18] ([15 June] 1659), p. 4. See also Su Fang Ng, *Literature and the Politics of Family in Seventeenth-Century England* (Cambridge, 2007), p. 127.
11 Mark S.R. Jenner, 'The Roasting of the Rump: Scatology and the Body Politic in Restoration England', *P&P* 177 (2002), 84–120; Alexandra C. Lumbers, 'The Discourses of Whoredom in Seventeenth-Century England' (DPhil thesis, Oxford University, 2005), pp. 217–19.
12 Angela McShane and Mark S.R. Jenner, 'Debate: The Roasting of the Rump: Scatology and the Body Politic in Restoration England [with Reply]', *P&P* 196 (2007), 253–86.
13 *Lucifers life-guard*, 669.f.25[34] ([May] 1660); *Bumm-foder*, Wing B5471 (1660); *The dragons forces totally routed*, 669.f.26[35] ([5 December] 1660); *The Rump roughly but righteously handled*, 669.f.22[63] ([11 January] 1660).
14 *Rump rampant*, Wing A34 (1660); *Fortunate rising*, 669.f.23[7] ([20 January] 1660).
15 *The Rump serv'd in with a grand sallet*, 669.f.23[70] ([1 March] 1660); *The petition of the Rump*, 669.f.23[44] ([15 February] 1660).
16 *A new-years-gift for the Rump*, 669.f.22[55] ([5 January] 1660).
17 *Mris. Rump brought to bed of a monster*, 669.f.24[44] ([28 March] 1660); *The life and death of Mris Rump*, 669.f.24[52] ([2 April] 1660); *The history of the second death of the Rump*, 669.f.24[5] ([7 March] 1660). See also *The Rump Carbonadod*, Wing R2270 (1660?).
18 *Mercurius fumigosus*, E.1019[3] (28 March 1660), p. 25; *The character of the Rump*, E.1017[20] ([17 March] 1660), p. 1. See also *The famous tragedie of the life and death of Mris. Rump*, Wing F385B (1660), which very closely resembled the original 1648 Mistress Parliament play-pamphlets.
19 *The Rump held forth*, E.1017[35] ([22 March] 1660), p. 5. See also *The Rump despairing*, Wing R2271 ([20 March] 1660), pp. 4–6.

20 John Tatham, *The Rump…a new comedy*, Wing T233 (1660).
21 [Alexander Brome], *Ratts rhimed to death*, E.1761[2] ([November?] 1660), sigs A2r–3r. See above for Thomason's problematic dating of this tract. See also Jenner, 'Roasting of the Rump', p. 94.
22 J[ohn] M[ilton], *The readie and easie way*, 2nd ed., Wing M2174 (1660), p. 81.
23 Sharpe, '"Darling and Desire"'; Erin Keating, 'In the Bedroom of the King: Affective Politics in the Restoration Secret History', *Journal for Early Modern Cultural Studies* 15:2 (2015), 58–82.
24 Robert Latham and William Matthews (eds), *The Diary of Samuel Pepys* (11 vols, Berkeley and Los Angeles, CA, 1970–83), iii, pp. 24, 82, 139, 175–6; iv, pp. 136–8.
25 Paul Hammond, 'The King's Two Bodies: Representations of Charles II', in Jeremy Black and Jeremy Gregory (eds), *Culture, Politics and Society in Britain, 1660–1800* (Manchester, 1991), pp. 13–48.
26 Nicole Greenspan, 'Charles II, Lucy Walter, and the Stuart Courts in Exile', *EHR* 131:553 (2016), 1386–414; Ronald Hutton, *Charles the Second: King of England, Scotland, and Ireland* (Oxford, 1989), p. 78.
27 BRBML, OSB MSS 5, Box 1:20.
28 *Pepys*, ix, pp. 57–9. See also Turner, *Libertines*, p. 124.
29 *MITM*, E.1046[3] (8–14 October 1660), p. 20.
30 David Foxon, *Libertine Literature in England, 1660–1745* (New York, NY, 1965), p. 9. See also Gerald MacLean, '1660', in Joad Raymond (ed.), *The Oxford History of Popular Print Culture, Volume One: Cheap Print in Britain and Ireland to 1660* (Oxford, 2011), pp. 619–28, at 628.
31 See for example [Richard Blome], *The fanatick history*, E.1832[2] ([July] 1660); *The holy sisters conspiracy*, E.1055[20] ([26 January] 1661); [James Heath], *Flagellum*, Wing H1328 (1663); William Yonge, *England's shame*, Wing Y44 (1663). See also Alexandra Walsham, 'Phanaticus: Hugh Peter, Antipuritanism and the Afterlife of the English Revolution', *Parergon* 32:3 (2015), 65–97.
32 [Samuel Butler], *Hudibras*, Wing B6296 (1663), p. 88.
33 [Alexander Brome], *Rump*, Wing B4851 (1662), sig. A3v.
34 Ibid., sig. A3v-4r.
35 Harris, '"There is None that Loves Him"', pp. 35, 41; Edward Legon, *Revolution Remembered: Seditious Memories After the British Civil Wars* (Manchester, 2019), pp. 23–4.
36 TNA, SP 29/10, fol. 58r.
37 *A proclamation for . . . suppressing of two books*, 669.f.25[70] ([15 August] 1660); WACML, DA396 A2G6. The book was rediscovered in 1667 when a new owner tore the stable down for renovations.
38 Roger L'Estrange, *Considerations . . . to the regulation of the press*, Wing L1229 (1663), sig. A2v.
39 Tim Harris, *London Crowds in the Reign of Charles II: Propaganda and Politics from the Restoration Until the Exclusion Crisis* (Cambridge, 1987), p. 28; Steve Pincus, '"Coffee Politicians Does Create": Coffeehouses and Restoration Political Culture', *Journal of Modern History* 67:4 (1995), 807–34.

40 Harris, 'Bawdy House Riots', pp. 554–5; Zwicker, 'Virgins and Whores'; Rachel Weil, 'Sometimes a Scepter is Only a Scepter: Pornography and Politics in Restoration England', in Lynn Hunt (ed.). *The Invention of Pornography: Obscenity and the Origins of Modernity, 1500–1800* (New York, NY, 1993), pp. 125–53, at 128.

41 Ibid., pp. 143–51. See also Julia Rudolph, 'Rape and Resistance: Women and Consent in Seventeenth-Century English Legal and Political Thought', *JBS* 39:2 (2000), 157–84.

42 Tony Claydon, *William III and the Godly Revolution* (Cambridge, 1996).

43 For late Stuart 'politeness', see Markku Peltonen, 'Politeness and Whiggism, 1688–1732', *HJ* 48:2 (2005), 391–414; Helen Berry, 'Rethinking Politeness in Eighteenth-Century England: Moll King's Coffee House and the Significance of "Flash Talk"', *TRHS*, 6:11 (2001), 65–81; Lawrence E. Klein, *Shaftesbury and the Culture of Politeness: Moral Discourse and Cultural Politics in Early Eighteenth-Century England* (Cambridge, 1994); Anna Bryson, *From Courtesy to Civility: Changing Codes of Conduct in Early Modern England* (Oxford, 1998).

44 *The parliament of women*, Wing P506A (1684); David M. Turner, *Fashioning Adultery: Gender, Sex and Civility in England, 1660–1740* (Cambridge, 2002), pp. 36, 109; Roy Porter and Leslie Hall, *The Facts of Life: The Creation of Sexual Knowledge in Britain, 1650–1950* (New Haven, CT, 1995), pp. 35–8; Tim Hitchcock, *English Sexualities, 1700–1800* (New York, NY, 1997), p. 29.

45 John McTague, 'Anti-Catholicism, Incorrigibility and Credulity in the Warming-Pan Scandal of 1688–9', *Journal for Eighteenth-Century Studies* 36:3 (2013), 433–48; Mark Knights, *Representation and Misrepresentation in Later Stuart Britain: Partisanship and Political Culture* (Oxford, 2005); Mary E. Fissell, *Vernacular Bodies: The Politics of Reproduction in Early Modern England* (Oxford, 2004); Harold Love, *English Clandestine Satire, 1660–1702* (Oxford, 2004); Melissa M. Mowry, *The Bawdy Politic in Stuart England, 1660–1714: Political Pornography and Prostitution* (Aldershot, 2004); Rachel Weil, *Political Passions: Gender, the Family and Political Argument in England, 1680–1714* (Manchester, 1999).

46 [Roger L'Estrange], *The committee*, Wing L1226 (1680).

# Conclusion

On 1 May 1652, just five months before Michael Sparke published the lines that opened this book, Henry Agarde wrote to a correspondent about an embarrassing family matter. 'It is so falne out', he penned in disgust, 'that my sister Anphiles not worthy the name of a sister is greate with childe'. Anphiles was evidently unmarried, for Agarde was deeply worried about the 'prejudice to my house' that would result 'should she returne to me againe', and he wondered if his friend's neighbours might 'suffer her there to stay till she be lighter'. Yet he expressed no sympathy at all for his sibling's plight. 'Let her begg with her bratt or starve', he wrote, 'for never more will I owne her'. Agarde concluded by pleading with his friend to 'pittie my condicon'.[1] Not one more word was spared for the eminently more pitiable state of his beleaguered sister.

Any modern reader would be unsurprised by Agarde's letter, which fully embodied the stereotype of the puritan killjoy that continues to flourish in Western popular culture. But there was also another side, literally, to the story. Scribbled on the letter's back in an eighteenth-century hand, a commentator identified only as 'J.A.' offered a different reading. Noting that Agarde – dubbed 'a Puritan & an Oliverian' – was 'very angry with his sister for obeying the second Law of nature', the anonymous writer next described in verse how 'the Saints' in those 'pious times' really felt about 'Fornication'. According to J.A., interregnum puritans

> were wont to creep & lurk in private Holes
> And in the dark securely damn'd their souls
> Wore vizzards of Hypochrysy, to steal
> And slink away in Masquerade to Hell.[2]

Here, long after the conclusion of the English Revolution, was the familiar image of the hypocritical puritan who preached moral reformation while secretly wallowing in sin.

J.A.'s comments encapsulate a lurid version of mid-seventeenth-century history that did not survive the Victorian professionalisation of English historical studies responsible for Samuel Rawson Gardiner's magisterial *History of the Great Civil War*.[3] Thereafter, the history of the English Revolution grew increasingly insular and empirical, with scant regard for the broader cultural, social and gendered contexts that shaped its causes, course and consequences.[4] Only recently have historians and literary critics begun to address those questions in detail; and even then, excepting the important work of a few specialists, J.A.'s vision of mid-century England as a sex-drenched world-turned-upside-down remains elusive. Recapturing that lost narrative, as it was promulgated and debated during the 1640s and 1650s, has been this book's central purpose.

The mid-seventeenth century propelled graphic sex-talk into print for the first time in English history. That process, in turn, transformed sexual politics from an underground, subversive form of prewar political commentary into a central feature of English public culture. This revolution owed its success to two key catalysts. First, the Anglo-Scottish troubles of the late 1630s and the concurrent polarisation of English political opinion shattered the various mechanisms through which early Stuart regulators had previously kept most obscene, libellous and subversive sexual rhetoric from print. Next, the collapse of press licensing in 1640/41 provided civil war pamphleteers with an opportunity to deploy those formerly taboo discourses in service to a variety of partisan causes. From there, mid-century apologists transformed graphic sex-talk into a set of coherent and increasingly complex political languages which only grew more explicit, libellous and daring as the period wore on: a process that owed much to the efforts of writers like John Taylor, Richard Overton, Marchamont Nedham and John Crouch to legitimate scurrilous satire as a particularly effective form of political discourse. By 1659, as the acrid anti-Quaker tracts of that year demonstrate, sexual politics – still largely of the post-Reformation variety – had thoroughly invaded polemical print. Long before the accession of the Merry Monarch, in other words, sex was already a regular feature of English public culture.

In civil war England, as in sixteenth-century Scotland and throughout Reformation Europe more broadly, the heightened stakes of internecine warfare therefore converted a powerful cultural taboo into a valuable polemical tool.[5] In the process, the increasingly participatory nature of mid-century England's surging print marketplace (not to mention the entrepreneurial spirit of the publishers who supplied it) helped to foster what Valerie Traub has dubbed a 'nascent sexual public'.[6] Throughout the period, contemporaries like Edward Finch and Edmund Chillenden took to print to explain (and, often, rebut) public statements about their personal sexuality. This incipient linkage between sexual discourse and sexual practice grew stronger as the upheavals continued, until some radicals – including both Abiezer Coppe's

Ranters and merrymaking interregnum royalists – even began advocating for new standards of sexual morality altogether: an innovation that, in the latter case, ultimately bore fruit in the form of the promiscuous Restoration court. Meanwhile, libellous exposés of leaders as august as Oliver Cromwell and King Charles I offered readers unparalleled access to the bedchambers of the elite, fostering a public discursive connection between political legitimacy and personal behaviour that would flourish into the eighteenth century.[7] Certainly, as we have seen, English men and women bought, read and discussed mid-century sexual politics with vigour, and even nonliterate contemporaries may have listened to them being read aloud or seen the graphic woodcut illustrations that adorned the period's anti-sectarian screeds. The reasons for their enthusiasm likely varied from genuine political interest to the simple desire for sexual gratification.[8] Regardless, English authors and publishers were more than happy to oblige them, and modern scholars have much to learn as a result.

First, as a uniquely potent mode of public politicking, graphic sex-talk shaped mid-century debates over partisan identity, religious heterodoxy and constitutional theory. From the mid-1640s, moreover, it received more-or-less explicit approval from high-ranking royalists and parliamentarians alike. Sex informed high-minded discussions of religious toleration and patriarchal kingship as well as the most trivial interactions between men and women on the streets of London. It played a crucial role in the politics of republican moral reformation and featured equally prominently in the development of libertine cavalier drollery during the mid-1650s. And it proved especially devastating for some, like the Quakers, who suffered horrific physical abuse that may well have stemmed from their oppressors' exposure to the lurid satires of interregnum polemicists. In every case, the sexualised human body (and especially the bodies of English women) provided a critical battleground over which the most serious mid-century debates could be, and were, fought.

That state of affairs is a testament to the catalysing impact of civil war on English political discourse. The sexual polemics that haunted the Quakers in 1659, like those that shaped the stereotypes of 'roundhead' and 'cavalier' some two decades prior, were cobbled together by partisan apologists scrambling to craft an effective mélange of satire, libel and porno-political theory amid a full-blown political collapse. Their efforts to organise, publicise and radicalise the disparate and largely underground sexual tropes of the Tudor and early Stuart periods into distinctive genres of political truth-claims after 1640 exemplify the creativity engendered by the revolutionary upheavals.[9] Moreover, as parliamentarians and royalists recast their respective claims to patriarchal and political authority in graphic sexual terms – most spectacularly, in the latter case, by conflating their monarch's sovereign political authority with the vigorous, explicit exercise of his sexual body – they did so knowingly, aware that they were engaging in a formerly transgressive form of public debate. In this sense, by attending to the growing respect afforded to explicit sex-talk by some prominent polemicists, we can appreciate anew the role played by the English Revolution in undermining early Stuart notions of social harmony and public decorum.[10]

The persistence of these themes across the entire period also reaffirms, as David Underdown and others have so compellingly documented, the centrality of inversion to seventeenth-century rhetorical strategy.[11] As distant as the royalist drolleries and republican apologetics of 1656 might seem from the cavaliers and roundheads of 1641, this study has illustrated that both groups (and, perhaps more importantly, their critics) continued to engage with the same fundamental arguments about patriarchy, morality and religion throughout the revolutionary decades, albeit in increasingly intense and novel formulations. By tracing the ways in which the polemical positions of 1640/41 were repeatedly appropriated, inverted and expanded by partisan apologists, therefore, it becomes possible to appreciate both the radicalising potential and the enduring continuities of mid-century political discourse. That storyline, in turn, provides a convincing explanation for the ongoing potency of gendered and post-Reformation politics after the Restoration.

On that note: this book has been devoted, in large part, to the argument that 1660 was not as much of a watershed as it has long been made out to be. I will say more about the implications of this claim for the broader history of Western sexuality shortly, but we should note that there are also grounds for positioning the story told here in relation to other historiographical settings. One suitable candidate, for instance, is the chronology sketched out by scholars of Western civility, politeness and obscenity, in which medieval vulgarity gives way to Renaissance civility and then Enlightenment politeness, with a brief counter-cultural interlude during the libertine Restoration.[12] In this context, the early-1640s emergence of explicit sex-talk in print arguably enhances the significance of the mid-seventeenth century as a meaningful disruption of what Norbert Elias famously dubbed the 'civilizing process' – and, in turn, provide grounds for seeing the resurgence of 'civil discourse' in England during the 1670s and 1680s as a reactionary, political response to the mid-century upheavals.

Alternatively, this account offers a chance to establish an entirely new periodisation for the history of sex-talk more broadly, stretching from the classical satires of ancient Rome to Steven Marcus's 'other Victorians' and beyond.[13] Such a chronology would necessarily extend beyond pornography (already well-trodden ground) to encompass sexual language in all its forms, and taking this approach would provide a useful opportunity to reflect on the relationship between, for instance, mid-seventeenth-century English porno-politics and the political pornographies that haunted pre-revolutionary France, or that linking the 1650s royalist drolleries with later erotic miscellanies of the eighteenth and nineteenth centuries.[14] Although the English Revolution would presumably play only a minor role in its most ambitious manifestations, such a history would be welcome indeed for scholars working across a bevy of otherwise unrelated fields.

But this story makes most sense as seventeenth-century political history. The sexual polemics that sprang into English print in 1640/41 had circulated for decades prior in manuscript and oral forms. After their mid-century transformation, many retreated into the shadows during the Restoration, while others enjoyed unprecedented visibility amid the celebratory early years of Charles II's reign. A combination of factors, from the culture wars of the 1670s and 1680s to the efforts of later Stuart moral authorities to tame England's acerbic public sphere before it sparked another civil war (evidence, again, of the political origins of late-seventeenth-century 'politeness'), soon put an end to that promiscuous moment; but the eventual accession of William and Mary only propelled a competing brand of anti-popish sexual politics back into prominence. The continuation of that history into the early eighteenth century – and, correspondingly, across the Channel, for of course the whole story is European, rather than narrowly English or British – remains to be explored. It is hoped that this book will provide later scholars with a productive starting point.

I want to end with a few final reflections on the implications of my argument for other corners of the historiography. First, this story highlights the fundamental inadequacy of empirical histories of the English Revolution that fail to take gender seriously. (I hope I have adequately made the same point about sex-talk.) In mid-seventeenth-century England, as in eighteenth-century France, it was impossible to divest politics from contemporary notions of patriarchy, masculinity and misogyny.[15] The sexual politics canvassed in the preceding pages were overwhelmingly, although not exclusively, the products of male writers who viewed women's bodies as a battleground for asserting their patriarchal – and therefore political – primacy. Indeed, in some sense, it is precisely the centrality of such claims to sexual mastery over English women at mid-century that explains their continued vitality after the Restoration.[16] But sex was only one arena in which gender intruded on mid-century affairs, and political histories of the period that continue to ignore its many resonances will inevitably prove wanting.

Scholars of the Restoration must similarly reevaluate the degree to which Charles II's personal appetites were uniquely responsible for the libertine sexual culture that prevailed after his accession. As we have seen, the new king's much-praised 'aesthetics of pleasure' can be linked to the royalist polemics of the later 1640s, when Charles I was repeatedly portrayed as a loving husband to his people who had been scorned by the whorish Mistress Parliament.[17] The promiscuous attitudes that prevailed among Charles II's courtiers similarly had their origins in the amorous, drunken frivolity of radical interregnum royalism. Moreover, each of these tropes, much like the sexual slanders directed at Charles II after 1666/67 by his disillusioned subjects, were products of the same post-Reformation frameworks that gave rise to early modern English sexual politics in the first place. To be sure, Charles's jovial promiscuity differed markedly from the moralism of his immediate predecessors, and his apparent willingness to license similarly transgressive behaviour among his followers represented a considerable (if temporary) sea-change in the long English tradition of patriarchal kingship. Even so, all of the necessary materials for promoting, contesting and condemning that new milieu were already simmering in print and manuscript alike when the new monarch ascended to the throne in May 1660. All Charles needed to do was activate them – which, it must be said, he did with singular flare.

Finally, there is an argument to be made for the long-term impact of these developments on Western sexual history writ large after 1660. Since the later 1970s, scholars of social history and demography,[18] gender,[19] and culture[20] – but rarely of politics – have produced a plethora of studies identifying early modern England as a key turning-point in the history of Western sexuality. Faramerz Dabhoiwala has dubbed the transformation from premodern notions of 'public discipline' into modern 'principles of individual privacy, equality, and freedom' the West's 'first sexual revolution': an event predominantly driven by later Enlightenment thinkers whose ideas were amplified in turn by the rise of new communicative media and public politics in the mid-eighteenth century.[21] Like most histories of Western sexual modernity, the bulk of Dabhoiwala's analysis begins after 1660, when the raucous celebrations of the Restoration court cemented the death of medieval 'public discipline' while simultaneously sparking a new sense of sexual celebrity that would lead, in time, to the birth of modern 'sexual liberty'.[22]

This book has argued instead that the English Revolution, not the Stuart Restoration, deserves pride of place in that story. It was civil war publicists, working in service to competing partisan agendas, who overcame the various regulatory mechanisms that had suppressed explicit sex-writing from print before 1640 to infuse English political culture with a potent mélange of increasingly graphic satires, libels, and porno-political theory that eventually came to encompass new visions of human sexual practice itself. Once mid-century polemicists – along with their printers, publishers and readers – had 'reconfigured the terms of what could be said and written about sex in public', as Traub puts it, there was no going back.[23] Even after the heyday of Restoration pleasure-politics, sex remained a visible element of English public life: too visible, as it turned out, to fall victim ever again to state-imposed 'public discipline' of the kind that had reigned in England prior to 1640. To be sure, very few civil-war pamphleteers intended to spark a sexual revolution, and in this sense the permissive society envisioned by Charles II certainly marked a new chapter in the development of a 'modern' Western sexual culture. Nevertheless, the crucial precondition for that novel milieu – Traub's 'nascent sexual public' – was entirely a mid-century invention; and, insofar as interregnum royalist sex-writing provided the ideological underpinnings for the promiscuous Restoration court, so too was that permissive society itself.

Indeed, it might be argued that the story told here provides an alternative origin-point for what Michel Foucault described as the 'great sexual sermon' of modern Western culture: a never-ending 'multiplication of discourses concerning sex' that, since its inception, has served at once to categorise, regulate and weaponise human sexuality.[24] For Foucault, that process was amorphous, undirected and gradual, unfolding slowly over a vague period between the seventeenth and nineteenth centuries; I, in contrast, have emphasised the importance of specific decisions, made by rational political actors, over a reasonably short timeline. Even more fundamentally, I break with his account in arguing that the proliferation of explicit sex-talk in English print after 1640 complicated, rather than encouraged, later efforts to regulate sexual morality. But although my story differs from Foucault's in these crucial senses, I am not sure that the paradigm itself is necessary to appreciate the enduring influence of mid-century sexual polemic on the political culture of Restoration England or, more broadly, its stage-setting importance for what David Turner calls the 'much greater visibility of sex and marriage in the burgeoning public sphere of later seventeenth-century England'.[25] The sheer volume of mid-century sex-writing tabulated here – not to mention its popularity among contemporary readers, writers and publishers, as we have seen again and again in these pages – is surely sufficient.

If there is one last lesson to be learned from this story, therefore, it is that historians of sexuality can benefit from reading not just books primarily about sex, but also books primarily about politics. And that brings us back to the central point: for it was ultimately a series of political arguments, contingent upon the ferocious post-Reformation upheavals and novel public culture of the English Revolution, that propelled graphic sex-talk into print for the first time in English history. There it continued to flourish into the eighteenth century, when – evidenced by J.A.'s knowing reference to 'the second law of nature' – new Enlightenment discourses of sex and the body emerged to usher in another transformation in Western sexual culture; but those developments, driven by the proliferation of new pornographies, seduction narratives, crim. con. literature and sexual polemics in print after the dissolution of the Licensing Act in 1695, also owed a debt to the pioneering efforts of mid-century apologists.[26] In this respect, the sexual politics of the English Revolution can be said to have set the pace for more than a century of British sexual culture to follow. They remain one of the period's most remarkable legacies.

# Notes

1. BL, Stowe MS 744, fol. 19r.
2. Ibid., fol. 19v.
3. S. R. Gardiner, *History of the Great Civil War, 1642–49* (4 vols, London, 1886–1901).
4. Ann Hughes, *Gangraena and the Struggle for the English Revolution* (Oxford, 2004), p. 9.
5. For these other contexts, see Steven W. May and Alan Bryson, *Verse Libel in Renaissance England and Scotland* (Oxford, 2016), p. vi; Allyson F. Creasman, *Censorship and Civic Order in Reformation Germany, 1517–1648: 'Printed Poison & Evil Talk'* (Farnham, 2012); Luc Racaut, *Hatred in Print: Catholic Propaganda and Protestant Identity During the French Wars of Religion* (Aldershot, 2002).
6. Valerie Traub, *Thinking Sex with the Early Moderns* (Philadelphia, PA, 2016), p. 116. See also Jason Peacey, *Print and Public Politics in the English Revolution* (Cambridge, 2013).
7. Marilyn Morris, *Sex, Money and Personal Character in Eighteenth-Century British Politics* (New Haven, CT, 2014).
8. Sarah Toulalan, *Imagining Sex: Pornography and Bodies in Seventeenth-Century England* (Oxford, 2007), p. 31.
9. Michael Braddick, 'Mobilisation, Anxiety and Creativity in England during the 1640s', in John Morrow and Jonathan Scott (eds), *Liberty, Authority, Formality: Political Ideas and Culture, 1600–1900* (Exeter, 2008), pp. 175–94.
10. For a reminder about the pitfalls of focusing too closely on the period's 'polarized languages' (among which its sexual politics undoubtedly numbered), see Anthony Milton, *England's Second Reformation: The Battle for the Church of England, 1625–1662* (Cambridge, 2021), p. 512.
11. E.g., David Underdown, *A Freeborn People: Politics and the Nation in Seventeenth-Century England* (Oxford, 1996); Susan Amussen and David Underdown, *Gender, Culture and Politics in England, 1560–1640: Turning the World Upside Down* (London, 2017).
12. Keith Thomas, *In Pursuit of Civility: Manners and Civilization in Early Modern England* (New Haven, CT, 2018); Melissa Mohr, *Holy Shit: A Brief History of Swearing* (Oxford, 2013); Joan DeJean, *The Reinvention of Obscenity: Sex, Lies, and Tabloids in Early Modern France* (Chicago, IL, 2002); Anna Bryson,

*From Courtesy to Civility: Changing Codes of Conduct in Early Modern England* (Oxford, 1989). The 'civilizing process' is detailed in Nobert Elias, *The Civilizing Process* (Oxford, 1982).
13 Amy Richlin, *The Garden of Priapus: Sexuality and Aggression in Roman Humor* (New Haven, CT, 1983); Steven Marcus, *The Other Victorians: A Study of Sexuality and Pornography in Mid-Nineteenth-Century England* (New York, NY, 1964).
14 Robert Darnton, *The Forbidden Best-Sellers of Pre-Revolutionary France* (New York, NY, 1996); Kathleen Lubey, *What Pornography Knows: Sex and Social Protest Since the Eighteenth Century* (Stanford, CA, 2022).
15 For French parallels, see Sarah Maza, *Private Lives and Public Affairs: The Causes Célèbres of Prerevolutionary France* (Berkeley, CA, 1993); Lynn Hunt, *The Family Romance of the French Revolution* (Berkeley, CA, 1992); Darnton, *Forbidden Best-Sellers*.
16 Hughes, *Gender*, p. 145.
17 Kevin Sharpe, '"Thy Longing Country's Darling and Desire": Aesthetics, Sex, and Politics in the England of Charles II', in Julia Marciari-Alexander and Catharine MacLeod (eds), *Politics, Transgression, and Representation at the Court of Charles II* (New Haven, CT, 2007), pp. 1–32, at 27.
18 Lawrence Stone, *The Family, Sex and Marriage in England, 1500–1800* (New York, NY, 1977); Keith Wrightson and David Levine, *Poverty and Piety in an English Village: Terling, 1525–1700* (New York, NY, 1979); Thomas Laqueur, *Making Sex: Body and Gender from the Greeks to Freud* (Cambridge, MA, 1990); Martin Ingram, *Church Courts, Sex, and Marriage in England, 1570–1640* (Cambridge, 1994); Paul Griffiths, *Lost Londons: Change, Crime, and Control in the Capital City, 1550–1660* (Cambridge, 2008).
19 Amanda Vickery, 'Golden Age to Separate Spheres? A Review of the Categories and Chronology of English Women's History', *HJ* 36:2 (1993), 383–414; Anthony Fletcher, *Gender, Sex and Subordination in England, 1500–1800* (New Haven, CT, 1995); Tim Hitchcock, 'Redefining Sex in Eighteenth-Century England', *History Workshop Journal* 41:1 (1996), 72–90; Karen Harvey, 'The Century of Sex? Gender, Bodies, and Sexuality in the Long Eighteenth Century', *HJ* 45:4 (2002), 899–916.
20 Alan Bray, *Homosexuality in Renaissance England* (New York, NY, 1995); Susan Dwyer Amussen, *An Ordered Society: Gender and Class in Early Modern England* (New York, NY, 1988); David Underdown, *Fire from Heaven: Life in an English Town in the Seventeenth Century* (New Haven, CT, 1992).
21 Faramerz Dabhoiwala, *The Origins of Sex: A History of the First Sexual Revolution* (London, 2012), pp. 2–3.
22 But Dabhoiwala does not ignore the English Revolution: see for example ibid., pp. 45–50, 82–3, 89–90.
23 Traub, *Thinking Sex*, p. 116.
24 Michel Foucault, *The History of Sexuality, Volume One: An Introduction*, trans. Robert Hurley (New York, NY, 1990), pp. 7, 18.
25 David M. Turner, *Fashioning Adultery: Gender, Sex and Civility in England, 1660–1740* (Cambridge, 2002), p. 8.

26 For these genres, see Lisa Forman Cody, *Birthing the Nation: Sex, Science, and the Conception of Eighteenth-Century Britons* (Oxford, 2005); Karen Harvey, *Reading Sex in the Eighteenth Century: Bodies and Gender in English Erotic Culture* (Cambridge, 2004); Tim Hitchcock, *English Sexualities, 1700–1800* (New York, NY, 1997); Peter Wagner, *Eros Revived: Erotica of the Enlightenment in England and America* (London, 1988); Dabhoiwala, *Origins of Sex*; Turner, *Fashioning Adultery*. On the dissolution of the Licensing Act, see Mark Knights, *Representation and Misrepresentation in Later Stuart Britain: Partisanship and Political Culture* (Oxford, 2005).

# Bibliography of archival sources

## Bedfordshire Archives, Bedford

MS J1368                St John papers

## Beinecke Rare Book and Manuscript Library, Yale University

GEN MSS 205             John Aston correspondence
Mellon Alchemical 100   Lilly, *Monarchy or no monarchy in England* (1651)
OSB MSS 5               Taaffe correspondence
Osborn MS b4            Poetic miscellany
Osborn MS b15           Sermons
Osborn MS b62           Commonplace book
Osborn MS b101          Assheton Commonplace book
Osborn MS b197          Commonplace book
Osborn MS b200          Commonplace book
Osborn MS b230          Commonplace book
Osborn MS fb77          Collection of English proverbs
Osborn MS fb106         Poetic miscellany
Z17 92c                 *Mercurius aulicus* (1648)

## Bodleian Library, Oxford University

Ashm. F 14              *Mercurius pragmaticus* (1647/48)
Marl. M 1               Edwards, *Antapologia* (1644)
MS Add. C. 209          John Taylor autograph pamphlets
MS Ashmole 36–37        Poetic miscellany
MS Ashmole 1153         'Pigges Corantoe'
MS Bankes 18/19         Star Chamber depositions
MS Bodley 878           Hatton-Cosin correspondence
MS Eng. Poet. C. 50     Poetic miscellany
MS Firth C.1            Richard Fanshawe poems
MS Rawlinson C 956      Diary of Sir John Holland
MS Rawl. Poet. 26       Poetic miscellany
MS Rawl. Poet. 71       Poetic miscellany

| | |
|---|---|
| MS Rawl. Poet. 216 | Poetic miscellany |
| MS Top. Oxon. C. 378 | Diary of Thomas Wyatt |
| Wood 326 (1) | Brome, *Ratts rhimed to death* (1660) |

## British Library, London

| | |
|---|---|
| 186.c.10 | Balcanquhall, *A large declaration* (1639) |
| Add. MS 4155 | Thurloe papers |
| Add. MS 4929 | Fairfax sermon notes |
| Add. MS 5829 | Committee for Scandalous Ministers |
| Add. MS 11045 | Rossingham-Scudamore newsletters |
| Add. MS 14827 | Diary of Framlingham Gawdy |
| Add. MS 18980 | Sir Lewis Dyves papers |
| Add. MS 18981 | Royalist correspondence |
| Add. MS 20065 | Whitehall sermons |
| Add. MS 21433 | Early Stuart commonplace book |
| Add. MS 21935 | Nehemiah Wallington, 'Historical Notes' |
| Add. MS 22084 | Wiltshire report on scandalous ministers |
| Add. MS 22603 | Poetic miscellany |
| Add. MS 23229 | Poetic miscellany |
| Add. MS 25348 | 'True Tragicomedy . . . ', c. 1654 |
| Add. MS 35297 | Journal of John Syms |
| Add. MS 35331 | Diary of Walter Yonge |
| Add. MS 36914 | Aston correspondence |
| Add. MS 46885A | Peter Heylyn papers |
| Add. MS 54332 | Commonplace book of Henry Oxinden |
| Add. MS 70005 | Robert Harley correspondence |
| Add. MS 70006 | Robert Harley correspondence |
| Add. MS 71448 | Thomas Chaloner correspondence |
| Add. MS 71532 | Henry Marten papers |
| Add. MS 78264 | Edward Nicholas correspondence |
| Add. MS 78298 | Letter-book of John Evelyn |
| G.15426 | Weldon, *The court . . . of King James* (1650) |
| G.16567 | Neville, *Newes from the New Exchange* (1650) |
| Harley MS 393 | Poetic miscellany |
| Harley MS 646 | 'Life' of Sir Simonds D'Ewes |
| Harley MS 3991 | Poetic miscellany |
| Harley MS 4931 | Poetic miscellany |
| Harley MS 7019 | Cambridge University public accounts |
| Sloane MS 29 | 'State of the Irish People', 1640 |
| Sloane MS 1457 | Wallington papers |
| Stowe MS 184 | Dering papers |
| Stowe MS 744 | Dering papers |

## Brotherton Library, University of Leeds

| | |
|---|---|
| BC MS Lt 31 | Commonplace book |
| BC Ms Lt 57 | Commonplace book |

*Bibliography of archival sources*

## Cambridge University Library

| | |
|---|---|
| MS Add.22 | Henry Smyth papers |
| MS Add.4138 | Early Stuart commonplace book |
| MS Baker Mm 1.39 | Baker transcripts |
| MS Baker Mm.1.46 | Baker transcripts |
| MS Dd 3.68 | Henley correspondence |
| MS Gg.4.13 | Political tracts and verses |

## Cheshire Archives and Local Studies, Chester

| | |
|---|---|
| QJF | Cheshire quarter sessions |

## Clare College, Cambridge University

| | |
|---|---|
| MS CCAD/1/1/2a | Clare College letter-book |

## Devon Heritage Centre, Exeter

| | |
|---|---|
| Exeter Chamber Act Book VIII | Chamber Act Book |

## Diocese of Westminster Archives, Kensington

| | |
|---|---|
| MS A.30 | Assorted papers |

## Dr Williams's Library, London

| | |
|---|---|
| DWL/RB | Richard Baxter correspondence |

## East Sussex Record Office, Brighton

| | |
|---|---|
| MS FRE 600 | 'A satire against sepretists' |

## Essex Record Office, Chelmsford

| | |
|---|---|
| D/DEb 14/1 | William Tutty deposition |
| Q/SBa | Essex quarter sessions |

## Folger Shakespeare Library, Washington, DC

| | |
|---|---|
| MS V.a.399 | Poetic miscellany |
| MS V.b.110 | Henry Oxinden miscellany |

## Houghton Library, Harvard University

| | |
|---|---|
| MS Eng 625 | Commonplace book |
| MS Mus 182 | Ridout commonplace book |

## Isle of Wight Record Office, Newport

| | |
|---|---|
| MS OG/AA/31 | Commonplace book of John Oglander |

## John Rylands Library, University of Manchester

| | |
|---|---|
| MS GB 133 NP/77/15 | Edward Nicholas correspondence |

## Lancashire Record Office, Preston

| | |
|---|---|
| QSP | Lancashire quarter sessions petitions |
| QSR | Lancashire quarter sessions rolls |

## London Metropolitan Archives, Clerkenwell

| | |
|---|---|
| CLA | City of London quarter sessions |
| MJ/SR | Middlesex quarter sessions |

## National Library of Scotland, Edinburgh

| | |
|---|---|
| MS Wodrow Fol.XXV | Douglas correspondence |
| MS Wodrow Fol.XXVI | Douglas-Wylie correspondence |

## Norfolk Record Office, Norwich

| | |
|---|---|
| C/S | Norfolk quarter sessions |
| MS FC 19/1 | Norwich church book |

## Nottinghamshire Record Office, Nottingham

DD/HU/1 Commonplace book of Lucy Hutchinson

## Palace Green Library, Durham University

Add MS 865 Sermons
Mickleton Spearman MS 9 Poetic miscellany

## Parliamentary Archives, Westminster

BRY/18 Proceedings in the Lords
HL/PO/JO House of Lords Main Papers

## Somerset Heritage Centre, Taunton

Q/SR Somerset quarter sessions

## Staffordshire Record Office, Stafford

Q/SR Staffordshire quarter sessions

## The Harry Ransom Center, University of Texas at Austin

Ah C380 645k *The Kings cabinet opened* (1645)
BX9081 .N53 1640 Corbet, *The epistle* (1640)
HRC 157 New England petition
Thomas Killigrew Miscellany Poetic miscellany

## The Huntington Library, San Marino, CA

EL Ellesmere Manuscripts
HA Hastings Papers/Hastings Irish Papers
HM 16522 'Rump Songs'
RB 54008 *The Kings cabinet opened* (1645)
RB 88529 Weldon, *The court . . . of King James* (1650)
RB 105648 Milton, *The tenure of kings and magistrates* (1649)
RB 147922 Symmons, *A vindication of King Charles* (1647)
STT Temple correspondence

### The John Carter Brown Library, Providence, RI

| | |
|---|---|
| DA643 .P973d | Prynne, *A fresh discovery* (1645) |
| DA648 .B682b | *The British bell-man* (1648) |
| DA651 F288d | Featley, *The dippers dipt* (1651) |

### The National Archives of the U.K., Kew

| | |
|---|---|
| ASSI 45 | Northern assizes examinations |
| C 115/107 | Scudamore correspondence |
| SP 16 | State Papers, Domestic, Charles I |
| SP 18 | Council of State papers |
| SP 21 | Committee of Both Kingdoms papers |
| SP 25 | Council of State papers |
| SP 28 | Commonwealth Exchequer papers |
| SP 29 | State Papers, Domestic, Charles II |
| SP 46 | State Papers, Domestic, Supplementary |

### The Newberry Library, Chicago, IL

| | |
|---|---|
| Case F 455 .66 | *A disingag'd survey* (1650) |
| Case J 5453 .17 | Finch, *An answer* (1641) |
| Case J 5453 .352 | Goodwin, *Anti-cavalierisme* (1642) |
| Case J 5453 .947 | Walker, *Anglo-tyrannus* (1650) |
| Case J 5454 .571 | *Mercurius pragmaticus (for Charls II)* (1649) |

### University of Nottingham Library

| | |
|---|---|
| MS Mi LM 15/1 | Commonplace book of Francis Willughby |
| MS PwV 4 | Earl of Clare's 'Private Affairs' |
| MS PwV 18 | Thomas Jordan's 'Medleys and Songs' |

### William Andrews Clark Memorial Library, UCLA

| | |
|---|---|
| DA396 A2G6 | Goodwin, *Hybristodikai* (1649) |
| DA400 C47 1645a | *The Kings cabinet opened* (1645) |
| MS.1951.011 | Sermon notes of John Harper, 1625–66 |
| MS.1970.004 | Commonplace book of Daniel Fleming |
| MS.1972.002 | Sermons of William Juxon |
| PR3570 D61 1645 | Milton, *The doctrine & discipline of divorce* (1645) |

## Wiltshire and Swindon History Centre, Chippenham

MS 865/587                'A catechisme calculated . . .'

## Worcester College, Oxford

MSS Clarke              Clarke papers

# Index

2 Corinthians 11:14 117, 204, 252
2 Timothy 3:6 109, 111, 117, 124–5, 249, 255

Adamites, 49–50, 84, 87, 113, 116–17, 131, 209, 220n47, 275
adultery 6–7, 14, 20, 31–4, 45, 57, 87, 93, 112, 115–16, 121, 124, 131, 151–62 *passim*, 169, 192, 226, 232, 242, 250, 274
    *see also* Adultery Act; Cromwell, Oliver, Lord Protector; David, King; Maria, Henrietta, Queen; Marten, Henry; Mistress Parliament
Adultery Act 203–5, 210, 214, 217, 232
Africa and Africans 93, 154
Aldermanbury accord 108, 111
Amsterdam 32–3, 108, 117
Anabaptists and Anabaptism 112–13, 123, 125–6, 131
    *see also* Munster Anabaptists
Anglo-Dutch War, 211, 213, 228, 231
Anne of Denmark, Queen 93–4, 104n122, 164, 175
Antichrist 16, 36, 41, 45, 205, 252
anti-court rhetoric 14, 32, 38–9, 44, 52, 58, 72, 87–8, 138, 274
antinomianism 17, 37, 73, 109, 111–12, 116, 119, 155, 191, 228, 238, 247–8, 250, 254
    *see also* Ranters and Ranterism
anti-popery 16–17, 31, 33, 36, 51–2, 75, 77–9, 85–6, 107, 115–16, 122, 129–31, 138, 157, 272–4, 283
    *see also* post-Reformation

anti-puritanism 11–12, 17, 37, 41–2, 51–7 *passim*, 73, 76–7, 83–4, 107–8, 111, 117–19, 125, 133–9, 188–9, 195, 202–4, 212–16, 226–7, 229–31, 238–41, 253, 258, 265, 269–72
    sexual hypocrisy 32, 48, 89, 132, 154–5, 212, 271, 279
    *see also* holy sisters; post-Reformation; royalists and royalism
Aretino, Pietro 18, 216, 229, 236, 242, 270
Atherton, Bishop John 40–1, 44–5, 88, 90
Atkinson, Christopher 248–9, 251–4, 256, 262n113
Attaway, Elizabeth 120, 124–26

Baillie, Robert 32–4, 42, 44, 118–19, 125–6, 139
Balcanquhall, Walter 33–5
Bale, John 16–17, 31
Baptists 112–13, 121, 124, 197, 226
Barebone's Parliament 217
bastardy 17, 35–6, 38, 70–1, 85–6, 91, 97, 119, 137, 152, 157–8, 162, 166, 170, 174–5, 198, 242–3, 253–4, 267
Bastwick, John 41–2, 239
Bauthumley, Jacob 192–3
Baxter, Richard 6, 11, 195, 244, 254
Berkenhead, Sir John, 76–7, 81, 84, 96, 132–3, 257, 269, 275
    *Mercurius Aulicus* 76–8, 81, 83–90 *passim*, 95–7, 120, 133, 136, 235

bestiality 2, 6, 74–5, 85–6, 133, 204, 209–10, 215, 228, 248–9, 254–7, 275
  see also Green, Ralph
bishops see episcopacy
Bishops' Wars 2, 8, 30–9 passim, 42, 44, 52, 57–9, 89, 207, 280
Blackleach, John 200–3, 211
Blasphemy Act 204, 245
body politic 6, 13, 16, 55, 141, 151, 163
  see also king's two bodies
Brisbrowne, Hugh 248–9, 254, 256–7
broadsides 5, 8, 74, 76, 133, 230–1, 256–7, 268, 271, 273
Brome, Alexander 264n134, 269, 271–2
Browne, John 44–5
Brownists and Brownism 37, 49, 73, 87, 108, 117–18, 125–6
Buchanan, George 31, 80, 171
buggery see bestiality; sodomy
Burges, Cornelius 73, 84, 87, 99n17
Burrough, Edward 248, 250, 252
Burton, Henry 42, 239

Castlehaven scandal 14, 19, 71–2
Catholics and Catholicism 8, 10, 14–18, 27n77, 29, 31, 44–5, 72, 83, 140n10, 170, 175, 236, 273–4, 278
  conspiracies against British Protestantism, alleged 35–6, 54, 79
  see also anti-popery; Ireland
cavaliers 30, 52–61 passim, 69, 72–4, 77, 80, 81–2, 85–93 passim, 127, 131, 139, 160, 188, 202–3, 207, 215–16, 227, 238, 268, 272, 281–2
  poets at the 1630s Caroline court 19, 38, 41, 227, 233
  see also malignants and malignancy; royalists and royalism
censorship see press regulation
Chaffin, Thomas 226–7, 230, 253
Charles I, King 1, 5, 32, 34, 37–40, 48, 52–6, 69, 75, 85, 96, 106, 121, 123, 126, 129–30, 133–5, 138–9, 156, 162–7, 172, 178, 212, 217, 227–8, 237, 239, 280–2
  aversion to impropriety 14, 29, 55, 60–1, 70–1, 78, 83, 235, 270, 284
  criticisms of 16, 35, 39, 58, 72–3, 75, 80, 82, 90–1, 93–5, 97, 107–8, 135, 139, 150, 162–76 passim, 200, 243
  defences of chastity 87–8, 95, 152–3, 164–5, 173, 175–6
  patronage of bawdy poets and dramatists 19, 38, 41, 44, 165, 168
  regicide 8, ch. 4 passim, 187–8, 191, 202, 214, 242, 244–5, 271
  see also Maria, Henrietta, Queen
Charles II, King 2–3, 13, 163, 168, 170, 174, 176, 187, 199, 206, 216–17, 227, 265–72, 280, 283–5
  criticisms of 206–9, 239, 242–4, 257, 269–70, 272–4, 284
Chillenden, Edmund 226–7, 280
Christian IV of Denmark, King 94, 164
civil war
  polemic and 2–5, 12–13, 20, 29–30, 69–70, 107–8, 139, 216, 280
  sexual consequences of 6, 8, 72, 93, 95, 131–2
civility and public decorum 18, 29, 37, 42–3, 52, 56, 71, 77, 83, 252, 282–3
  see also politeness
Clarkson, Laurence 192–3, 204
Clement, Gregory 210–11, 217, 226
Clotworthy, Sir John 40–1, 48
community of women see polygamy
Congregationalism see Independents and Independency
conjugal kingship 14, 16, 55, 92–3, 148–53, 156, 158, 162–3, 165, 167–9, 173, 175–6, 178, 201, 209, 244, 270
Conway, Edward, Viscount 230–1, 241, 271
Coppe, Abiezer 1, 188, 191–4, 197, 203–4, 246, 250, 280
Corbet, John 34, 37–8
Corbet, Miles 74, 137

Council of State 149, 153, 159, 167, 189–90, 198–9, 202, 206–8, 210–12, 232, 240, 263n122
Covenanters and the Covenanting movement 30–42 *passim*, 59, 86, 89, 92, 106, 110, 116, 209
  *see also* Presbyterians and Presbyterianism; Solemn League and Covenant
Cowley, Abraham 233–4, 237
Cromwell, Elizabeth 160–1, 201, 267, 269
Cromwell, Oliver, Lord Protector 130–1, 138–9, 149, 153, 187, 190, 200, 206–7, 216–17, 226–7, 231–2, 240, 244–5, 255, 265, 270, 272, 281, 284
  criticisms of 150–63 *passim*, 178, 190–1, 228, 244, 267, 271
  relationship with Frances Lambert 159–61, 201, 268–9
Cromwell, Richard, Lord Protector 265–7
Crouch, John 189, 201–3, 206, 211–18, 228–33, 235, 241, 247, 257, 267–8, 270–1, 280
cuckoldry 17, 32, 45–6, 52–4, 56, 59, 69, 76, 91, 115, 127, 133, 136–8, 160, 162, 235, 267, 274
  *see also* Devereaux, Robert, earl of Essex

D'Ewes, Sir Simonds 11, 43
Dabhoiwala, Faramerz 3, 12–13, 284, 287n22
David, King 153, 173, 184n104
  adultery with Bathsheba 7, 170, 173–4, 200, 239
Denham, Sir John 256–7, 264n134, 267, 269
Devereaux, Robert, earl of Essex 14, 53, 72, 74, 78, 87, 90, 130, 137, 231, 268
  *see also* Overbury affair
Diggers 187, 198–9, 251
drolleries 227, 236–42, 258, 270, 282–3

ecclesiastical courts 36, 43–4, 53, 73, 75, 91, 202
Edgehill, battle of 59, 69–70, 72, 239

Edward VI, King 14, 17
Edwards, Thomas 107, 111, 115, 118, 120, 126, 195
  *Gangraena* controversy 118–26 *passim*, 135
Elizabeth I, Queen 1, 14, 17, 170, 244
English Commonwealth 147–9, 151, 153, 172, 179, 187–9, 193, 199–200, 213, 216–17, 230–1, 239, 265, 267
  press corps and polemic 148, 161, 167–76 *passim*, 194–201 *passim*, 204–12, 243–4
  *see also* reformation of manners; republicans and republicanism
English Republic *see* English Commonwealth
episcopacy 1, 16–17, 30–1, 33–7 *passim*, 41, 44–5, 59, 108, 115, 118, 155, 202, 250
erotic writing 8, 18–20, 37, 41, 188, 194, 201, 212, 218, 229, 236, 238–9, 258, 267, 270–1, 283
  *see also* pornography
evil counsellors 16, 40–5, 48, 54, 71–2, 78–9, 96, 163

Fairfax, Anne 145n116, 150
Fairfax, Sir Thomas 92–3, 117, 120, 127, 130–1, 134, 138, 157, 200
Family of Love and familism 17, 49, 72, 84, 109, 111, 116, 125–6, 153–5, 211, 220n47, 247, 250
favourites 14, 16, 38, 40, 60, 164, 171
  *see also* evil counsellors
Featley, Daniel 112–14, 119, 121, 126, 158
Fell, Margaret 249, 252
Filmer, Sir Robert 148, 176
Finch, Edward 43, 45–8, 51, 60, 83, 90, 257, 280
flyting 31, 238
  *see also* libel
Foucault, Michel 285
Fox, George 242, 245–7, 249, 252–6
France 6, 14, 22n20, 35, 58, 79, 82, 133, 172, 176, 178, 209, 215, 233, 235, 236, 238, 272, 274, 283
Franklin, William 194, 199
Frewen, Archbishop Accepted 11, 57

gendered and sexual disorder 14, 39, 75–7, 93–6, 109, 129, 131–2, 161, 187, 248
  Antipodes and the world-turned-upside-down 5, 10, 130, 155, 157–8, 161, 213–18, 239, 267, 280
  *see also* civil war; inversion; patriarchy; women
Gianoutsos, Jamie 12, 168, 188
Gilpin, John 247–9, 256
Goodwin, John 58–61, 75, 120, 169, 273
Great Seal 82, 87
Green, Ralph 256–7, 267, 269, 275
Griffith, John 73, 77–8, 86–7, 95, 97, 127, 129
Gwin, John 45–6

Harrington, James 244
Henrietta Maria, Queen 14, 16, 31, 36, 45, 58, 88, 130, 152–3, 176, 221n63, 237
  criticisms of 19, 39, 72–3, 94, 97, 152, 164, 174–6, 272
  rumours of adultery with Henry Jermyn 79, 82, 90–1, 93, 104n122, 174, 272
Henry VIII, King 13–14, 16, 170
heresiography 8, 107, 111, 115–19, 121, 125, 132–3, 137–8, 154, 195, 249
*Hero and Leander* 235–6, 271
Heylyn, Peter, 76–7
High Commission, court of 42, 73, 116
Hobbes, Thomas 10, 148, 176–9, 187
holy sisters 9, 37–8, 41, 48–9, 53–4, 57, 81, 89, 122, 133, 137, 154, 159, 212, 214, 226, 229–30, 239–41, 247, 253–4, 256–7, 271, 275
homosexuality 6, 8, 267
  *see also* sodomy
Hotham, Sir John 54–5, 74, 163
Hughes, Ann 12, 107, 119, 189
Hutchinson, Anne 112, 118
Hutchinson, Lucy 204

incest 33–6, 40–1, 45, 73, 87, 112, 116, 154, 161, 168, 170, 175, 236, 241
*Little non-such* 122–3, 126
Independents and Independency 106–25 *passim*, 129–31, 134–9, 149, 151
inversion 8, 16, 115, 125, 139, 151–7, 165, 169, 246, 282
Ireland 34, 40, 75, 88, 90, 149–50, 159, 168, 187, 199, 213
  1641 Catholic rising 52, 56, 58, 79
Isle of Wight 75, 122, 138, 164, 166

James I, King 14, 78, 92, 94, 165–6, 147, 166
  criticisms of 16, 35, 72, 93, 152, 165, 168, 170–1, 174, 237
Jermyn, Sir Henry *see* Henrietta Maria, Queen
Jordan, Thomas 241

*Kings cabinet opened, The* 94–7, 152, 164
king's two bodies 13, 55, 147, 162–78 *passim*, 199, 244, 270, 273

L'Estrange, Sir Roger 273, 275
Lambert, Frances *see* Cromwell, Oliver, Lord Protector
Lambert, John 160–1, 268
Laud, Archbishop William, 34, 40, 43–5, 79, 91–2, 97
Laudianism 40, 43, 47, 76, 108, 116, 257
Levellers 12, 120, 127, 131, 157, 187–91, 198, 202, 206
Leslie, Alexander 38, 207
Leslie, David 207
libel 1, 8, 10, 17, 20, 32–3, 38, 41–2, 45, 53, 60, 71, 73, 77–9, 119–22, 130, 132–9 *passim*, 161, 164, 189, 202, 211–12, 229–30, 238, 246, 248, 265, 271, 281, 284
libertines and libertinism 10, 109–10, 115–16, 121, 135, 176, 191–8, 228, 238, 246–50, 252, 254, 269, 281–3
  *see also* Ranters and Ranterism

liberty of conscience *see* toleration and its critics
Lilburne, John 127, 189–91, 199
Lilly, William 174–5, 187
London, City of 1–2, 19, 31, 35–6, 40, 43–4, 54, 56, 69–71, 78, 84, 93, 108, 110, 118–21, 129–33, 162, 197, 202, 209, 211, 226, 242, 245, 265, 268–70, 273–4, 281
    printing in 32–3, 36, 42, 53–4, 75–7, 80, 87, 132–3, 151, 189, 201, 212, 240
    royalist criticisms of 57, 59, 76, 81, 85, 133–6, 151–2, 155–7, 213–15, 228–31, 257, 268
Long Parliament 31, 43, 154, 267–8
Louis, Charles I, Prince Elector of the Palatine 137
Lucretia *see* Tarquin

McElligott, Jason 12, 107, 135
major-generals 232, 238, 240–1
malignants and malignancy 40, 45, 55, 72, 74, 77, 79, 82–3, 87–8, 96, 130, 206
manuscript culture 5, 11, 16–20, 29, 31–42 *passim*, 51, 53, 55, 57, 60, 72, 93, 122, 171, 197, 227, 230–1, 233, 236, 241–2, 257, 271, 273, 283
Marprelate, Martin 17, 33, 35–6, 49, 107, 114–15
marriage 6, 72, 110, 120–4, 147, 163–4, 169, 176, 192, 194, 217, 238, 247, 258, 285
    metaphor for rule *see* conjugal kingship
Marston Moor 89–90, 111
Marten, Henry 74, 89, 130, 135–7, 151, 169, 189, 201, 203–4, 210, 216–17
Mary I, Queen 170, 175
masturbation 6, 11, 214, 270, 274
Mennes, Sir John 234, 240
Millett, Kate 4
Milton, John 167–74, 178, 240, 269
    divorce tracts 110–11, 118–20, 123–6

Mistress Parliament 150, 153, 156–8, 161–2, 168, 178, 214, 268, 276n18, 284
mobilisation 2, 30, 52, 56, 68–70, 78–9, 81, 83–4, 86–7, 96, 120, 133–4
monarchy 7, 13–16, 40, 58, 71, 80, 88, 92, 147–50, 168, 179, 200, 237, 243–5, 265, 270
    royal succession 35, 72, 79, 94, 97, 152–3, 158, 171, 200
    *see also* Charles I, King; conjugal kingship; king's two bodies
Monck, George, General 265, 268
monstrosity and monstrous births 5, 9, 14, 16, 38, 55, 57, 61, 76, 83, 97, 112, 118–19, 139, 154, 157–9, 161–2, 214–15, 229, 268
moral control *see* reformation of manners; sexual regulation
Mortimer, Roger, earl of March, 82, 175
Munster Anabaptists 17, 37, 109, 111–13, 116, 119, 126, 198, 247, 250, 255–6

Naseby 93–5, 115
Nayler, James 245–7, 253–4, 256, 275
Nedham, Marchamont 81, 90, 94, 133, 169, 208, 211–13, 230, 243–5, 257, 266, 269, 280
    *Mercurius Britanicus* 81–92 *passim*, 152
    *Mercurius politicus* 206, 208–9, 243
Neville, Henry 1, 127–32 *passim*, 135, 138, 143n73, 156, 201–2, 235
New England colonies 81, 108–12, 118, 136, 155, 220n46
New Model Army 92–3, 113, 117–22, 125–30, 133–4, 138, 149, 153, 157, 194, 208, 216–17, 226, 245, 265–8

Oates, Samuel 121–2, 125
Oglander, Sir John 75–6, 96, 122
oral culture, sexual politics in 16, 20, 35, 56, 60, 75, 84, 91, 97, 162, 175–6, 211, 244, 246, 272

Overbury affair 14, 53, 72, 78, 171
Overton, Richard 35–6, 113, 122, 126–7, 138–9, 150, 189–91, 198–9, 250, 280
  Marpriest tracts 107, 114–16, 118, 122, 129, 152, 191, 193
Oxford 53, 69–71, 84–6, 93, 97, 106, 122, 127, 156, 176, 231
  hotspot of royalist malignancy 75, 77, 82, 87–8, 92, 120, 127, 129
  royalist press at 74, 76–8, 81, 86–7, 89, 95–6, 132, 152, 233, 235

Pagitt, Ephraim 116–17, 154, 250, 262n103
Parker, Henry 72–3, 94, 170, 174
parliament 5, 20, 29, 35–6, 39–43, 48, 52, 55, 69, 73–6, 82, 88, 92–3, 106–7, 122–3, 129–30, 134–5, 138–9, 147–51, 164, 202–5, 211, 216–17, 231–2, 245
  depicted as female 16, 156, 168, 179n2
    see also Mistress Parliament; Parliament of Ladies
  press corps and polemic 56–9, 71–2, 78–82, 85–95 passim, 161, 164–5
  radical critics of 187–99 passim
  royalist family conspiracy about 38, 153–9
    see also Long Parliament; Rump Parliament
Parliament of Ladies 125–32 passim, 135, 138, 156, 201, 235, 269, 274
  see also Neville, Henry
Parnassus biceps 238–40
patriarchy 3–4, 7, 10, 29, 38, 49, 54, 59, 70, 78, 109, 119, 124, 178, 194, 198, 203, 212, 214, 217, 227, 238, 254, 265, 281–3
  effeminacy and hyper-sexuality 38, 58, 160
  kingship and 13–14, 79–80, 91, 94–5, 97, 147–8, 152–3, 155, 160–2, 283–4
  republicanism and 161, 188, 199–201, 217

Pepys, Samuel 270
Peter, Hugh 81, 118, 136–7, 205, 271
petitions 41–5, 48, 51, 53–6, 71, 110, 122, 131, 217, 220n47, 231, 241–2
Peyton, Edward 174–5, 207
Phillips, John 240
'Pigges Coranto' 39, 59
politeness 274, 282–3
  see also civility and public decorum; sex-talk
polygamy 17, 37, 82, 95, 111–12, 116, 190, 198, 252, 254–5, 263n122
Poole, Elizabeth 165–6
Popish Plot (1678–81) 121, 275
porno-politics 4–5, 11, 38, 53, 55, 76, 83, 86–7, 92–3, 97, 108, 116, 118–19, 139, ch. 4 passim, 189, 194, 200, 214, 239, 268, 270, 281–4
pornography 2, 8–10, 266, 270, 274, 282, 285
  see also erotic writing
post-Reformation 3, 7, 10, 16–17, 29–31, 37, 44, 49, 52, 58–60, 70, 88, 106–7, 115–18, 126, 135, 137, 139, 245–7, 257–8, 274, 280, 282, 284–5
pox see venereal disease
pregnancy see procreation
Presbyterians and Presbyterianism 17, 29–34, 81, 106–23 passim, 125, 127–34, 136–9, 149, 153–4, 166, 193, 195, 206–9, 240, 247, 254, 271, 275
press regulation 29, 32–3, 37, 42, 187, 211–12, 229–33, 240–1, 265, 267, 270, 273, 284–6
  episcopal licensing system 1–2, 17–18, 39, 280
  September 1649 press act 151, 161, 189, 199, 202, 211, 214, 234
Preston, 138–9, 147, 149, 151
Pride's Purge 147, 149, 267

print culture
  licensing and 'official' publications 42, 69–70, 76, 78–83, 85–6, 90, 96, 168, 174, 195, 200, 208, 273, 281
    see also press regulation
  'para-propagandists' 69, 72
  'print explosion' 5, 42–5, 130–1, 280
  printers and publishers 2, 5, 9, 19, 32, 36, 48, 70, 75, 84, 107, 130, 132–3, 216, 235, 237, 240, 269, 270, 274, 280
  unlicensed and anonymous print 29–31, 36–8, 43, 48, 51–2, 55, 70–2, 75
procreation 37, 49, 53, 115–16, 118, 122, 154, 187, 214, 239, 279
  see also monstrosity and monstrous births
Protectorate 217, 227–32, 234, 240, 242, 244–5, 265–7
Protestants and Protestantism, 8, 14, 16, 18, 31, 35, 41, 59, 83, 94, 154, 191, 231
  radicals, sectarians and separatists 17, 37, 43, 48–50, 53, 108–9, 112–13, 118–25, 132, 188–9, 192, 198, 213, 227, 238, 245, 257, 271
    see also Adamites; Brownists and Brownism; Family of Love and familism; Quakers and Quakerism; Ranters and Ranterism
  see also post-Reformation
Prynne, William 42, 78–81, 83, 87, 90–2, 97, 112, 117, 150, 165, 168, 170, 239
  *Histriomastix* and punishment 19–20, 39, 72, 87
public culture
  definition of 5–6
  sex-talk in 2–4, 8–9, 13, 29, 42, 47, 51, 61, 69, 85, 91–2, 97, 120, 139, 176, 188, 252, 256–7, 269–70, 275, 280, 284–5
public discipline *see* sexual regulation
puritans and puritanism 6, 17–19, 29, 32–6, 41–3, 45, 48, 51, 56, 70, 73, 81, 88, 106, 108–9, 117, 122, 153–4, 188, 191–4, 202–4, 206, 217, 226, 232, 248, 271, 274, 279–80
Pym, John 40, 42, 48, 53, 55–6, 60, 71, 73, 81, 84, 201, 230–1

Quakers and Quakerism 2, 227–8, 245–58 *passim*, 265, 269, 280–1
  Ranter comparison 246–7, 250–2, 254–5

Ranters and Ranterism 1, 8, 187–8, 191–9 *passim*, 203–4, 207–10, 212–15, 220n47, 227–8, 246, 250–2, 255, 275, 281
  see also Quakers and Quakerism
rape *see* sexual violence
reformation of manners 9, 44, 53, 72–3, 150–1, 154, 160, 163, 187, 202–6, 210, 216–17, 227–8, 232, 234, 237, 258, 279
republicans and republicanism 1, 11, 74, 80, 127, 130, 135–7, 147–8, 161–76 *passim*, 179, 187–9, 198–203, 206–10, 216–17, 227–8, 242–5, 258, 265–7, 269, 272–3
  see also English Commonwealth
Restoration 2–4, 8, 60, 178, 218, 233, 238, 247, 258, ch. 7 *passim*, 281–2, 285
  sexual politics of 4, 10, 13, 176, 216, 238, 266, 269–75, 283–5
root and branch petition, 41, 117, 126, 138, 238
roundheads 30, 52–60 *passim*, 69, 73, 139, 211, 227, 241, 268, 281–2
royalists and royalism 30, 51–2, 59, 69–71, 75, 78, 84–6, 93, 95–7, 106, 113, 122, 127, 130–1, 138, 149, 163–4, 168, 175–8, 187–8, 190, 206–16 *passim*, 226–8, 232–3, 242–3, 250, 265–72, 281
  press corps and polemic 11–12, 37–8, 53, 56, ch. 2 *passim*, 107–8, 132–8 *passim*, 150–62 *passim*, 176, 189, 201–3, 211–16, 228–30, 233–45 *passim*, 247, 266–9, 272, 283–5

radicalisation of 3, 8–9, 212, 216, 218, 227, 231, 235, 241, 258, 266, 281
  *see also* cavaliers; malignancy
Rump Parliament 149, 265–9
Rump satires 230–1, 265–9, 271–2
Rupert of the Rhine, Prince, 74–5, 77, 82, 87–90, 129
Rutherford, Samuel 116, 195

Salmasius, Claudius 172–4, 185n115
Salmon, Joseph 192, 194
Saltmarsh, John 120, 129
Scot, Thomas 137, 268
Scotland 30–9 *passim*, 42, 52, 80–1, 84, 108, 155–6, 159, 167, 170–1, 206–9, 254, 268, 280
  *see also* Bishops' Wars; Covenanting movement
Scottish prayer book 29–32, 34, 37, 39
serial print 57, 70, 76–7, 84–9, 97, 107, 133, 228, 232
sex-talk
  anxieties about 18–20, 30, 34, 188, 208, 239, 241–2
  connection with sexual practice 4, 8–9, 47, 60, 74, 97, 135, 188, 193, 266, 280, 284
  legitimate discourse 188, 191, 208, 233, 237, 280
  partisan stereotypes and 30, 52–60 *passim*, 70, 96, 188, 281
  truth-claim 4–5, 29, 32, 60, 109, 148, 281
sexual liberty 4, 13, 111, 188, 192, 284
sexual regulation 6–7, 217, 283–5
  *see also* ecclesiastical courts; reformation of manners
sexual violence 14, 16, 34–5, 38, 45, 52, 54, 56–8, 72–3, 82, 86, 109, 123, 134, 167–9, 179, 209, 243–4
Sharpe, Kevin 13, 167, 265–6
Sidley, Elizabeth *see* Griffith, John
Simmonds, Martha 253–4
Society of Friends *see* Quakers and Quakerism
sodomy 11, 14, 16, 40–1, 72–5, 77, 85–6, 93, 109, 115, 159, 193, 204, 229, 236

Solemn League and Covenant, 81, 110
Song of Songs 18, 194, 246
Sparke, Michael 1–2, 9, 218n3, 279
spiritual and sexual error, link between, 10, 31–2, 34, 49–50, 83, 97, 106, 109–17 *passim*, 120, 123–5, 132, 192, 197, 247, 250
  *see also* post-Reformation; toleration and its critics
*Sportive wit* 237–8, 240, 271
Star Chamber 29, 32, 42
Stationers' Company 2, 18, 42, 140n15
Stokes, Edward 197, 209
Stuart dynasty 2, 12, 18, 35, 93, 148, 150, 161–4, 170–1, 173–5, 188, 199–200, 243–4, 274
  *see also* Charles I, King; Charles II, King; James I, King; Stuart, Mary, Queen of Scotland
Stuart, Mary, Queen of Scotland 31, 35, 80, 170–1
Suckling, Sir John 44, 58, 234
Symmons, Edward 89–90, 96, 134–5, 216

Tarquin 13, 80, 169, 209, 243
Taylor, John 49–53, 57, 73, 76, 81, 85–7, 90, 95–6, 133, 137, 154, 212–13, 280
theatre 2, 17, 19, 173, 202, 232, 236, 270
Thirty Years' War 29, 34
Thomason, George 1, 9, 66n113, 93, 125–8, 158, 172, 185n115, 238, 240, 256, 264n134, 267
Thurloe, John 229–30, 234, 240, 242–3, 269
toleration and its critics 106, 108–25 *passim*, 129, 132, 137, 157, 195, 245–7, 258
Town Bull of Ely 153, 159–60, 190–1, 201
  *see also* Cromwell, Oliver, Lord Protector
Traub, Valerie 2, 13, 280, 284–5
tyranny 12–13, 58, 80, 91–2, 129, 148–50, 153, 159–61, 167–72, 176, 179, 188–90, 198, 230, 243–4, 267, 274
  *see also* Tarquin

venereal disease 34–5, 37, 53, 58–9, 84, 109, 132, 136, 159, 162, 190–1
Villiers, George, duke of Buckingham 16, 20, 32, 34, 38, 40, 93, 171, 173, 236
virginity 14, 45, 49, 71–2, 90, 131, 170, 214–15, 227, 243–5, 258, 266
Vote of No Further Addresses 135, 149, 164

Walker, Henry 51–2, 85, 137
Waller, Lady Anne, 89, 131
Wallington, Nehemiah 59, 88
Walter, Lucy 207, 242–3
Walwyn, William 120, 190
Warner, John 136–7
Webbe, Thomas 195, 197
Weld, Thomas 111–12
Weldon, Anthony 170–1
Wentworth, Thomas, earl of Strafford 40–5, 91
Western sexuality, historiography of 3–4, 12, 282, 284–6
Westminster, City of 56, 86, 129, 134, 149, 165, 175, 195, 199, 245
Westminster Assembly of Divines 108, 110, 115–16, 118, 120–2, 133, 157, 193
Whigs and Whiggism 179, 274–5
White, John 43, 48, 82–3, 86–8, 90, 96
Whore of Babylon 8, 16, 31–3, 36, 41, 45, 56, 58, 75, 79, 93, 112, 115–16, 155–8, 193, 205, 248, 252, 269
whores, whoremongers and whoredom 1, 11, 16, 19, 22n29, 34–5, 40, 43–4, 56, 74, 77, 83, 87, 93, 120, 136–7, 152, 156–7, 161, 190, 194, 200, 207, 209, 211, 216–17, 227, 229, 244–6, 253–4, 266–8, 270, 272
Whorwood, Jane 164, 166
William III, King, 274, 283
William the Conqueror 38, 170, 198
Wilmot, John, earl of Rochester 24n41, 176, 270
Winstanley, Gerrard 198–9, 220n46, 251
Wiseman, Susan 5, 11, 136
witchcraft 93, 210, 248–9, 255
Wither, George 174, 207
women 7, 14, 38, 47–8, 56–9, 67n128, 92–3, 111–13, 117, 125, 127, 129–31, 136, 157, 160, 168, 173, 187, 190, 204, 209, 214, 226–9, 231, 239, 244, 268
  bodies as rhetorical battleground 4, 60, 188, 281, 283
  radical Protestantism and 49, 54, 84, 109, 112, 117, 119, 121–4, 197, 214–15, 246, 249, 254–5
  see also 2 Timothy 3:6; holy sisters
  victims of sexual politics 20, 93, 203, 217, 246, 281
  see also sexual violence
Worcester 125, 207, 209–11, 215
Wren, Bishop Matthew 45, 90
Wyatt, Thomas 54–6, 59, 84, 95, 176

EU authorised representative for GPSR:
Easy Access System Europe, Mustamäe tee 50,
10621 Tallinn, Estonia
gpsr.requests@easproject.com

www.ingramcontent.com/pod-product-compliance
Lightning Source LLC
Chambersburg PA
CBHW051601230426
43668CB00013B/1933